Cross of Fellowship

That I may   know Him
and the power of His resurrection
and the fellowship of
His sufferings...
Philippians 3:10

When He opened the fifth seal, I saw under the altar

the souls of those who had been slain for the

word of God and for the testimony which they held.

And they cried with a loud voice, saying,

"How long, O Lord, holy and true,

until You judge and avenge our blood on

those who dwell on the earth?"

Revelation 6:9-10

"This volume provides the fulfillment of our Lord's Word
and the history of 'the blessed' who were persecuted, rejoiced,
and have been rewarded in Heaven (Matthew 5:11-12).
Here is the ennobling record of a long line of Christ's martyrs
by whose sacrifice He has built His church.
It's the most inspiring of all Christian history."
—John MacArthur
Pastor-Teacher of Grace Community Church
President of The Master's College & Seminary

"*FOXE: Voices of the Martyrs* is the one book none of us want to be
in, but it's the one book that should be in the hands of every Christian
and chained to every pulpit."
—Ray Comfort, Evangelist
Co-host of The Way of the Master TV program

"Christians in every generation have given witness to their faith in
Jesus Christ with the sacrifice of their lives. Whether in the
times of the Roman Empire or in the dictatorial regimes of today,
Christian martyrs follow the loving example of the Lord
Who gave His life for our salvation."
—Tom Coburn, M.D., United States Senator

"It has been said that the blood of the martyrs is the seedbed of the
church. Every Christian needs to read the stirring accounts of those
who have given their all for their faith in the Lord Jesus Christ."
—Pat Robertson, Host of The 700 Club
Chairman/CEO, The Christian Broadcasting Network

"The fresh publication of this classic is needed by a generation
which could be destined in learning its lessons and repeat the valor of
those whose witness has carried the banner of faith
through deadly fires into eternal glory."
—Dr. Jack W. Hayford, Founding Pastor, The Church on The Way
President, International Foursquare Churches
Chancellor, The King's College and Seminary

"Anyone who wants to seriously live a godly life in Christ Jesus must read this book."
—Bob (Xiqiu) Fu
President, China Aid Association
Former Chinese house-church pastor

"As a new Christian, a teenager, in 1969 I read *Foxe's Book of Martyrs*. Those powerful stories ignited me, raised the bar of my commitment to Christ, and gave me a love for persecuted Christians. I pray this wonderful book from Voice of the Martyrs will do the same for countless readers. Hebrews 11 is still being written throughout the world. May we learn from those stories, and, empowered by Christ, may we live in such a way that our own stories might one day be worth telling."
—Randy Alcorn
Author of *Heaven, Heaven for Kids* and *Safely Home*

"If you want proof that Jesus is real then hear it in the words of those who have given their all to serve Him."
—Everett Piper, Ph.D., President, Oklahoma Wesleyan University

"When John Foxe completed his first edition of the Book of Martyrs in Latin in 1559 (the first English edition came out in 1563) the 'book' on Christian martyrdom was certainly not closed. In fact the number of those who have died for their faith in Jesus Christ has steadily risen to the point that now more men and women are dying for Jesus than at any time in the history of the Christian movement. This new 'update' will sadly be obsolete before it even goes to print."
—Michael Card, Singer and Author

"In a day when the Gospel is scorned as intolerant or irrelevant, and so-called martyrdom is purchased by some through violence, the counter witness of Christ's humility, grace, and triumph in the face of persecution is writ large upon the biographies in this new volume. I highly recommend it."
—Ravi Zacharias, Author and Speaker

FOXE

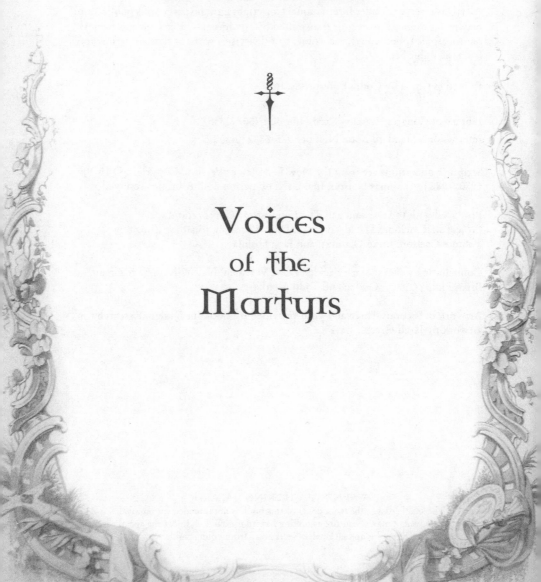

Voices
of the
Martyrs

Bridge-Logos

Orlando, FL 32822 USA

Foxe: Voices of the Martyrs
by John Foxe and The Voice of the Martyrs

Printed in China by Codra Enterprises, Inc.

Library of Congress Catalog Card Number: 2007923553
International Standard Book Number 978-088270-330-5

Scripture quotations are from the New King James Version. Copyright © 1979, 1980, 1982 by Thomas Nelson, Inc. Used by permission. All rights reserved.

Produced with the assistance of The Livingstone Corporation.
Project staff includes David Veerman, Dana Veerman, Jonathan Ziman, Thomas Carlson, Brian Dennert, and Jana Holiday.

Contributing writers: Mark Fackler, Dana Veerman, Neil Wilson, Kari Ziman, Brian Fidler, Cheryl Odden and Todd Nettleton.

Artwork in Sections Three and Four provided by Lookout Design. Research for artwork by Jared Given.

WARNING! CHOKING HAZARD
The small cross in the front cover of this book is not intended for removal.
If it is removed, it may constitute a choking hazard for children under the age of three.
Keep this and all small objects away from young children.

TABLE OF CONTENTS

Part One: Martyrs of the First Century

Part Two: Martyrs from the Second Century to the Twentieth Century

Part Three: Modern Martyrs in the Twenty-first Century

Acknowledgements

Firstly, I acknowledge the martyrs themselves, those who "did not love their lives to the death" (Rev. 12:11) but instead laid their lives down willingly for the cause of Christ. Not all of their stories are contained in these pages, but we honor each of them with this volume and with our ongoing work.

When we initially considered this work, the scope was challenging. Collecting, verifying, writing, and editing stories of hundreds of Christian martyrs, from the days of the apostles until today, was a daunting task. I admire the commitment of those who have worked with me to complete it.

I am thankful to our friends at The Livingstone Corporation, who put together a team with the expertise not only to accomplish this work, but also to accomplish it with heart and dedication. David Veerman led this effort, and I am thankful to him and to his team: Dana Veerman, Jonathan Ziman, Thomas Carlson, Brian Dennert, Jana Holiday, Mark Fackler, Neil Wilson, and Kari Ziman.

Additional martyr testimonies were identified and written by Cheryl Odden, Brian Fidler and Todd Nettleton. Gary Lane researched and wrote the persecution survey contained in the final section of this book.

Throughout the entire process that has brought you this volume, Guy Morrell and his team at Bridge-Logos Publishers have shown an uncommon commitment to telling the stories of the martyrs, putting ministry and excellence ahead of bottom-line profits. This finished book is a tribute to the commitment of Guy and his team: Steve Becker, Sue Teubner, Elizabeth Nason and, early in the process, Beverly Browning. In addition, Guy called on the expertise of others, including Pat Judd.

Steve Cleary and Todd Nettleton managed this project on behalf of The Voice of the Martyrs, working with the publisher and finding writers. They also wrote and edited some of the testimonies in this book. I have worked side-by-side with each of them, and I appreciate their commitment to the persecuted church and to the ministry of VOM.

May you and I be faithful, as the martyrs were, until the number is complete (Revelation 6:11).

Tom White
Executive Director
The Voice of the Martyrs—USA

FOREWORD

Foxe's *Book of Martyrs* has been called the second most important book in history, second only to the Bible itself. John Foxe wanted the church to know the stories of those who had gone before—those who stood firmly for their Savior even to the painful point of death. It wasn't only that they had died, or even the details of how they died. Foxe wanted the church to be encouraged by their testimonies, that even in the lowest moments of torture and tribulation, they had found Christ worthy of their devotion and love. He wanted Christians to be blessed and encouraged by the testimonies of those who had gone before, who now formed part of the "great cloud of witnesses" in the stadium of history (Hebrews 12:1-2).

That same drive motivates The Voice of the Martyrs ministry today. We want to tell the stories of the persecuted church as a challenge and an encouragement to Christians around the world. That same desire brings you this work.

John Foxe's masterpiece was first printed in English in 1563. He lived long enough to see the Council of Bishops order that a copy of the work be placed in every cathedral and church in England. Foxe died in 1587. But martyrdom obviously didn't end when he died; it has continued more than 400 years since. The Bible says it will continue until Christ returns for His faithful ones, to take us with Him to heaven.

John Foxe painstakingly collected the stories of the martyrs up to his time, and his son carried on the effort. The full title of Foxe's book was *Acts and Monuments of Christian Martyrs.* He considered it a written memorial to those who had been faithful unto death and a reminder of their suffering. We have carried on his mission, collecting in this volume the stories of martyrs dating from ancient times all the way to today.

Some people were offended by Foxe's stories. To them, it was a collection of murder, blood and mayhem. We sometimes hear the same complaints about the stories we publish today. But where others see only tragedy and suffering, discerning Christians like Foxe find courage, faith, and blessing.

I wish I could tell you that persecution is waning, that our brothers and sisters are being treated with fairness and justice. Instead, I must tell you that persecution of Christians is more common in our generation than ever in history. The oft-quoted statistic is that more people died for their Christian faith in the past century than in all the other centuries of recorded history combined. (David B. Barrett, International Bulletin of Missionary Research, January 2007)

Jesus told His followers that the world hated Him, and that if they followed Him the world would hate them too (John 15:18-19). His words are coming true right now in China, India, Sudan, Egypt, North Korea, Saudi Arabia, and thirty-five other nations. Each month in VOM's newsletter we continue to chronicle the acts of martyrs for the gospel around the world.

Foxe's Book of Martyrs was one of my first contacts with the powerful, life-changing testimonies of persecuted Christians. As a thirteen-year-old, I couldn't get enough of the stories of people who stayed true to their faith in Christ even as their lives were being snuffed out. I wasn't sure how these people achieved such faith, but I knew I craved more of it.

Foreword

When I was in prison in Cuba, I remembered some of the stories now in this book. I drew strength from those who had gone before me into the prisons of Rome and Romania, Siberia and Shanghai. Many of them never came out alive; thankfully God saw fit to bring me safely to my earthly home instead of my heavenly one.

I carried into prison an amazing legacy of faith; this book is a way to pass that legacy on to the believers of today and tomorrow. Even now, new stories are being written by faithful servants of Christ who are laying down their lives for His cause. We will need many more pages in the years to come as this "living" book of Acts unfolds.

The apostle John, in the closing of his Gospel, said that Jesus did many other things that he did not record. "If they were written one by one," John said, "I suppose that even the world itself could not contain the books that would be written." (John 21:25). In collecting the martyrs' stories included between the covers of this book, we've run into a similar dilemma—there simply aren't enough pages to include them all.

The stories you read here have been carefully researched, and we offer them as a representative sample of lives given for the gospel message. Countless others who have also given their lives are known only to God. In heaven we will hear a complete accounting; we will read a complete *Acts and Monuments of the Christian Martyrs*. Until then, may these stories encourage and challenge you to walk with the Savior, no matter the cost.

For those in bonds,

Tom White
Executive Director
The Voice of the Martyrs, USA

"Father, forgive them;

for they do not know what they do." Luke 23:34

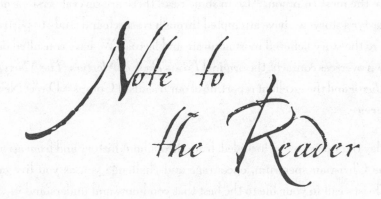

It's been both an honor and a challenge to collect and share the stories of courageous believers that you are about to read. We know that no book on Earth could contain the stories of all those who have laid down their lives for the gospel cause. Any attempt to assemble a list of Christians is fraught with opportunities to offend, and there will no doubt be readers who are offended by some of the stories in this book. Followers of Christ come in many doctrinal shapes and stripes. Thankfully, the final answer is not given by man here on Earth but in eternity by our Father, when true followers hear the words, "Well done, good and faithful servant" (Matthew 25:21).

Christ founded the church with a call to love one another, but those who claim His name have not always lived out that call. In looking back across church history, there are even times when persecution of His followers has come from other so-called believers.

In working through the stories on these pages, we have included men and women from a variety of theological and doctrinal backgrounds. They don't share doctrine, but they do share a commitment to follow Christ and to live out His call in the way that they know. By including them here we honor their commitment to Him, though we know some may question their doctrine.

Sometimes in translating names and places from another language into English, there are multiple spellings. In those cases, we have attempted to use the most common. Also in some cases there are several versions of a martyr's story; we have attempted through research and study to portray here the story believed most accurate and factual. We have consulted our own overseas contacts, the original *Foxe's Book of Martyrs, The Martyrs' Mirror* and the excellent reporting of our friends at Compass Direct News Service.

May the stories we've included, from throughout history and from across the Christian spectrum, encourage and challenge you as you live out Christ's call in your life to the best that you know and understand it.

—The Voice of the Martyrs

PART ONE

Martyrs
of the
First Century

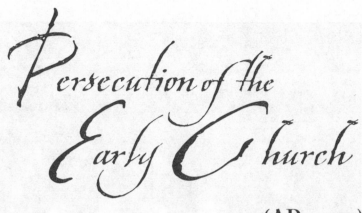

Persecution of the Early Church

(AD 40—110)

By the time the apostle John put the finishing touches on the book of Revelation, he alone among the original disciples remained alive. All of them suffered for Christ, with most dying violently for His sake. The witnesses of the bodily resurrection of Jesus Christ willingly exchanged their lives for the high privilege of declaring that life-transforming miracle. As has often been pointed out, people don't usually endure torture and painful death for something they know to be a lie. Those who told the world, "He is risen!" stood by their claim in the face of threats, suffering, and death. Their examples in dying left a lasting legacy. They set a high bar of faithfulness for generations to come.

The passage of time and the proliferation of accounts make it difficult to verify many of the specific details of the martyrdom of the original disciples and their closest companions. While the untimeliness and brutality of their deaths are almost universally acknowledged, the locations and particulars of their sacrifices are more difficult to ascertain. In the accounts that follow, the dominant versions of the deaths of the apostles will be given, with some reference to other possible or intriguing reports and circumstances.

Make no mistake, the shoot that grew from the root of Jesse was abundantly watered by the blood of the martyrs, some whose names we are honored to know; others whose stories wait to be told in the great account of God's ways in the throne room of heaven.

1

The stoning of Stephen

Stephen (AD 34)

The charges were false, even ludicrous. Those who couldn't refute his arguments or silence him by threats drummed up false accusations. Stephen took control of the room with his voice, unexpectedly holding his audience spellbound. His words resonated with the kind of passion that flows from a simple man who has grasped a great idea, or has been grasped by a vision larger than himself. He told an old familiar story once again, highlighting parts of it that had been curiously overlooked and even forgotten over the years. He traced God's amazing ways down through the centuries until, like the weaver's final pass of threads in a seamless garment, Stephen confronted his audience with the truth about their condition.

Stephen presented his case, beginning with Abraham, the father of Israel and Israel's faith (Acts 7:2–53). Then he unfolded an extended history lesson highlighted by God's faithfulness despite the faithlessness of His people. Because the accusations had focused on Stephen's alleged words against the Temple, his case demonstrated that even God had words of warning about the Temple. That was not, after all, a place on which God had staked His reputation. Having dismantled the accusers' sham case against him, Stephen swiftly stated God's case against them. Despite all God's gifts and blessings to His people, they had ultimately rejected Him and His Son. Then Stephen's closing thunder had to provoke either a storm of resistance or an outpouring of repentance. He said, "Which of the prophets did your fathers not persecute? And they killed those who foretold the coming of the Just One, of whom you now have become the betrayers and murderers, who have received the law by the direction of angels and have not kept it " (Acts 7:52–53).

The crowd had gathered to judge Stephen, but history and truth passed judgment on them. They rose in rejection of the truth and killed the messenger. Stoning is perhaps one of the most effective *ad hominem* arguments (an attack against a person rather than an idea), but it doesn't stop or silence the truth.

Stephen must have seen the murder in their eyes. But he also saw something better when he looked up. "I see the heavens opened and the

Son of Man standing at the right hand of God" (Acts 7:56), he declared. The mob dragged Stephen out of the city and began to stone him. He didn't expect to escape, so he asked God to receive his spirit. Then, with his last breath, he prayed, "Lord, do not charge them with this sin" (Acts 7:60).

Luke, the writer of this account, was not present at Stephen's martyrdom, but he knew well a man who had been there. That man would have remembered details like the last words Stephen uttered. That man was the apostle Paul, at that time known as Saul, a fierce persecutor of Jesus' followers. But Saul didn't know he would have an appointment on the road to Damascus with the same Jesus whom Stephen had seen just before he died.

"Lord, **do not** charge them

with this **sin**."

— Stephen, the first Christian martyr,

as he was being stoned to death

James the Great (ca. AD 44)

Arrests, beatings, and intimidation had become common. A group of believers were randomly rounded up and carted off to Herod's dungeon. Among them happened to be one of the apostles—James. The event seemed little more than the usual inconvenient harassment that the Roman leaders felt obligated to perform at the insistence of certain Jewish leaders, who seemed obsessed with the followers of Jesus. But things took a sudden turn when James was hauled out without fanfare and summarily executed by the sword. The church in Jerusalem was stunned; their opponents were elated (Acts 12:1–2).

James's death turned out to be a political experiment on Herod's part. He must have been sick and tired of the bickering in his court over the Christ-followers who seemed to be spreading like an infection. They didn't do anything wrong except provoke extreme hatred from others. But when the old politician saw the excited response to James's death among his political allies, Herod decided he could afford to eliminate a few more of these Christians. His attempt to kill Peter failed, and before he could devise a further plan, he was distracted by a crisis in another part of his kingdom. Herod died shortly thereafter when "immediately an angel of the Lord struck him, because he did not give glory to God. And he was eaten by worms and died" (Acts 12:23).

James, the son of Zebedee, has the noteworthy distinction of being the first apostolic martyr. His death came within fourteen years after Jesus' resurrection and ascension. Only Stephen anteceded James among the well-known early martyrs. Stephen's death and Saul's persecution must have made it clear to the apostles that things were not going to go well in the area of personal safety. After all, His *presence*, not preservation, had been Jesus' promise in the Great Commission, when He said, "I am with you always, even to the end of the age" (Matthew 28:20).

Curiously, James and his brother John were confronted by Jesus at one point after their mother asked the Lord for a special privilege for her sons. Jesus asked, "Are you able to drink the cup that I am about to drink?" (Matthew 20:22). Though they most likely had no idea to what He was referring, the brothers immediately said, "We are able." They thought they were about to get a privilege above the other ten disciples.

Jesus responded, "You will indeed drink My cup" (Matthew 20:23). His words were prophetic. James was the first to die; John the last. Their deaths formed the bookends in the stories of apostolic martyrdom.

Of the three disciples with whom Jesus spent extra time (Peter, James, and John), we have the least information about James. His own brother John never mentions him (or himself, for that matter) by name in the Gospel he wrote. James, the son of Zebedee, is called "the Great" merely to differentiate him from James, the son of Alphaeus ("the Less"), one of the other disciples.

In the context of history, fourteen years doesn't represent a large time span. But Jesus' active ministry only covered three years. The question becomes, then, what were James and the other apostles doing during those first fourteen years before James died at the hands of Herod's soldiers?

During the years following Jesus' ascension, an uneasy relationship developed between the growing movement of Christians in Jerusalem, those Jewish leaders who had rejected Christ's claims and helped to have Him killed, and the Roman authorities who were charged with keeping the peace. Order was often maintained by the use of threats and torture. The early chapters of the book of Acts provide glimpses of the ebb and flow of the persecution of believers. But Luke records a significant moment involving Gamaliel, the rabbi who was Saul's mentor. He wasn't opposed to the persecution of believers, but he cautioned his fellow members of the Sanhedrin against *killing* Christians. He understood the power of martyrdom. Gamaliel said, "And now I say to you, keep away from these men and let them alone; for if this plan or this work is of men, it will come to nothing; but if it is of God, you cannot overthrow it—lest you even be found to fight against God." (Acts 5:38–39). This tactic of toleration may have kept many believers in Jerusalem and thus slowed down the process of taking the gospel to the world. Stephen's and James's deaths eventually changed all of that. (The fall of Jerusalem in AD 70 scattered the church to the winds.)

The death of Stephen almost seems like an unusual case in which things got out of hand. But packing Christians off to prison became part of life in Jerusalem. Saul apparently had success in intimidating Christians to the point that many left Jerusalem for safer places. This had the benefit of spreading the gospel, something that Saul certainly didn't intend at that point in his life. Nor did he intend to be confronted by the Lord on the road to Damascus. But when Saul (Paul) defected as the chief persecuting official of the Sanhedrin, the situation in Jerusalem became a stalemate again for a number of years.

An ancient church in Spain claims to contain at least some of the remains of James's body. This gave rise to the tradition that James may have left Jerusalem for a number of years on a mission journey to Spain before his death. There seems to be little reason why Luke would not have included some reference in Acts to that effect among his notes about outreach. But it does appeal to our pioneering view of missions that one of the apostolic fishermen would embark for a long voyage to the far end of the Mediterranean—the ends of the Earth—and seek to carry out Christ's commission there.

The apostle James (the Great) beheaded in Jerusalem, AD 44

Philip (AD 54)

Two men named *Philip* occupied the stage in the early church. One was Philip the apostle, the first person called by Jesus to follow Him. The other was Philip the evangelist, one of the seven chosen by the church to help with the special needs of the growing band of believers in Jerusalem. Both men had similar evangelistic hearts, and the accounts of their lives have often been intertwined in subsequent history. Their stories are further complicated because they each appear to have fathered several daughters. Philip the apostle is mentioned several times in the Gospel of John but only once in the book of Acts (1:13). Philip the deacon appears in Acts and is instrumental in the conversion of the Ethiopian eunuch as well as in the spiritual outbreak among the Samaritans, recorded by Luke in Acts 8. Philip the deacon later hosted the apostle Paul on his last journey to Jerusalem (Acts 21:8). They may have had further contact during the two years that Paul was imprisoned in Caesarea before his journey under guard to Rome.

Philip the apostle came from Bethsaida, a town in northern Israel close to Capernaum and the Sea of Galilee. His non-Jewish name may indicate the degree to which Bethsaida was influenced by the Greek culture and government language that preceded the Roman occupation, a time when Alexander the Great had spread Greek influence across the world. The fact that Koine Greek, and not Latin, was a trade and official language of the times, indicates that Rome didn't rule everything.

John gives us four glimpses of Philip in action. When Jesus called Philip to follow Him (John 1:43), the young disciple immediately sought out his friend Nathanael and invited him to meet Jesus. He was clearly a young man more prone to see himself as a channel than a destination. Once he received information, he determined to act on it. Philip also spoke up in the discussion before the feeding of the five thousand, offering his estimate of what it would cost to buy food for such a large crowd (John 6:7). His practical observation regarding the lack of means or money simply highlighted Jesus' miraculous action. Circumstances that look and *are* impossible do not hinder God from working. On another occasion, when a group of Greek speakers wanted to approach Jesus, they contacted Philip to act as an intermediary. John mentions Philip's connection with Bethsaida as the reason for their strategy (John 12:21).

John also remembered Philip's request to Jesus during the Last Supper, "Philip said, 'Lord, show us the Father, and it is sufficient for us'" (John 14:8). Jesus' answer to Philip was for all the disciples: "Have I been with you so long, and yet you have not known Me, Philip? He who has seen Me has seen the Father; so how can you say, 'Show us the Father'? Do you not believe that I am in the Father, and the Father in Me? The words that I speak to you I do not speak on My own authority; but the Father who dwells in Me does the works" (John 14:9–10).

Jesus told the disciples everything they would need to remember later, after the reality of the Resurrection had wiped out their tendency toward unbelief. Philip's Greek name, his multilingual abilities, and his outgoing personality all combined with his vibrant faith in the risen Christ to make him an equipped messenger for the gospel.

One of the unique features surrounding the apostle Philip is his connection with the area we now know as France. He is the only apostolic figure claimed to have carried the gospel to the Gauls, the ancient inhabitants of that region. Philip the apostle has also been traditionally linked with Hierapolis in western Turkey. The church he led in that city was just outside the circle of seven churches mentioned by John in the first chapters of Revelation. His proximity to the apostle John may explain why John's Gospel features Philip's words and actions.

Culturally, Hierapolis had a Phrygian background, and the regional religion focused on the god Sabazios, represented by a snake. Geographically, Hierapolis was the site of magnificent mineral springs— rumored to have healing powers—that drew people from many parts of the world. This gathering of various nationalities would have attracted an apostolic missionary. Historically, Hierapolis became a largely Christian city. The church may have been planted as a result of Paul's journeys, though the city is not mentioned in his itineraries. The ruins of Hierapolis today include the remains of several ancient churches. Philip may have paid with his life in order to sustain the church. The pagan priests of

Hierapolis may have been delighted to profit from visitors from many places of the world, but they didn't appreciate having their religion directly challenged as Philip's message would have done.

Crucifixion was a favored punishment by the Romans, but the practice may have become even more widely known because of its prominence in the preaching of Jesus' followers. This could explain why so many of the early missionaries were themselves crucified. In Philip's case, the religious establishment apparently arranged for him to be crucified and stoned. Obviously, their tactic once again proved ineffective in stopping the gospel.

If you **abide** in My word,
you are My **disciples** indeed.
And you shall know the **truth** , and
the **truth** shall make you **free**.

John 8: 31, 32

Matthew (AD 60)

Matthew and his brother James the Less (the son of Alphaeus) are the lesser known of three sets of brothers whom Jesus chose to be disciples. Peter and Andrew (sons of John), along with James and John (sons of Zebedee), were the other two brotherly pairs. Matthew also went by the name Levi, a thoroughly Jewish name for a man whose original career as a tax collector placed him among the despised in Capernaum and brought shame to his family. But Jesus saw something in Matthew. One day as Matthew was collecting taxes along the main thoroughfare in Capernaum, Jesus walked by and called him to follow, so "He arose and followed Him" (Matthew 9:9b). Based on the existence of the Gospel he recorded, we imagine that all Matthew took with him from his old life were his writing tools.

The next stop for Jesus after calling Matthew to be a disciple was a dinner party at Matthew's house. Apparently both guests and critics showed up. Since the place was packed with obvious sinners (particularly tax collectors), certain Pharisees confronted Jesus' disciples. "Why does your Teacher eat with tax collectors and sinners?" (Matthew 9:11) The question reveals Matthew's reputation as well as the Pharisees' reluctance to confront Jesus directly. In this case, the disciples couldn't or didn't reply. But Jesus had an immediate answer that accomplished a number of purposes in a single statement. "Those who are well have no need of a physician, but those who are sick. But go and learn what this means: *'I desire mercy and not sacrifice.'* For I did not come to call the righteous, but sinners, to repentance" (Matthew 9:12–13). Jesus revealed His mission—to call sinners. He offered an invitation—those willing to acknowledge their sinfulness could claim His call. He rebuked the judgmental attitude of the critics by referring to the Old Testament Scriptures, "I desire mercy, not sacrifice." That quote also offered Jesus' listeners a subtle clue about His identity. God in Christ was demonstrating in the flesh His priorities with people. Matthew never went back to his old job.

The extent of Matthew's conversion can, in some ways, be measured by the fact that this prodigal from Israel, who had cooperated with the enemy as a taxing agent, became the author of a Gospel written with his own people in mind. Matthew remained a son of Abraham. His Gospel is filled with notes and highlights designed to clarify for the chosen people that their Messiah had come. One of the persistent ancient traditions about Matthew is that he was the only Gospel author to write his account of Jesus' life in Hebrew.

Given Matthew's passion to reach Israelites with the good news about their Messiah, we shouldn't be surprised to discover various traditions about Matthew's ministry among the widely scattered communities of Jews throughout the Roman Empire. As an itinerant missionary, it's quite possible that Matthew visited many locations. Matthew's apostolic assignment was to Ethiopia. In ancient times, that name was used for two locations: the familiar African one as well as an area of Persia. Traditional consensus has leaned toward placing Matthew in African Ethiopia, where he was beheaded while carrying out Jesus' commission to reach the world.

Matthew the evangelist pinned to the ground and beheaded
in Haddayar, Ethiopia, AD 70

James the Less (AD 63)

When the stones rained down on him, we don't know what he said, but he had good examples to follow. And the legacy of his death remains with us even today.

Among the "James trio" in the New Testament, James, son of Alphaeus, (or James the "Less") has the smallest profile. He receives no credit for a single question, comment, or action during his years with Christ. He was simply one of the Twelve. This James never stood out for ridicule or praise. James, son of Zebedee (the "Great"), and James, son of Joseph, both held far more prominent roles in the history of the times. James, son of Zebedee, was one of the famous Sons of Thunder among the disciples. James, son of Joseph and the half-brother of Jesus, eventually took a significant leadership role in the church of Jerusalem. But James, son of Alphaeus, lived in the background of the story.

At some point, tradition tells us, the apostles assigned themselves certain areas of the world as destinations for outreach. Syria was the appointment of James the Less. During the early persecutions of Christians in Jerusalem, one of the popular escape destinations was Damascus in southern Syria. So much so that when Saul began to run out of believers to hound in Jerusalem, he set his sights on Damascus as a concentration of Christians that he could raid for prisoners. Fortunately, God had other plans. Those who had been targeted for suffering in Damascus ended up giving shelter to Saul following his confrontation with Jesus on the road to their city.

In Jerusalem, persecution was creating what sheer obedience had not accomplished. Eventually, Paul's bold example and the successes of those like Peter and Philip, who had been drawn out of Jerusalem on specific missions, began to overcome inertia. Christ's final words, "You shall be witnesses to Me in Jerusalem, and in all Judea and Samaria, and to the end of the Earth" (Acts 1:8), were coming true one way or another.

James's mission in Syria was met by three audiences: transplanted believers such as Ananias, who would have probably welcomed someone with apostolic credentials; transplanted Jews who would suspect James as a troublemaker; and the wider mixed culture typical of territory on a major trading route. Apparently the Jews in Syria rejected James's preaching by stoning him to death.

One account says he was appointed the first overseer of the church at Jerusalem shortly after Christ's death. This account says the high priest Ananias summoned him before the judges to deny Jesus is the Christ. He was placed on the pinnacle of the temple where he was to deny Christ before the people. Instead, he boldly proclaimed Jesus Christ is the promised Messiah. The multitudes praised God. However, James was cast down and stoned. But the fall and stoning only broke his legs, so on his knees he prayed to God for those who were attacking him, saying, "Lord, Forgive them; for they know not what they do." Then he was struck in the head and died.

James contributed to an eastern expansion of the gospel that eventually left a lasting arm of the church on the distant end of the arched trade route that connected Jerusalem and Damascus on the west to ancient Iraq on the east. The gospel traveled even farther east into India, pushing toward the ends of the Earth.

And they **overcame** him by the **blood** of the **Lamb** and by the **word** of their **testimony**, and they **did not love their lives** to the **death**.

Revelation 12:11

Matthias (AD 70)

Matthias was the alternate apostle. He was chosen to fill the vacancy among the Twelve created by Judas's betrayal and abrupt departure (Acts 1:23–26). Based on the requirement that each of the candidates had to meet—a long association with Jesus as a disciple—it is almost certain that Matthias was one of the seventy evangelists the Lord sent out (Luke 10:1). He was a witness to the full scope of Jesus' ministry.

After his appointment in the first chapter of Acts, Matthias is not mentioned by name again in the New Testament. But neither are most of the original twelve disciples. Luke based his account in Acts of the development of the early church primarily on the ministry of Peter and then Paul.

For Matthias's role, we rely on the general participation by the Twelve in the affairs of the church in Jerusalem, and we also turn to the various accounts from tradition that include Matthias. As one of the apostles, he was under the public pressure of persecution that broke out when Saul and others decided they needed to stamp out the followers of Jesus.

Matthias was one of those apostles whose missionary assignment took him north. Even Sebastopol (present day Sevastopol) on the northern side of the Black Sea is frequently mentioned as one of his destinations. Eventually, Matthias appears to have made his way back to Jerusalem, where he was stoned to death. Some say he would not sacrifice to the god Jupiter. Others state he was to be hung on a cross, stoned and then beheaded with an ax for the blasphemy he had committed against God, Moses and the law. When Matthias would not deny Christ, he is believed to have said, "Thy blood be upon thy head, for thine own mouth hath spoken against thee."

Andrew (AD 70)

Undoubtedly with his brother Simon's permission, Andrew temporarily left the fishing nets behind and journeyed to hear a man called John the Baptist. John was the talk of the town and wharf. He urged people to get right with God because the long-awaited Savior was coming. Andrew saw and heard something in John that he liked. This wild man was not only a scathing critic of society's flaws, but he also offered people hope through repentance. He had a knack for making people feel very bad before he showed them how they could be forgiven. So Andrew became a follower of John the Baptist. Eventually, he was likely joined by his friend John, the son of Zebedee, who recorded the initial steps Jesus took in choosing a group of disciples to train. At some point, at least five of the original apostles were in the area where John the Baptist was carrying out his ministry.

According to the biblical account, Andrew was the first of the apostolic band to discover Jesus in his unique role as Lamb of God who takes away the sins of the world. Andrew was standing beside John the Baptist when the fiery prophet pointed out Jesus as the one he had come to announce. We don't know if Andrew witnessed Jesus' baptism, but John the Baptist probably identified Jesus, who had just returned from His forty-day wilderness experience that had immediately followed His baptism.

Andrew and his unnamed companion (probably John) approached Jesus. Jesus invited them to spend time with Him. They immediately broadened that invitation to include Simon. Within a couple of days, both Philip and Nathanael joined that small group of seekers. They were with Jesus when He returned to Cana for a wedding, witnessing Jesus' first miracle. Not long after this, Jesus called Simon and Andrew to leave their nets and follow Him. Andrew never looked back.

Andrew took time for individual people. He noticed their needs and qualities and understood them. He quietly took action. He connected people with each other. He connected them with Christ. He introduced his big brother to Jesus. He was instrumental in other significant introductions, making an impact in people's lives, one by one. In the end, tradition tells us, this great quality in the first disciple got him killed.

Andrew is seldom mentioned in the accounts of Jesus' action, but he was a constant presence. His few moments in the spotlight reveal that he was always aware of what was going on and looking for ways to be helpful.

In John's account of the feeding of the five thousand (John 6:4–13), Andrew is the one who offered the quiet suggestion that he had just spoken with a lad who had five loaves and two fishes. Not much, but something! And what Jesus did with that little gift was astounding. John 12:20–26 describes a group of Greeks who wanted to meet Jesus. They singled out Philip to approach, probably because of his Greek name, but it's worth noting that Philip asked Andrew to help him make the introductions. Andrew's last appearance by name in Scripture occurs in Acts 1:13 where he is listed among the eleven disciples as they chose Matthias to replace Judas. He was doubtless present during those exciting and turbulent early years in Jerusalem, serving among the leaders of the church.

While Andrew's eventual missionary travels may have taken him as far north as Scythia (southern Russia) and included time around Ephesus with John, he likely ended up on the Greek peninsula in the city of Patras. There he began to relate to individuals and introduce them to the Savior. Among the converts was a woman named Maximilla, the wife of a high Roman official, a governor named Aegaeas, who was so angry at his wife's conversion he threatened Andrew with death by crucifixion. To this, Andrew replied, "Had I feared the death of the cross, I should not have preached the majesty and gloriousness of Christ."

Andrew was arrested and tried. Threatened, scourged, and tortured, he remained steadfast. It is said that the judge pleaded with Andrew not to cast aside his life, and the old apostle responded with equal passion, urging the judge not to cast aside his soul.

Unwilling to recant his faith in Christ, Andrew was tied to an "X"-shaped cross to die a slow and painful death. This particular cross is still called St. Andrew's cross. One source says that when Andrew came near the cross, he said, "O beloved cross! I have greatly longed for thee. I rejoice to see thee erected here. I come to thee with a peaceful conscience and with cheerfulness, desiring that I, who am a disciple of Him who hung on the cross, may also be crucified. The nearer I come to the cross, the nearer I come to God; and the farther I am from the cross, the farther I remain from God."

Andrew hung for three days on the cross; and during this time he taught the people who stood near him, saying such things as: "I thank my Lord Jesus Christ, that He, having used me for a time as an ambassador, now permits me to have this body, that I, through a good confession, may obtain everlasting grace and mercy. Remain steadfast in the word and doctrine which you have received, instructing one another, that you may dwell with God in eternity, and receive the fruit of His promises." Only heaven will reveal the thousands upon thousands of lives that were eventually transformed by Andrew's quiet and persistent work behind the scenes, touching one life at a time.

Precious in the sight
of the Lord
is the death of His saints.

Psalm 116:15

Mark (AD 64)

One of the unexpected shared characteristics of the biblical records of Jesus' life and the spread of the gospel is the almost painful and sometimes humorous honesty of those recording the events. Mark, also known as John Mark, "signed" his Gospel with an embarrassing footnote in chapter 14 when he seems to have described his own reaction to Jesus' arrest. "Now a certain young man followed Him, having a linen cloth thrown around his naked body. And the young men laid hold of him, and he left the linen cloth and fled from them naked" (Mark 14:51–52).

We tend to justify John Mark's qualifications to record his Gospel based on the tradition that he based his writings on Peter's account of Jesus' ministry. But events like the one above and the fact that Mark's home in Jerusalem was used as a gathering place for the early church certainly place this young disciple in the center of history as an eyewitness. The clipped and almost breathless format of Mark's Gospel (his favorite connecting phrase is "and then") combines all the action of a storyteller's style with a young man's impatience to get the story told. Mark knew the people about whom he was writing. He may not have been part of all the events, but his personal awareness of the participants gives his Gospel a ring of authenticity.

As a young man at the time of Jesus' resurrection, Mark had a long life ahead of him. Some of his learning trajectory was recorded by Luke in Acts. Mark's uncle Barnabas, and his mother Mary, were recognizable figures in the early church. Barnabas is the one who first brought Mark and Paul together shortly before the first missionary journey out of the Antioch church. Although Paul and Barnabas were specifically sent out by the church, "they also had John as their assistant" (Acts 13:5). Apparently the rigors, pressures, and suffering on the road got to Mark early in the trip. By the time they reached Pamphylia in southern Turkey, he left Paul and Barnabas and returned to Jerusalem (Acts 13:13).

Mark's departure became an issue between Paul and Barnabas that led to their split as a partnership (Acts 15:36–40). Barnabas insisted that Mark deserved another chance. In the final outcome, Barnabas proved to be a better judge of Mark's character than Paul, who later acknowledged that fact by expressing his appreciation of Mark's capabilities (Colossians 4:10, 2 Timothy 4:11, Philemon 23–24). After a stint with Barnabas, Mark spent time traveling with Peter (1 Peter 5:13). These various apprentice trips took him from Jerusalem to Antioch to Babylon to Rome.

By the time Peter and Paul were martyred, Mark was a capable evangelist in his own right. He had a longstanding connection with the city of Alexandria in Egypt and was instrumental in founding and nurturing the church there. As was often the case, the good news about Jesus was bad news for the existing pagan religious structures in communities. So within days of his arrival in Alexandria, Mark was a "marked" man. Though years passed before action was taken, a mob eventually exercised their demonic energy against him. Mark was tied with ropes (hooks may have also been used) and dragged through the cobblestone streets of Alexandria until his body was ripped, wounded, and badly injured. After a night in prison, the same treatment was repeated until Mark died. Though the crowd intended to burn Mark's body, there is a persistent account that a storm delayed the process and allowed other Christians a chance to retrieve and bury his remains.

Peter (AD 69)

Simon, son of John, grew up in Capernaum, on the north end of the Sea of Galilee. Raised along with his brother Andrew in a fishing family, Simon seemed headed for a career in that business. Then Jesus came walking along the shore and invited Simon to follow him into a life of fishing for people. Simon accepted both the invitation and a new name given by Jesus—*Peter* (from the Greek word *petros*, meaning "a piece of rock"). For three years, Peter was Jesus' constant companion.

We find it easy to imagine Simon Peter, the rock, smiling over the immense irony of Jesus' call in his life as Peter wrote these lines: "Coming to Him as to a living stone, rejected indeed by men, but chosen by God and precious, you also, as living stones, are being built up a spiritual house, a holy priesthood, to offer up spiritual sacrifices acceptable to God through Jesus Christ. Therefore it is also contained in the Scripture, *'Behold, I lay in Zion a chief cornerstone, elect, precious, and he who believes on Him will by no means be put to shame.'"* (1 Peter 2:4–6).

Peter knew firsthand the depth of that promise of never being put to shame. He knew the unspeakable joy that comes when, in the midst of the overwhelming facts and feelings of failure, Jesus steps in and says, "I still have work for you to do." In the biblical record, Jesus' first and last words to Peter were, "Follow Me" (Mark 1:17; John 21:22). History tells us Peter did just that. From the out-of-the-way shore of Galilee to the center-of-the-world hallways of Rome, Peter followed Jesus. From laying down his nets to laying down his life, Peter learned and practiced fishing for men and women. It remains clear that Peter is one of our finest examples of what it means to be a martyr. He lived a full life and he died a faithful death for Christ.

Given the obvious leadership role that Peter had among the disciples and in the early church, it is interesting to see how faithfully the Gospels record his fumbling efforts. The disciples as a group neither comprehended what Jesus was doing nor why, and Peter usually made public their lack of understanding. His impulsive nature allowed him to sometimes blurt out the truth, but more often to state the mistake. Though the resurrection of

Jesus transformed an average group of disciples into a powerful force for the gospel, those who knew them never forgot their background. The Gospel writers could have easily shaped the stories of the ministry days with Jesus in order to make the first leaders of the church more heroic. They resisted that temptation. Instead, they gave us the truth –God's Word. They gave us accounts into which we can fit ourselves. The ordinary people who spent time with Jesus are people with whom we can relate. The fact that they became apostolic witnesses simply reminds us that God desires also to do something through us in order to bring glory to His name.

When it comes to Peter's missionary efforts, the first twelve chapters of Acts record the exciting events of the initial years of the movement that began with Jesus' command to make disciples throughout the world. Peter's first sermon on the Day of Pentecost seemed to open the floodgates of new believers, but the spread of the gospel was at first limited to Jews and proselytes (those Gentiles who had become "naturalized" Jews). God used Peter's visit to a Roman soldier's household to confirm Jesus' inclusion of people from every nation as candidates for the good news of salvation. Cornelius became the test case for Gentile conversions.

Peter departs the Acts account suddenly in chapter 12. He had just been miraculously freed from prison and had briefly visited the believers who were gathered together praying for him at Mary's house. They had prayed for Peter's safety, and God had answered by having Peter knock at the door. Because he was technically a prison escapee, Peter's life was in added danger. Luke notes Peter's parting message: "But motioning to them with his hand to keep silent, he declared to them how the Lord had brought him out of the prison. And he said, 'Go, tell these things to James and to the brethren.' And he departed and went to another place" (Acts 12:17).

The "other place" where Peter went has been the subject of both tradition and legend. Traditional accounts for Peter's travels focus primarily on time spent in Babylon (to the east) or Rome (to the west). In support of Peter's ministry in Babylon, we have the apostle's apparent location mentioned in 1 Peter 5:13, "She who is in Babylon, elect together with you, greets you; and so does Mark my son." The Eastern branch of the church claims that Peter was instrumental in planting the gospel there. In support of Peter's ministry in Rome, we have the obvious case that he did end up in Rome and was martyred there. As to his founding the church in Rome, we have little direct evidence, but someone did bring the gospel to the Roman Empire's capital, for when Paul wrote his letter to Rome, there was already a thriving church there. But if Peter was already in Rome at the time, it seems strange that Paul didn't mention him among his various detailed greetings in that letter. What we know from Acts is that Peter was somewhere, busy sharing the gospel.

It has often been noted that when Jesus and Peter walked on the shore of Galilee for the last time, the Lord not only reinstated His call on Peter's life, but also gave Peter an inkling of the end that awaited him.

> "Most assuredly, I say to you, when you were younger, you girded yourself and walked where you wished; but when you are old, you will stretch out your hands, and another will gird you and carry you where you do not wish." This He spoke, signifying by what death he would glorify God. And when He had spoken this, He said to him, "Follow Me" (John 21:18–19).

It's not where we go and what happens to us that matters all that much. What does matter is how we respond when Jesus comes to us and says, "Follow me."

Peter's final days in Rome are not described in the Scriptures, but various traditional accounts have survived. Reportedly he spent horrific months in the infamous Mamertine Prison, a place where incarceration was often itself a death sentence. Though manacled and mistreated, Peter survived the tortures and apparently communicated the gospel effectively to his guards. Eventually he was hauled out of the dungeon, taken to Nero's Circus, and there crucified upside down because Peter did not consider himself worthy to be crucified with his head upward, like Christ.

Paul (AD 69)

In contrast to most of the other apostolic figures, little confusion exists about the place of Paul's death. He always had a passion to preach the gospel in Rome, and he died there. Paul spent time in Rome twice, on both occasions at the expense of the Roman Empire. Neither Paul's travel arrangements nor his accommodations were first class, but they suited the apostle well. Throughout Acts and his letters, Paul conveys an unmistakable sense that his time was short, and he was grateful for every moment he was given. Paul understood God's grace, not simply as a great theological concept, but also as his own reason for living. He appreciated God's grace because he knew he needed so much of it.

His final thoughts had little to do with regrets and much to do with the satisfaction that flows from grace-drenched living. He wrote to Timothy: "For I am already being poured out as a drink offering, and the time of my departure is at hand. I have fought the good fight, I have finished the race, I have kept the faith. Finally, there is laid up for me the crown of righteousness, which the Lord, the righteous Judge, will give to me on that Day, and not to me only but also to all who have loved His appearing" (2 Timothy 4:6–8).

While he lived, Paul certainly traveled broadly, proclaiming the gospel everywhere he went. Perhaps his statement to the Colossians sums up his heart the best: "Him we preach, warning every man and teaching every man in all wisdom, that we may present every man perfect in Christ Jesus. To this end I also labor, striving according to His working which works in me mightily" (Colossians 1:28–29).

One of the greatest ironies in Paul's life is that he accomplished a lot to spread the gospel even while he was persecuting the church. His rabid efforts to hunt down Christians in and around Jerusalem scattered believers to the wind, planting the gospel seeds everywhere they went. Truly God uses even the plans and efforts of evil men to accomplish His will. But once Paul turned around after his confrontation with Jesus on the road to Damascus, all the fiery intensity of his former life was now channeled into his efforts for Christ. He produced almost half the New Testament writings with the letters he sent to the churches. He set the standard for missionary living. He pioneered evangelistic practices. He planted several dozen churches. He fearlessly applied God's love and grace to the non-Jewish world, and was hounded for his faithfulness by those who should have cheered him on. The one who once persecuted Jesus Christ became the one who spent the rest of his days promoting Christ.

Fortunately, Paul has given us an idea of the treatment he received as part and parcel of his work as an evangelist in the ancient world. While the following list of highlights may make us shudder at the cost paid by God's servant, it also serves as an indicator of the common experiences of those who followed Jesus. They risked everything for the good news. The salvation we have Jesus bought for us on the cross—a price beyond measure. The faith we claim has been delivered to us by many willing to pay the price of faithfulness.

> "From the Jews five times I received forty stripes minus one. Three times I was beaten with rods; once I was stoned; three times I was shipwrecked; a night and a day I have been in the deep; in journeys often, in perils of waters, in perils of robbers, in perils of my own countrymen, in perils of the Gentiles, in perils in the city, in perils in the wilderness, in perils in the sea, in perils among false brethren; in weariness and toil, in sleeplessness often, in hunger and thirst, in fastings often, in cold and nakedness—besides the other things, what comes upon me daily: my deep concern for all the churches" (2 Corinthians 11:24–28).

We miss a significant lesson from Paul's life if we make suffering our goal. Suffering is not an accurate measurement of obedience or faithfulness. Disobedience and faithlessness can also bring suffering. When suffering becomes a goal, pride is often the hidden motivation. Suffering is an unpredictable by-product of obedience and faithfulness. But it's only a small part of an even greater unpredictable aspect of life in Christ – joy! The example of the great martyrs of the faith is one of joyful, carefree living. They didn't relish suffering, but they didn't run from it either. They learned, as did Paul, the principle of radical contentment:

"Not that I speak in regard to need, for I have learned in whatever state I am, to be content: I know how to be abased, and I know how to abound. Everywhere and in all things I have learned both to be full and to be hungry, both to abound and to suffer need. I can do all things through Christ who strengthens me" (Philippians 4;11–13).

Paul let nothing but God's Spirit hinder him from going to the ends of the Earth. The timeline of his life, stories from tradition, and references in Scripture to places, such as his desire to minister in Spain (Romans 15: 23-24), allow us to consider that the range of his travels took him from Arabia to the British Isles. The six years of silence between his two Roman imprisonments provide room for wide travels.

The apostle's final destination this side of eternity was a spot on the Ostian Way just outside the walls of Rome. Tradition has it that Paul and Peter were martyred on the same day—the former fisherman crucified in the city, and the former Pharisee beheaded beyond the gates. Both of them fought the good fight, finished the race, and kept the faith. They are two significant reasons why we can do the same today.

The apostle Paul was beheaded in Rome.

Judas / Thaddaeus (ca. AD 70)

At least three men named *Judas* had prominent roles surrounding Jesus. Two were disciples Jesus chose: Judas from Iscariot and Judas/Thaddaeus, son of James. The third was Jesus' half-brother, Judas, who did not believe in Christ until after the Resurrection. This half-brother of Jesus wrote the letter that bears his name, Jude, in the New Testament. Our subject here is the faithful disciple Judas, also known as Thaddaeus.

Even the Gospel writers sensed the need to indicate when they were talking about Judas the betrayer of Jesus or Judas the faithful disciple. Both disciples named Judas died violent deaths: the first by his own hand out of remorse (Matthew 27:3–10; Acts 1:18–20); and the second by the hands of others with whom he was carrying out Jesus' command to spread the gospel to the world.

Although we can be sure that Judas/Thaddaeus was present throughout the Gospel accounts when the disciples are mentioned, he rarely appears on his own. John's Gospel records a poignant question Judas asked: "Judas (not Iscariot) said to Him, 'Lord, how is it that You will manifest Yourself to us, and not to the world?'" (John 14:22). In that comment we catch a glimpse of difficulties the disciples had in grasping Jesus' purposes. Their problem wasn't that they didn't believe He was the Son of God; it was their mistaken expectations of what the Son of God would do in the world. Judas's question was basically, "How can you rule the world and not show yourself to the world?" Jesus' response made it clear again that His kingdom was not of this world, "If anyone loves Me, he will keep My word; and My Father will love him, and We will come to him and make Our home with him" (John 14:23).

The Great Commission in both its versions (Matthew 28:19–20 and Acts 1:8) includes the command to take the gospel to the world. The kingdom would be global, but personal, lived out in the hearts and lives of individual men and women. Jesus gave them a monumental task and equipped them with power and understanding. At the core of their understanding of their mission was the fact that the way would not be easy. They could expect to receive the same kind of welcome their Master received. Jesus promised them victory and suffering.

The traditional accounts of Judas's ministry have him preaching north and east of Jerusalem, even as far as India. Like fellow disciple Bartholomew, Judas has a strong historic bond with Christianity in Armenia, an ancient land between the Black and Caspian Seas, spilling down into what we now call eastern Turkey. Armenia has long been recognized as the first Christian nation, based on early evangelization and the "official" declaration by the state designating itself a nation for Christ in the fourth century. But the source of that early influence for Christ goes back to Judas and then Bartholomew. Judas/Thaddaeus arrived first, and carried on a ministry that lasted eight years. He was executed as a martyr with arrows or a javelin sometime around AD 70. The specific events surrounding his death are not known, but the gospel frequently generated both faith and resistance in new lands. And when the message could not be killed, the messengers often were.

One story may explain the original reason behind Judas's journey to Armenia so soon after the Resurrection. The following events have not been historically confirmed, but they provoke all kinds of curiosity about the way information traveled in the first century. According to an account recorded by a bishop and early church historian named Eusebius, news about Jesus reached as far as the kingdom of Edessa in eastern Armenia. The king, Abgar, sent a letter to Jesus, offering asylum and a more receptive audience than He was having among his own people. Abgar was also hoping Jesus could heal him from a disease. Jesus replied that though His responsibilities required Him to stay in Israel until God's plan had been fulfilled, He would arrange to send a personal emissary, one of His disciples, soon after He returned to heaven. Tradition identifies that messenger as Judas.

Stories that come from the "silences" in the Gospels or the rest of the New Testament are not inspired as are the Scriptures, but they do lead us to appreciate and pay attention to the Bible in new ways. Did Jesus receive and respond to correspondence? We have no specific examples in God's Word, but it's not difficult to imagine that such things occurred. They were simply too numerous for special attention or not considered central to the account. The ripples of good news that began in the sea of humanity with Jesus' resurrection certainly did spread a long way in every direction.

And perhaps the news spread quite widely even during Jesus' lifetime. Only heaven will reveal the extent of the original surge and the full adventures of those who first carried the gospel to the ends of the Earth.

For to you it has been **granted** on behalf of **Christ**, not only to **believe** in Him, but also to **suffer** for His sake.

Philippians 1:29

Bartholomew / Nathanael (ca. AD 70)

Bartholomew came as a reluctant seeker, brought to Jesus by Philip, who couldn't wait to spread the word about the Messiah. Bartholomew's initial response to news about Jesus was a mixture of skepticism and sarcasm: "Can anything good come out of Nazareth?" (John 1:46).

As he had done the day before when meeting Simon, Jesus greeted Bartholomew with perceptive and challenging words. Jesus immediately let Bartholomew know that He really understood him. Imagine a person greeting you with, "Behold, an Israelite indeed, in whom is no deceit" (see John 1:47).

Bartholomew was stunned. "How do You know me?" he blurted. Jesus had just identified his central impulse. He didn't feel complimented; he felt completely known. He was curious about how Jesus did it; to which Jesus responded with a description of Bartholomew's location when Philip found him. Jesus' perception was enough to convince Bartholomew that Philip was correct. This was in fact the Promised One. And he said so: "Rabbi, You are the Son of God! You are the King of Israel!" (John 1:49). Jesus received Bartholomew's declaration, with the promise that he would eventually have many more reasons for recognizing the Son of God.

Bartholomew was one of the group of five apostles who began to follow Jesus shortly after His wilderness experience. He joined Andrew, John, Simon, and Philip in a movement away from John the Baptist toward becoming followers of Jesus. We know him under two names: Bartholomew and Nathanael. He is mentioned in the naming of the Twelve (Matthew 10, Mark 3, and Luke 6) as Bartholomew, and as Nathanael one other time as part of the group of seven disciples who went fishing after Jesus' resurrection, and then had breakfast with Him on shore (John 21:2). Bartholomew is not credited with any words or actions throughout the Gospel accounts of Jesus' ministry. He was simply there—watching, listening, and following. With someone around like Simon Peter, always eager to leap into the verbal breach, men like Bartholomew were content to observe and learn.

The apostolic career of Bartholomew is linked with that of the apostle Judas / Thaddaeus. Both are credited with the spread of Christianity into Armenia. Traditions have him traveling east, as far as regions called India, but the historical consensus locates his ministry and martyrdom in Armenia—a land to the northeast of Palestine, between the Black and Caspian Seas.

As has been demonstrated repeatedly during the worldwide spread of the gospel, those who bring the message of Christ often lose their lives as a direct result of their effectiveness. Even while living peaceably and doing good, believers have often been cruelly persecuted. The mixed response by the world often parallels the response Jesus received in His own time. Some who hear the message simply decide they would have to give up too much in order to acknowledge Christ; they decide instead to eliminate His messengers.

We may long to equate faithfulness with safety and success, but there's little reason for us to do so. Some of Christ's most effective and faithful servants have suffered the same fate as their Master, being despised and rejected by the very people whom they approached with good news.

Under Bartholomew's influence, the gospel apparently penetrated every facet of Armenian life except the stronghold of local pagan religious leaders, who rightly perceived Christianity as anathema to their belief systems and demonically energized practices. Their powers were no match for the power of God exercised by Thaddaeus and Bartholomew. Their idols were proven impotent. Believers from royal rank on down began to worship Jesus and the God of the Bible. Many were baptized, and the church grew by leaps and bounds.

Meanwhile, the pagan priests conspired with the king's brother to protect their power and system of beliefs. Underhanded maneuvers led to Bartholomew's arrest and torture. He suffered flaying, a particularly gruesome form of abuse in which a person's skin is almost entirely removed by the use of whips. He was then crucified in agony (some accounts say head down) and allowed to die a martyr's death for Christ.

One of the startling historic witnesses to the effectiveness of Bartholomew's ministry in Armenia is the obvious link between the Holy Land and Armenian tradition. Pilgrimages to the lands of the Bible became popular even in the apostolic era. Many of the biblical sites in the Holy Land are even today marked by shrines and churches constructed by Armenian believers many centuries ago.

Blessed are those who are persecuted for righteousness' sake, for theirs is the kingdom of heaven.

Matthew 5:10

Thomas (ca. AD 70)

With the exception of Peter and Paul, we have more information on the subsequent life of Thomas than on any of the other apostles. Most of the material comes from tradition. For a disciple with a doubtful reputation, he certainly left behind a variety of regions that name him among the founders of their ancient traditions of faith.

The account in John's Gospel gives us the most glimpses of Thomas, but they come within the last few weeks of Jesus' ministry. Apparently his character traits became more obvious under the growing pressure of opposition. Keenly aware of the danger waiting for Jesus in Jerusalem, Thomas voiced the outlook that must have been on all their minds when he said, "Let us also go, that we may die with Him" (John 11:16). Perhaps more clearly than the other disciples, Thomas thought that if their hopes of a kingdom with Jesus as the leader fell through, death would result. Jesus' frequent references to His death may have confused some of the disciples, but it seems to have unsettled Thomas.

Our next glimpse of Thomas comes during the Last Supper when he reacts to Jesus' comforting words about His Father's house. Thomas reveals that his heart is indeed troubled when he blurts out, "Lord, we do not know where You are going, and how can we know the way?" (John 14:5). We can be grateful for Thomas's boldness, for it allowed Jesus to make one of His clearest claims about His role as Lord and Savior, "I am the way, the truth, and the life. No one comes to the Father except through Me" (John 14:6).

Thomas's third outburst came the evening of resurrection Sunday (or very early on Monday). Jesus had appeared to ten of the disciples on Sunday evening, with Thomas as the only absentee. Perhaps he was reacting differently than the rest of the disciples to the news that Jesus had arisen. They gathered, but Thomas stayed away. When informed of Jesus' visit, Thomas responded with daring doubts:

> "The other disciples therefore said to him, 'We have seen the Lord.' So he said to them, 'Unless I see in His hands the print of the nails, and put my finger into the print of the nails, and put my hand into His side, I will not believe'" (John 20:25).

The apostle Thomas was tortured by the natives in Calamina,
thrown into an oven, and stuck through with spears, AD 70.

A week later, that dare was met. Jesus appeared before all of them, and Thomas's doubts vaporized as he declared, "My Lord and my God!" (John 20:28). Jesus used the occasion to make another crucial point about the nature of faith: "Thomas, because you have seen Me, you have believed. Blessed are those who have not seen and yet have believed" (John 20:29).

The passion Jesus awakened in His disciples drove them out to bless thousands who would not have the privilege of seeing, but would believe the testimony of those gladly willing to lay down their lives for their convictions. Once Thomas left Jerusalem, there's no evidence that he ever returned. He left his doubts behind. He headed for the ends of the Earth. He undoubtedly found that Jesus was true to His promise of companionship to the end.

Thomas traveled north and east from Israel, passing through Babylon and Persia and making an impact for the gospel as far as the southern regions of India. Long-standing traditions about his journeys far beyond the boundaries of Roman control remain even today. Many of the places and kings associated with Thomas that were thought to be merely legendary have been confirmed by independent historical and archeological studies. Undeniably, developed civilizations lay beyond the horizon to the east, and Jesus' words, "to the ends of the Earth," must have constantly echoed in the apostles' minds. The trade routes he would have used have existed for thousands of years. Portuguese mariners and explorers in the sixteenth century reported evidence of Thomas's ministry, including a sizeable band of believers known as the St. Thomas Christians. The fact that Thomas has been so uniquely connected with India among the apostles makes a strong case for his ministry there.

Various versions of Thomas's martyrdom agree that he ran afoul of the Hindu priests who envied his successes and rejected his message. Thomas was speared to death. The location of his tomb can still be visited in Mylapore (Meliapore), India.

Luke (AD 93)

Luke was the official historian of the early days of the church. His account parallels the other acknowledged biographies of Jesus: Matthew, Mark, and John. We have confirmation in extra-biblical sources such as Josephus. But when it comes to the historical record, the two-volume effort called Luke-Acts gives us a carefully compiled, continuous record of Jesus' life and the immediate results of His ministry on Earth.

Although Luke was not a member of the inner apostolic band, he had access to many of those individuals. In the introductory paragraphs for the Gospel of Luke and for Acts of the Apostles, Luke outlines his approach to writing: "It seemed good to me also, having had perfect understanding of all things from the very first, to write to you an orderly account, most excellent Theophilus, that you may know the certainty of those things in which you were instructed" (Luke 1:3–4). The intimate information that Luke includes about the birth of Jesus in chapters 1 and 2 of his Gospel has the tone of an eyewitness account. In this particular case, the obvious eyewitness would have been Mary. All the things she treasured in her heart for a lifetime she recalled and shared with the gentle physician who had so many questions.

One of the characteristics of Acts involves what has come to be known as the "we" sections. When Luke narrates events of Paul's travels, he sometimes uses "we" as a subtle indicator that he was a participant. (If this is correct, then Luke first joined Paul's missionary band in Troas.) Paul calls Luke the "beloved physician" (Colossians 4:14). Having a doctor on the team would have been a real benefit. During their travels, Luke must have served as a medic for the group, not only tending to Paul's long-standing illness but also mending the occasional abrasion and contusion resulting from the beatings, stonings, and other assorted violent treatment received by those who preached the good news. Since Luke was an assistant and keeper of the record rather than a public speaker, he may have been spared some of the harsher handling his companions suffered.

Luke, however, clearly experienced his own share of suffering for Jesus' sake. He accompanied Paul on the final journey from Caesarea to Rome.

Luke the evangelist hanged from an olive tree in Greece, AD 93.

The time of the year made a normally perilous trip even more hazardous. Describing the desperate struggle for survival by the crew of their ship as they were driven by hurricane winds (Acts 27), Luke included the details of an eyewitness and the detachment of a survivor. That two-week ordeal tested every participant. After the shipwreck on Malta, with his physician eyes Luke describes two incidents that caught his attention. Paul was bitten by a venomous serpent and escaped unharmed, creating quite a stir among the islanders. Also, he diagnosed the illness of an important man on the island as "fever and dysentery." But God provided healing through Paul's prayer. Out of that disaster came many opportunities to preach the gospel to a new audience. The suffering had an immediate purpose.

Tradition disagrees over the manner of Luke's death. By some accounts, Luke was with Paul until the end in Rome and then carried on an extensive ministry of his own. By that account, Luke died as an old man in a place called Boeotia (which may have been a region in ancient Greece). But given the violence of the time in which he lived, the traditional echoes that point to Luke's martyrdom somewhere in Greece cannot be ignored. The beloved physician certainly brought about by his writing the healing of many more souls than he ever touched in his lifetime.

"For to me, to **live is Christ**, and to **die is gain.**"

Philippians 1:21

Simon the Zealot (AD 74)

Simon may have been the most volatile among the disciples. All of them had histories; Simon may have been a wanted man. He joined the followers of Jesus with a reputation as a Zealot. He was connected with a loosely organized resistance against Rome that today the Romans would have called terrorists. What an odd and remarkable mix! Alongside fishermen and workingmen, Jesus chose two men at the opposite end of the spectrum: Matthew and Simon. As a tax collector, Matthew represented those who had apparently sold out to Rome and were collaborating with the enemy. As a Canaanite Zealot, Simon represented angry and frustrated Jews who were willing to kill even their own countrymen in their efforts to harass the Romans. Simon's original motive for following Jesus may have been mixed. Jesus' miracles and methods were not violent, and the people flocked to Him. Perhaps Simon felt, as most of the disciples felt in one way or another, that Jesus would usher in a kingdom and would usher out the Romans.

Other than his place in the lists the Gospel writers provide, Simon isn't singled out by word or deed in the Gospels. As a person used to operating under cover, his inclination would have been to avoid the spotlight, even among the disciples. He watched, learned, and was gradually transformed. Interestingly, of all the disciples whose background might have led them to lash out at the guards who came to arrest Jesus, Simon is the most obvious candidate. But Peter, the impulsive fisherman, took a swipe with a blade.

The Acts of the Apostles by Luke mainly highlights the ministry of Peter and Paul, with some attention given to the contributions of other apostles and deacons along the way. Our evidence for the journeys and actions of the *other* apostles comes primarily from tradition. We do know that Christianity spread like wildfire during the first century. Someone had to deliver the message in a compelling way. We know that the *Pax Romana* (the peace of the Roman Empire's control and infrastructure) allowed for extensive and relatively easy travel (by the standards of that day). The apostle Paul certainly traveled thousands of miles on his missionary journeys. Why not the other apostles?

The traditional account of Simon's missionary travels has him taking the road less traveled. He went south and west from Jerusalem, crossing the full breadth of northern Africa, passing through Egypt, Libya, and Mauritania, and then up through Spain and even into the islands we now call Britain. All of these destinations fell within the boundaries of the Roman Empire. Subsequent flourishing Christian communities in far-flung places such as Carthage and Alexandria require some explanation. The grand international evangelistic explosion that occurred at Pentecost in Acts 2 may partly explain the way God's Spirit prepared the mission fields, but the apostolic follow-up best explains the widespread and vibrant spread of Christianity. Another factor to consider is the presence of Jewish exiles in every direction from Jerusalem. If Paul's approach gives us a clue, those Jewish synagogues in exotic locations provided a foothold for the gospel, for the apostles brought the good news that the long-awaited Messiah had come!

Later we pick up Simon back in the Middle East doing missionary work north and east from Jerusalem with Jude, taking the gospel as far as Persia. Long-standing traditions have both apostles suffering martyrdom about the same time, with the detail that Simon was sawn in half.

The vivid descriptions of persecution that conclude Hebrews chapter 11, the "roll-call of faith," may well have been written with abundant examples of then current martyrs on the writer's mind. Those verses read as an accurate sample of the suffering experienced by the followers of Jesus:

> Women received their dead raised to life again. Others were tortured, not accepting deliverance, that they might obtain a better resurrection. Still others had trial of mockings and scourgings, yes, and of chains and imprisonment. They were stoned, they were sawn in two, were tempted, were slain with the sword. They wandered about in sheepskins and goatskins, being destitute, afflicted, tormented—of whom the world was not worthy. They wandered in deserts and mountains, in dens and caves of the Earth (Hebrews 11:35–38).

John (ca. AD 98)

Unlike his apostolic companions, John died quietly in the city of Ephesus, serving the church he loved. But he didn't live a quiet life. By the time he died, John had been part of the twelve disciples of Jesus, participated in the early life of the church in Jerusalem, traveled widely, and had written five New Testament books (the Gospel of John, the letters 1 John, 2 John, 3 John, and Revelation). John certainly had an impressive resume of accomplishments, but he would probably have been the first to point out that anything he had done in life paled in comparison with what Jesus did for him. John's character résumé tells us a lot about the ways Jesus changes a person's life.

The fact that John survived the other apostles points to the kind of unique suffering he endured. All of the other disciples suffered and died; John suffered and lived. Though not technically a martyr, John's life displayed a martyr's qualities. He was a living sacrifice worthy of imitation. And as we shall see, he only escaped actual martyrdom by God's intervention on several occasions.

John and his brother James were two of the more fiery members of Jesus' disciples. Artistic renditions and personal impressions often create a distorted picture of John. Yes, he was the disciple Jesus loved, but that didn't mean that he was particularly lovable. He was more likely a typical fisherman of his time: rough cut, hardworking, brash, and short on social graces. Jesus called John and his brother, "Sons of Thunder," which was probably more a term of endearment than a compliment. Mark reports that special name early in his Gospel (3:17), indicating that their character traits were obvious from the beginning. They certainly lived up to that nickname.

On one occasion, after Peter, James, and John saw Jesus transfigured on the mountain, a revealing argument broke out among the disciples over their internal pecking order: Who was the greatest? After Jesus disarmed that argument, John reported that he and the others had confronted someone who was casting out demons in Jesus' name. They had told that man to stop "because he does not follow with us" (Luke 9:49). If John

41

expected Jesus' approval, he was taken aback by Jesus' insistence that others should be encouraged to make use of the power in Jesus' name.

But the jockeying for power and prestige were not over. Luke immediately describes the final journey to Jerusalem and an incident in Samaria in a town where Jesus was not welcomed. John and James, eager to flex what they might have considered heightened authority among the Lord's followers, volunteered to take action: "Lord, do You want us to command fire to come down from heaven and consume them, just as Elijah did?" (Luke 9:54). We are simply told that Jesus "turned and rebuked" them for this suggestion, raising the possibility that Jesus said nothing, but turned so they could see his face. The look may have been a more devastating rebuke than words. The process of discipleship Jesus practiced with the first disciples was painstaking and time-consuming. And it continued throughout the apostles' lives.

John learned to love the hard way. When he consistently leaves his name out of his Gospel but describes himself as the disciple Jesus loved (John 13:23), he's revealing what transformed him from a son of the thunder to a son of love. Jesus loved him. John never lost his hunger for truth. Even a casual reading of his Gospel and the three letters of John gives the impression that the writer was a champion for truth. But an even greater impression arises in John's writings that he was a man of love. Ancient witnesses like Eusebius record that by the end of his life, John had simplified his message to one gentle command: "Children, love one another." Apparently, whenever he was asked to speak or comment, that was his chosen statement. When asked about it, he responded that everything else necessary would be taken care of if that one command were faithfully carried out.

That simple but profound message still describes the difference between authentic discipleship and inconsistent following of Jesus. Since the beginning, believers haven't been persecuted and killed just because they held a set of beliefs. Their lives have provoked reactions. The darkness has violently resisted and tried to destroy Christ's followers because of the awesome power that love brings into any human situation. The message of the God who loves and who changes people into genuine lovers represents everything the darkness abhors.

John certainly did not live a long life unscathed by pain and suffering. His emotional trials must have been considerable. He lived during times in which those who killed or abused Christians had nothing to fear from the law. If fact, they were sometimes carrying out the law. The painful death of friend after friend must have taken a heavy toll on John. Tradition holds that on one occasion, John was scheduled for boiling in oil. He escaped by divine intervention. His exile on Patmos could have easily been a death sentence. When Emperor Domitian, who had exiled him to Patmos, had died, John was brought back to Ephesus, where he was confined for two years. It is written that he was compelled to drink poison but was unharmed and finally died in peace.

The apostle John

PART TWO

Martyrs from the Second Century to the Twentieth Century

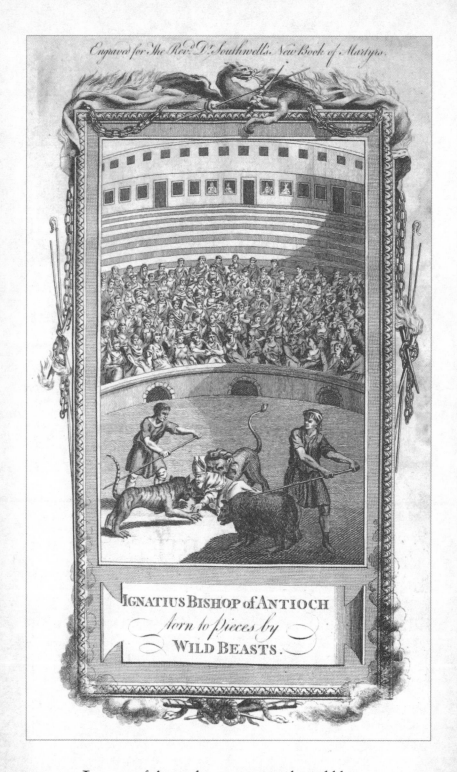

IGNATIUS BISHOP of ANTIOCH torn to pieces by WILD BEASTS.

Ignatius of Antioch torn to pieces by wild beasts

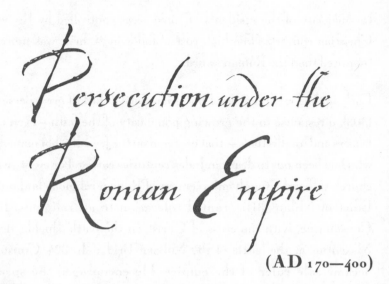

Persecution under the Roman Empire

(AD 170—400)

round the time of Jesus' birth, the government of the Roman Empire changed. The older republican constitution was exchanged for the principate, an innovation introduced by Gaius Octavius, the adopted son of Julius Caesar. Octavius became the first principate, ruling as Augustus (from which we get the name of our eighth month) from 27 BC to AD 14. The principate was a lifelong appointment, and while this person was still subject to the constitution and cooperated with the Senate, the principate had broad powers that could easily turn into tyranny, as it did in Nero's reign around AD 64.

Rome burned in AD 64, and Christians were blamed. Until then, Christians had enjoyed the same privileges as Jews, who were permitted to worship even though their monotheism challenged the cult of Roman religion. When Paul began building churches among non-Jewish populations of Asia Minor, however, Rome felt the threat of this religion as a challenge to its hegemony. Nero killed many Christians, including Paul.

The next great persecution came under Emperor Decius in 249–251. Rome had lost territories, population, and power. Decius determined to regain Rome's eminence by prohibiting cults that refused to worship the emperor. A short period of calm followed; then Valerius (257) resumed state persecution of Christians. Despite this, by the end of the third century, the majority of the residents of some areas controlled by Rome were Christian converts. The high cost of following Christ was more to be treasured than the Roman sword.

Early in the fourth century, Diocletian started the last great persecution (303), a response to the growing popularity of the faith—even among leaders and intellectuals—that centered on the Jewish rabbi named Jesus, who had been put to death in Judea centuries earlier. For eight years the church suffered a tough enforcement of Roman religious law, until the Edict of Milan (311) granted toleration to all religions. In 312, Constantine, with the cross of Christ on the battle shields, defeated Maxentius at the battle of the Milvian Bridge. In 324, Constantine became sole ruler of the empire. He encouraged the spread of Christianity and was himself baptized shortly before his death in 337. With his support, the faith took hold, and then the towering figure of Augustine (354–430) gave Christians their most elegant spokesman and convert. Christians still suffered, but mostly on the frontiers where barbarians threatened the once mighty Roman legions. Within the empire itself, the church grew and official persecutions ended.

"Now I **begin** to be a **disciple.**
Come fire and cross and grapplings with wild beasts, the rending of my bones and body ...

only let it be mine to **attain**

Jesus Christ."

– Ignatius of Antioch

Ignatius of Antioch (ca. AD 30–ca. 107)

"I hope indeed, by your prayers, to have the good fortune to fight with wild beasts in Rome," wrote Bishop Ignatius on his journey from Antioch in Syria, to the Roman Empire's capital city. Around seventy years old at the time, Ignatius was one of the "post-apostolic fathers"—the generation of leaders who had been mentored in the faith by the apostles themselves; Ignatius was likely mentored by John. It is also believed that his appointment as a bishop came from Peter. Legend suggests that Ignatius was the child blessed by Jesus in Matthew 19.

After his trial and condemnation, Ignatius wrote seven letters while he traveled to his martyrdom in the Coliseum, sometime during Emperor Trajan's reign (98–117). Under military guard between Philadelphia and Troas, Ignatius was welcomed at Smyrna by fellow bishop Polycarp. There he wrote the first four letters. Later, he addressed two letters to two churches and one personal note to Polycarp.

Ignatius adopted the name *Theophorus*, which means "God-bearer" or "God-inspired." He wrote with a focus on Christ and the unity of the church—themes he sounded before the trial court where he faced trumped up charges of disloyalty to Rome for failing to bow to the pagan deities. Like all Christian leaders of that era, Ignatius' treason was easy to prove. Officials had only to listen to the bishop preach, or ask him a simple question about whom he followed, or speak with the growing band of Christians to realize that a new and powerful spiritual movement was underway whose followers could never again offer Rome ultimate loyalty. For Ignatius, the heart now belonged to the triune God, and he seemed to gladly accept the punishment of the court for his crimes of faith and devotion. Readers today hear echoes of Paul's writing as Ignatius begins his letters:

> Heartiest greetings of pure joy in Jesus Christ ... Out of the fullness of God the Father you have been blessed with large numbers and are predestined from eternity to enjoy forever continual and unfading glory. The source of your unity and election is genuine suffering, which you undergo by the will of the Father and of Jesus Christ, our God.

Ignatius believed the "last days" had arrived. Whether he lived or died meant little to him. Ignatius delighted in his journey to Rome, calling it a victory, not a death march. He urged believers to "keep on praying" and to "gather together more frequently to celebrate God's Communion and to praise Him." In such devotion "Satan's powers are overthrown."

Bishop Ignatius knew nothing of the wealth and power later bishops would enjoy. In his era, a bishop was more likely to be the leader of a single congregation rather than the head of a diocese in a well-organized hierarchy, into which the position later expanded. Thoroughly devoted to Christ, Ignatius was part of that great generation who taught and built the church, buried the apostles, collected their writings, stood before the emperor's psychotic wrath, and fought heretics and swindlers infiltrating the movement.

Their church fathers and grandfathers had told these leaders about the great silence of God, but Ignatius knew the "Son, Jesus Christ, who is the Word issuing from the silence ... our perpetual Life." He followed this Word-made-flesh until his own flesh was torn by lions. On his way to Rome, the old man wrote to the churches: "You deserve to be happy in God's good news of salvation," and by every account, Ignatius was.

"Now I begin to be a disciple. I care for nothing of visible or invisible things so that I may but win Christ. Come fire and cross and grapplings with wild beasts, the rending of my bones and body ... only let it be mine to attain Jesus Christ."

Polycarp of Smyrna (ca. AD 70–ca.155)

An elderly man in his eighties sat at a table eating dinner. Polycarp knew his life was in danger. A group of Christians had just been executed in the arena on account of their faith. But Polycarp refused to leave Rome. The Romans were executing any self-proclaimed Christians, and pagans were betraying those they knew to be Christians. After the recent executions, the crowd in the arena had chanted for Polycarp's death.

A renowned follower of Christ and bishop of Smyrna, Polycarp had become a Christian under the tutelage of John the apostle. Recently, the Roman proconsul had been looking for him for days. After arresting and torturing one of Polycarp's servants, they finally learned where he was staying. The soldiers came into the house, but instead of fleeing, Polycarp calmly stated, "God's will be done."

Polycarp asked that food be brought for the soldiers, and he requested an hour for prayer. Amazed by Polycarp's fearlessness, especially for a man his age, the hardened Roman soldiers granted his request. He prayed for two hours for all the Christians he knew and for the universal church, and the soldiers let him.

As Polycarp entered the stadium, several Christians present heard a voice from heaven say, "Be strong, Polycarp, and act like a man." Because of his age, the Roman proconsul gave Polycarp a final chance to live. He just had to swear by Caesar and say, "Take away the atheists" (at that time Christians were called atheists for refusing to worship the Greek and Roman gods). Polycarp looked at the roaring crowds, gestured to them, and proclaimed, "Take away the atheists!"

The proconsul continued, "Swear, and I will let you go. Reproach Christ!"

Polycarp turned to the proconsul and boldly declared, "Eighty-six years I have served Him, and He has done me no wrong. How can I blaspheme my King who saved me?"

The proconsul urged him again, "Swear by the Fortune of Caesar."

But Polycarp replied, "Since you vainly think that I will swear by the Fortune of Caesar, as you say, and pretend not to know who I am, listen carefully: I am a Christian!"

The proconsul threatened, "I have wild beasts. I will throw you to them, if you do not repent."

Polycarp replied, "Call them! For we cannot "repent" from what is better to what is worse; but it is noble to turn from what is evil to what is righteous."

Then the proconsul threatened Polycarp with fire, but he responded: "You threaten me with a fire that burns an hour and is soon quenched, for you are ignorant of the fire of the coming judgment and eternal punishment stored up for the ungodly. But why do you delay? Do what you want."

Finally, the proconsul sent a herald to the middle of the stadium to announce that Polycarp was confessing his faith as a Christian. The crowd shouted for Philip the Asiarch to send a lion against Polycarp, but he refused. Then they shouted for Polycarp to be burned. They moved him to the marketplace and prepared the pyre. Polycarp undressed and climbed up. But when they were going to nail him, he told them, "Leave me like this. He who gives me to endure the fire will also give me to remain on the pyre without your security from the nails." So they did not nail him but tied him up. Bravely, Polycarp prayed as the soldiers prepared the wood:

"O Lord God almighty, Father of Your beloved and blessed Son Jesus Christ, through whom we have received knowledge of You, God of angels and powers and all creation, and of the whole race of the righteous who live before You, I bless You that You considered me worthy of this day and hour, to receive a part in the number of the martyrs in the cup of Your Christ, for the resurrection to eternal life both of soul and of body in the incorruptibility of the Holy Spirit. Among them may I be welcomed before You today by a fat and acceptable sacrifice, just as you previously prepared and made known and You fulfilled, the deceitless and true God. Because of this, and for all things, I praise You, I bless You, I glorify You, through the eternal and heavenly high priest Jesus Christ, Your beloved Son, through whom be glory to You with Him and the Holy Spirit both now and for ages to come. Amen."

The Romans had threatened Polycarp with beasts and with fire, but nothing would make him turn against Christ. After his prayer, the men lit the pyre, which sprang up quickly. But even the fire wouldn't touch him as it formed an arch around Polycarp's body. The Romans didn't know what to make of this. In the end, the Romans commanded an executioner to stab him. A great quantity of blood put out the remaining fire, and Polycarp bled to death.

That the genuineness of your **faith**, being much more **precious** than gold that perishes, though it is **tested** by **fire**, may be found to praise, honor, and **glory** at the revelation of **Jesus Christ**.

1 Peter 1:7

Justin Martyr (ca. AD 100–165)

For all his intelligence, Justin Martyr never quibbled with the prospect that he, too, would die violently at the hands of the Roman state. In his day and time, execution was more or less the expected means of passing from this life to heaven. After all, a Roman magistrate need only order the smallest reverence toward the emperor or the pagan deities, the shortest nod of worship, and the faithful Christian, utterly refusing, was condemned. Justin might have anticipated such a fate, but he lived into old age (for his era) before the choice confronted him.

Justin was a scholar devoted to ideas, debates, and arguments—by modern standards undramatic, yet immensely significant for the early church in the decades after the apostles. Born to a pagan family living at the site of ancient Shechem in Samaria, this bright lad mastered the writings of the Stoics and the Platonists, the best minds of Rome and Greece. Unsatisfied and yearning for the peacefulness of truth, he responded to the witness of an unknown "old man," and around age thirty committed his life and mind to Jesus Christ, who alone taught "the one sure worthy philosophy."

Thereafter Justin employed his mind to spread that truth with zeal and determination. Armed with passion for God and the tools of ancient rhetoric, he debated with Jew and Gentile the merits of the gospel, the truth of the Messiah, and the coming judgment of the one righteous and merciful God. It is often said that Justin was the first Christian thinker after Paul to grasp the universal implications of Christian faith: God's love reached to all; the resurrection of Christ was a once-for-all answer to sin's horrendous judgment.

Strong in faith and articulate in early theology, Justin did not neglect the horizontal view. He was astute and appreciative of culture, and knew, as a sociologist might today, the times and people who comprised his dynamic world.

He taught that one can find truth in the philosophies of pagans; God had given pagan philosophers a glimpse of truth through the mercy of Christ. But the glimpse was only foretaste, not substance. The pagans cannot fully find truth until they come to Christ, as Jesus is the Reason, the Logos of the universe come to Earth. Justin's breadth would pave the way for other Christians to recognize the good, the true, and the beautiful in non-Christian cultural works and writings. With courage and conviction, Justin's "apology" for the faith affirmed that only Christ was Lord and refused all compromise with lesser gods.

He resented the widespread notion that Christians were traitors, immoral, weak, or rebellious. A large part of his work described the social benefits of faith. The followers of Jesus should be admired and promoted as model citizens, he told the Roman authorities. Because of faith, because of the goodness of Christ, these Christians gave the state its noblest strength. "We are in fact of all men your best helpers and allies in securing good order." But he warned: "Don't demand that they bow before falsehood."

And just that demand sealed Justin's fate after thirty-five years of teaching and preaching (he never held an official church office). Early in the reign of Marcus Aurelius, Justin and six others were arrested and brought before the prefect Rusticus. Justin was the group's spokesperson, of course; but as soon as he began his confession and defense, the prefect, obviously bored at the prospect of a sermon, made the fatal demand to renounce Christianity and bow before Caesar. Everyone refused, and Rusticus pronounced the standard brutal sentence. Soon after, Justin and his fellows were scourged and beheaded, but the truth was not silenced. "The lover of truth ought to choose in every way, even at the cost of his own life, to speak and do what is right, though death should take him away," Justin wrote at the beginning of his *First Apology*. "You can kill us, but cannot do us any real harm."

Martyrs from Scillium (180)

It was a hot summer day in Scillium (near the ancient city of Carthage; present-day Tunis) in the Roman province of northern Africa. Six prisoners stood before the Roman proconsul in the hall of judgment. This was their last chance before being sentenced. Saturninus, the proconsul, addressed the prisoners: "You can have our Lord the Emperor's indulgence, if you come back to a sound mind."

Speratus, the spokesman for this small band, declared their innocence: "We have never done wrong, but when mistreated we give thanks, because we listen to *our* Emperor."

The proconsul tried to reassure them, "We are religious, too, and our religion is simple: We swear by the Emperor's genius, and pray for his health, which you should do, too."

Speratus offered, "If you will lend me your ears in peace, I will explain the mystery of simplicity."

But Saturninus angrily retorted, "When you speak evil of our sacred rites, I will not listen. Instead, swear by the genius of our Emperor!"

The prisoner calmly responded, "I do not recognize the empire of this world, but rather I serve that God, 'whom no man has seen or can see' (1 Timothy 6:16). I have not stolen, and I pay taxes on what I buy, because I know my Lord, the King of kings and Emperor of all nations!"

Saturninus turned to the other prisoners and said, "Cease to be of this persuasion."

But Speratus answered again, "It is an evil persuasion to commit homicide, or to speak false testimony."

Ignoring him, Saturninus commanded, "Do not be participants in this madness!"

Cittinus, another prisoner, spoke up, "We have no one to fear except our God who is in heaven!" One of the three women prisoners, Donata, added,

"Honor to Caesar as Caesar, but fear to God." Vestia shouted aloud, "I am a Christian!" The third woman, Secunda, confessed, "I wish to be what I am."

Saturninus asked Speratus, the spokesman, "Do you remain a Christian?" Speratus answered, "I am a Christian." And the rest of group agreed.

Then Saturninus changed tactics. "Will you have a time to consider?" But Speratus immediately answered, "There is no deliberation in so straightforward an issue."

The proconsul inquired, "What things are in your book-bag?"

Speratus answered, "Books and letters of Paul, a just man."

The proconsul insisted, "Wait thirty days and rethink."

But Speratus insisted back, "I am a Christian!" And the rest of the group agreed.

Finally, the proconsul read the decree:

> "Speratus, Nartalus, Cittimus, Donata, Vestia, Secunda, and the rest have confessed to living by the Christian rite. Since they obstinately persist, after an opportunity to return to the Roman custom, it is decided to punish them with the sword."

Speratus said, "We thank God." Nartalus echoed him, "Today we are martyrs in heaven, thanks to God."

The proconsul commanded the herald to announce their condemnation, along with six previously condemned prisoners. The group was executed on July 17, 180. They did not fear those who kill the body but are unable to kill the soul. Having confessed Christ before men, they were confessed by Him before His Father in heaven (Matthew 10:28, 32).

Perpetua, Felicity and Blandina (203)

Perpetua bravely held Felicity in her arms, anticipating their death together as sisters in Christ. The bull's horns had already wounded Felicity, and the crowd wanted the *coup de grâce*. Then, abruptly and inexplicably, the bull stood still. The crowd hushed. This animal was not following the script. Now the crowd let loose with demands for blood, and gladiators rushed forward to finish the work. Felicity died quickly. When Perpetua's executioner hesitated, she herself helped guide his blade into her body.

The Coliseum had never before seen such a spectacle. Perpetua came from a wealthy family. Her father was pagan but her mother and brothers were Christians. Perpetua had a nursing baby at the time of her arrest for confessing Christ. Her father urged her to renounce faith, for his sake and for her family. Even Roman authorities urged her to offer a simple sacrifice to Roman power. She refused. She would not renounce Christ as Lord, claiming that the name that belonged to her was the name of a Christian.

Felicity was a slave—and pregnant. Since Roman law prohibited the execution of pregnant women, sentence was delayed. Felicity gave birth in prison to a baby girl that would be adopted by Christians. When prison guards wondered how she would handle facing beasts in the arena, especially so soon after her child's birth, she responded, "Now my sufferings are only mine. But when I face the beasts there will be another who will live in me, and will suffer for me since I shall be suffering for Him."

These two women from different classes showed fortitude, determination, and, remarkably, even joy at the prospects of public humiliation and suffering. Several times they refused offers of acquittal and ignored pleas to save themselves. Together they clung to heavenly hope, and to each other, for endurance through the ordeal. Rather than acquiesce to Roman demands, they asked to be baptized while in prison. Perpetua stated, "The dungeon is to me a palace." Amazingly, when Perpetua was told beasts would devour her, she and her companions returned to prison in high spirits at the prospect of death for the glory of God. Three men imprisoned with them were forced to run the gladiator gauntlet; two were killed by beasts; one was beheaded.

As for Perpetua, she was the picture of poise in the center of chaos and blood. When the bull tossed her but did not hurt her, Perpetua's hair came undone. She asked to be allowed to put her hair up because undone hair was a sign of mourning, but this was a day for triumph and joy.

Blandina, a slave girl, was the last to die. She was hanged from a post and exposed to wild animals, but they would not attack. She was repeatedly tortured and eventually trapped in a net, trampled by a bull. All of the martyrs' bodies were left unburied and guarded by soldiers.

Such courage made a mark on the Romans. These three women and Christians had stood together and died together. Several spectators converted to Christianity as a result, including the governor of Rome.

Origen (185–254)

An early church father, Origen was one of the first textual scholars of the Bible, one of the first Bible commentators, and one of the first to write a systematic statement of faith. Yet this early genius, an Egyptian raised by Christian parents, would do his traveling and teaching between persecutions. Indeed, the persecutions of Emperors Septimus Severus (202), Caracalla (215), and Decius (250) are markers on his life.

As a teenager, Origen felt the pain of persecution when his father Leonidas was captured and martyred in 215. Indeed, Origen wanted to die as well, and he would have rushed to join the martyrs had not his mother hid his clothes, preventing him from leaving the house.

Origen began teaching at a local catechetical school. Many of his students were martyred and he stood by them in their trials and sufferings, but was allowed to go free. He lived a humble life—giving money to the poor, owning only one coat, and sleeping on the floor.

To escape the persecution of Caracalla, Origen went to Palestine to preach and teach. He would return there fifteen years later to be ordained a priest.

Around the age of sixty-five, Origen was caught by the zealots of Decius, put in chains and tortured. He was eventually released, but never recovered. He died soon after.

His writings are studied today by historians and scholars, and criticized for the influence of Greek philosophy on his thought. Nonetheless, his book, *On Prayer*, reveals a heart intent on love and service to God. His life was characterized by the endurance such a heart enables.

Cyprian (ca. 200–258)

The church was divided and angry. Believers in Carthage had stood strong against the persecution of rabid Emperor Valerius. But not all of them. Some had caved in, made their ritual sacrifice to Rome's statute gods, and renounced their allegiance to Christ. Now that Valerius was gone and his persecution done, should the cowards and compromisers be re-admitted to the church? Bishop Cyprian must decide, then lead the church toward harmony and growth—a difficult mandate made even more difficult by the fact that he himself had gone into exile to avoid persecution. Did Cyprian have the moral prestige to lead the recovery?

Little is known of Cyprian's early life. Likely he came from a wealthy Christian family and received a good education. Well respected in Carthage, he converted around age forty, but the story of his coming to faith is lost to history. Not lost, however, is the evidence of his new life in Christ. Cyprian took vows of poverty and celibacy; he gave up reading secular authors in favor of the Bible exclusively to avoid distractions as he grew in faith. He won the respect of fellow believers, for he was made bishop of the church in Carthage in 248, only two years after his conversion. But those were dangerous times for bishops everywhere.

Decius became emperor of Rome in 249, as Goths to the north threatened the empire from without as much as immorality threatened it from within. Decius would fix that by a new loyalty campaign aimed particularly at leaders of the Christian sect. He ordered that everyone do a general sacrifice, pouring out a libation to the Roman gods and eating the sacrificial meat. Roman authorities would certify compliance by issuing a *libellus*, essentially a "ticket" out of persecution.

Never before had so many Christians compromised faith as during Decius's two-year persecution, called at the time the bloodiest in the history of the church. Those who bowed to Rome (or bribed an official) carried their libellus, also a ticket of apostasy. In Carthage, eighteen Christians were martyred before Decius died in battle and his persecution ended. Cyprian survived by self-imposed exile. Now in 251 he was back to deal with the damage.

Another wave of persecution swept the Roman world in 258 under Valerian. This time Cyprian stayed. He was among the first arrested and ordered to reveal the roster of other Christian leaders. He refused. Awaiting his execution, Cyprian wrote to nine Christians exiled to the mines in nearby Sigua: "Let cruelty, either ignorant or malignant, hold you here in its bonds and chains as long as it will. From this Earth and from these sufferings you shall speedily come to the kingdom of heaven. The body is not cherished in the mines with couch and cushion, but it is cherished with the refreshment and solace of Christ."

Cyprian used his execution to preach the greatness of knowing Christ as Lord. After kneeling in prayer, he gave his executioner a gift, and then placed the blindfold on himself, surrendering life in peace and treasuring the life to come.

"You can **kill us**, but you cannot do us any **real harm.**"
— Justin Martyr

Valentinus (ca. 269)

The great day celebrating romantic love is named after him, yet who he really was, no one knows. Nonetheless, February 14 is his legacy, and we piece together a little fact and a lot of legend to get his story.

Three third-century martyrs all carry the name Valentinus. One was a priest in Rome, one a bishop of Interamna, and one a Christian in the Roman province of Africa. About the lives of these three we know nothing. About the death of Valentinus at the decree of Claudius II, we think the story hinges on soldiering, marriages, and a cold-hearted emperor—all the ingredients of passion and power that prompted Pope Gelasius in 496 to declare St. Valentine's Day as a replacement for the Roman pagan holiday of Lupercalia.

Apparently, recruits for Claudius's army were complaining about their long separations from wives and lovers, for the edict went forth that no soldier of Rome—may their hearts grow bloodlessly cold—could weaken his will or soften his courage in marriage. Of course, edicts do not command passions, so marriages simply went underground with an assist from the sympathetic priest Valentinus, to whom soldiers and their betrothed surreptitiously fled.

In time, the priest was caught and his treasonous disobedience duly sentenced by the Prefect of Rome. He was beaten by clubs and beheaded on February 14 in 269 or 270.

It's an unlikely subplot, but nonetheless another story is told that during his imprisonment, Valentinus tutored his jailor's daughter Julia, who was blind from birth. On the eve of his martyrdom, Valentinus sent her a note of encouragement and faith, including on it a yellow crocus. When Julia opened the note, the story goes, her blind eyes fixed on the flower and she was healed. In gratitude, Julia planted an almond tree near Valentinus's grave. Today the almond tree remains a symbol of abiding love and friendship.

The Theban Legion (286)

To how many loyalties can a person be loyal? How many oaths can one person keep? After the first one, all others are conditional. So the young Coptic Christians from Thebes in Upper Egypt, recruited and trained into a legion of 6,600 men in the Imperial Roman army, gave their oath of allegiance to the emperor—after they had pledged first loyalty to God.

Records of the Theban Legion are remote and sometimes contested by scholars. Evidence of their courage and sacrifice was uncovered sixty-four years after the event, in 350 by Theodore, bishop of Octudurm. Not until around 490 was their story written, at least in surviving records, by Eucherius, Bishop of Lyons. If these two bishops are dependable, the Theban Legion has given to the history of faith one of the most remarkable episodes of solidarity, duty, and hope ever told.

Commanded by Mauritius (called "St. Maurice" in Switzerland, where his memory is celebrated), the legion was ordered by Emperor Maximian to march west over the Alps to help put down an insurrection in Gaul. Of course, they obeyed. A long march followed; then a brief military campaign. Maximian was a man of immense self-importance, similar to other emperors. Wishing to celebrate the victory, he ordered all his troops to take the Oath of Allegiance, with its not so subtle notion that Maximian was divine, and then to help exterminate all Christians remaining in the Burgundy region.

Mauritius replied that because his own men were Christian, he would withdraw from the main encampment and permit the other battalions to reckon with their own consciences. He and his men could not kill innocents without dishonoring their first oath, taken at baptism, to love and serve God above all else.

This response from a legion commander was a slap to the ego of the commander-in-chief, who replied with an order of decimation: every tenth man in the Theban legion was to be executed.

So it was done. By picking names out of caps, 660 of the emperor's warriors were killed on his own order.

Despite their losses, still the Legion could neither take the Oath nor draw swords against brothers of faith. Maximian ordered a second decimation. Another 600 troops were slaughtered.

The twenty-first-century reader must gasp and gather the senses to imagine the mix of faith and fury racing through the souls of these Theban survivors. They had choices to make. Defend themselves? Comply with the order? Stand by for another massacre? Mauritius and his lieutenants replied to Maximian with as clear a statement of loyalty as any soldier could offer:

> "Emperor, we are your soldiers but also the soldiers of the true God. We owe you military service and obedience, but we cannot renounce Him who is our Creator and Master, and also yours even though you reject Him. In all things which are not against His law, we most willingly obey you, as we have done hitherto. We readily oppose your enemies, whoever they are, but we cannot stain our hands with the blood of innocent people [Christians]. We have taken an oath to God before we took one to you. You cannot place any confidence in our second oath if we violate the other [the first]. You commanded us to execute Christians; behold we are such. We confess God the Father the creator of all things and His Son Jesus Christ. We have seen our comrades slain with the sword. We do not weep for them but rather rejoice at their honor. Neither this nor any other provocation has tempted us to revolt. Behold, we have arms in our hands, but we do not resist, because we would rather die innocent than live by any sin."

Maximian might have been proud at their bravery and delighted that such resolute men stood ready to defend his empire. Instead, in a rage he condemned them all, the entire Legion, which order was carried out on September 22, 286. The Legion did not attempt to muster a defense or to find a hiding place. Those who were posted away from the encampment did not run. Nearly 6,000 battle-hardened troops were killed for their first allegiance to Christ, by their second-in-command, Emperor Maximian.

Centuries later, in 515, a monastery was built near the site of the martyrdom through a gift from the king of Burgundy.

Alban (304)

Alban lived near Verulamium, a town in Roman Britain situated near the modern city of St. Albans in Hertfordshire on what is now park and agricultural land. A pagan and a soldier in the Roman Army, Alban became the first Christian martyr in Britain and is listed in the Anglican calendar of England and Wales as "Saint Alban."

In 303, the emperor of the Eastern Roman Empire, Diocletian, published his edict against the Christians. At some point, Alban gave shelter to a Christian priest who was fleeing the authorities. Impressed by the priest's lifestyle and devotion, and through their many conversations, Alban was converted to Christ and baptized.

Hearing that the priest was in that vicinity, the local magistrate sent soldiers to search for him. As they approached Alban's cottage, he changed clothes with the priest, wearing his hooded cloak, and was arrested instead. Alban was brought before the magistrate as he was offering sacrifices to the pagan gods. Seeing that the prisoner was Alban and not the priest, the magistrate became enraged that Alban had freely offered himself to the soldiers in place of his guest.

The magistrate ordered Alban to be dragged to the pagan gods and ordered the punishment for Alban that the priest would have received, if Alban had indeed become a Christian. Alban declared, "I worship and adore the true and living God who created all things."

Alban, who had voluntarily given himself up to the persecutors as a Christian, was not in the least afraid of the magistrate's threats. Instead, he openly declared that he would not obey the government's commands. Then the magistrate said: "Of what house and stock are you?"

Alban replied: "What business is it of yours of what lineage I am born? If on the other hand you desire to hear the truth of my religion, know that I am now a Christian and devote myself to Christian service."

Angered even more, the magistrate ordered Alban to be beaten, hoping that he would recant. But Alban patiently endured the torture. Realizing that Alban was determined to confess Christ, he ordered him to be beheaded.

Alban was taken out of the town Verulamium to the top of the hill across the river. The place of his beheading is where St. Alban's Cathedral now stands. The most probable date for Alban's martyrdom is 304.

Alban, thus, became the first martyr in Britain. The second was the executioner that was ordered to kill him, who after hearing his testimony became a Christian on the spot and refused to follow the order. The third was the priest, who after hearing that Alban had been arrested in his place, hurried to the court to turn himself in and save Alban.

If anyone desires to come after Me,
let him deny himself, and **take up his cross,** and **follow Me.**
For whoever desires to **save his life**
will **lose it,** but whoever **loses his life**
for My sake will **find it.**

Matthew 16:24-25

The Forty Martyrs of Sebaste (320)

In 320, Constantine, the Roman emperor of the West, pressured Licinius, the emperor of the East, to legalize Christianity in his region—and Licinius conceded. Later, however, fearing treason among the troops, Licinius broke his alliance and decided to eliminate Christianity from his territory. He authorized Agricola, the commander of his forces in the Armenian town of Sebaste (now Sivas, Turkey), to carry out his evil intentions.

Agricola knew of forty soldiers who were devout Christians and skilled in battle. In an attempt to force them to renounce their faith, he announced to these men, "Either offer sacrifice to the gods and earn great honors, or, in the event of your disobedience, be stripped of your military rank and fall into disgrace." Then Agricola had the soldiers imprisoned to think about what he had told them. That night they encouraged themselves by singing psalms and praying.

The next morning Agricola brought out the forty men and tried to persuade them with flattery, praising them for their valor and good looks. These Christian soldiers were determined, however, not to fall prey to the commander's empty words. So Agricola sent them back to prison to await the arrival of an official. While the soldiers waited, they prepared themselves for martyrdom.

When the official arrived, he again attempted to persuade the men. Unsuccessful, he ordered the forty men to be taken to a frozen lake. There, they were told to strip off their clothing and stand in the middle of the frozen mass of ice. A guard watched over them while warm baths were set up along the shore, along with fires, blankets, clothing, and hot food and drink, in order to tempt them to turn their backs on Christ and sacrifice to the pagan idols. One of the soldiers could no longer bear the cold and ran to the shore. Seeing this, the remaining soldiers cried out to God to help them. Their prayer was answered as a light warmed the shivering men. One of the guards was so moved by the resolve of the Christian soldiers that he stripped off all his clothes and joined them. One version of the story reports that all the men were frozen to death by morning.

Another account, however, says that in the morning, the men, still alive, were taken back to the prison and tortured to death. Then their bones were crushed with sledgehammers.

Regardless of which version of the story is correct, the forty soldiers of Sebaste courageously refused to deny Christ. May we remember their courage and stand strong against anything that might lure us away from Christ. May we, like them, show God's grace even in the midst of great trials!

Telemachus (404)

In the Greek myths, the character Telemachus (meaning "far-away fighter") was a timid and diffident child. But as an adult he defended the honor of those he loved and became a fighter and a hero. Unlike his mythological counterpart, the fourth-century monk Telemachus was anything but a fighter. Or perhaps it can be argued that his greatest fight was his effort to eradicate fighting.

An ascetic hermit from the East and unknown except for his final act, Telemachus journeyed to Rome just in time for the victory celebrations. After years of aggressive invasions from the continent, Rome had finally defeated the Goth king Alaric in northern Italy in 403.

As was common in those times, extravagant gladiatorial contests were held in celebration of military victories. The twenty-year-old emperor Honorius decreed that this particular celebration would be held in the 50,000-capacity Coliseum, a battleground named for the colossal 130-foot statue of Nero nearby, the emperor made famous for condemning Christians into human torches. If there was one place in all of Rome that a pacifist Christian might consider avoiding, the Coliseum was it. Telemachus, a "rudely clad man of rough but imposing presence," resolved to interrupt, indeed to stop, the bloody contest in the Coliseum.

Thousands had gathered that day. Cries of "habet, hoc habet" erupted from the crowds—"He has had it!" they cried every time a fighter was mortally wounded. In this atmosphere Telemachus jumped from the crowd into the arena itself, no longer spectator but activist, peacemaker, preacher.

"Do not requite God's mercy," he screamed, "in turning away the swords of your enemies by murdering each other!" Certainly the crowd heard him, but the gladiators continued fighting. Telemachus ran between the gladiators, pleading with them to stop. "Sedition! Sedition! Down with him!" roared the crowd. "This is no place for preaching! The old customs of Rome must be observed! On gladiators!" Still, Telemachus continued to turn from one encounter to another, stopping gladiators in mid-fight. Then, frustrated by the annoyance of one man interrupting the games, someone pulled a sword and thrusting it, Telemachus fell. Joining in, the crowd threw stones down from their seats to the arena below.

News quickly spread throughout Rome that the murdered man was the hermit Telemachus. Rome was shocked, as was Emperor Honorius, that such a gentle man had been slain. Telemachus's courage and boldness to speak God's mercy and love changed the games forever. A man bent on peace, Telemachus lost his life fighting in the grandest battleground of Rome. Soon after his death, gladiatorial battles were banned from the Coliseum. Telemachus had achieved the impossible.

Representation of the Tortures used in the Inquisition

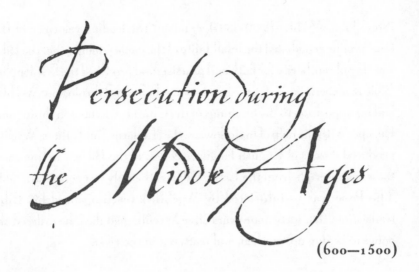

Persecution during the Middle Ages

(600—1500)

 hough Emperor Julian (361–363) tried to revive paganism in the Roman Empire, that old way was doomed. Theodosius established a policy that suppressed pagan worship (392) and freed the church to expand its missionary efforts. Patrick took Christian faith to Ireland in the fifth century. Scottish monks evangelized lower England around 600. Irish monks returned to Europe as missionaries from 500 to 1000.

The Bishop of Rome came to be seen as the leader of the church, and often, when the Pope was strong, the bishop was also the leader of the secular monarchs who ruled Europe. Hildebrand (Pope Gregory VII, 1073–1085) was such a figure. His papal armies fought Emperor Henry IV of the Holy Roman Empire, who eventually gave his confession and allegiance to Hildebrand.

During this era, the great Crusades were organized to roll back Muslim influence in the East, Spain, and North Africa. Jerusalem was twice won and lost by crusaders bent on Holy War. At the same time, the seemingly invincible pagan armies of Genghis Khan captured much of Asia Minor.

From 1232, the church's Inquisition turned its fearsome power against "heresies" such as the Waldensians and Lollards, early "Bible-for-everyone" activists, and later, against the leaders of the Reformation.

Note: John Wycliffe (1329–1384) stands as the leading reformer of this era. Wycliffe repudiated the infallibility of the papacy, taught that the Bible was the sole authority for faith and practice, and produced the first English Bible manuscripts. An Oxford professor, scholar, and theologian, Wycliffe, and his opposition to the teachings of the Church, was known throughout Europe. With the help of his followers, the "Lollards," and others, Wycliffe produced dozens of English language copies of the Bible. He translated these manuscripts from the Latin Vulgate, the only text source available. The Pope was so infuriated by Wycliffe's teachings and his Bible translation, that forty-four years after Wycliffe had died, he ordered the bones to be dug up, crushed, and scattered in the river.

Wycliffe's Bones Burned by Papists

Boniface (ca. 680–755)

He never lost his passion for missionary service. The archbishop of Germany, Boniface, could have enjoyed the honor of his office at an age when most men dream of a settled life. But the mission field held more purpose and challenge than presiding over monasteries or maintaining cathedrals. Boniface was seventy-five years old when he left Germany to preach the gospel once again.

Boniface is probably the most widely known name, apart from popes and kings, of the eighth century. He was born "Winfrid" in England around 680. Early in life, to his father's dismay, he chose a vocation in the church. He took training in Benedictine monasteries and wrote the first Latin grammar in England. He was ordained a priest when he was thirty years old, but he wanted the frontier.

In 716, Winfrid set out on a missionary expedition to Friesland, or Frisia. His own Anglo-Saxon language was similar to the spoken language of the Frisians. The mission was frustrated, however, by a war raging between Charles Martel (who later stopped the "Mohammedans" from entering Europe in the battle of Potiers, 732) and the Frisian king.

In 719, during a visit to Rome, Winfrid was given the name *Boniface* by Pope Gregory II, who commissioned him to evangelize Germany. For five years Boniface preached and baptized in Hesse and Thuringia. In 722 he was named bishop of the Germanic territories.

A year later Boniface performed one of those simple acts of defiance that gives birth to legends. He felled a large oak tree near the town of Fritzlar in northern Hesse, a tree known to locals as Thor's Oak. Indeed, many locals were present as Boniface worked at the oak's tough base. These onlookers grew steadily more curious and angry with this foreigner who was infuriating their gods with each stroke of the axe. Indeed, they expected Thor or one of his agents to fell the bishop with a thunderclap. When the oak hit the ground, it split into four parts, so the story goes, and the people instantly knew that a superior divine power was at work. Most converted as Boniface had the wood sawn to make a chapel—today the site of Fritzler Cathedral.

Boniface made other trips to Rome, each time receiving honors and more territory to win for Christ. He was made archbishop of Germany in 732 and put his headquarters at Mentz. More structures were built and movements begun.

In 755, Boniface was restless again about the heathen in Frisia. He organized a large group of priests and lay helpers, and he preached there with extraordinary success. On Whitsun Eve (the eve of Pentecost) in 755, he called all new converts to a great meeting near Dokkum. Instead of converts, however, Boniface was ambushed by a gang of local vigilantes, who mercilessly killed fifty-two Christians, including Boniface.

His reputation had already been won, his legacy established, his titles and honors awarded. The powers in Rome would have made his old age comfortable. Instead, Boniface chose missions, and in Frisia he died a martyr.

You did not **choose** Me, but I chose you and **appointed** you that you should go and **bear fruit**, and that your **fruit** should **remain**...

John 15:16

Alphage (954–1012)

He wanted the hermit's life: quietness, meditations, and seclusion. Instead he was given leadership, travel, international peace negotiations, and finally martyrdom. The twenty-ninth archbishop of Canterbury might have said at the end, "Not my plan, but God's."

Alphage was born to a noble English family, but early in life he chose God over temporal power and privilege. He entered the monastery at Deerhurst and then Bath, where he became abbot and was known for his piety and austerity. In 984, Dunstan (the twenty-seventh archbishop) appointed Alphage bishop of Winchester.

In 1006, Alphage succeeded Aelfric as archbishop of Canterbury. At that point, Alphage's life became more difficult as his country became more vulnerable to Scandinavian marauders. Apparently Alphage persuaded King Olaf Tryggvason I of Norway not to attack the English coast, but he did not succeed in putting off the Danes. When marauders from Denmark sacked Canterbury in 1011, Alphage was taken hostage and held for ransom at an encampment near Greenwich.

The Danes commanded: "Give us gold!"

Alphage replied, "The gold I give you is the Word of God."

On Easter Sunday in 1066, after months of captivity, Alphage was bludgeoned to death, the promised consequence of failure to pay the ransom. It is said that a sympathetic Dane ended his torment with an ax-blow to the head.

Alphage (also known as Alfege, Elphege, Alphege, or Godwine) was buried at St. Paul's Cathedral, London, but his body was later moved to Canterbury. The anniversary of his martyrdom in the Anglican calendar is April 19, St. Alfege's Day.

Bishop Gellert (980-1046)

In one respect, Christians have no homeland on Earth; our citizenship is in heaven with Christ. However, since "the Earth is the Lord's," every place is God's (Psalms 24:1). Bishop Gellert, who gave his life while teaching the gospel to the people of Hungary, understood his dual citizenship well. He died a missionary martyr.

Gellert was born in Venice, Italy, around 980, and given the name Giorgio di Sagredo. He grew up in a noble family. While young, Gellert caught a dangerous sickness. Fearing for the boy's life, his parents took him to a monastery and dedicated him to God. Gellert recovered and joined the Benedictine order of monks. Tragedy would come to his family, though, when his father died during a religious pilgrimage. This prompted the young monk to adopt his father's name, Gellert.

At the monastery Gellert excelled in studies and prospered in life. Fellow monks elected him abbot at San Giorgio Maggiore. Around 1015, he decided to give up that honor to make a pilgrimage to the Holy Land. The trip would change his life.

Gellert's travels took him through Hungary, where King Stephen I had sought to bring the faith to his people. Stephen took note of the young teacher-traveler, and invited Gellert to tutor his son, Prince Imre. Gellert tutored the prince for seven years, and then spent another seven in solitude in the Bakony Mountains, studying Scripture and writing commentaries for the Hungarian people.

In 1035 King Stephen appointed Gellert the first bishop of Csanád. Contemplative practices, care for the uneducated Christians, and concern for the heathen marked Gellert's ministry. He evangelized the Hungarians, trained monks for missions, and established monasteries for outreach. Gellert's missionary work played a major role in converting Hungary to Christ.

In 1038, Stephen died, leaving no heir. He was succeeded by the son of his sister, whose harsh rule would lead to political revolt, uprisings by pagans, and targeting of Christians. Nonetheless, Gellert continued his missionary work until September 24, 1046. That morning, he held service near the Danube River. Crossing later, his boat was rocked in a barrage of stones thrown by pagan rebels. Gellert was caught, stabbed, his body tucked in a barrel and thrown down a hill into the river; while Gellert prayed the prayer of the first Christian martyr, Stephen: "Lord, do not charge them with this sin" (Acts 7:60).

Hungarian Christians remember Gellert today as a father of the faith in Eastern Europe. The hill on which he prayed and died carries his name, and a monument in Budapest recalls his faithfulness in a foreign land, a way station that became his mission field and home.

So when this **corruptible** has put on **incorruption**, and this **mortal** has put on **immortality**, then shall be brought to pass the saying that is written: **"Death is swallowed up in victory."**

1 Corinthians 15:54

The Great Schism between
Orthodox and Roman Churches (1054)

Political power and the great geographical distances from West (France and England) to East (Constantinople) created controversy and division in the medieval church. When Charlemagne was consecrated emperor in 800, the Eastern churches felt threatened. The insertion of the term *filioque* (an effort to define the deity and humanity of Jesus) in the Nicene Creed in 885 was unacceptable to Russian and Greek church leaders.

In 1054 the Great Schism began in Constantinople, when delegations from Pope Leo IX and Patriarch Michael Ceralarius parted without a treaty or a plan for unity. Not until 1417, at the long Council of Constance (1414–1418), did the "conciliar" efforts bear fruit. The Council of Constance induced the Roman pope to abdicate and then deposed two other claimants. Elected in 1420, Pope Martin IV reestablished a united papacy in Rome.

This was a time of frustration and loss for the church. The Crusades had failed; clergy were abusing ordination vows; the papacy was so entangled in secular power struggles that the mood was disillusionment and distrust.

John Wycliffe translated the first written English Bible from the Latin in 1380. This printed Bible was also a threat to papal hegemony. Itinerant preachers sent throughout England started a spiritual revolution. As Europe became more literate, Christians sought the comfort of the Scriptures, which seemed increasingly contrary to encrusted procedures and policies of the church. The Bible printed in vernacular languages began to make every reader a "priest." The conciliarists who worked for papal unity were also responsible for condemning Jan Hus (1415). After the Council of Constance, no pope made spiritual reform a priority for a century. The most zealous reformer before Luther, Savonarola, denounced clerical misconduct and was condemned by the church in 1498.

The Crusades (1095–1291)

Perhaps Christendom's greatest historical embarrassment, the Crusades, at the time were a brilliant strategic move by papal leaders to unite a warring Europe against heathen enemies threatening the Byzantine church. Not that Pope Urban II in Rome cared much about Constantinople or vice versa. Each part of the church had excommunicated the other in the great schism of 1054. But internal feuding needed alternative war-games, and the call to defend the Holy Land and the Eastern Church against invading Turks presented a quite legitimate target for knights and lords otherwise bent on battling each other.

The First Crusade, led by Peter the Hermit in 1095, was a military disaster. The same could be said for one of the last crusades—the Children's Crusade of 1212—when hundreds of youngsters sailed from Marseilles toward Palestine and fell into the hands of slave traders. Between these, however, many great medieval reputations were made. Richard the Lion-Hearted of England was one of many who led armies to victory, his soldiers bearing the famous sign of the Red Cross. In 1099 Jerusalem was taken. When Godfrey of Bouillon was offered the throne of Jerusalem, he refused to wear a crown of gold in the city where his Savior had once worn a crown of thorns. Instead, Godfrey took the title "Defender of the Holy Sepulchre."

But holding conquered territory was not so easy as winning it. Most of Europe's warriors returned home after winning the victory, leaving the remainder vulnerable to counterattack. The great Muslim general Saladin struck back in 1187, and a horrified Europe sent the third wave of Crusaders in response. Richard defeated Saladin in 1191, and Pope Innocent III, considered the greatest of the medieval papal leaders, launched the Fourth Crusade. His commanders wanted first to control Constantinople, so this Crusade became Christian against Christian. Pope Innocent was powerless to stop it.

Events far from Christendom, however, led eventually to the exhaustion of military resources and the settlement of disputed territories. From far away in Asia, Genghis Khan's Mongols presented an unstoppable military force, which fought against anyone and everyone with savage success. The Khan's tactic was total war, and refusal to submit to him meant extermination.

The fall of Acre in 1291 is generally regarded as the end of the Crusades; the Mongols converted to Islam. A few small Christian settlements remained, but on the Asian mainland Islam was triumphant. The Crusades had failed.

But I say to you,

love your **enemies**,

bless those who **curse** you,

do good to those who **hate** you,

and **pray** for those who **spitefully use**

you and **persecute** you.

Matthew 5:44

The Waldensians (ca. 1173)

Also called the Waldenses, this movement is believed to have been founded by Peter Waldo, or Valdes, in 1173. Some sources earlier than Waldo suggest that Waldenses were active even in the ninth century. Others have claimed this movement to be the child of the early church, rejecting the infusion of power and prestige that followed Constantine's conversion.

The Waldenses sought to teach from the Bible alone and believed in voluntary poverty. They rejected doctrines of purgatory, masses for the dead, indulgences, saints as mediators, and adoration of the Virgin Mary. They were mostly pacifists, except in cases of extreme peril to family and faith. Historically, the movement favored artisan callings and avoided business as morally perilous.

Waldenses were targets of Catholic reaction and endured a long series of persecutions throughout the twelfth and thirteenth centuries. Often they were chased into mountain hideaways. New settlements outside of Europe were hounded mercilessly. As late as 1541, inhabitants of twenty-two villages in France were massacred. In 1655, the settlements in Italy's Piedmont Valley were attacked and slaughtered.

Through all these martyrdoms, the Waldensian church survived, principally in Italy. In 1893 a colony founded Valdese in North Carolina. During the Second World War, they were responsible for helping many Jews escape the Nazis. The Waldensian church is still alive today—many times joined with the Presbyterian Church—in places such as South America, Italy, Germany, and the United States.

William Swinderby (1401)

John Wycliffe began the trouble. He claimed the Bible taught what the church did not, and the church taught what the Bible did not. In 1380, Wycliffe translated the first Bible from Latin into English. Others followed who called themselves Lollards. They read, studied, and preached a faith that sought genuine conversion and renewal from old forms and rituals, deposits from the past encrusted with residue of power and privilege. A stroke took Wycliffe's life in 1384. Forty-four years after John Wycliffe died, the Pope ordered his bones to be exhumed and burned.

But other Lollards carried on. William Swinderby was reputed to be among their ablest preachers, thus also one of Wycliffe's most dangerous protégés. Of his work little is known, except that his effectiveness and lack of conformity drew the attention of church officials five years after Wycliffe's death. Swinderby was a priest in the Lincoln diocese when a board of examiners found his teaching outrageous and ordered him to never speak again, lest the dry wood they had carried to the examination be used to reduce his body to ashes.

Such threats would quickly silence most men, but Swinderby kept talking and teaching. In 1392 another order was issued against this persistent priest, this time by King Richard II. Swinderby was apprehended, questioned, and found wrong on matters of baptism, church policy, governance, salvation and the sacraments.

Records indicate that nine years passed between this second arrest and Swinderby's torturous death at the stake in London in 1401. What happened during those years one cannot tell, but the final chapter of his life shows that Swinderby's heart and mind were convinced that the Bible was intended to be the Christian's foundational document, that its way of salvation—God's mercy expressed in personal faith—was the Christian's hope. He surrendered neither that hope nor his integrity nor conscience during his long testing and confinement. And when his day of pain came, it was a small price for the reward of a faithful life and the sure hope of life to come.

Jan Hus (1370-1415)

His accusers made it clear at the trial that Jan Hus would not only die, but that he would die without hope. "We take from you the cup of redemption," the prosecutors solemnly intoned before sentencing. But Hus replied, "I trust in the Lord God Almighty … that He will not take away from me the cup of His redemption, but I firmly hope to drink from it today in His kingdom."

The communion cup was key to Hus's crimes. Born in 1362 in the village of Husenic in southern Bohemia (today the Czech Republic), this son of peasants learned to pray at the feet of his mother. It was his mother who prompted young Jan toward the priesthood, where he might find, among other benefits, the money and prestige to escape his family's poverty. An average but hard-working student, Hus received a master's degree in theology from the university in Prague and became preacher in that city's Bethlehem Chapel in 1402. Shortly before, news had arrived from England of a certain John Wycliffe, a reformer, whose ideas soon split the university faculty. Chief among those ideas was the nature of the communion cup. Was the wine of the Lord's Supper really changed into Christ's blood during the Mass? Yes, argued the German and Roman theologians. No, countered many Czechs and Wycliffe supporters. Thus the cup would become a symbol of reform that Hus, by some accounts, would carry to this pyre.

Times were dangerous in the early fifteenth century. The church was split between two popes, one in France, the other in Rome. The so-called Great Schism (1378–1417) meant that every leader, politician or churchman must take sides and hope his pope emerged the winner. Survival and the future of the church hung in the balance.

Meanwhile, Wycliffe's influence on the preacher Hus was becoming a clear and present danger. In 1405 Hus began to speak against the sins of the clergy and denounce their hoaxes perpetrated on common parishioners. When the Bohemian church claimed that Christ's blood was appearing on communion wafers, Hus exposed the scheme in language sure to make its point: "These priests deserve hanging in hell" for they are "fornicators," "parasites," "money misers," and "fat swine." Strong words in a volatile

Jan Hus burned at the stake

"Do not believe that I have taught
anything but the **truth**.
I have taught no error.
The truths I have taught
I will **seal** with **my blood**."

— Czech reformer John Hus

church climate. "They [priests] are gluttons whose stomachs are overfilled until their double chins hang down." Later came Hus's outrage against indulgences, the selling of heavenly favor used to finance papal wars. "Shall I keep silent?" he asked. "God forbid."

Four times Hus was excommunicated. For two years (1412–14) he went into exile working in villages in southern Bohemia, writing, preaching, and keeping his head down.

Then in October 1414, Pope John XXIII convened the Council of Constance and invited Jan Hus to attend. Two grand purposes filled the Council's agenda: End the schism and eradicate heresy from Europe. Promised safe conduct, Hus accepted the invitation, joking that "the goose [*hus* in Czech means "goose"] is not yet cooked and is not afraid of being cooked."

Within a week he was arrested. For several months Hus wasted away in a cell in the Dominican monastery on an island in Lake Constance, saved from death there only to face accusations that surely foretold a bitter death to come.

Hus's critics brought the common charges: dangerous heretic, unworthy of the name Christian, wicked man, teacher of a fourth person in the Godhead—all charges to which Hus was forbidden to reply.

On July 6, 1415, amid shouts and jeers, the church committed his soul to the devil. Hus was pushed by a crowd through the streets of Constance to the piled tinder, wrapped by the neck to a stake, and set ablaze. He died singing, "Jesus, Son of the living God, have mercy on me."

Jerome of Prague in the Stocks

Jerome of Prague (1416)

Three months before the death of Jan Hus in Constance, Germany, a Bohemian scholar named Jerome secretly snuck into the city. He had already escaped from prison in Vienna, and had boldly made his way to Germany, without protection, to try to help his friend Hus. Jerome had translated the writings of John Wycliffe into the Czech language, which Jan Hus had read and followed. Feeling perhaps that it was he, Jerome, who should have been arrested, he bravely wrote letters to the emperor and the Council of Constance, pleading for safe conduct and to be heard on behalf of Hus—but they refused. Having done all he could, he made his way back to Bohemia.

He never made it home. As he traveled through a small town in Germany, the Duke of Sulzbach sent an officer to illegally arrest him. Chained around the neck and shackled, he was led back into Constance as if he was the center of a parade. Surrounded by men on horseback and many more guards, they took him to a degrading prison to await trial.

Later, during which time Jan Hus was martyred, the Council of Constance still refused to let Jerome speak. They knew he was a persuasive, intelligent scholar, and were afraid of his ability to defend the Christian faith. He asked to defend himself, and they refused again. Held against his will, with no trial or opportunity to plead his own case, he yelled out:

> "What cruelty is this? For 340 days I've been confined in various prisons. There is not a misery or a want that I have not experienced ... and you have denied me the smallest opportunity to defend myself ... You are a general council, and in you is contained all that this world can impart of wisdom, solemnity, and holiness; but you are still men, and men are often fooled by words and appearances. The higher your character is for wisdom, the more you should be careful not to fall into foolishness. The cause I wish to plead is my own cause, the cause of men, the cause of Christians. It is a cause that will affect the rights of future generations, no matter in what way the testing process is applied to me."

After accusing him on six accounts of ridiculing and persecuting the papacy, and of being a "hater of the Christian religion," they tortured him for eleven days by hanging him by his heels. Threatened with worse torture, he faltered. He verbally affirmed that the writings of Hus and Wycliffe were false. However, after returning to prison, albeit with better treatment, he retracted his statements and vowed full support of Hus and Wycliffe. The council brought 107 new charges against him, but finally let him speak before burning him at the stake.

Jerome eloquently reminded them that throughout history, men of truth have openly voiced their opinions and differences. All that Jerome had done, all that Wycliffe had done, was to unveil the misguided teachings of the Roman Church at that time to the people of their own land, and in their own language. They taught that the Gospel itself is enough to rule the life of every Christian; that the Pope is no different from any other priest; that communion is not the actual blood, body, and bones of Christ; and many other doctrines that follow more Protestant lines of thought.

The Roman Church at that time had already martyred Jan Hus, banished the teachings of Wycliffe, and now Jerome of Prague was on the pyre. Singing hymns as the pyre was lit, his last known words were, "This soul in flames I offer, Christ, to Thee."

His death was not in vain. Jerome, like Hus and Wycliffe, was simply encouraging people to know what the Bible actually said, and not to blindly follow those who claimed to have the utmost authority over Christianity. The work of Jerome, Hus, and Wycliffe led the way for men like Tyndale to translate the Bible into English, and later into other languages, so that everyone had access to the Word of God.

John Oldcastle (1417)

To be a friend of the king is both advantageous and dangerous. Such friendship may lead to wealth and power so long as the friendship serves the king's greater wealth and power. But friends once strong have been known to split over trifles or women. How much greater is the split when the difference is conscience—for here a man must declare himself, and no one can long live when conscience shows itself to be independent from the king.

John Oldcastle was destined for leadership. Strong, brave, and capable of devotion, he served in the armies of the English King Henry IV, a gallant soldier in an era of fighting with clubs and swords. The old king loved him. But King Henry was not immortal, and Oldcastle was not merely a warrior. The king died, and Oldcastle came under the influence of John Wycliffe and the early English reformers known as the Lollards. The Lollards opposed the church of Rome, the priesthood and its privileges, the Eucharistic sacrament and its miracle, and the veneration of saints and icons in place of the Lord Christ, to whom alone confession may be made, and who alone forgives all sinners.

Married to an heiress of title, Oldcastle entered Parliament during the reign of Henry V, and likely fought with his army in France in 1411. But he was a Lollard, and the steely Archbishop of Canterbury, Arundel, wanted the English Church cleansed. The young king was finally persuaded to summon Oldcastle to a hearing, which the latter ignored until his very honor was at stake.

Heresy trials were predetermined affairs, each side aware that the debate only fixed positions. On September 13, 1413, Oldcastle presented his confession of faith to the church, including his views on the Eucharist and the confessional. Arundel condemned him as a heretic.

Execution normally quickly followed judgment. But Oldcastle was the king's friend; as a gesture he was granted forty days to change his mind. During that time, Oldcastle escaped and became leader of a Lollard conspiracy against the crown. He devised a plot to kidnap the king, but the scheme was betrayed. Henry captured most of the conspirators; Oldcastle escaped.

Further plots developed and failed. Finally in 1417, Oldcastle's hideout was discovered and he was captured after suffering extensive injuries. He was taken to London and ordered to a double death: hanged as a traitor and burned as a heretic. The same day he was carried to the town of St. Giles's Fields, the site of his most recent failed plot. There he was hoisted by chains between two gallows and a low fire set beneath him. Throughout his agony, he is said to have praised God and commended his soul to God's keeping.

In 1598, William Shakespeare adapted an old play written when King Henry and Oldcastle were still the closest of companions. But Shakespeare knew his limits, and in his play *Henry IV* he substituted the name *Falstaff* for the old heretic, changing the character into someone quite unlike the Lollard leader.

The persecution of English dissenters would continue through several more King Henrys, and reach its apex when Queen Mary tried unsuccessfully but brutally to purge her island of Oldcastle's successors and compatriots.

"I am ready to die for my Lord; that in my blood the Church may obtain liberty and peace."

— Thomas a Becket, the Archbishop of Canterbury, who was martyred in 1170

Catherine Saube (1417)

By any measure, Catherine was a minor player in fifteenth-century religious life. She lived in Thou, Lorraine, France. As a young girl she presented herself to the leaders and priests of Montpelier as a candidate for life in the nunnery, essentially living as a recluse, away from the world, without contact or friend except for other nuns. Quite obviously Catherine felt a call to pray.

But she did more than pray. After the leaders of Montpelier led her to the nunnery on the Lates Road and "shut her" there, Catherine talked and taught so convincingly, it appears, that after only nine months she was put on trial for offenses against the faith. She no longer believed that the communion bread was made into the body of Christ or that confession should only be made to a priest. Indeed, Catherine had shared these revisionist ideas with the other nuns. She had infected the entire group.

In orderly fashion, a vicar of the inquisitor, M. Raymond Cabasse, D.D., pronounced Catherine a heretic on October 2, 1417, and remanded her to the bailiff for the cleansing and purifying of the church. Catherine was burned at the stake that afternoon.

How did Catherine come to her convictions? There is no record. Did she seek the nunnery as the only viable platform from which a woman living then might teach her contrary convictions? No record. Did she win converts in the nunnery? Apparently so, for the Montpelier town book records that Catherine was burned, together with all the Lates Road nuns.

Apart from brief court records, no doubt kept to show the loyalty and rectitude of Montpelier parish officialdom, the story of Catherine and the Lates Road nunnery would be known to God alone. How many other quiet martyrs will one day raise the choir's call when heaven's record is opened and judgment is fairly rendered?

Martin Luther

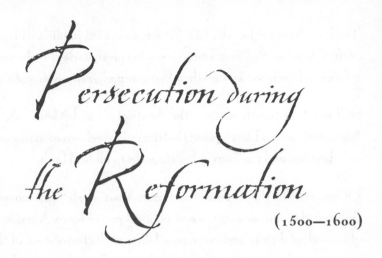

Persecution during the Reformation

(1500–1600)

Martin Luther wanted to address discrepancies between theology and practice, to set right the disorder he painfully observed in the church, and to open up discussion and debate on points of doctrine encrusted by centuries of politics and mismanagement. He did not intend to start a new church. But his *Disputation on the Power and Efficacy of Indulgences* (known as the *Ninety-five Theses*) nailed to the church door at Wittenberg on October 31, 1517, led to a massive protest against church abuses such as indulgences and church office as patronage and, finally, to the worldwide Protestant movement. Many would die for their faith in the process.

Luther was a scholar and an activist. When he was finally labeled a heretic in 1520, he took the official document and publicly burned it. Excommunicated the next year, Luther still appeared before the Diet of Worms in April, where he uttered his famous "Here I Stand" defense. The result: Luther was regarded an outlaw, and his writings were contraband. Luther owed his survival to the protection of Frederick of Saxony, his terrestrial ruler and staunch supporter.

Other centers of reform took up the movement launched by the German monk. In Zurich, Ulrich Zwingli, a parish priest, rose to prominence both supporting Luther's reforms and proposing others, primarily, that Christ's presence in the communion bread and wine was spiritual only.

The French lawyer John Calvin, in Geneva in 1536, published his *Institutes of the Christian Religion*, and so provided present-day Presbyterians and reformed church bodies with their first comprehensive systematic theology.

Still in the sixteenth century, the Anabaptists and Mennonites (led by Menno Simons, a Dutch priest) led the radical reformation toward adult-only baptism and pacifism as benchmarks of biblical faith.

Of course, the Reformation was more than a religious movement. It threatened economic engines and political power bases. A renewed sense of individual dignity and autonomy followed the translation of the Bible into vernacular languages. A renewed sense of wonder at God's creation emerged when science shed its accountability to the medieval church.

Blood, fire, and sword also played their painful parts in the emergence of a renewed church, or churches. To many martyrs we all—Catholic, Orthodox, and Protestant—owe a debt for a clearer vision of God's grace and truth that most medieval believers could have learned or enjoyed.

Henry Voes, Johann Eck, and Lampertus Thorn (1523)

Reading the wrong book may cost you your life.

Throughout Europe after 1521, reading any book by Martin Luther was a crime. Luther had presented his theological views at Worms that year. The Church had responded with the famous Edict of Worms, outlawing his writings. Because Martin Luther was an Augustinian monk, however, his work was widely accepted by that Order. In Antwerp, the Augustinians enthusiastically read and preached the gospel as Luther taught.

But Antwerp was close enough to the University of Leuven for the doctors of theology there to hear and react to these unlawful ideas. In 1522, the entire Order was placed under arrest and its facility demolished as you would a building condemned for irreparable safety violations—in this case, irreparable spiritual violations, so they thought.

The prior, James Probst, eventually escaped the dragnet; his assistant, Melchior Mirisch, recanted and joined the Inquisition. Three Augustinian monks, among others, resolved to stand by their minds and consciences, and so became among the first to die for disavowing the papacy, the communion substance, and all other church regulations for which they could find no scriptural base. Henry Voes and Johann Eck died on July 1, 1523, without doubt or wavering. Lampertus requested time to contemplate his recantation but eventually died, too, for a clear gospel of faith in Christ.

The trials of these monks were unlike trials elsewhere. Here, the charges in the indictments were less tied to politics and were much more a matter of theology and doctrine. The prosecutors urged that the accused "return" to faith, and would have pardoned each one for just a word of agreement. When told that Martin Luther had led them astray, Henry Voes replied: "Yes, we were led astray by him, as were the apostles led astray by Christ." Asked if they had no fear at breaking the Pope's edict, they answered: "We believe God's commandments, and not human statutes, save or condemn." Such responses were like sparks to the dried sticks, which eventually took their lives.

Martin Luther himself was overcome with sorrow at the news of their public and painful executions. "The cause which we defend," he said, "is no longer a simple game; it looks for blood, it seeks for life." Then he wrote "Song about Two Martyrs of Christ in Brussels, Burned by the Sophists at Leuven":

> The old enemy had captured them, terrified them with threats.
>
> They were told to deny God's Word, trying to trick and deceive them.
>
> For this purpose he gathered many of the Sophists of Loewe.
>
> They were impotent with all their tricks. The Spirit showed them up as fools.
>
> They were unsuccessful.

My brethren, count it all **joy** when you fall into various trials, knowing that the **testing** of your **faith** produces **patience**.

James 1:2-3

Patrick Hamilton (1527) and
Henry Forest (1529)

No one was more surprised by the court's sentence, or treated with greater cruelty, than the early Scottish martyr Patrick Hamilton. He was royalty after all, related to the Stuart King James V. Through that relation he was educated in Paris, and knew Erasmus, one of Europe's premier scholars.

Hamilton had been appointed abbot of Ferne the same year Martin Luther posted his *95 Theses* on the church door at Wittenberg. Hamilton had met the German reformer and also knew Philip Melancthon, whose written works powered the Lutheran Reformation. Patrick was a gifted musician, composing and directing in his home cathedral. This promising young man, brilliant and connected, faltered at only one life skill, so it seemed: a sense for danger.

In the summer of 1523, Hamilton returned from Europe to join the faculty at St. Andrews University. Recently challenged on the Continent to reconsider the meaning of Christian faith, he took every opportunity to teach and debate his recovery of biblical truth: God's mercy in Christ apart from indulgences and other contrived interventions. But the archbishop, James Beaton, was scrutinizing the young scholar from afar. Utterly devoted to the papacy, the archbishop would make sure this vile teaching of faith and grace at St. Andrews would not ruin the church.

Dispatching Hamilton was a quick decision and a sub-humanly slow process. In late autumn, 1527, just after Hamilton's wedding, he was invited to participate in a conference of learned church leaders who were gathering, so it appeared, to debate the "new doctrines." Hamilton responded without delay, anticipating a lively colloquy. Instead, Archbishop Beaton conducted a short theological examination and ordered Hamilton's arrest. The next morning the young scholar was questioned by bishops on thirteen charges of heresy, found guilty, and condemned to die that afternoon. The sentence was to be quickly carried out lest his friends exploit the heretic's royal connections and Hamilton be pardoned or acquitted. He had, of course, agreed to every charge. He very much believed what he taught. He could not deny what he and all those around him plainly knew.

Doubtless stunned by the quick turn of events, Hamilton nevertheless walked to the place of burning in a spirit of prayer. Once fixed to the stake, a bag of gunpowder was tied under each armpit and a pile of still-green faggots and kindling placed around him. The gunpowder burst into flames but did not explode; the faggots burned but with insufficient heat to kill. So there Hamilton hanged, flames smoldering, but his blistered, burned body writhing. While more wood was gathered, he begged for an end to the misery. A full six hours he suffered in front of the crowd at St. Salvator's College, who heard him cry amid the agony, "Lord Jesus, receive my spirit. How long will darkness overwhelm this land?"

Two years later, in 1529, a Benedictine monk, Henry Forest, began to illustrate his sermons with the story of teacher Patrick Hamilton, a martyr for the truth. Archbishop Beaton was no more inclined to Forest's perverse teaching than to Hamilton's. Yet Beaton had an increasingly uneasy parish to contend with. The faithful had seen uncommon courage only too recently, and Beaton feared their reaction should he move too openly against another.

Instead of confrontation, Beaton sent a friar to hear Forest's confession, always a confidential matter between sinner, priest, and God. But in this case, the confessional was really a pretext for intelligence gathering, which Beaton quickly used to condemn his mark. Instead of the stake, however, Beaton ordered Forest smothered in a cellar jail away from the people, a private affair within the church.

As the Scottish Reformation grew, Hamilton and Forest were honored as early heroes, and the man most widely known for changing the soul of Scotland, John Knox, took his place in their wake, preaching and teaching the gospel that the abbot and the monk knew and died for.

William Tyndale (ca. 1494–1536)

So great is our passion to know the truth that some seekers will give everything, even their lives, for the treasure of knowing one certain thing.

William Tyndale was a well-educated scholar who was frustrated at the distance between English education and the Bible, the source of truth. Studying at Oxford and then at Cambridge, he bristled at the barriers and longed for the nourishment his mind and heart treasured. "In the universities," he said, "they have ordained that no man shall look on the Scripture until he be nozzled in heathen learning eight or nine years, and armed with false principles with which he is clean shut out of the understanding of the Scripture." Tyndale's life would be devoted to overcoming just this obstacle. For him, the Bible "for the people" would become the answer to corruption in the church. The Bible "for the people" meant that all could drink from the truth itself, without pressure or pretext; and most clearly, without a priest to read or interpret.

Tyndale was born sometime around 1494 in Gloucester, England, near the Welsh border. Ninety years earlier the Church had banned the only English Bible in the world, the hand-copied work of John Wycliffe. It was a flawed translation, based on the Latin Vulgate, but it was all English speakers had. And to have it was a crime. Tyndale's passions eventually settled on a mission as dangerous as any in his century: to work from the Greek and Hebrew texts to create a Bible in vernacular English, so readable and accurate that an Englishman could depend on it, learn from it, and find God's voice in it. All this was clear to the multilingual Tyndale by the age of thirty.

To do that work, Tyndale had to leave England. No bishop in the realm would protect him, much less encourage the project. Tyndale traveled to Germany where he completed the New Testament in 1525. Then he went on to Antwerp, one step ahead of English agents, where the first five Old Testament books were translated and printed. In Belgium he met a community of English merchants, and though agents were searching the continent to find him, Tyndale felt secure enough to relax his guard. His lack of caution would prove fatal.

Tyndale took up a friendship with Henry Phillips, who won Tyndale's confidence but secretly sought the bounty offered for his capture. In May 1535 the trap was set. Tyndale was taken under guard to the castle at Vilvoorde, near Brussels, where he suffered in dank and cold for eighteen months before standing trial for "maintaining that faith alone justifies ... that to believe in the forgiveness of sins, and to embrace the mercy offered in the gospel, was enough for salvation." The complete list of charges included direct attacks on church teaching, among them that "neither the Virgin nor the Saints should be invoked by us."

Tyndale knew how these trials ran. He would have no chance at defense, and death was the remedy. With his body shaking from cold and the winter's light dim for writing, he worked to complete the English Bible, helped by a sympathetic prison governor.

In August 1536, Tyndale was condemned as a heretic and defrocked. For two more months he was kept at Vilvoorde. Then in early October, just past dawn, he was led from prison to the stake. Formalities included placing the Mass once more in his hands, then quickly snatching it back, the offer of last-minute reprieve if he would only recant, and always the shouts of a crowd gathered to witness a "heathen" die.

Secured to the stake, surrounded by brush and logs, Tyndale was heard to pray, "Lord, open the King of England's eyes." Then the executioner snapped hard on the rope, strangling Tyndale before the blaze consumed his body.

That final prayer was for the bully King Henry VIII, whose pursuit of a male heir had already cost Anne Boleyn her life and Catherine her marriage. So full of his own power and pomp, would this king's eyes ever fall favorably on Tyndale's English Bible?

Indeed they did. Two years after Tyndale's death, King Henry authorized the distribution of the *Matthew Bible*, much of it Tyndale's work. And then in 1539, all printers and sellers of books were ordered by the king to provide for the "free and liberal use of the Bible in our own maternal English tongue." Tyndale's dream and his last earthly appeal had come true.

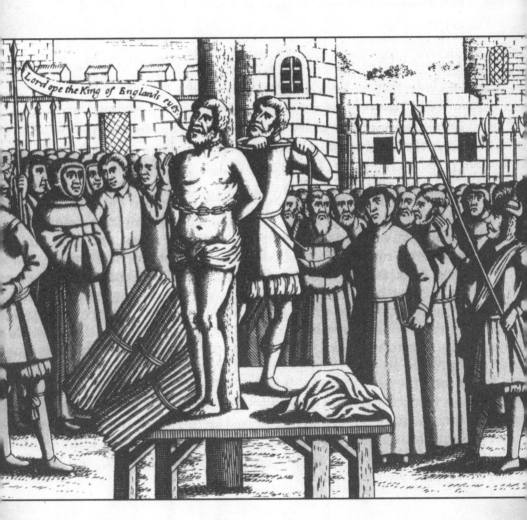

William Tyndale burned at the stake for translating the Bible
into English language.

George Wishart (1546)

Educated at King's College in Aberdeen, Scotland, Wishart the preacher became "infected" with Reformation teaching, and was forced into exile in 1538 after charges of heresy put his life in danger. He returned to Scotland in 1544.

That year Wishart was in Dundee tending to those afflicted by the plague that had consumed the city. "They are in trouble and need comfort," Wishart said about his mission, while Beaton recruited an assailant. There in Dundee, priest John Weighton, on Beaton's orders, confronted Wishart with a cloaked dagger after listening to one of Wishart's sermons. "My friend, what would you have?" called out Wishart, as he noticed Weighton's weapon and realized his intent. Terrified, the would-be assassin fell to his knees pleading for forgiveness. But the congregation of the sick cried out, "Deliver the traitor, we will take him by force." Wishart rebuked them. Holding Weighton by his arms, Wishart insisted, "Whatsoever hurts him shall hurt me; for he has done me no mischief, but much good, by teaching more heedfulness for the time to come." Unfortunately, that time would come sooner than Wishart expected.

Cardinal Beaton finally caught up with Wishart in December 1545, again having assigned the dirty work to another, this time the Earl of Bothwell. In a show trial, Wishart was convicted of refusing to accept that a confession was a sacrament, for denying free will, and for rejecting the idea that an infinite God "could be comprehended in one place" between "the priest's hands." Instead, Wishart proclaimed that the true church was anywhere that Christ's Word was truthfully taught.

Wishart dedicated his life to bringing the Reformation to Scotland, yet more importantly he recognized the everyman, the sick, the down-and-out. Wishart administered the grace of God to all equally. "I have offered you the Word of salvation," Wishart once said. "With the hazard of my life I have remained among you; and I must leave my innocence to be declared by my God." Even minutes from death, Wishart had others in mind, ironically the very people who wished him death, as he prayed: "I beseech thee, Father of Heaven, forgive them that have, from ignorance or an evil mind, forged lies of me. I forgive them with all my heart. I beseech Christ to forgive them that have ignorantly condemned me." His friends were obviously not so forgiving.

On March 1, 1546, George Wishart was burned outside St. Andrews Castle in Scotland. The betrayer, Cardinal Beaton, watched from inside the castle window, thinking all was well.

The Nagasaki Martyrs (1597)

The Jesuits arrived in Japan in 1549, the great missionary St. Francis Xavier leading the campaign to convert the island people. Along with them came traders, whose goods were valued even if the God-words of the priests were greeted with respectful curiosity but not much enthusiasm. Yet a small church grew.

In 1597, Japan's ruler, Toyotomi Hideyoshi, came to believe that his troubles were due to a loss of nationalistic fervor. Thus he directed the cleansing that outlawed Christian worship and led to the arrest of twenty-six Christian men, nineteen of them Japanese. Following a month-long winter march, the men were crucified on Nishizaka Hill on crosses cut to fit the dimensions of each of the condemned. It is said that when the column of prisoners saw their crosses lying in the wheat field beside the hill, they each embraced theirs, and one of the condemned asked that his hands be nailed to the crossbar. For the rest, chains and iron straps kept the men suspended until a squad of executioners finished the work by pushing spears into their chests.

The men were a mix of ages and backgrounds. Louis Ibaraki was only twelve years old. He died with a child's vision of flying from his cross into heaven. John of Goto was nineteen, born to Christian parents who had him educated by the Jesuits. He took his first Jesuit vows the morning of his death. Paul Miki was thirty, the son of a samurai soldier. He was not ordained but was the most gifted preacher in the group. From his cross, he told spectators they could find no salvation apart from Jesus Christ. "I have committed no crime," he said. "The only reason why I am put to death is that I have been preaching the doctrine of our Lord Jesus Christ. I am very happy to die for such a cause." Brother Philip was Mexican. He died while his mother, far away, was preparing vestments for his first Mass. Brother Anthony (aged thirteen) watched his Japanese mother weeping in the crowd in front of him. All the martyrs prayed and sang together before Hideyoshi's executioners brought silence to the hillside.

For nearly 200 years, Christians in Japan met as an underground church, and were finally discovered by French priests permitted into Japan in the 1850s. Today the Shrine of the Twenty-Six Martyrs stands in a replica of the Nagasaki church where those "hidden Christians" first emerged. The original church was destroyed by an atomic bomb in 1945.

The Anabaptists

The term *Anabaptist* means "rebaptizer" and was used by critics of these sixteenth-century radical reformers. The Anabaptists believed the Bible taught "believer's baptism," while the church followed infant baptism. They did not think of themselves as rebaptizing anyone, since the first baptism done to infants, they believed, was illegitimate. The Anabaptists simply called themselves "believers" or "brethren" or "Christians." These reformers did not form a communion or church, such as the Lutherans, but were rather a collection of different movements, which today range from the Amish, Hutterites, and Mennonites (who trace from Menno Simons) to English Baptists, and in the most general sense to all who restrict baptism to adult believers. Moreover, some Christians in the first centuries followed this practice, yet the Anabaptist movement has its origins in the Reformation.

In Zurich in 1525, three men—Conrad Grebel, Felix Manz, and George Blaurock—met to continue the reforms they believed had stalled in compromises made by Martin Luther and Ulrich Zwingli. Grebel and company wanted nothing to do with an established church and its half-hearted followers. For them, a commitment to follow Christ was total and meant not only belief but also practice. The sign of one's joining Christ's church was baptism, which only adults could receive. These radicals therefore refused to have their children baptized.

In the modern era, no civic authority would consider baptism to be state business, and the social response would be on the order of "live and let live; to each his or her own." But in sixteenth-century Zurich, civil and religious authorities were not two distinct spheres. Convergence and order required the city to recognize one way of worship only. Thus the radicals presented to the city an unacceptable disunity.

The solution offered was a debate. The radicals were to meet in a public forum with Zwingli himself. Afterwards, the city council would settle the matter in law. Indeed, the debate resulted in laws expressly forbidding the "rebaptizers" from meeting, teaching, or having fellowship together. The group was to be treated as nonexistent. Obviously the passing of these laws set up a classic conflict of conscience for Grebel and the others.

Against the law, the radicals met for prayer on January 21, 1525. Thus the Swiss Brethren were born as fellows of the Reformation, yet they were rejected and made pariahs by the reformers. Succeeding generations of Anabaptists would resist the neighboring culture (Amish) or assimilate incompletely (the pacifist Mennonites). Certainly the tragic misuse of doctrine and power against Grebel and his Brethren would be repeated in succeeding centuries. The migrations of Brethren from Europe to the New World in the seventeenth and eighteenth centuries attest to their continuing effort to find a safe place to worship and raise families. And in some corners of positive Christian radicalism, the prayers of Grebel, Manz, and Blaurock are echoed today.

Felix Manz (1527)

Today a disaffected churchgoer can simply choose another place to worship. Options are many; choices seem limitless. Not so in sixteenth-century Europe, even in enlightened Switzerland, which was a bit freer in polity and conscience than any of its neighbors.

Felix Manz rose up from a difficult childhood—his father was a priest, his mother thus an unmarried woman—to become a bright, well-educated young adult. He became enamored with the teachings of Ulrich Zwingli in 1519, and associated himself with Zwingli's reform movement. But two years later, he wondered if Zwingli himself, the great teacher, was holding back, settling for compromise when he should have moved forward. Baptism was the issue. Manz and a few others—Conrad Grebel and George Blaurock—could not find infant baptism in the Bible, despite Zwingli's teachings. What was not in the Bible, they reasoned, must be human invention. Sound faith cannot be based on inference or imagination. This small group dissented, even after the Zurich City Council found in favor of Zwingli's ideas on January 17, 1525, following a public debate intended to settle the matter in their city.

Four days later Manz and his group met to pray. "Who should we follow?" they asked. What law governs one's relationship with God? At the meeting (cited as the beginning of the Mennonite Church), Grebel baptized Blaurock, and Blaurock baptized the others. Their act was a crime against the state.

For the next two contentious years, on several occasions Manz was arrested and detained. Finally authorities had suffered his defiance enough. Manz was imprisoned and ordered to cease his "radical" reforms. Of course he could not, on pain of denying his faith, so the law had its way. On January 5, 1527, he was placed on a boat, taken out on River Lammat near Lake Zurich, bound, weighted, and thrown into the water. His mother and brothers urged Felix to remain strong as he walked to his icy death. Manz left for them these words written in prison: "I praise thee, O Lord Christ in Heaven, that Thou dost turn away my sorrow and sadness . . . already before my end has come, that I should have eternal joy in Him."

Not yet thirty years of age, Felix Manz became the first of the radical reformers to be martyred by other reformers. Manz and his group were simply known as the Brethren. (The name by which his church is known today, the Mennonites, was still a decade ahead.) Others called them Anabaptists, for they rebaptized adult believers in defiance of the law. But for Manz, church reform simply needed to go further, for "He instructs us with His divine graces, and shows love to all men."

Michael Sattler (1495–1527)

Michael Sattler was born in 1495 and became a monk. As many Reformation-era monks, he wrestled with his sensual passions and his love for God. Sattler broke his oath of celibacy for an equally unavailable woman named Margarita, a nun who also broke her oath for marital love. Later, the Sattlers would die for a far greater love: their bond with God.

In 1526 the Sattlers had returned to the Anabaptist movement, which Michael had been forced to renounce years earlier to avoid imprisonment. Now, with his Anabaptist convictions strengthened, Michael dedicated his life to preaching at a church in Horb, a strongly Catholic region of Austria. On February 4, 1527, in the small German town of Schleitheim, the Anabaptists met and introduced to the world a new way of understanding church and gospel. The Sattlers traveled to Germany from Horb for the deliberations that produced the "Seven Articles of the Faith," also known as the "Brotherly Union." Michael Sattler helped write this founding document of the Anabaptist movement.

But traveling home from that meeting, Michael and Margarita Sattler were captured and their articles confiscated. They were transformed from Anabaptist advocates to Anabaptist martyrs—a twist of events that propelled the church further than Sattler could ever have imagined.

Tried before a judge on May 17, 1527, Michael, Margarita, nine other men, and eight women were charged with various violations of doctrine and practice. Particularly grievous were the charges against the Eucharist, baptism, unction, and the veneration of the saints.

"Michael Sattler shall be committed to the hangman," read the court's sentence, "who shall take him to the square and there first cut out his tongue, then chain him to a wagon, tear his body twice with hot tongs there and five times more before the gate, then burn his body to powder as an arch-heretic."

Amid cries of "Almighty eternal God, Thou are the way and the truth," the sentence was carried out on May 21, 1527. Eight days later Margarita met the same fate, burned in the city of Rottenburg near the Black Forest.

Finding completion in the love of wife and Lord, Sattler had set himself to making the Anabaptist movement a light of truth for all nations. Soon after their deaths, Anabaptists began carrying the "Brotherly Union" and an account of the Sattlers' deaths in miniature version on their persons, and no threat of torture could stop them. Something deeper than the fear of fire and mutilation burned in their souls. And this can be said about the soul of Michael and Margarita Sattler: for love they lived, and for Love they died.

And though I **bestow all** my goods to **feed the poor**, and though I **give my body** to be burned, but **have not love**, it profits me **nothing**.

1 Corinthians 13:3

George Wagner (1527)

Only three matters separated Herr Wagner from the normal life of good men. These three matters were the difference between life and death in Munich in the sixteenth century: a priest's power to forgive sin, transubstantiation of the communion bread and wine, and water baptism as a rite that saves a person from God's judgment. Herr Wagner believed none of these tenets, having been converted to the Anabaptist movement, the radicals of the Reformation. For George Wagner, what the Bible did not directly teach, he was under obligation from no human being to believe.

The prince of Bavaria who arrested Wagner for his petulance was neither a bloodthirsty man nor one to take innocent life. Rather, he preferred a simple confession and then a return to more pleasant business. Oddly, George refused, even when the prince politely asked. George refused again when the prince brought Frau Wagner and their child before him. For even these loves, a normal man or woman would usually admit to mistakes on a few doctrinal points so clearly taught by the church. But not *this* man.

George Wagner, Anabaptist, was burned on February 8, 1527, for heresy. "Today I will confess my God before all the world," he said on his way to the fire.

That very night, Wagner's executioner died in his bed. Some said it must have been the wrath of God, a sad and bitter end to a public servant's life. George on the other hand had walked to his death with a smile—a most unusual man, but a happy one at the end.

Balthasar Hubmaier (1480–1528)

He was the scholar of the Anabaptists, the radical movement that parted company with Luther on grace, and with Calvin on election, and with both on infant baptism. Hubmaier was the only Anabaptist leader to earn a doctorate in theology. His writings continue to inspire Christians around the world.

As a scholar, Hubmaier knew that most arguments had some good reasons and some not-so-good ones, some logic but also some disconnects. It was perhaps his advanced learning that troubled him whenever his courage fell victim to the manifold operations of his productive mind.

For example, while in Zurich and trying to escape the army of King Ferdinand of Austria, Hubmaier was arrested for teaching against infant baptism—*utterly useless*, he thought. In his defense, he quoted the great reformer Zwingli, also in Zurich. Imagine Hubmaier's surprise when Zwingli refuted Hubmaier, claiming the latter had misunderstood him. Embarrassed and without an ally, Hubmaier agreed to recant. Yet the next day, his conscience in turmoil, Hubmaier retracted his recant. With those words, Hubmaier was sent to prison and put on the rack to determine if pain would clarify his theology. Indeed it did. Hubmaier agreed to his recantation after all. He was released from prison and left Switzerland. Yet his conscience was troubled. He wrote his *Short Apology* in 1526: "I may err—I am a man—but a heretic I cannot be ... O God, pardon me my weakness."

Hubmaier did more than soul-searching, however. He preached and taught widely from his base in Bavaria, and he baptized adults throughout the region. These radical Protestant offenses had unsettled the peace of the Austrian empire, concluded King Ferdinand. When Hubmaier finally committed his views to paper, Ferdinand's forces captured him and brought him to Vienna. Eight months later, on March 10, 1528, he was burned at the stake, with his wife Elizabeth urging him to be strong. Three days after his execution, Elizabeth was thrown into the Danube River with a rock around her neck.

The legacy of their faith includes their writings, which taught God's love for all sinners, baptism as a witness to saving faith, and pacifism as a Christian obligation. Neither atheists nor pagans were to be tormented, Hubmaier wrote, but rather kindly confronted with God's eternal longing for their trust and obedience. Hubmaier had given the radical reformation its strongest theological statement. It cost him his life.

George Blaurock (1491–1529)

When Blaurock started a project, he went all the way.

Born in Bonaduz in the Grisons, Switzerland, Blaurock had studied for the priesthood and had been ordained. At some point before 1524, however, he abandoned his vows, took a wife, and attached himself to the reformers' movement. George arrived in Zurich that year to hear Ulrich Zwingli debate key doctrinal questions, but he found himself pulling past Zwingli's reforms toward a small group of radicals called the Anabaptists. Indeed, Blaurock was the baptizer of all the new communicants, after he himself was baptized, at the famous first meeting of the Anabaptists, or Brethren, on January 21, 1525.

Trouble lay ahead, of course. On the day Felix Manz was martyred, Blaurock, not a citizen of Zurich, was merely beaten and expelled. He went to Bern, Biel, the Grisons, and Appenzell, at each place being arrested and banished. From Switzerland he went to Tyrol and took the pastorate of Michael Keurschner, who had been burned at the stake. In August 1529, authorities in Innsbruck, Austria, apprehended Blaurock and commenced a trial.

The details of his trial are lost, except that Blaurock endured torture to extract information about the radical reform movement. On September 6, 1529, he and his pastoral associate Hans Langegger were burned at the stake.

A letter and two hymns constitute the legacy of Blaurock's writing. In the hymn "Gott, dich will ich loben," he wrote what would become his own triumph song:

Thy Spirit shield and teach me,

That in afflictions great

Thy comfort I may ever prove,

And valiantly may obtain

The victory in this fight.

John Frith (1503-1533)

An English Protestant priest, John Frith lived only thirty years on this Earth.

Born in 1503, John eventually attended Eton College and then graduated from King's College, Cambridge. After graduation, in 1525, John became a junior canon at Wolsey's College, Oxford. There he helped William Tyndale translate the New Testament into English. But that work earned him three years in prison.

After his release, John went to Marburg where he translated Patrick Hamilton's book, *Loci Communes*. Known as "Patrick's Places," this work clearly set forth the doctrine of justification by faith and the contrast between the Gospel and the Law. The young Rev. Frith also wrote *Disputacion of Purgatorye*.

When John returned to England in 1532, he was arrested and tried for heresy. But even then, imprisoned in the Tower of London, he continued to write, formulating the Protestant views on the Sacraments.

Frith received his sentence—death—but was offered a pardon if he would say that he believed in purgatory and in transubstantiation (the Roman Catholic teaching that in the Eucharist, the bread and wine become the actual body and blood of Christ). John answered that neither doctrine could be proven by Holy Scriptures.

Thus, John Frith was burned at the stake on July 4, 1533, at Smithfield, London. In 1573, forty years after his death, John's works were published by John Foxe.

John Lambert (1538)

Branded a "heretic" by the Catholic Church and Henry VIII's Church of England, John Lambert was burned to death on November 22, 1538, at Smithfield in London.

Lambert was born "John Nicholson" in Norwich. As a young man, he was educated at Queens' College, Cambridge. After graduation, Catherine of Aragon nominated John as a fellow at that prestigious institution. But after some theological disputes, John changed his name and went to Antwerp, where he served as a priest to English workers. There he became friends with John Frith and William Tyndale, and he joined the theologians who would meet regularly at the White Horse Tavern. This group included the future Lutherans Edward Fox and Robert Barnes and the archconservative Stephen Gardiner.

John returned to England in 1531 and immediately came under the scrutiny of Archbishop William Warham. But he was not accused of anything, because the Archbishop died in 1532. In 1536, the Duke of Norfolk accused Lambert of heresy, but he escaped and avoided the authorities for a couple of years. In 1538, John was captured and put on trial, charged with denying the real presence of Jesus in the bread and wine of the Eucharist. He was convicted and, thus, condemned to death at the stake.

As flames consumed John, he raised his hands and declared, "None but Christ! None but Christ!"

My flesh and my heart fail;
but God is the strength of my heart
and my portion forever.

Psalm 73:26

Contributions of Calvinism

The two great names in Reformation history are Martin Luther and John Calvin. Neither one anticipated that his writings would lead to churches or movements, which now bear their names. Calvin's primary contribution was a fresh statement of God's supreme power and grace in *The Institutes of the Christian Religion*, written in 1536 but expanded in 1559. Popularly, Calvin is known as the teacher of the ominous doctrine of predestination, according to which God decides who is saved and people can do nothing to change God's mind. In the *Institutes*, however, and in almost every Calvinist confession, the question is never whether people should or can respond to God's gospel in faith, but always that God Himself gets credit for that faith. For Calvin, even saving faith was clearly a gift from God. The dead cannot make themselves live, apart from God's power, Calvin insisted.

Two Protestant families claim a Calvinist heritage: the Presbyterians of Scotland and the Reformed Church of the Netherlands. But even this is too simple. Many other Protestants—Baptists, independents, and others— have adopted Calvinist theology. In addition to God's sovereignty, Calvinists also stress vocation, the teaching that God calls His people to work in all parts of His kingdom. This was an important breakthrough. With God's interest in redeeming all of creation now recovered, a convert no longer need become a priest or pastor to "follow God's will," but could work in business, health care, or any vocation that reflects and advances God's redemptive purpose in Christ.

Calvinism secured the idea that God saves us and that our service to God as artists or teachers or laborers, done to God's glory, becomes a holy calling. As a result, Christians in the eighteenth century worked to help educate the poor in decrepit city centers, in the nineteenth century to end slavery, and in the twentieth century to save victims of the Holocaust, or to harness new energy sources.

Dirk Willems (1569)

He saved the man who tracked him down, only to have the bounty hunter turn him in.

Dirk Willems was a Protestant in Catholic Holland, but the details of his faith and work are lost to history. We do know that when the authorities issued a warrant for his arrest, there was a chase—Willems running for his freedom, and a bounty hunter in pursuit. Willems took a risky path over some thin ice and made it across safely. His pursuer did not. When the sinking man's cries reached Willems' ears, the safety of the other took priority over his own. Willems turned back to rescue the man from the icy waters. Grateful for life, the bounty hunter offered Willems his chance to run. But from the far shore, a town official yelled for the deputy to perform his duty after all. Willems was brought in.

The only record of Dirk Willems's trial and punishment reads: "After severe imprisonment and great trials, he was put to death in a lingering fire by these bloodthirsty, ravening wolves, enduring it with great steadfastness, and confirming his faith."

No last words of Dirk Willems are recorded. Only two last deeds—one, saving a man's life, and then dying with dignity and faith in the God who ultimately rescues all who trust in Him.

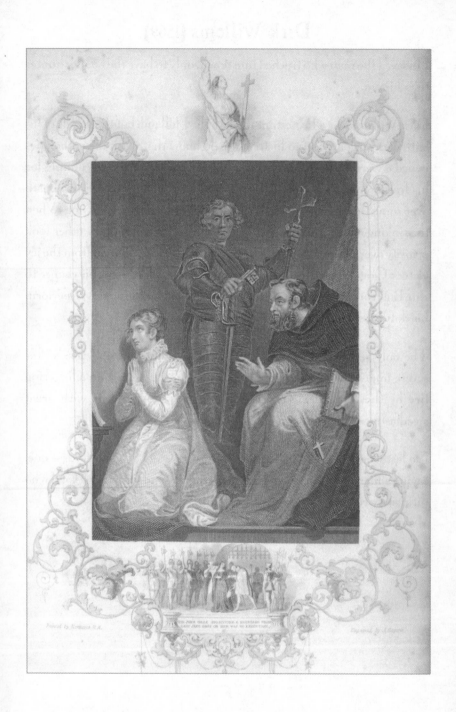

Lady Jane Grey

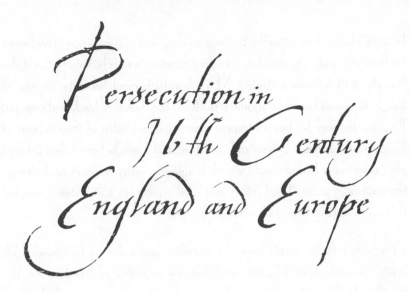

Persecution in 16th Century England and Europe

(1553—1595)

ngland's King Henry VIII won his battle with Rome, securing a host of wives and becoming head of his national church. When he died in 1547, his successor, Edward VI, was still a child and sickly. To stabilize power, the Duke of Somerset became adviser to the king, but he so disturbed wealthy landowners that he was executed in 1557. The Duke of Northumberland took over; and as Edward grew weaker, he plotted to bring to the throne Lady Jane Grey, also young. Northumberland forced Grey to marry his son, securing his own place in the kingdom.

Surely temporal and religious reasons combined in these plots and plans. Edward VI was agreeable to the growing Protestant movement. Grey herself was a sincere Protestant. But Edward's legitimate heir was his half-sister Mary, daughter of Catherine of Aragon, who was as devoted to Rome as anyone in Europe.

Nine days into Jane Grey's rule, Mary's army arrived in London and proclaimed her queen. Northumberland was beheaded despite his pleas to live. Archbishop Cranmer, who had instigated several reforms and had written the *Book of Common Prayer*, was imprisoned. The Queen reversed her earlier clemency for Jane Grey and had her beheaded, along with Grey's tiresome husband.

In 1555, Parliament passed a law reinstating burning as proper treatment for heretics, and only days later the first martyrs were chained to the stake. Nearly 300 followed, giving Mary her historical identity as one of England's most heartless monarchs. But Mary failed to lead, and angered English leaders by her unhappy marriage to Philip of Spain, son of Emperor Charles V. Many of her influential lords believed that Mary's allegiance with Rome would wreck England's independence and change the country's polity. Had Mary not died young (in 1558), many suspect that a revolution would have swept her out.

Elizabeth I (1558–1603) brought stability and calm to England. Her religious settlement in 1559 established a new day of freedom for the English Reformation, but set the stage for the persecution of Puritans and their search for a new place to worship and live. As a result, North America became home to European religious refugees.

Lady Jane Grey (1554)

The morning of July 9, 1553, arrived for Lady Jane Grey just as any other summer morning in the English countryside. But much to her surprise and somewhat against her will, on that day Lady Jane was crowned queen. It was a day that her parents had dreamed of, that she dreaded, and that her cousin Mary feared and disdained.

King Edward was ill, and Jane's mother-in-law had come six days earlier to tell Jane that she had been named heir to the throne. This came as quite a shock to Jane, as Mary was closer in bloodlines than Jane. On July 6, Edward passed away. The news was kept a secret for several days in hopes of prohibiting the Catholic Mary from making a claim to the throne. But on July 9 the news leaked out, and Mary proclaimed herself queen.

Meanwhile, that same day Jane was brought to her father-in-law's house, the residence of the Duke of Northumberland, himself a power monger. As she walked down the familiar corridors, something unfamiliar happened. Everyone she passed curtsied or bowed. She heard murmurs of "Your Majesty" and stopped suddenly, realizing what was happening. Someone steered her toward a room which contained an empty throne. As she approached it, Jane swooned and fell, crumpling to the floor. She cried, "The crown is not my right and pleaseth me not. The Lady Mary is the rightful heir." Lady Jane took a moment to gather her strength and consider what her best course of action would be as her family sought to persuade her of the imperative nature of her acceptance of the crown.

Jane did what was natural to her: She prayed for divine guidance. After a moment, she ascended the throne and allowed those present to swear allegiance to her, because she had asked God to give her "such spirit and grace that I may govern to Thy glory and service, and to the advantage of the realm."

But Jane's greatest challenge was yet to come. Jane made her state entrance into London amidst few cheers, as public opinion was on the side of Mary. For several days Jane lived as Queen, but soon her father-in-law, Lord Northumberland, mustered an army to meet Mary, who was encroaching on London with an army of her own. While he was gone, a royal council decided to declare Mary Tudor as queen, which Jane herself supported. In a desperate attempt to save himself, Lady Jane's own father swore allegiance to Mary, in spite of his previous actions to place his daughter on the throne. Lord Northumberland also quickly changed his position, but it was too late.

Jane, her husband Guilford, her father-in-law, and her father were all sentenced to the Tower of London. Jane's father was pardoned (temporarily, as it turned out), her father-in-law was executed in August, and Jane and her husband were assured of Mary's pardon. But an ill-timed insurrection of other enemies of Mary's hardened her heart, and she rescinded her forgiveness, particularly because Jane refused to convert to Catholicism.

February 11 was the date of Jane and Guilford's execution. Jane was brought to the block, recited the 51st Psalm, and asked that the deed be done quickly. Her final sentiment echoed that of her Lord's: "Father, into your hands I commit my spirit." In the end, Jane died a martyr for her faith. She was a political pawn from the first, acquiescing to the wishes of her family to her own detriment in the end. Yet, her faith was firmly grounded in the truth of Scripture, and Jane died with the strength and dignity God provided for her.

Yet in all these things
we are **more than conquerors**
through Him who loved us.

Romans 8:37

John Bradford (1510-1555)

For saving a life, he lost his own; for owning an oath, he was condemned as a liar. A humble, sometimes timid man, this martyr gave us one of today's most frequently used quotations, yet few know of him.

The sixteenth century was one of the most religiously dangerous times in English history. Survival required changing one's color like a chameleon, depending on the whim of the monarch. Many souls, once captured by the gospel, dared to remain loyal to God at any cost. For John Bradford, the cost was a promising career in government, and eventually his life.

Bradford was born into a wealthy family and received early training in business and law. His skill led to service in the government of the notorious Henry VIII, whose quest for a male heir forced his break with the Roman Church and the death or banishment of wives unable to bear a son.

While a law student in London, Bradford came to faith in Christ and soon afterward turned his studies toward theology at Cambridge University. He was ordained a chaplain in 1550, during the short reign of Protestant King Edward VI. As chaplain, Bradford once watched a column of prisoners being led to their execution, when he said, "There but for the grace of God go I." His words were a gift to the ages and a premonition of his own untimely death.

In 1553, Edward died, and Mary Tudor took the throne. Known as "Bloody Mary," she condemned more than 300 martyrs in her effort to return England to the Catholic Church. Any preacher or prelate could see the tide turning; many turned with it. Yet for Bradford, it was an act of interfaith heroism which Mary used against him.

On a hot August Sunday during Mary's first year, her loyal bishop of Bath preached a sermon critical of the recently deceased king. The crowd grew angry and threatening. One listener threw a knife at the bishop, who was shaken but unhurt. Bradford, present that day, quieted the crowd, urged them to good order, then at his own risk escorted the panicked bishop to safety. Three days later Bradford was arrested for sedition.

John Bradford burned at the stake

For two years Bradford lived inside dank English cells, preaching and writing. His word was so trusted that guards would release him occasionally at night, fully confident that he would return before daybreak. He always did. Finally examined by an ecclesial court that was determined to find fault, they asked whether he would accept the queen's mercy. Bradford replied, "I shall be glad of the queen's favor on terms that correspond with my duty to Him whose favor is life, but whose displeasure is worse than any death mortals can inflict."

The immensely popular preacher was led to the stake on July 1, 1555. Upon arriving, he asked forgiveness of any he had wronged, granted forgiveness to the soldiers around him, then picked up a nearby stick and kissed it. He was bound to the stake with a younger prisoner, who heard from Bradford this assurance as flames lifted around them: "Brother, be of good comfort, for we shall have a merry supper with the Lord this night, where all our pains will end in peace, and our warfare in songs of joy."

John Hooper (1555)

Awaiting execution at the Newgate prison, John Hooper scribbled with coal on the prison wall: "Fear not death, pass not for bands. Only in God put thy whole trust. Death is no death, but amens to live." Sentenced days earlier by a magistrate of Queen Mary of England, Hooper sat in a prison cell at the very church where he once preached, a prisoner of the Word he had so boldly announced.

Born in Somerset, England, to a well-to-do Catholic family, Hooper left home in 1515 to attend Oxford University. With a Bachelor of Arts in hand, Hooper spent the next twenty years straddling the line between overindulgence and temperance, committing himself to a monastery, only then to become steward to a wealthy family. At times admittedly a "brute beast ... a slave to my own lusts," Hooper ultimately conceded that "living too much of a court life in the palace of our king" was not his calling. In the Puritan Reformation, John Hooper found his passion.

But this was unfortunate timing. Henry VIII, desperate for national solidarity in England, demanded ecclesial unity from his subjects. Puritans either went underground or else faced the king's wrath. When Henry died in 1547, Hooper was made chaplain to Edward Seymour, first Duke of Somerset, where he championed the tenets of the Swiss Reformation. Then the impossible happened. John Hooper, the radical, outspoken Puritan preacher, was offered the bishopric of Gloucester by the English crown, a distinguished appointment and certainly a fortunate career move toward power and public influence. Hooper's response? He said no.

Citing the "shameful and impious form of the [acceptance] oath" and the vestments Hooper would be required to wear, he declined the position. Several months in the Fleet prison followed, until Hooper conceded various points and officially assumed the position of Bishop of Gloucester in March 1551.

Two years later, in 1553, the consummate Catholic monarch, Mary Tudor, became Queen of England. Her policy was no compromise, no concession. Defrocked and imprisoned in March 1554, Hooper had one chance left to renounce his beliefs before a Commission of Bishops in January 1555. His response was as clear as his Queen's indictment of him: no compromise.

Hooper accused the Pope and the entire Catholic Church of opposing the teachings of Christ. Firm in his beliefs about divorce, marriage, and the Eucharist, Hooper was condemned to death on January 29.

> Charge #1: "He [a priest] had himself married and openly maintained and taught the lawfulness of the marriage of the clergy."

> Charge #2: His teachings that "married persons, in the case of adultery [can be] divorced from one another."

> Charge #3: Hooper's position that the Eucharist was "not truly the true and natural body of Christ and His true and natural blood under the species of bread and wine."

As noted in the execution document written by the Commission of Bishops, Hooper was "a most obstinate, detestable heretic, and, committed to our secular powers, [should] be burned according to the law." Led on February 9 from his cell to the pyre, Hooper was forbidden to speak, being a "vainglorious person [who] delighteth in his tongue." The silent John Hooper was tied to the stake and given one last chance to repent, with a box containing a pardon placed in front of him. The ban on speech lifted for a moment, and he replied, "If you love my soul, if you love my soul, away with it!"

John Rogers (ca. 1500–1555)

Life was a string of successes and honors for this Cambridge University graduate and rector of Holy Trinity Church in London. That is, until the death of the English king he had chosen to serve and the accession of a queen his convictions forced him to challenge. John Rogers, a minister, Bible editor, and father of eleven children, holds the dubious distinction of being Mary Tudor's first victim.

In 1534 Rogers took a post as chaplain to English merchants in Antwerp. There he met his wife, and also befriended William Tyndale, who convinced Rogers that the recovery of biblical truth, indeed the Bible itself, was the first and only foundation of God's truth. It was God's Word.

John became a Protestant and helped compile the *Matthew Bible*, the first English edition authorized for distribution by Henry VIII himself. From Antwerp, Rogers went to Wittenberg, where he pastored a church and studied further the doctrinal reforms sweeping Europe. In 1548, Rogers returned to England, where Edward VI welcomed reform, and leaders such as Ridley and Cranmer were drafting and planning a new era of Christian worship. Their efforts would be cut short, however, by Edward's untimely death and the subsequent reign of Mary Tudor.

By August 1553, Rogers knew that his life as leader and reformer would soon change. Early that month he preached on the foolishness of "popery, idolatry, and superstition." This was a direct challenge to Mary's vision for the future of the English church. The sermon led to John's examination and house arrest. His employment as chaplain and rector was ended and his church office stripped.

Six months later, a new bishop of London had Rogers transferred to Newgate Prison. Mary was preparing Parliament to pass her "crackdown" laws, and offenders were being put in line so that the coming legislation could be practiced and its bitter lessons taught to the people.

Rogers waited a year at Newgate without trial. Then in January 1555, he was brought before Mary's hatchet man, Bishop Stephen Gardiner of Winchester. Gardiner declared Rogers a heretic because he denied the change of substance in the communion bread and wine. Then, because Parliament had outlawed heresy and clarified its punishment, Rogers was condemned to be burned.

Treatment of the man was unnecessarily cruel. John requested a meeting with his wife—he was denied. He was asked to recant—this *he* denied. But such stalemates and discourtesies were short-lived. On February 4, Rogers was marched to the stake. His children joined the crowd lining the street as he walked to his death. His youngest child was there, at mother's breast. All who knew the gravity of the day encouraged him to go with strength. Indeed, John's final conversation was a witness in itself.

"Will you revoke your evil opinions of the Sacrament?" the sheriff asked.

"That which I have preached I will seal with my blood," Rogers answered.

"You are a heretic then," declared the official.

"That shall be known at the day of judgment," Rogers assured him.

"I will never pray for you," the sheriff finished.

"But I will pray for you," Rogers said, moments before the flames rose.

John Philpot (1555)

Like many before him and after, John Philpot was caught in the pincers of changing worldviews, where ideas once favored become dangerous, and people who are guided by fear and ambition are placed in positions of judgment.

Philpot was privileged. His father was a knight, and his college was Oxford. With a good mind to complement a sturdy character, Philpot grew into a leader and church reformer. He traveled widely, gaining exposure beyond England's shores. He returned to his homeland in what appeared to be its prime. The boy-king, Edward VI, favored Philpot's reformational faith. And John became the new archdeacon of Winchester. The future appeared open, favorable, challenging.

Situations soon changed. Edward died, and after the brief and most unhappy try-at-queen by Lady Jane Grey, Mary I took the throne. She was a staunch Catholic and opposed the Protestant reformers as deeply as anyone in her day. Philpot, a thoughtful man, no doubt acknowledged the new difficulties confronting him. But how could he—the knight's son, Oxford trained, church leader—have foreseen the end?

In the pogrom that Mary inspired, Philpot was relieved of duty and summoned to defend his views. He did this with conviction and intelligence through thirteen colloquies, separated by various depredations of prison and confinement. For several of these prison terms he was not allowed books or pen, as if the absence of the tools of the mind would eventually bend him to recant and join the Queen's spiritual cadre.

Intellectually defeated but politically strong, England's Privy Council convened the fourteenth examination to finally rid themselves of the Philpot pest. He had been in various prisons for more than twenty months.

His last interrogation had a stark simplicity about it. Whatever Philpot's reason for believing as he did, he could either recant or die. The realm was no longer interested in windy monologues that seemed to end in the quietude of defeat for the side that was supposed to win. Absent a complete change of heart and mind, Philpot was sentenced to be burned.

John Philpot praying at the place of his martyrdom

On December 18, 1555, the sheriff, escorting the prisoner across a muddy track on the way to the stake, asked if he would like the courtesy of being carried by two officers, thus avoiding the mud. He replied sharply: "Would you make me a pope? I will finish my journey on foot."

Then at the place of execution, Philpot said: "Shall I disdain to suffer here at the stake, when my Redeemer did not refuse to suffer the most vile death upon the cross for me?"

As the fire at his feet grew hot, Philpot recited Psalms 107 and 108. In moments the realm's will was done. Another voice was gone, another martyr's crown won.

Lawrence Saunders (1555)

Blood was spilt in this chaotic middle decade of England's sixteenth century. Passionate faith and politics ran strongly together, and the power of the combination was both a testament to faith and a threat to life.

Lawrence Saunders was a gifted young man. Educated at Eton and Cambridge, he obtained a license to preach during the brief reign of the boy-king, Edward VI. The king, fond of tennis and some revelry, caught a cold in the winter of 1552–53 and succumbed to tuberculosis on July 6. He and his counselors had planned that Lady Jane Grey would succeed him and thus keep Protestant faith paramount. But the people wanted King Henry's rightful heir, Mary; so nine days into Jane's patched-together queenship, Mary rode into London and took the throne for herself. Mary ordered all those involved in the Lady Jane plot to be killed, sparing her half-sister Elizabeth. But how does one kill a church, a faith, and turn it back toward Rome? Mary's plan was to listen well to what the preachers had to say.

On October 15, 1553, Saunders delivered a sermon meant to clarify the teachings of Protestant faith and perhaps as well, to boost Jane Grey's chances for reinstatement. The sermon was theologically astute but politically futile. Whether by plan or serendipity, Saunders' sermon was heard by royal sympathizers. He was accused of treason, and the Bishop of London ordered his arrest.

The plot to bring Jane back failed completely. Jane, her husband, and other culprits were executed. Saunders waited in prison for Parliament to pass the law, which permitted heretics to be burned. On February 8, 1555, preacher Lawrence Saunders was marched barefoot to the fire. His last words: "Welcome the cross of Christ, welcome everlasting life."

Nicholas Ridley (1500–1555) and Hugh Latimer (1485–1555)

The fire that quenched the lives of these two pastors was lit to cleanse English soil of traitors and heretics. Instead, it silenced scholars, committed churchmen, and forceful humanitarians.

Both Nicholas Ridley and Hugh Latimer had reached pinnacles in their careers. Ridley was the bishop of London and confidant to Archbishop Thomas Cranmer. He influenced Cranmer's *Book of Common Prayer*, began pastoral work in inner-city London, and founded hospitals and schools.

Latimer, an extraordinary preacher, was an ardent Catholic who converted to reformation faith upon hearing of a confession by Thomas Bilney, whose confidence in the God of the Bible reduced Latimer to tears. Latimer advised the intemperate King Henry VIII and flourished under Henry's successor, Edward VI.

But Edward died, and Mary Tudor, the daughter of Henry's first wife, took the throne. Now was the time to cleanse England of so-called reformers and restore it to Rome. Nicknamed "Bloody Mary," the new queen arrested Ridley, Latimer, and Cranmer—in all, about three hundred people met death by her decree.

Engraved for The Revd Dr Southwell's New Book of Martyrs.

Dodd delin.   Taylor sculp

MARTYRDOMS of the Bishops RIDLEY and LATIMER, who were burnt together in one Fire at Oxford.

Bishops Ridley and Latimer were burned together in one fire.

Because each man refused to repent of his convictions about church and sacrament, both were condemned to be burned, a testament to the people that stature and age do not insulate a heretic from the queen's wrath (and from God's, in her view). When the queen's court passed judgment, the men were told to prepare immediately for the stake. A blacksmith approached Ridley to fix a chain around his waist. The deposed bishop replied: "Good fellow, knock it in hard, for the flesh will have its course." When executioners laid a lighted faggot at Ridley's feet, Latimer turned to him and said, "Be of good comfort, Dr. Ridley, and play the man. We shall this day light such a candle by God's grace in England, as I trust never shall be put out."

Latimer died quickly, but Ridley's fire waned. His lower parts burned through, but the flames barely hurt his upper body. In agony he moaned, "I cannot burn ... Lord, have mercy on me." At last, flames ignited the gunpowder sack hung around his neck, and his life passed from Earth to Heaven.

Thomas Cranmer, deposed Archbishop, his own heart and mind wavering, his every sinew fearing the fire, watched his friends die from his cell in London Tower. He too was eventually burned at the stake.

Rowland Taylor (1510–1555)

Nothing in the training, preaching, or patriotism of Rowland Taylor would have led him to predict that in the prime of his life, he would be violently killed and his children left fatherless. Indeed, Rowland's own father was a distinguished rector and public servant, not wealthy but well connected, ensuring as best a man can that his lively offspring would prosper.

Rowland certainly did. By the time his father died, Rowland, at age twenty-four, had earned a degree from Cambridge University and was well on his way to a lifetime of preaching and influence.

But certain ideas were lining up for Rowland that history now reckons to be among the most dangerous of his era. For Rowland, in his education and through his royal service, had come to reject doctrines such as priestly celibacy and the miraculous transubstantiation of the wine and bread during Communion. Indeed, even Rowland's marriage might be seen as a harbinger—his beloved Margaret is widely thought to have been the sister of William Tyndale, who was burned at the stake in 1536 for promoting an English-language Bible and other reforms.

Nonetheless, Rowland enjoyed clergy duties, and even shared the home of Archbishop Thomas Cranmer, serving as his chaplain. He maintained the parish at Hadleigh, in Suffolk County, and was much beloved for his pastoral care.

Then everything changed. The friendly young Protestant king, Edward VI (successor to Henry VIII), died. Lady Jane Grey, likely with Rowland's support, took the throne but kept it for only nine days before Edward's half-sister, Mary, became Queen and launched her crusade to recapture the realm for Rome.

Only a couple of days after Mary's coronation, Taylor's parish at Hadleigh was "invaded" by John Averth. He was a neighboring priest with strong Catholic sympathies, who conducted a Mass protected by armed guards, and who ejected Taylor from the church when he protested. That night the die was cast.

Averth's co-conspirators wrote of the altercation to England's Lord Chancellor, Stephen Gardiner, to whom Queen Mary had given the job of enforcing her ecclesial will. A summons from Gardiner was tantamount to a death sentence, so when that summons arrived at Hadleigh, many of Taylor's churchmen begged him not to go. Some, citing Matthew 10:23, urged that he save himself for later ministry once the storm had passed. Taylor replied: "Flee yourselves, and do as your conscience leads you. For myself, I am fully determined, with God's grace, to go to the bishop, and to his face tell him that what he does to me is insignificant. God will raise up teachers after me who will teach His people with more diligence and fruit than I have done."

Rowland Taylor's interview with Chancellor Gardiner in London was bravely confrontational. He begged the bishop to remember his own vows made to Henry and Edward, vows to reform the church, to create the Church of England, to support forms recently set forth in the *Book of Common Prayer*. Gardiner dismissed these vows as "Herod's oath—unlawful, and properly broken." Then Gardiner turned the tables, accusing Taylor of treason (because he had objected to the Mass at Hadleigh parish) and heresy.

Taylor replied, "My lord, I am parson of Hadleigh. It is against all right, conscience, and laws, that any man should come into my parish and dare to infect the flock committed to me." And so went charge and countercharge, with the winner predetermined and the outcome grimly obvious.

Taylor was imprisoned for two years until his formal trial on January 22, 1555. The charge was heresy and schism, and the sentence cited a law revived just two days earlier in Parliament—heretics should be burned. He was taken by sheriff's escort on February 9 to Aldham Common, Hadleigh. There he was allowed a last reunion with Margaret and their children, and then chained to the pole. To his young son Thomas he gave these words, the blessing of a father about to die:

> "Almighty God bless thee, and give thee His Holy Spirit, to be a true servant of Christ, to learn His word, and constantly to stand by His truth all the life long. And my son, see that thou fear God always. Fly from all sin and wicked living. Be virtuous; serve God daily with prayer. In anywise see thou be obedient to thy mother, love her, and serve her. Flee from whoredom, remembering that I thy father do die in the defense of holy marriage. And another day when God shall bless thee, love and cherish the poor people, and count that thy chief riches to be rich in alms. And when thy mother is waxed old, forsake her not, but provide for her to thy power. For so will God bless thee, give thee long life upon Earth, and prosperity, which I pray God to grant thee."

Taylor was only the third victim of hundreds who were burned during Queen Mary's short reign. John Hooper, Mary's fourth victim, was burned later that day. Perhaps because the gruesome event was not yet well practiced and the spectators not conditioned, one of the sheriffs, as the flames were just ascending, struck Taylor's head with his halberd, killing him instantly. An unhewn stone marks the site: "Dr. Taylor, in defending what was good at this place, left his blood."

William Hunter (1555)

Provide all the incentives a young adult might want—those were the bishop's tactics. Just offer the lad what he needs and doesn't have. Offer him money. Offer him a bit of public honor. That's enough for any boy. He'll take it. London's Bishop Bonner was confident. He knew the mind of London's youth. But Bonner, trying to buy William Hunter's obedience, instead brought the judgment of history upon himself and his queen.

William Hunter's case was clear enough. Raised in a Christian home, he learned the Bible and loved it. He trusted God and distrusted the established church. The charge against him was just as clear. Queen Mary had decreed that everyone in London must take Mass. No ambiguity there. But young Hunter did not take Mass. Even in the big city, he could hide only so long.

The lawbreaker was finally caught. He explained to the sheriff that reading the Bible, even alone, was worship. He had obeyed the edict, just not in the edict's required way. Then the bishop got involved, even though he certainly must have had more important responsibilities. Who was this young boy? Why should he be petulant? Failing to coax him by money, Bonner had William Hunter placed in the stocks. For two days Hunter crouched in the wood frame without food or water. Now will you obey the Queen? No? To Newgate prison then. No honor awaits you there.

For the next nine months William Hunter carried chains around the dismal prison—all for reading a Bible, for not taking the Mass, for defying the Queen's express order. By February 9, 1555, Bishop Bonner had troubled himself enough with this boy. Still no? Then back to Brentwood with you, your home village, to be burned as a heretic.

On March 26, with Psalm 51 on his lips, William Hunter, Bible reader, age nineteen, died in the fire lit by bailiff Richard Ponde, acting on orders of the state.

As the wood ignited, William's brother yelled to him, "Think on the holy passion of Christ, William, and be not afraid of death."

The sheriff said to his convict: "I would no more pray for you than for a dog."

"I am not afraid," William replied.

Today a monument in Brentwood carries this message:

William Hunter. Martyr.

Committed to the flames March 26 MDLV.

Christian Reader, learn from his example to

value the privilege of an open Bible.

And be careful to maintain it.

Thomas Cranmer (1489-1556)

Only one thing did old Thomas Cranmer lack as he faced his last day of life. He had been leader of the English church, counselor to kings, writer and compiler of one of the most famous religious books ever published. The former archbishop had traveled widely, married twice, and held the hand of a dying monarch. Only one thing more he needed: courage to face execution.

Thomas Cranmer rose from a humble home to achieve renown throughout the Christian West. He was a Cambridge graduate, ordained a priest, and concluded while he was young that God had vested all earthly power in sovereign heads of state. His own sovereign at the time was the infamous Henry VIII, who would regularly return subjects' loyalty and love with the cool emotional distance of a mercenary. Indeed, Henry could watch wives and trusted friends die as traitors if it served his remote interests. Thus when Henry appointed Cranmer as the archbishop of Canterbury, he assumed the new prelate would last only as long as his usefulness.

Indeed, Cranmer did prove useful. Every marriage Henry needed, Cranmer granted. Every divorce Henry demanded, Cranmer found lawful. Finally England had an archbishop who understood the church's one true doctrine—the ecclesial supremacy of the king.

This was even more the case when Henry's successor, Edward VI, moved England closer to Protestant faith. Cranmer basked in the glow of leadership and influence. Secretly, he took as his wife the daughter of German reformer Andreas Oslander. (His first wife, before ordination, had died in childbirth.) Publicly he compiled and wrote the Anglican liturgy, called the *Book of Common Prayer*, and still being used today.

But history took a different turn. Edward died. The timorous archbishop threw his support to Lady Jane Grey, the Protestant great-niece of Henry VIII. She got the job, but only for nine days, when into London rode Mary Tudor, daughter of Henry's first wife, Catherine of Aragon, and a devout Catholic. The subsequent reign of "Bloody Mary" is the story of dark ages in the English church.

In November 1553, Cranmer was charged with treason and imprisoned. He stood a mock trial with reformers Nicholas Ridley and Hugh Latimer, whom he was forced to watch burn. Mary's agents wore him down, shaved his head, and scraped the tops of the fingers of his right hand—those that had been anointed in his ordination years earlier.

Then in jail on the night of March 20, 1556, Cranmer succumbed to his ultimate humiliation. Shivering with fear of the stake awaiting him the next morning, he signed decrees recanting every reformational conviction and affirming the Bishop of Rome as true head of Christ's church. He quivered at how far he had fallen.

On the next day, perhaps even Cranmer himself was surprised by the calm and courage of his last hour. Asked to make public his true convictions, Cranmer clearly recanted his midnight recantations, boldly declared his faith by the Nicene Creed, clearly separated himself from Rome, and declared he would thrust his right hand first into the flames to purge the cowardice of last evening's signatures.

At nine o'clock in the morning, he was bound by a steel band to the stake. "This hand hath offended," he said, lowering it into the flames. "Lord Jesus, receive my spirit," he moaned, and then collapsed into the fire.

Death is swallowed up in victory.

O Death, where is your sting?

O Hades, where is your victory?

1 Corinthians 15:54, 55

Julius Palmer (1556)

An excellent scholar and committed Catholic, Julius Palmer could not understand how the Protestant martyrs endured their painful deaths with apparent joy and goodwill. It confounded him; it troubled him. Their faith, after all, was false and therefore groundless, he thought. Being false, they would have no reason to suffer for it, much less to suffer bearing so little ill will toward their persecutors. And not just the absence of ill will but the positive presence of peace. He watched them burn and the experience upset him.

Julius Palmer was born in Coventry, where his father was mayor. At Oxford, he became a top student and scholar of Latin and Greek. Julius excelled in debate, and the passion to learn was so strong that he normally woke as early as four in the morning to begin research and writing. He became a reader in logic at Magdelan College, Oxford. He was heading toward academic brilliance.

The short reign of the Protestant boy-king, Edward VI, was not easy for Catholic scholars, especially debaters who projected their beliefs and taught younger scholars their ways. In early 1553, Julius was dismissed from his post at Magdelan. Unable to find university employment, he became a tutor to a wealthy family until good fortune came his way in the early death of the sickly king and the subsequent rule of the rigorously pro-Catholic Queen Mary. Palmer was promptly reemployed at Magdelan.

But not all was well with him. Catholic as he was by practice and intellect, he did not enjoy, and, in fact, struggled greatly over the burning of Protestants as part of Queen Mary's purge of the English church. Moreover, Julius began to study these stalwart "heretics," who seemed so convinced of their beliefs that not even the flames could budge their thinking. He inquired into their motives, and he studied the judicial records of their trials. In 1555, Palmer watched Latimer and Ridley burn and heard their strong and sure testimonies. And in his studies, Julius himself was changing.

Because of these changes and in good faith, Palmer resigned from Oxford and became a schoolmaster in the town of Reading. Soon he was exposed as a sympathizer, however, and he left when confronted by townsmen who had discovered his Protestant bent. Out of money and without employment, he went to his mother to request his share of the inheritance his father's estate had left him. His mother replied, "Thy father bequeathed naught for heretics."

Palmer returned to Reading to gather his belongings, technically a violation of his agreement to leave the town. He was promptly arrested and offered all the goods necessary for a comfortable life, if only he would recant the errors of his new convictions. Unable to accept the bribe and now willing to follow the path of those he had so closely studied, Julius Palmer stood condemned by the court. He was burned along with two others on July 15, 1556. The last words of these courageous martyrs came from Psalm 31: "Be of good courage, and He shall strengthen your heart, all you who hope in the LORD."

Julius's mind and then his heart led him to that place. Perhaps he himself was surprised by it; yet convinced by the truth he followed, he was obliged to accept its consequences.

One of Palmer's judicial examiners had offered this sage advice while Julius still had time: "Take pity on thy golden years, and pleasant flowers of lusty youth, before it is too late." But Palmer, ever the scholar, had turned the metaphor back: "Sir, I long for those springing flowers that shall never fade away." In death he danced among them.

Hans Smit (1558)

When the Spirit of God moves and people obey, the consequences belong to God alone.

Hans Smit, along with five other men and six women, all Anabaptists, were sent on a preaching mission through the Netherlands and into Germany. It was a short mission indeed, for only days passed before they were arrested and interrogated in Aix-la-Chapelle, Germany, on January 9, 1558.

Hans was the leader of the group. His own interrogation followed questions on the conventional topics that Catholic monarchs considered most essential to the peace of the realm: baptism, the sacraments, the nature of salvation and judgment, and the authority by which these strangers presumed to teach about God. In every case, Smit responded in a manner true to his beliefs, but utterly contrary to the monarch's way of thinking. Neither did the rack seem to sway Smit's mind on these questions, as convincing a teacher as the rack was in many cases. No, Hans had come on his mission with full knowledge that his message could lead to this; when it did, he wasn't about to doubt the truth of it.

Apparently the leaders investigating these intruders/missionaries were reluctant to take their blood upon themselves. Smit warned them that *they* might own the gallows here, but *Christ* owned His judgment throne before which they would surely stand. The leaders chose to stretch the limbs a bit more for these malcontents; then let them go.

If only Smit had left the city quietly. Instead, he opened a loud prayer and revival meeting. What could the authorities do? Hans was re-arrested, along with the others.

Patience running thin, and fear of a royal backlash if they appeared soft, authorities this time imposed a sentence that Smit seemed all too content with. On October 22, 1558, Hans Smit was hanged and burned. On the way to his execution, Smit remarked, "Oh what a beautiful feast day we shall have. So many people are coming."

Three days later, Hendrick Adams was also hanged and burned. Three other men of the group were given three months to consider the options. They were executed on January 4, 1559. Only one came to believe the rack's teaching and was spared. The women? A scourging with rods was sufficient to satisfy their crimes. They returned home singing.

Lest torture and intimidation win the day, one other death weighed heavily on the leaders of that city. The most aggressive leader, the one most eager to see the Anabaptists dead, had received a prophecy from Hendrick Adams as he was sentenced: "You yourself will not live to see this sentence carried out." Indeed, on the eve of Smit's execution, this councilman himself lay dying in mortal fear, plucking out his own beard and mumbling incoherently about fears of the afterlife. His own body was stone cold before Adams was ever burned.

Walter Mill (1558)

As he was about to be burned at the stake, Walter Mill confidently and courageously exclaimed:

> "I marvel at your rage, ye hypocrites, who do so cruelly pursue the servants of God! As for me, I am now eighty-two years old, and cannot live long by course of nature; but a hundred shall rise out of my ashes, who shall scatter you, ye hypocrites and persecutors of God's people; and such of you as now think yourselves the best, shall not die such an honest death as I do now. I trust in God, I shall be the last who shall suffer death in this fashion for the cause of this land!"

His words were prophetic because he was, in fact, the last martyr of the early reformation in Scotland.

Born in 1476, Walter became a priest in Angus County, Scotland. Impressed by the teachings of the reformers, he questioned the church hierarchy and theology and stopped saying Mass. So as a young man, he was condemned to death for his defiance of the church. Eventually, in 1538, Mill was arrested, but he escaped to Germany where he ministered for twenty years.

At the age of eighty-two, he returned to teach the Protestant faith and live out his remaining days in his homeland. But he was hunted down and imprisoned, even though as an old man he was not a threat. At his trial, Walter entered the courtroom at the cathedral of St. Andrews and fell to his knees in prayer. Feeble from his imprisonment, the judge, guards, and audience assumed that he would be unable to speak in his defense. Yet Mill spoke with force. And Walter Mill was condemned to be executed for heresy.

While being bound to the stake, Mill continued to speak to his captors and the assembled onlookers. Many admired his bold declaration of faith. Some complained aloud about the cruelty of his persecutors. Walter prayed quietly for a short time. Then, as the fire was being lit, he cried out, "Lord have mercy on me. Pray, pray, good people, while there is time." Then, cheerfully, he left this life to live with God.

John Knox wrote: "That blessed martyr of Christ, Walter Mill, a man of decrepit age, was put to death most cruelly the 28th April, 1558."

Petrus Ramus (1515–1572)

Peter Ramus had three strong, positive attributes that eventually put him in harm's way. First, he was intelligent. Born into a poor family in Picardy, France, not far from John Calvin's birthplace, Ramus lost his father when he was a young boy. To compensate, indeed to overcome this immense social deficit, he worked hard as a soldier, then as a servant, and eventually as a student, earning a Master of Arts degree in logic and rhetoric.

Second, Ramus was creative. His studies were not merely to fill his brain with the learning of others—whether teachers or book writers, holy men or dilettantes. Rather, Ramus was interested in finding the clue to hidden mysteries, unknown links, and in putting the ideas of others through the crucible of his own intellectual powers. Aristotle, for example, the ancient Greek revered by the church since Thomas Aquinas, received no free pass through Ramus's grid. This quality caused him no end of trouble.

Third, Ramus was loquacious. He loved debate. And he published books at a pace unequaled in France at the time: more than fifty, and some in multiple editions as his own thinking developed. No one in Europe needed to wonder what Ramus thought. He was happily telling as many souls as his tongue and pen could reach.

Two other events guaranteed Ramus a life of trouble and, finally, a shorter life than he anticipated. Ramus converted to Protestantism in the 1560s, entirely because his brilliant mind led him there. He became a Huguenot, a French believer in church reform. With that move, he lost the support of the Cardinal of Lorraine, whose help was vital to Ramus's teaching career. As a result, he was forced to leave Paris and the university, spending several years in Switzerland and Germany, feasting at the table of Reformed and Lutheran theology that was spreading in those countries.

All this would have led Ramus perhaps to a reputation equal to Calvin or Luther, had not his last attribute been so prominent. As Ramus found stillness contrary to his every impulse, so also he considered hiding, cowering, or running to be a fool's errand. When he returned to Paris in 1570, he had no permit to lecture and was therefore unable to attract the large audiences his writing and education had earned. His statement, "I had rather that philosophy be taught to children out of the gospel by a learned theologian of proved character than out of Aristotle by a philosopher," angered professors and other philosophers. It was also the wrong time to be a Huguenot in that city.

On August 24, 1572, a wave of killings began, as a political tool to cement the hold of Charles IX to his crown. On this St. Bartholomew's Day eve, a spirit of massacre and bloodletting was unleashed throughout France. As a result, thousands of Protestants were slaughtered. Charles had ordered Ramus to be spared, but no one could control the Paris mob. Ramus was captured in his study at the College de Presles, where he was killed and his body mutilated, decapitated, and thrown into the Seine River.

If only Ramus had been less intelligent, less willing to follow his convictions, less talkative, a more conforming chap, and a less-determined Christian—think of the long life he might have enjoyed, the bitter end he might have avoided. Given his place and time, Ramus was like a magnet for trouble, a magnet that won him a martyr's crown.

John Penry (1593)

If the Queen and the Archbishop had their way, Puritan preacher John Penry would simply and quietly disappear from the face of the Earth. Why else would he be dragged suddenly, at about the dinner hour, from his cell near Old Kent Road and told to prepare for death? Why else were the gallows so quickly erected and the sheriff ordered to deny the condemned man a customary courtesy: a farewell speech affirming his innocence and loyalty? Why else, apart from sheer hatred, would the father of four young daughters be condemned as a traitor on the basis of writings never published or released to the public?

Penry was born on a farm near Llangammarch, Cefn Brith, Wales, and converted early in his life to Protestant faith. In England, to be a proper Protestant was to be a member of the Church of England, which recognized the Queen as its head. An improper Protestant was part of the dissenting or free church movement, which was tantamount to disloyalty to her majesty, potentially an act of treason. That potential could be a powerful tool in the hands of political enemies, and Penry had one—the Archbishop of Canterbury, John Whitgrift. Penry had indirectly criticized the archbishop for failing to provide Wales with Christian nurture in his 1587 tract entitled *Equity of a Humble Supplication*.

So incensed was the archbishop that he directed the Northampton sheriff to search Penry's home for incriminating papers. Indeed, the same unlicensed press that produced Penry's work was also producing the now famous Marprelate tracts, a series of satirical jabs at Church of England priests and bureaucracy. Because the Marprelate tracts were unlicensed, Elizabeth I's Star Chamber court took a serious interest in finding and stopping those very popular satires. Perhaps the sheriff could nab two birds with the same stone.

Penry slipped into Scotland to evade the sheriff, but he returned to London in 1592 to take up preaching at the Puritan meeting hall whose two pastors, Frances Johnson and John Greenwood, had just been arrested (and would later be executed). In March of the next year, Penry was captured by authorities and placed under arrest for writing such vehement criticisms of Queen Elizabeth in his journal. The journal, unpublished and simply a personal notebook, was judged to contain "feloniously devised and written words with intent to excite rebellion and insurrection in England." The one who had begged for pastors for Wales was now in a position to plead for his life, and if not for his own sake, yet for his four young daughters.

But mercy was not to come. A week after his trial the verdict was rendered; and four days after that, Penry was suddenly ordered to prepare for his execution. To his daughters—named Deliverance, Comfort, Safety, and Sure Hope—he wrote: "I, your father, now ready to give my life ... do charge you ... to embrace this my counsel ... and to bring up your posterity (if the Lord vouchsafe you any) in this same true faith and way to the Kingdom of Heaven."

Penry was led to a quickly constructed gallows, the sheriff carrying his certificate of death by hanging, signed first, among several other names, by Archbishop Whitgrift, whose laxity toward the churches in Wales had first prompted Penry to take a public stand. Penry died a Protestant martyr killed by offended Protestants, part of the struggle for worship free of state control.

The Jesuits

Founded by Ignatius of Loyola in 1540, the Jesuits have been the most successful missionary movement in the Catholic Church. Their achievements in education and scholarship are profound. In the United States alone, nineteen universities are Jesuit-related.

Ignatius, a Basque nobleman, was converted in 1521 while recovering from battle wounds. The intensity of his devotion attracted followers, including Francis Xavier, who was to be the Jesuits' leading missionary until his death in 1552. Jesuits, who pledge fidelity to the Pope, were also instrumental as agents of the Catholic Inquisition.

The Jesuits began and continue today with two purposes: the sanctification of the individual believer and the evangelization of all people. Indeed, Catholic mission efforts on all continents owe much to the zeal of this order. These missionaries persisted despite setbacks and persecutions, even in North America, where eight French missionaries are remembered as the Jesuit martyrs—tortured and killed by Mohawk and Iroquois Indians in the seventeenth century.

The discipline and hierarchy of Jesuit life became a threat to European monarchs in the late seventeenth century, to the point where Pope Clement XIV suppressed the order. After the Napoleonic wars, Pope Pius VII restored the Order, which grew until the Second Vatican Council in 1962. That Council led to sweeping changes in the Catholic Church. Some Jesuits adopted social activism as their calling, a direction not shared by conservatives in the order. Jesuit leadership since Vatican II has sought middle ground between liberal and traditional life and discipline.

Edmund Campion hanged, drawn and quartered in England

Edmund Campion (1540-1581)

His best-known work, still read today in some circles, is called *Campion's Brag*. It is a booklet he published clandestinely, but so polished an argument for Catholic faith, so refined in its rhetorical power, that its formal title, "Challenge to the Privy Council," was replaced by detractors and admirers both with the author's name and a backhanded tribute.

For all his learning, mastery of argument, and Catholic conviction, Edmund Campion was the "most wanted" man in England in 1581. He was wanted by the Catholics to conduct masses. He was wanted by the enemy Protestants and the Protestant Queen Elizabeth I in England. And he was wanted and harassed in Ireland by the 1559 Act of Supremacy, which required all subjects to confess that the Queen was supreme governor of the church.

Campion had returned secretly to England in 1580. Years earlier, he had so impressed the Queen with his youthful talent that his peers believed he was destined for the highest offices of power and privilege. Indeed, Edmund had taken Anglican orders in the 1560s. But his trip to Dublin in 1569 and his work on the "History of Ireland" had shown him clearly that the faith he had celebrated as a precocious teenager during Mary Tudor's reign was his heart's passion. Thus, when Parliament passed into law the thirty-nine Articles of the Anglican Church in 1571, Campion left England for Douay, now part of France. He entered the Society of Jesus (Jesuits) and was ordained a priest in 1578. Two years later his superiors included him in a team bound for England, where Catholic families were worshiping in secret, and a small band of priests traveled from safe-house to safe-house, conducting Mass and offering the services of the church.

But Edmund was "wanted" by English authorities. They nearly apprehended him at Dover when he arrived, but by a narrow escape Campion had become lost in London. His "Challenge to the Privy Council" booklet had embarrassed the Privy Council. If that were not enough, his booklet, *Ten Reasons* (opposing Anglican worship), appeared on the seats at Oxford's commencement ceremony that June. Then, too, Campion's reappearance in England coincided with the arrival of papal military forces at Munster, Ireland—no small threat to the hegemony of Elizabeth over that isle. Edmund Campion was a very wanted man.

With a price on his head, Campion did not survive long. A bounty hunter posing as a devout Catholic caught up with him at Lyford Grange, west of London. Campion's host quickly put the priest and his two companions in a secret chamber supplied with food and water, but the small enclosure was not secret enough. Campion was discovered, captured, and taken to London Tower. There followed the usual torments and opportunities to end torment if only the prisoner would submit to the Act of Supremacy and end his rebellion, so to speak, against the Queen. Edmund replied, "If our religion do make traitors, we are worthy to be condemned; but otherwise we were and have been true subjects as ever the queen had."

On November 20 the court condemned Campion, and on December 1, he was executed by one of the cruelest means ever devised: hanging, drawing, and quartering. Campion left England and life with this challenge:

> "In condemning us, you condemn your own ancestors, you condemn all the ancient bishops and Kings, you condemn all that was once the glory of England."

"Oh what a **beautiful** feast day we shall have. **So many** people are coming."

— Hans Smit

Robert Southwell (1595)

In the days of Queen Elizabeth I of England, a law was passed that forbade any English-born subject who had taken priest's orders in the Catholic Church from remaining in England longer than forty days. In effect, being a part of the Roman priesthood had become a capital crime. For the likes of Robert Southwell, a devout Jesuit whose heart and mind were filled with images and emotions nurtured by Catholic faith, this law was incentive for missionary action, a journey back to England. On the eve of his installment as a priest, Southwell wrote to his superior: "I address you, my Father, from the threshold of death, imploring the aid of your prayers ... that I may either escape the death of the body for further use, or endure it with courage."

Robert had been raised a Catholic. At an early age he had left England to be educated at Douai. His young faith was strongly influenced by one of history's great Jesuits, Leonard Lessius. While a student, Robert also met John Cotton, who operated a safe-house for Catholics in London. Southwell became a priest in 1584.

Two years later he requested the dangerous English mission. Most English Catholics at the time lived in the countryside and waited for a priest to arrive for confession and last rites. Southwell traveled in disguise providing services and succor, and urging his own father and brother to return to Catholic faith.

In 1586 Robert became domestic chaplain to Ann Howard, whose husband, the Earl of Arundel, was in prison. For three more years (six altogether) Southwell did his secretive work, until the daughter of one of his regular contacts, herself imprisoned, betrayed him. One of Elizabeth's most notorious priest-hunters, Richard Topcliffe, captured Southwell during a Mass in a private home.

The priest in full vestments was taken immediately to Topcliffe's home, and there hanged by his wrists during an interrogation intended to reveal the names and locations of Robert's colleagues. From all reports, Robert endured the torture, admitting only that he was a Jesuit and prayed daily for the Queen, whose rule, apart from the ban on Catholic worship, he respectfully obeyed. Unable to break him, Topcliffe had Southwell's battered body transferred to the gatehouse at Westminster. A month later at his examination it was discovered that he had been so ill-treated that his wounds were infested with lice. Southwell's family, appealing to common decency, begged the Queen to treat him as the gentleman he was. Mercifully, Robert was transferred to the Tower of London, allowed a change of clothes, a Bible, and the writings of Saint Bernard. His incarceration lasted three years, during which he was put on the rack thirteen times.

Finally, in 1595, the Privy Council resolved to try Southwell on charges of treason. To break him further, if that were possible, the Council moved him to an underground dungeon called Limbo.

Three days later Robert was brought before the court. He declared himself "not guilty of any treason whatsoever" and admitted being a priest that served Catholics who wanted the comfort of the Church. When Southwell appealed to "our Savior," the court stopped to rebuke him. When Robert gave his age as the same as Jesus at his trial, the court gasped at his "insupportable pride." When Southwell referred to himself as "a worm of the Earth," the court ordered that the next day, February 20, 1596, he would be hanged (by the neck), drawn (before death, cut out entrails and genitalia and burn before victim's eyes), and quartered (beheaded and body divided into four parts).

From his cart on the way to the gallows Southwell preached from Romans chapter 14, and then, "In manus tuas, Domine" (into your hands, Lord). The court's intention was that Southwell would hang until death was near, and then be taken off the rope to have his extremities torn from their sockets; finally, his torso opened and organs removed until he died. In another moment of mercy, his agony was shortened when onlookers pulled on his legs while he hanged by the rope.

Southwell left a collection of prison poems and tracts still read today, though lost for centuries after his death. His *A Hundred Meditations on the Love of God* was first printed in 1873. The famous English playwright and poet Ben Jonson said that he would have willingly destroyed many of his own poems were he able to claim as his own Southwell's *Burning Babe*, which depicts a vision of the suffering Christ appearing to the poet on Christmas Day:

> Alas, quote he, but newly born in fiery heats I fry,
>
> Yet none approach to warm their hearts or feel my fire but I.
>
> My faultless breast the furnace is, the fuel wounding thorns,
>
> Love is the fire, and sighs the smoke, the ashes shame and scorn.

Yet indeed I also count
all things **loss** for the
excellence of the **knowledge**
of Christ **Jesus** my Lord,
for whom I have **suffered**
the **loss** of all things, and
count them as **rubbish**, that
I may gain **Christ**,
and be **found** in Him.

Philippians 3:8-9

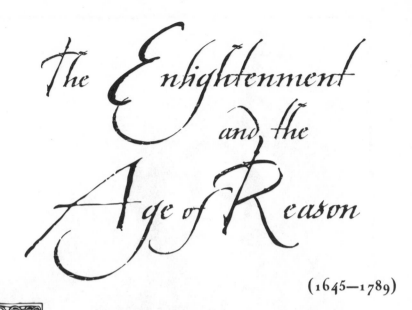

The Enlightenment and the Age of Reason

(1645–1789)

The French *philosophes* had seen enough. By the eighteenth century, Denis Diderot and other philosophers had had enough of religious faith and its institutions. Across Europe a new day was dawning. Credible evidence from the material world was replacing religious doctrine as the standard of rational belief. Intellectual leaders were tiring of the suppression of science by clerics and the dominance of a holy text over systematic observation.

The *philosophes* were but one in a series of challenges to the control of the church over commerce, politics, the arts, and the marketplace. In Germany, one philosopher (so regular that people set their timepieces at the start of his afternoon walks) revolutionized the way people in the West made moral decisions and how they understood the world of ideas. Immanuel Kant proposed a purely rational basis for value judgments and a largely humanistic basis for the origins of all ideas, including those about God and the afterlife.

At the same time, notions of "natural rights" (rights enjoyed by all people by virtue of their humanity) challenged notions of rights conferred by faith or penitence. Similarly, natural law challenged the authority of divine law. The disciplines of scientific discovery expanded knowledge of disease, mechanics, and the Earth as part of a vast uncharted universe. Yet despite this shift from faith to philosophy, followers of Christ were still dying for the privilege of knowing Him.

Mary Dyer hanged for heresy by Puritans in Massachusetts

Mary Dyer (ca. 1611–1660)

Convinced that the intolerant law of Massachusetts Colony banishing Quakers violated God's law, Mary Dyer would not stay quiet or stay away. Mary was a Quaker, and Quakers believed that God could communicate directly to us and that salvation could be assured. This was considered heresy by the Puritans in Massachusetts, so they banished her from the colony.

Mary challenged that law with a persistence that finally led authorities to a critical decision: Agree with Mary and change the social structure of the colony, or silence her. Mary Dyer died on the gallows on June 1, 1660, affirming her stand against the government that persecuted her Quaker faith. "Nay, man," she said at the last, "I am not now to repent."

Mary had other alternatives. For one, she was married to a respected colonial official, William Dyer, who more than once had rescued her from a Massachusetts jail through his political connections. He too was a Quaker but less militant than Mary, who never dodged a fight over religious freedom, especially when her "inner light"—God's voice to the soul—bade her confront the secular powers.

For another, Mary had the testy patience of Massachusetts Governor John Endicott on her side. When her fellow Quaker "lawbreakers," William Robinson and Marmaduke Stephenson, were hanged in 1658, Mary stood right behind them, awaiting the same fate. To her complete surprise, she received a last-minute reprieve and was ordered never to return. She left under guard, with her husband's promise that she would comply with the Massachusetts edict of banishment.

Finally, Mary had a mission to Native Americans on Shelter Island, teaching and converting them to the Quaker faith. Had she been content with her work and obedient to the law, she might have seen the last of her eight children reach adulthood. But she was neither content nor submissive.

In April, 1660, Mary returned to Boston, led by her conscience and fully aware of her danger. She didn't tell William, who nonetheless wrote a moving letter to Governor Endicott asking again for mercy toward his driven wife. This time, however, the stakes were too high.

At issue was more than Quaker nonconformity. To survive in the New World, settlers had learned to build strong communities. If food security, weather, the forest, disease, and hostile Indians were not enough, tough-souled London businessmen had given up on the colonies, leaving them to their own wits and devices. Religious nonconformity was a further strain on the social system, and defiance of law was finally a capital offense. Who could waste precious resources maintaining a prison system? Mary wanted religious freedom; Massachusetts wanted order and survival. Leaders such as Roger Williams in Rhode Island had found middle ground, granting wider freedom of expression in and around the city of Providence. Mary and her husband lived there for a while, but Mary was not a person to take refuge there.

Thus, on May 31, 1660, the General Court of Massachusetts summoned Mary Dyer and convicted her of willful violation of the banishment decree. Replied Mary, "I came in obedience to the will of God, desiring you to repeal your unrighteous laws, and that is my work now and earnest request."

The next morning she was escorted to the gallows, a troop of drummers in front and behind to keep Mary from preaching to the gathering crowd. She left behind engraved on the wall of her jail cell: "My Life not Availeth Me / In comparison to the Liberty of the Truth."

In 1959, on the 300th anniversary of her death sentence, the Massachusetts General Court decreed that a bronze statue of Mary Dyer be erected in her memory on the grounds of the State House in Boston, recognizing the truth and social value of Mary Dyer's "earnest request."

The Scottish Covenanters

The late sixteenth and early seventeenth centuries were times of immense religious and political upheaval for England and Scotland. Politically, the English kings were desperately trying to roll Scotland into a single unified British state. Religiously, battle lines were being drawn between competing models of worship and governance.

The Scottish Covenanters were named for a series of covenants made during the late sixteenth and early seventeenth centuries that preserved the Presbyterian doctrine as the only religion of Scotland. At first, the Covenanters merely promoted and developed Presbyterianism as a form of church government favored by the people, in contrast to Episcopacy, which was favored by the crown of England. Later they came to represent a rallying cry for complete independence for Scottish independence—a cause worth dying for.

The first of the covenants was made in 1557 in opposition to the Catholic faith, when Scotland was ruled by Mary of Guise, the Catholic Queen-Regent. After her imprisonment, a relatively peaceful time followed when James I became king. He was more religiously tolerant, and in 1581 the King's Covenant was signed, which allowed for the continued existence of Catholicism in England and Scotland, Calvinism in Scotland (to which the Scottish Covenanters subscribed), and the growth of Puritanism in England.

Problems for the Covenanters began in the early 1600s, when James I tried to unify Scotland and England with "high-church" Protestantism by appointing his own bishops over the church in Scotland. Later, James's son, Charles I, was less tolerant and sought to move the Church of England toward a high-church form and away from Calvinism. Rebels and men of action, the Scottish Covenanters established the National Covenant in 1638, denouncing the Pope and all rule by the king's bishops. Charles I saw this as a direct challenge to his royal authority, as did his son, Charles II. They both sought to crush the "rebellion." A period of time followed, from 1679–1688, called the "Killing Time." Most Covenanters that were captured during these years were executed by hanging, with hands and sometimes heads displayed on pikes for all to see. A few were even sentenced to be slaves in American plantations.

However, the Scottish Covenanters boldly clung to their faith. Rebel ministers preached at secret services or "conventicles" in the fields, despite the harsh persecution that followed. Anyone associated with the Covenanters was suspect to arrest and consequent execution. Because of the fierce oppression and heavily biased trials that took place, Covenanters eventually organized to take up arms and tried to fight back. Unfortunately, they were no match for British forces and their rebellion was crushed, first at the Battle of Drumclog in 1679, and then at the Battle of Bothwell Brig a year later.

James Guthrie (1612–1661)

Guthrie was born into a wealthy Scottish family in 1612, at a time and place fraught with risk for trusting souls. Power was shifting and realignments created quicksand that could surprise and swallow the cleverest person.

While attending St. Andrews University, Guthrie met the esteemed theologian, Samuel Rutherford, whose reformational convictions won James's heart, soul, and trust. He became a Presbyterian minister.

When the King of England, Charles I, tried to impose his bishops on the Scottish church, Guthrie opposed it, along with many of his countrymen. James signed the National Covenant, a document sure to be reckoned as political rebellion, despite its focus on the church as God's house, free from the state and ruled by Christ alone. Those who signed this National Covenant were known as "Covenanters." Given notions of kingship in the seventeenth century and King Charles's need to tap the wealth of his entire realm, only heretics or traitors would dare propose a church independent from the crown.

Pastor Guthrie guided his parish through the Puritan Revolution, which led to the beheading of King Charles I in 1649 and Oliver Cromwell's decade of power. But the monarchy was again restored in 1660, when Charles's son, Charles II, became king. Consolidation of power was the order of the day. Certainly churches were subject to the realm. Obviously the king's bishops would be the church leaders.

Guthrie had come to trust Charles II. During Cromwell's reign, the heir apparent, safe in Scotland, had taken an oath to uphold the National Covenant and promote Presbyterian polity. Now this same man, sitting at last on his father's throne, was demanding that the Scottish church become Anglican. This new king had given his promise, had he not? Even on Scottish soil he had made his solemn pledge. Guthrie joined a group of twelve Scottish pastors who made a formal petition to Charles II to uphold the National Covenant. But power finds its own purposes. The entire band of Scottish Covenanters was imprisoned.

Guthrie, forty-nine years old, was sentenced to be hanged. His head was fixed to a pole for public humiliation and his belongings confiscated. Guthrie's trust had been tragically misplaced. Facing the loss of life and family fortune, Guthrie gave these words to the crowd gathered on June 1, 1661, to watch him die.

> "I take God to record upon my soul, I would not exchange this scaffold with the palace and mitre of the greatest prelate in Britain. Blessed be God who has shown mercy to me such a wretch, and has revealed His Son in me ... Jesus Christ is my Life and my Light, my Righteousness, my Strength, and my Salvation and all my desire. Him! O Him, I do with all the strength of my soul commend to you. Bless Him, O my soul, from henceforth even forever. Lord, now lettest Thy servant depart in peace, for mine eyes have seen Thy salvation."

For almost three decades, James Guthrie's severed head was spiked above the Netherbrow Port in Edinburgh. But Guthrie, not Charles, had come to know the One whom he could trust, and so died in confidence and hope.

Hugh McKail (1666)

He was young and brave, a Scotsman who believed that no human, peasant or king, was head of Christ's church, but Christ alone. Hugh McKail said so in the last sermon he preached, on the Sunday before all Presbyterian Covenanters were deposed in favor of Charles II's episcopacy. His words that day were food to the people but poison to the state. Young Pastor Hugh fled to Europe and safety.

Virtually nothing is known of Hugh's birth and growing years. After studying at the University of Edinburgh, McKail was ordained at the age of twenty, only a year after Charles II had rejuvenated the monarchy following Oliver Cromwell's failed experiment in popular sovereignty.

Hugh was a Scotsman. He could not travel forever nor ignore his calling to the Scottish church. Four years in hiding was enough. He returned to Galloway to watch and wait. When his fellow Covenanters took up swords and clubs against the British, he couldn't be content sitting quietly at his hearth.

Whether McKail became a fighter is uncertain, but certainly he knew the Covenanter captains and likely traveled with them. In November 1666 he was captured and tortured for information, which apparently he withheld despite a metal wedge being hammered into his leg, shattering the bone.

A month later, on December 18, he was tried with other prisoners and sentenced to be hanged. During the next four days he prepared for death, composing an eloquent gallows farewell and asking his father, who was with him for a last dinner on the night before the hanging, "I desire it of you, as the best and last service you can do me, to go to your chamber and pray earnestly to the Lord to be with me on that scaffold; for how to carry there is my care, even that I may be strengthened to endure to the end." Then he asked his father to leave him, or else he would stir emotions that would deflect his purpose the next day.

At the gallows, McKail spoke at some length, begging the audience to listen to his "few words," as his years on Earth were few as well. At the end of his testimony and admonition to courage, he said:

> "And now I leave off to speak any more to creatures, and turn my speech to thee, O Lord! And now I begin my intercourse with God, which shall never be broken off. Farewell father and mother, friends and relations; farewell the world and all delights; farewell meat and drink; farewell sun, moon, and stars. Welcome God and Father; welcome sweet Lord Jesus, the Mediator of the new covenant; welcome blessed Spirit of grace, and God of all consolation; welcome glory; welcome eternal life; welcome death."

Then Hugh climbed the ladder to the waiting rope and prayed for some time before the executioner released him to gravity and heaven.

It was said that Charles II had sent a letter of reprieve, which Archbishop Burnet of Glasgow had hidden so that McKail and other Covenanters would die. It was a dangerous decade to be a free-church Christian in Scotland.

Richard Cameron (1680)

Zeal was his hallmark, passion his shield, and a prophetic sense his special gift. The eldest of three sons to a small shopkeeper in Scotland, Richard Cameron was converted by Covenanter preachers as a young adult. Leaders of this movement quickly realized what a gifted preacher he was. They urged him to quit teaching school and licensed him to preach. They soon came to regret this decision, however, for Cameron was more radical than any Covenanter before him. He felt they were timid, shortsighted, and fearful of the implications of their doctrine, and he said so. This resulted in being censured in 1677 by the Presbyterian clergy in Edinburgh. This experience put Cameron into a depression, for his gifts were great and his passion for an independent church knew no bounds. He went to Holland to cool down.

In the Netherlands, Cameron caught the attention of free-church ministers, who laid hands on him, ordaining him to the gospel ministry.

His spirits recovered, Cameron returned to Scotland in early 1680 and immediately began to preach sermons that moved the crowds gathered in fields to hear.

"Will you take Him? Tell us what you say! These hills and mountains around us witness that we have offered Him to you this day. Angels are wondering at the offer. They stand beholding with admiration that our Lord is giving you such an offer this day. They will go up to the throne to report everyone's choice," he proclaimed.

Cameron was also busy with plans of sedition against Charles II, king of England—at least that's how Charles saw it. King Charles's indulgences and additional restraints to worship practices had many Christians more willing to suffer than to resist. Richard Cameron refused to give in to King Charles. When Cameron and his followers met in Sanquhar Town on June 12 to read and declare that Charles was a tyrant, without any right or title to authority in Scotland, Charles needed no further evidence. He issued a writ to arrest them with suitable bounty attached, and Cameron fled to the hills to hide.

On June 20, 1680, Richard Cameron was camping with his brother Michael and twenty others at Meadowhead Farm, owned by William Mitchell. That morning he carefully washed at a stone trough and then said to Mrs. Mitchell, "This is our last washing. I have need to make [my hands] clean, for there are many to see them." At four that afternoon, a troop led by Bruce of Earlshall appeared at the farm. Cameron quickly gathered his band at the ready, loudly pleading with God "to spare the green and take the ripe." Outnumbered, the Covenanters were no match. Cameron and his brother were killed. A half dozen escaped. The rest, taken captive, were hanged in Edinburgh.

Richard Cameron's head and hands were carried to Edinburgh and there placed high on Netherbow Gate, an example to others of the terrible cost of defying the king. Before putting them on display, the sheriff pulled Cameron's head from the bag in front of another prisoner, the old Alan Cameron, Richard's father, mockingly asking if he recognized the parts. "I know, I know. They are my son's, my own dear son's. It is the Lord.

Good is the will of the Lord, who has made goodness and mercy to follow us all our days."

Cameron's hands were tied fingers upward at the sides of his head, as if he were praying. The display intended to show his weakness, even the futility of his protests. But Richard Cameron is known to history as the "Lion of the Covenant," and King Charles, apart from his title, was only one in a line of Stuarts easily forgotten.

Donald Cargill (1681)

Who should govern the church? Bishops appointed by a monarch? Or elders and deacons called by God and endorsed by the church itself? Who is head of the church, Christ or king? This question, along with the role of Scripture and the path of salvation, were critical issues during the Reformation, fought over with argument and sword.

Donald Cargill was a fighting Scotsman, a preacher, and a warrior. Educated at the distinguished universities of Aberdeen and St. Andrews, he was appointed minister to the parish of Barony in Glasgow in 1655. A Covenanter, Cargill was starting his ministry in the calm eye of a hurricane. Ill winds would soon carry him into exile and eventually to his death.

Scottish Covenanters were Presbyterians devoted to church leadership by elders. Thus they were utterly opposed to a church led by bishops, who were titled with a religious mandate but empowered by the English crown. King Charles I of England had sought to impose the Anglican Church in Scotland since 1625. But Charles had met his own doom at the hands of Cromwell's army in 1649. When Cargill started preaching, England was without a king. Yet the Glorious Revolution was unwinding, and Charles II would ascend the throne in 1660. Cargill thus had five years of peace.

Charles II clearly had territory to recover and an island empire to regain. He must suppress the Scots, and that meant placing his bishops in charge of the Scottish church. Enough of the independents, the elder-ruled churches, and their pastors who, to his thinking, mixed salvation with too clear a hint of political liberation. Charles II declared Covenanters to be traitors, their churches illegal, and the church's new leader—himself— the sovereign of state and of church.

Cargill responded by "excommunicating" Charles II and his bishops, saying, "The church ought to declare that those who are none of Christ's are none of hers." For such carefree boldness, Cargill's capture now carried a bounty, and the preacher was urged to find refuge in the Scottish lowlands where the king's agents had fewer allies.

Even during this internal exile, however, Cargill preached and taught, kept moving, and avoided sheriff and hunter. Finally in 1662 Cargill fled to the remote north of England, away from danger.

But could he stay away? He had inspired people with such words as, "If believers loved Christ as He loves them, they would be more in haste to meet Him." Was that a sermon to preach in exile, fleeing the king's agents?

Cargill's conscience said no, and his exile was short. Returning to Scotland again as an outlaw, he resumed his itinerant ministry, careful to keep his whereabouts within the counsel of close friends. Twice he escaped capture; once he suffered wounds during the getaway. Finally in 1679, he joined in a showdown of force at the Battle of Bothwell Bridge where Covenanters were viciously defeated. Cargill again fled, this time to the Netherlands.

Within months he was back, committed to a more open confrontation with the king. Cargill and fellow Covenanter Richard Cameron issued the Sanguhar Declaration, calling for war against Charles II and resistance to his brother, James II, who stood in line of succession.

On July 10, 1681, Cargill preached an inspired sermon in County Lanarkshire in southern Scotland, the site of battles lost against English forces. Before sunrise the next morning, he was seized and taken to Glasgow. He and several other Covenanters received a trial and sentence of death.

When Cargill mounted the scaffold on July 27, he said, "The Lord knows I go up this ladder with less fear and anxiety than I ever entered the pulpit to preach. Farewell all relations and friends in Christ; farewell all earthly enjoyments, wanderings, and sufferings ... Welcome joy unspeakable and full of glory." A moment later the executioner's axe severed his head. Cargill was again absent from his beloved Scotland, this time home with his beloved Savior.

Isabel Alison and Marion Harvie (1681)

Two young Scottish women were caught in the British wars of religion and executed for little more than being present at a Covenanter's open-air revival meetings. Both women were uneducated. Marion Harvie was a servant to the wealthy, and so little is known of Isabel Alison that she is described simply as "living in Perth." Their deaths signaled no victory for the British crown, no gain in the battle to suppress the Scottish spirit. Caught in events to which they were quiet observers, nonetheless they went to the gallows singing.

The first of the Scottish covenant bands appeared in 1557, and for a century these religious dissenters preached a clear gospel, while simultaneously mounting a military campaign for independence from England. A "killing time" followed the 1679 assassination of the king's archbishop, James Sharp. Charles II had restored the monarchy in England in 1662, and was not about to allow another rebellion like the one that severed the head of Charles I. The Covenanters must be stopped—annihilated. So in late 1680 the crown's agents conducted raids against commoners who had any association with the likes of Donald Cargill or Richard Cameron.

Isabel was taken from her home in Perth and Marion from Borrowstounness. Each was interrogated concerning the Sanguhar Declaration, a Covenanter creed, and other differences of doctrine and practice. Of these matters the women knew little beyond the preaching they had heard. But they did strongly affirm that their sins had been forgiven through faith in Jesus Christ. Credited by the court with good sense and uncommon intellects, they were nonetheless condemned as traitors and rebels, and then further condemned to hell by the king's churchmen.

On January 26, 1681, Isabel and Marion were led with five other female criminals to the Grassmarket, Edinburgh's outdoor gallows. Isabel testified: "So I lay down my life for owning and adhering to Jesus Christ, He being a free king in His own house, for which I bless the Lord that ever He called me." Marion wrote before her hanging: "I die not as a fool or evildoer, or as a busybody in other men's matters; no, it is for adhering to Jesus Christ, and owning Him to be head of His church."

Together on the platform they sang Psalm 84. As the winter wind carried their voices to heaven, the hangman pushed them over the edge. The king had won a short moment of silence at Grassmarket Square, but many more voices were singing in the angelic choirs above them.

"Blessed are those who spread joy that arises out of their own suffering. He who denies himself for others clothes himself with Christ."

— Prince Vladimir of the royal House of Ghica, who was imprisoned in a harsh dungeon

John Dick (1684)

The Scottish Covenanters were ever-present pests to Charles II, king of England. His cavalry and the Covenanters' militia played cat-and-mouse in the highlands for years. But in 1679, the battle of Bothwell Bridge was a full-fledged military encounter, and the Covenanters lost badly. A year later, Richard Cameron and others signed the Sanguhar Declaration—a declaration of independence from England based on two claims: The head of the church was Christ alone; and Charles, usurping that position, was no longer the head of Scotland. Charles saw treason in the statement and sent his army to find Covenanter leaders.

John Dick was among the Bothwell battle veterans who were rounded up and put in two cells of the Canongate Tollbooth in September 1683. None of the prisoners expected to see the sun again, except on their march to the gallows. But in one of the cells, the men managed to obtain a file and saw, enough to cut through a bar to the outside. Slowly they worked the metal, concealing their work, then fitting the displaced bar in place until the appointed day. When it came, all twenty-five men escaped.

John Dick thus enjoyed six months of freedom until a peasant woman, eager for the crown's reward, betrayed him. Dick was the only escapee to be recaptured. Within a day or two, John was taken to the scaffold, where he spoke to the crowd:

> "I am come here this day, and would not change my lot with the greatest in the world. I lay down my life willingly and cheerfully for Christ and His cause, and I heartily forgive all mine enemies. I forgive all them who gave me my sentence, and them who were the chief cause of my taking; and I forgive him who is behind me [the executioner]. I advise you who are the Lord's people, to be sincere in the way of godliness, and you who know little or nothing of the power thereof, to come to Him and trust God. He will not disappoint you. I say trust in the Lord, and He will support or strengthen you in whatever trouble or affliction you may meet with. Now blessed be the Lord, here is the sacrifice and freewill offering. Adieu, farewell all friends."

John Paton (1684)

Captain John Paton, a legendary Scottish soldier and Covenanter, is best known for his stirring testimony delivered from the scaffold on May 9, 1684. He fought bravely for Gustavus Adolphus in Germany, and also for his Covenanter brethren against the English crown in pitched battles going back to 1644. His last testament to faith has become Captain Paton's gift to the ages:

Dear Friends and Spectators,

You are come here to look upon me a dying man ... I am a poor sinner, and could never merit but wrath, and have no righteousness of my own; all is Christ's and His alone; and I have laid claim to His righteousness and His sufferings by faith in Jesus Christ; through imputation they are mine; for I have accepted of His offer on His own terms, and sworn away myself to Him, to be at His disposal, both privately and publicly. Now I have put it upon Him to ratify in heaven all that I have purposed to do on Earth, and to do away with all my imperfections and failings, and to stay my heart on Him ... I now leave my testimony, as a dying man, against the horrid usurpation of our Lord's prerogative and crown-right ... for He is given by the Father to be the head of His church ... Oh! Be oft at the throne, and give God no rest. Make sure your soul's interest. Seek His pardon freely, and then He will come with peace. Seek all the graces of His Spirit, the grace of love, the grace of holy fear and humility ...

Now I desire to salute you, dear friends in the Lord Jesus Christ, both prisoner, banished, widow and fatherless, or wandering and cast out for Christ's sake and the Gospel's; even the blessings of Christ's sufferings be with you all, strengthen, establish, support, and settle you ... Now as to my poor sympathizing wife and six small children upon the Almighty Father, Son, and Holy Ghost, who hath promised to be a father to the fatherless, and a husband to the widow, the widow and orphans' stay. Be Thou all in all to them, O Lord ... And now farewell, wife and children. Farewell all friends and relations. Farewell all worldly enjoyments. Farewell sweet Scriptures, preaching, praying, reading, singing, and all duties. And welcome, Father, Son, and Holy Spirit. I desire to commit my soul to Thee in well doing. Lord, receive my spirit.

Margaret Wilson and Margaret MacLachlan (1685)

Eighteen-year-old Margaret Wilson could see the older woman, Margaret MacLachlan, roped to a stake, waiting for the tide to cover her. This slow, methodical death by drowning was ordered by the court at Wigtown for their refusal to swear allegiance to Charles Stuart, King of England, and to his church. Wilson, too, had refused the oath, yet her stake was deliberately closer to shore so that she, witnessing the death throes of the other woman, might think better of her Covenanter convictions and save her own life.

The elder Margaret MacLachlan farmed the pitiful soil granted to peasants near the small village of Wigtown, Scotland. Not educated, yet intelligent and full of wisdom, widow MacLachlan had been convinced by Presbyterian preacher James Renwick that the Church of England had surrendered its integrity to the corrupted English king. It was a lost church, loyal to the Stuarts above all, not to be confused with Christ's church of the gospel and true sacrament. Against both tradition and law, MacLachlan declined to worship in her parish church but met with Covenanters in her own home. For this she was a marked woman.

The teenager Margaret was the oldest of three children of a prosperous farmer near Wigtown names Gilbert Wilson, who had complied with the law and worshipped where and how the king demanded. His two daughters and son, however, were religious rebels. When the children were too frequently absent from Sunday worship, officials used intimidation and threats so intense that the children fled to nearby mountains for safety. The boy, Thomas, was not heard from again, at least in history's records.

But the two sisters, cold and hungry, sought refuge in the home of fellow Covenanter Margaret MacLachlan. All three were betrayed by neighbors, arrested and imprisoned.

Their trial was a farce of justice. The court, perhaps all too aware that it had become a laughingstock, demanded that the three criminals sign the Oath of Abjuration, certifying that they were not aligned with the Cameronians (led by Richard Cameron), who had challenged Charles II both politically and as head of the church. In effect, the Oath was a pledge of loyalty to the king. All three refused.

Frantic, Gilbert Wilson raised enough money to buy his younger daughter's freedom, but not Margaret's, who was sentenced on April 13, 1685, to be "tied to stakes fixed within the flood-mark in the water of Blednoch ... there to be drowned." As for Margaret MacLachlan, the crown was simply glad to be rid of her. "Don't speak of that damned old bitch," one accuser said. "Let her go to hell."

At low tide on May 11, the two condemned Margarets were each fixed to their stakes. MacLachlan, weak from prison, was put farthest from shore. She died first, after a short struggle for life. Guards allowed the surf to nearly quench Wilson's life before they pulled her from the sea. They demanded again she pledge fealty to the crown. Margaret replied, "May God save the king, if He will."

Tied once more to her stake, guards pushing her under the tide, Margaret Wilson died singing:

"Do not remember the sins of my youth,

nor my transgressions;

According to Your mercy remember me,

For Your goodness' sake, O LORD."

Psalm 25:7

John Nesbit (1685)

John Nesbit was a fighter, a soldier in the Thirty Years War on the Continent, a warrior among the Scottish Covenanters. But he suffered scars and wounds of the heart nearly more severe than those of the body. By the time he was captured and tried, he was already taking leave of the struggles he had seen on Earth and was eager for Heaven.

When Nesbit returned from war in Europe, King Charles II had begun to impose his will on Scotland and the Scottish church, a will opposed by the determined free-church Covenanters. They resisted any king as church-head and the king's priests as intermediaries. The Covenanters believed with equal ferocity in Christ alone as head of the church and armed resistance as the right of all who seek to worship that way. The Covenanters would not bow to Charles without a fight.

But Nesbit had other business, too. He married Margaret Law and they raised a family. He kept a handwritten New Testament passed on to him from a great-grandfather who was one of the barefoot preachers sent to England in the fourteenth century by John Wycliffe. He studied, learned, worked, prayed, and often hid from Charles's dragoons.

But John could not hide forever. Severely injured on the field at Rullian Green, he was left for dead, but he escaped and recovered. He fought again at the Battles of Drumclog and Bothwell Bridge, both Covenanter disasters, which Nesbit survived after a brave fight. By then he was marked and a bounty was put on his head.

To draw him out from hiding, the king's troops forced Margaret and the children out of their home. Unable to secure shelter that winter, she died of exposure. A daughter and son followed her. Nesbit apparently found them as his daughter was being prepared for burial. His surviving son later wrote this account of it:

> "Friends were putting his little daughter in her rude coffin. Stooping down, he kissed her tenderly, saying, 'Religion does not make us void of natural affection, but we should be sure it runs in the channel of sanctified submission to the will of God, of whom

we have our being.' Turning to a corner where two of his sons lay in a burning fever, he spoke to them but they did not know him. He groaned, saying, 'Naked came I into this world and naked I must go out of it. The Lord is making my passage easy.'"

He buried his family and quickly went into hiding again. For two years he evaded his captors, despite the growing price on his head. Then one day, in the company of three others, a squad of dragoons led by a Captain Robert, John's cousin, surrounded them. A brief fight followed. Nesbit's three colleagues were injured, then executed. John, however, was worth more alive than dead. He was taken to Edinburgh, where he told his prosecutors that he was more afraid to lie than to die; that he was more willing to give his life than even they were to take it.

Quickly convicted, John was sentenced to be hanged. A few days before his death, he called aloud in prayer, "O for Friday: O for Friday! O Lord, give me patience to wait Thy appointed time." In prison he wrote his Last and Dying Testimony:

> "Be not afraid at His sweet, lovely and desirable cross, for although I have not been able because of my wounds to lift up or lay down my head, yet I was never in better case all my life. He has so wonderfully shined on me with the sense of His redeeming, strengthening, assisting, supporting, through-bearing, pardoning, and reconciling love, grace, and mercy, that my soul doth long to be freed of bodily infirmities and earthly organs, that so I may flee to His Royal Palace."

On the gallows he recited from the eighth chapter of Romans, then dropped and was gone. A warrior's heart was home at last.

John Brown (1685)

John Brown was a Scottish farm lad full of passion for Christ. He came from the homeland of the Lollards, the Shire of Ayr. Reared in reformational and free-church faith, Brown was a close friend of Richard Cameron, called the *Lion of the Covenant*, and Alexander Peden, the *Prophet of the Covenant*. At John's wedding in 1685, Peden told the new Mrs. Brown: "Ye have a good man to be your husband, but ye will not enjoy him long. Prize his company, and keep linen by you to be his winding sheet, for ye will need it when ye are not looking for it, and it will be a bloody one."

A speech impediment kept Brown from becoming a preacher, but in his humble cottage he ran a Bible school where he taught youth in what may have been the first regular Sunday school.

The year 1685 has been called the worst killing time in a terrible era. Scottish Covenanters were relentlessly pressed, harassed, and murdered, as recorded by historian Lord McCauley and author Daniel Defoe. When troops arrived at John Brown's door that year, they were seeking Alexander Peden, whom they believed was nearby. They ransacked Brown's cottage and found a few papers. They wanted to know about these writings and to know Peden's whereabouts. Instead, Brown gave them prayers and lessons, cut short by the commander's order to assemble a firing squad.

Brown turned to his wife, "Now, Isabel, the day is come."

She replied, "John, I can willingly part with you."

"That is all I desire," he said. "I have no more to do but die." He kissed her and his child, saying he wished gospel-promise blessings to be multiplied upon them.

The six soldiers ordered to shoot Brown were apparently so moved by the scene and its disregard for law, that they lowered their muskets and refused to fire. Their officer placed his own pistol at Brown's head and ended his life, just outside his cottage.

Isabel Brown set her child on the ground, took her linen, and wrapped her husband's body. She mourned alone until neighbors, told of the murder, gathered to support her and to remember anew their own losses of that terrible year. Scotland was fighting for its identity and for freedom to worship in the form and fashion they deemed right. Brown's murder was simple cruelty, yet the reason for it eventually won the day.

James Renwick (1662–1688)

Kill a martyr; make a follower. If only England had known what the deaths of Scottish Covenanter leaders would do for the movement, and how those courageous men and women would light a fire of faith among the next generation. So it was for nineteen-year-old James Renwick, a graduate of the University of Edinburgh despite his family's humble means. James had watched Donald Cargill die, had heard Cargill's stirring last words, and had seen his head and hands strung up on Netherbow Gate. That day Renwick determined to carry the mantle, to be a Covenanter preacher.

James turned out to be a very good one. He was clear, sincere, and passionate. In the meetings he held along hillside heather and valley stream, hundreds would hear him preach about a gospel centered on Christ, a church free of state control, and a destiny of joy that God had prepared for each person who trusted the Savior. Cargill would have been proud to hear him and see him evade capture time and time again.

One time, Renwick traveled to Newton Stewart for a series of outdoor meetings, called *conventicles*. During his stay at the town's inn, an officer of the king's army, also passing the night at the inn, engaged him in conversation. The two talked into the night, each equally delighted by the lively interchange. At length they retired. When the officer inquired the next morning about his new friend, he was told the man named James Renwick had left early to escape capture. The stunned officer simply returned to his barracks, convinced that such a winsome, harmless young man as Renwick was not worth arresting.

On another occasion, James sought a hiding place in a shepherd's cottage from which he had heard loud singing. He surmised it to be a Covenanter's cottage because of the exuberance of the music. But no, this shepherd was merely drunk and free-spirited. Still Renwick spent the night. In the morning while his own clothes were drying, Renwick used one of the man's old plaids for a morning walk, roaming the valley to pray and enjoy the early hour. Suddenly, a troop of soldiers appeared. They stopped the plaid-draped Scotsman to ask the whereabouts of the preacher they were hunting. Satisfied with the old man's empty-headed innocence, the soldiers rode on. Another narrow escape for Renwick.

Finally, in 1684, a frustrated Privy Council issued an edict naming James Renwick and all who gave him aid as enemies of the state. To withhold information or to hide him was tantamount to collusion in his crimes. Even then, three years would pass before the king's men would catch him.

In December 1687, Renwick was seized in Edinburgh when an officer heard praying inside a house and recognized the voice. The charges against James were three: refusing to accept the king's authority, refusing to pay the tax, and counseling his listeners to attend outdoor meetings with arms. Renwick pleaded guilty to all three and declined offers of pardon. On February 17, 1688, he was hanged in the Grassmarket, Edinburgh, and his head and hands hung on Netherbow Gate.

Who might have been watching that day in the Grassmarket? What young Christian might have been inspired when they heard him say, "I go to your God and my God. Death to me is a bed to the weary. Now, be not anxious. The Lord will maintain His cause and own His people. He will show His glory yet in Scotland. Farewell."

The French Huguenots

Who would rule sixteenth-century France, and how would the nation worship? These questions were eventually settled after a century of warfare and persecution. At the beginning of the century, however, was the immense influence of French exile John Calvin, who trained a cadre of missionaries and sent them back into France. These French Protestants were known as Huguenots. They built up the Protestant movement and also served as a magnet for political forces dueling for control of the crown.

The House of Bourbon favored the reformers. The Chantillon family, notably Gaspard de Coligny, joined forces with them and split French culture along religious affiliation. Civil war resulted. The Huguenots, while still a religious reform movement, became more and more dominated by secular princes bent on power. Violence was part of the movement from 1560 until Henry IV came to the throne in 1589. He was a Huguenot sympathizer, but converted to Catholicism in 1593. In 1598 he issued the Edict of Nantes, which made Catholicism the official religion of France, but permitted Huguenots freedom of worship and rights to keep a militia for self-defense, especially at their fortified city, La Rochelle.

In 1685, however, Louis XIV revoked the Edict of Nantes. Protestantism was now illegal in France. Four hundred thousand Huguenots sought refuge from persecution in Prussia, Holland, Britain, Switzerland, and North America.

Later, the French Revolution eventually destroyed the Catholic Church as a political power in France. Full religious liberty was finally guaranteed by the Napoleonic code of 1802.

For I am **persuaded** that neither **death** nor **life,** nor **angels** nor **principalities** nor **powers,** nor **things present** nor **things to come,** nor **height** nor **depth,** nor **any other created thing,** shall be able to **separate** us from the **love** of God which is in Christ **Jesus** our Lord.

Romans 8:38-39

Theophane Venard imprisoned and beheaded in Tonkin (Vietnam)

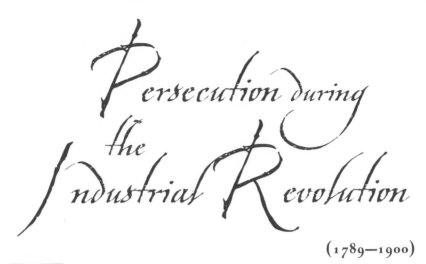

Persecution during the Industrial Revolution

(1789—1900)

s communication and transportation technologies began to shrink the world, Catholics and most of the Protestant movements engaged in the evangelization of North and South America, the vast malaria-plagued African continent, and the Hindu-Asian subcontinent. Clearly, missionaries from different movements overlapped, but the broad expanse of these territories seemed like limitless opportunity to missionary-sending agencies and churches.

There were plenty of obstacles though. Missionaries often followed in the path of colonizing armies, and frequently they bore the brunt of tribal and regional backlash. The church too often shrank from urban centers where destitute workers were put in virtual slavery to work the factories of industrial growth. And the era's towering intellectual giants—Karl Marx, Charles Darwin, and Sigmund Freud—each took aim at the full orbit of Christian belief. They believed the age of faith was finished and done as a kitchen floor is swept clean of dust and crumbs.

In the Christian West, the age of martyrdom was over. Democratic governance would not tolerate every religious idea and teaching, but state-sanctioned killings of religious non-conformists largely ended. Certainly some sects saw persecution. The Namugongo martyrs died at the order of the Buganda king in East Africa. Disease more than martyrdom was the great killer of Christian missionaries who took the gospel to the Southern hemisphere. We must also pause to acknowledge uncounted deaths for faithful discipleship in the movement that outlawed slavery.

The Industrial Revolution redirected Western religious aspirations from world evangelism to wealth, from sacrifice to a regime of efficiency, and from geographic churches to widespread acceptance of the notion that people must live and work together with different faiths in order to reap the benefits of progress and products promised by new machines.

"**Love** your enemies ... **pray** for those who spitefully **use** you and **persecute** you."
— Bishop Hannington's last words as he was killed by the Ugandan cannibals he tried to reach with the gospel of Jesus Christ

John Smith (1790–1824)

Demerara was one of three counties in the Caribbean colony of British Guiana (now Guyana). Slavery was the rule in Demerara, the way of life, the engine of its sugar cane economy. Whatever else happened there, slavery must never be questioned or threatened. Of those who might do so, missionaries were the most culpable.

The London Missionary Society (LMS) sent John Smith to British Guiana in March 1817. In Demerara he took over from the Reverend John Wray, who had been transferred to neighboring Berbice County. Such transfers helped keep relations transitory between the missionary preacher and the slave population. Bonds of sympathy were dangerous to the economy.

Smith's first interview with Governor Murray made it quite clear: Teaching the African slaves to read was forbidden. The job of the mission station was to teach contentment, not to educate, nor to "insinuate anything which might ... lead them to any measures injurious to their masters." In British Guiana, sugar cane was lord and king.

So the honorable Rev. John Smith set about his work in one of the most thankless, humid, and oppressive mission stations in the world—far from the British homeland where William Wilberforce and other Christian leaders were challenging the foundation of slavery and mapping out its legalized extinction.

Smith did his job perhaps too well. For one, he became a friend and counselor to his congregants, not merely their preacher. Second, he distributed books sent by the LMS for worship and nurture. One can hardly distribute books if the writing inside remains undecipherable. Teaching church leaders to read was a natural consequence of his teaching them the responsibilities of Christian discipleship.

Five years into his work, Smith was caught in a crisis that he and others must have seen coming. Certain slaves, having acquired reading skills and aware of Britain's anti-slavery movement, came to believe that plantation owners and the colonial government had already received orders for their emancipation but had suppressed them. With injustice piled upon wretchedness, a slave revolt was planned. Then an old slave named Quamina, a deacon at Smith's church, rose to advise that a work strike was the better alternative to bloody rebellion. Quamina wanted the advice of the preacher before he or others took up arms.

Smith advised patience. If new laws were coming, let them come. Even the governor himself would be obliged to enforce Acts of Parliament. After all, Britain was a civilized country. But counseling patience when freedom was in the air was unsuccessful. About 13,000 of the 74,000 slaves in Demerara rounded up plantation managers on August 20, 1823, and put them under house arrest. The governor mustered his militia, however, and quickly disarmed the disorganized rebels, with enough loss of life to teach the required lesson. Quamina was hunted down and killed. Smith was arrested at the urging of plantation managers. They figured that he must have known about it, had failed to warn the governor, and thus was, in their eyes, a co-conspirator as guilty as an African slave carrying a gun or club.

Smith was tried by a military tribunal, which included officers who had directed field operations against the slaves. They sentenced Smith to be hanged.

Outraged that a British missionary might be executed by the British military after a mock trial on British soil, the LMS and others tried to save him. But before calmer minds from the homeland could send his commutation to Governor Murray, Smith was dead, the victim of pneumonia, caught in the stink and stench of the Guyana jail awaiting word from London.

Smith's journal quietly acknowledges his guilt:

> Guilty of distributing Christian literature to slaves: "The Bibles and Testaments were sent from the Bible Society in allowing me a discretionary power in the disposal of them."

> Guilty of befriending slaves: "No missionary can properly discharge his sacred functions without having some intercourse

with his people besides that of public teaching."

Guilty of discouraging fieldwork on Sunday: "What crime have I committed? Are their masters greater than God?"

Guilty of sacrifice and service to the gospel: After his death, the African workers called him the Martyr of Demerara.

Parliament stopped the British slave trade in 1807. All African slaves in the Empire were granted freedom in 1833.

Henry Lyman (1809–1834)

The life-change for Henry Lyman was dramatic. A fellow alumnus of Amherst College described him as "one of the worst, boldest in wickedness, defying the authority of God." But after his conversion, "he became as ardent and bold for Christ as before he had been in opposition to all good."

After studying theology at Andover Seminary and medicine in Boston, Henry became one of the first missionaries sent to Indonesia by the American Board of Commissioners for Foreign Missions. Less than a year into his service, Lyman and his companion, Samuel Munson, met some Batak warriors near Tapahuli in northern Sumatra. Servants traveling with the missionaries reported that each was speared and then eaten by the Batak.

Lyman's intense, shortened, but dramatic life ended in violence, but work among the Batak continued. Today the Batak worship Christ and train others for missionary service in the region.

John Williams (1796–1839)

John Williams was an unlikely missionary. He apprenticed with an "ironmonger" as a teenager—a suitably rough and difficult trade for a lad whose life was skidding away from the faith he had been taught by pious parents near London. At age eighteen, however, John was converted so enthusiastically that he determined to go to the earth's remote corners, and the London Missionary Society agreed. But the LMS had misgivings. John was not schooled in theology, and his enthusiasm for searching out remote tribes exceeded prudent considerations.

To his credit, John was a good mechanic and problem solver, and he was gifted at languages and preaching. He excelled at team building, always leaving trained nationals behind to follow up his initiatives. Those efforts constitute a remarkable record of adventure and achievement. He brought Christian faith to the Hervey Islands after starting a mission on Raiatea. He preached on Rurutu and Rimatara. When he ran out of money, he sold his schooner, the *Endeavor*, and built his own, the *Messenger of Peace*, to get to Samoa and Tonga, then back to Raiatea and Raratonga, where he worked to revise the New Testament.

After eighteen years of missionary work, John and his wife Mary (plus two sons) returned to England in 1834. Their public meetings drew great interest. Another ship, the *Camden*, was purchased and fitted. Meanwhile, John wrote one of the most popular accounts of the region, plainly titled *Narrative of Missionary Enterprises in the South Sea Islands*. He was able to state that every known island along a 2,000-mile line had received the gospel.

John and Mary returned to Polynesia in 1837. Two years later, John was exploring the New Hebrides, where traders had recently exploited the natives. When John landed, trouble was imminent. John and his companion James Harris were attacked and killed at Erromango, their bodies eaten by the islanders.

News of his death inspired many new missionary voyages. Chalmers from Scotland, whose death so closely mirrored Williams's, and the Gordons from Canada, are but two examples of those who went to fill the space made empty by John's murder. Eventually the Martyr's Church was built on Erromango as a memorial to the many, including Polynesian pastors and teachers, who gave their lives for the gospel there.

George and Ellen Gordon (1861)
James Gordon (1872)

The South Sea Islands were there for the taking, if only the takers could survive disease, cannibals, and loneliness. The legendary explorer Captain Cook noted how barbaric the islanders had become and how unlikely the Christian gospel would ever be adopted there. His words only challenged the bravest souls to come. So to Erromanga Island they came.

The first to die, Williams and Harris, were likely the victims of revenge killings directed against white-skinned people who had been selling, cheating, and exploiting the Erromangans for years. That these two had come to build a church was a distinction lost on local chiefs. Yet their deaths inspired nearly forty national Christians from neighboring islands to come. Perhaps these brown-skinned Christians would escape the hatred felt toward whites. But most of these people either starved to death or were also killed.

Then a Canadian linguist and doctor, George Gordon and wife Ellen, sailed for Erromanga, arriving in 1857. On the way, they learned all they could of the island's four languages—simple phrases and greetings—but enough to get them on shore and ease their entry. For four years they taught the Bible and tended the sick. Then in the spring of 1861, a measles outbreak took the lives of two children under Gordon's care—two children of a chief. On May 20, George and Ellen were clubbed to death.

Back in Canada, George's younger brother James heard the news and knew he must take his brother's place. When he finished theological training in Halifax in 1864, James sailed to the strange, exotic, and treacherous mission station where his brother and sister-in-law had served and perished. To his surprise, he found a church there.

It was small, to be sure, but nonetheless a church had taken root on Erromanga in the three years since the Gordon murders. So James was welcomed by Christians. Single and eager, he traveled widely, translated the Bible into two island languages, and sent back to Canada detailed reports of the island cultures and history.

For eleven years James invested his mind and heart on Erromanga Island. Then on March 7, 1872, for reasons unknown, he was killed by a blow from a stone axe as he sat translating Stephen's words in Acts 7:60: "Lord, do not charge them with this sin."

Eight years later, a church building at Dillar's Bay was named the Martyr's Church, and by the century's turn, nineteen of every twenty islanders identified themselves as Christians. Captain Cook had miscalculated by far the power of God's message to take root and grow in the South Seas. And few could have calculated the cost of its planting.

But without **faith** it is impossible to **please** Him, for he who comes to God must **believe** that He is, and that He is a **rewarder** of those who diligently **seek** Him.

Hebrews 11:6

Andrew Kim Taegon (1820–1846)

Kim Taegon was the first Korean to be ordained a Catholic priest. He died at age twenty-six in a wave of persecution intended to cleanse Korea of foreign intrusions threatening its customs and traditions.

Born to Christian parents, Andrew Kim Taegon was baptized at age fifteen. Determined to work in the struggling Korean church, he traveled 1,300 miles to study in a seminary in Macao, China, and was ordained in Shanghai. He secretly re-entered Korea in 1845.

Only nine months later, he was arrested, kept in prison for three months, and then beheaded along the Han River near Seoul. His father also had been martyred years earlier.

While awaiting his execution, the priest sent this letter to his parish:

> "My dear brothers and sisters, know this: Our Lord Jesus Christ upon descending into the world took innumerable pains and built the Holy Church through His passion ... I pray you to walk in faith, so that when you have finally entered into heaven, we may greet one another. I leave you my kiss of love."

"I leave you my **kiss of love**."

— Andrew Kim Taegon

Allen Gardiner starved to death off Tierra del Fuego

Allen Gardiner (1794-1851)

His mother knew there was no stopping youthful Allen. He had always dreamed of adventure on the seas. But at fourteen he seemed so young. Surely his mother knew, despite her prayers, that his heart was turning away from God.

Allen left home, still an adolescent, but with a heart so primed for travel that he moved successfully through Britain's Naval College at Portsmouth, and began a long career that took him to China and South America.

During these journeys, Allen Gardiner searched and made three discoveries: first, the pursuit of the divine through Buddhism was futile; second, God did indeed love him; third, he would be transformed from captain in the Royal Navy to missionary to the world's most remote tribes. All his youthful energy still intact, Gardiner set out to take the Word of God to people and places where no missionary had ever succeeded.

In 1838 he crossed the Andes Mountains on muleback, searching for people who could understand his language and hear the gospel. The results? No converts at all. He went to preach among the Zulu in southern Africa (where he founded Durban). He traveled to Indonesia but was rebuffed as an enemy.

In 1850, Gardiner turned his attention to the Yagan peoples of Patagonia, a tribal group that Charles Darwin encountered and judged too savage to ever be civilized. Gardiner recruited a doctor, a fellow missionary, and four hardy Cornish sailors to join his party. They spent twenty months trying to make contact with the Yagan people. But the Yagans chased them from their shores, stole their provisions, and left the band with one boat wrecked, and digging in for the winter at Spanish Harbour on Picton Island, off Tierra del Fuego. Every man died of scurvy or hunger. The results? No meaningful contact with the Yagan, no converts, nothing accomplished.

Allen was the last to die, at least the last to write a journal entry. Considering his ordeal, one might expect a message less buoyant. But to the last, Allen was thinking of the next journey. In the journal, he urged that the Patagonia Missionary Society be renamed the South American Missionary Society (it was!) and that Christians from Britain return to bring the gospel to these people. (They did, and more died. Altogether, fourteen missionaries gave their lives before any Yagan came to the faith.)

Following the death of John Maidment, who had been searching for food for the two of them, with his strength at last waning, Gardiner wrote:

> "Lord, at your feet I humbly fall. And I give you all I have. All that your love requires. Take care of me in this hour of test. Do not let me have the thoughts of a complainer. Make me feel your power, which gives me life. And I will learn to praise you ... Wonderful grace and love to me, a sinner."

Gardiner died of starvation at age fifty-seven in August 1851, beside his boat named *Speedwell*. The British ship *Dido* discovered his camp in January 1852. Anglicans celebrate September 6 as Allen Gardiner Day, remembering these saints and heroes of the faith.

John Mazzucconi (1826–1855)

Missionaries traveling to the South Seas in the early nineteenth century said their goodbyes, knowing full well that returning home was unlikely. Distance over water, the islands' suspicious peoples, and tropical diseases constituted a triumvirate of risk. Father Mazzucconi's goodbyes came with this added burden: His father begged him to stay home, to find his calling near native Milan. The old man had already lost three children in their infancies; another six children had entered religious life. Why did John have to go so far away to serve God?

But John convinced his father, Giacomo, that the risk was no match to the reward. His mission would be to evangelize remote islands around present-day Papua New Guinea, places few Westerners were willing to explore. John asked how those islanders would find their way to heaven if not by the gospel brought through God's chosen servants.

John graduated from the Pontifical Institute of Foreign Missions, founded in 1850. He would be traveling with four other priests and two brothers. Seven years earlier a group of thirteen priests and brothers had ventured to Melanesia. Malaria and islanders had battered and beaten that first group. John was going as part of the second wave. God's will be done. His father finally consented.

In late summer 1852, the new missionaries arrived in Sydney, then on to Rook Island. On John's first night there, he contracted malaria. Soon all the missionaries on Rook were sick.

As malaria comes and goes, taking its toll of strength and sometimes of life, the first missionary fatality occurred in March 1855. Apparently John had recovered from his first bout, but then the worst of malaria put him down. His Father Superior ordered him back to Sydney. There John recuperated and purchased supplies for the mission.

Not long after, a spat of deaths in the families of local chiefs caused the islanders to conclude that their "spirits" were angry because of these white invaders. Their decision to exterminate the missionaries led to an evacuation at the same time John was leaving Sydney to return. His ship probably passed his fleeing colleagues at sea.

Thus on September 25, 1855, a group of natives, led by a man known to dislike missionaries, met the ship, the *Gazelle*, in Woodlark Bay and offered to help guide and unload. Under their few clothes were knives and hatchets. The black-robed Mazzucconi was their first target. One thrust of the hatchet split open his skull. The natives finished off the ship's crew quickly.

A setback to evangelization in the South Pacific? Certainly. A grief to a father in Milan? Indeed. But today two-thirds of the population of Papua New Guinea is Christian, a blessing that John Mazzucconi could not have imagined as he wrote in his journal before he left for his mission station:

> "I do not know what He is preparing for me in the journey I begin tomorrow. I know one thing only—If He is good and loves me immensely, everything else, calm or storm, danger or safety, life or death, are merely passing expressions of eternal love."

Theophane Venard (1829–1861)

The young French boy, on a hillside near his home, watched his father's goats grazing. He saw the wind sweep through distant trees and nearby grasses. He watched clouds take shape and move along. He wondered about life. And he read from the *Propagation of the Faith Review*, a missionary magazine, about the story of Father Cornay, a French priest who had died as a martyr the previous year in far-away Tonkin (Vietnam). On that hillside, nine-year-old Theophane said, "I want to go to Tonkin. I want to die a martyr too."

Such youthful quests are so rarely completed, but Theophane meant it, and set about his schooling to achieve it. He would also need to convince his family, especially his father, who would not want the oldest child, the son, to abandon France for a mission so distant. In all this, Theophane persisted, first at a minor seminary in Montmorillon, then a major seminary in Poitiers, then with his family. At his last dinner with them on February 27, 1851, he asked for his father's blessing. Through tears the old man said slowly, deliberately: "My dear son, receive this blessing from your father, who is sacrificing you to the Lord. Be blessed forever in the name of the Father, and of the Son, and of the Holy Spirit."

Theophane had strength of will and purpose, despite a weakened body. He suffered typhoid fever, seasickness, and later pneumonia and asthma. Yet people around him could not fail to see his deep inner joy that carried his spirit through the goodbyes to family and France and into the port of Hong Kong and then Tonkin.

Tonkin at last—from hillside reverie to reality. Yet the same dangers awaited missionaries in 1854 as Cornay had faced in 1837. Here and there were pockets of Christians and functioning parishes. Politically, however, the situation was dangerous, leaning toward desperate. By 1859, Emperor Tu-Duc determined that the "Jesus religion" and all people associated with it must go—and go permanently. Tu-Duc's edict called for death to Christians and their accomplices and rewards for informants and betrayers. Theophane took refuge in the home of a Christian widow, but the woman's cousin went to the authorities, who came for Theophane on November 30, 1860, and put him in a narrow, short wooden cage.

During the interrogations and trials that followed, Theophane gathered admirers even among the emperor's guards. God's mercies came in the form of paper to write letters home, a slightly larger cage, a mosquito net, an occasional visitor, and a secret confession to a priest.

Finally, on February 2, 1861, Tu-Duc signed the death warrant. Theophane was beheaded that day. At the place of death, the executioner asked him what it was worth to kill him quickly. Little did he know that for this priest, the next moment would be the fulfillment of a boyhood vision and reunion with his beloved mother and father, the fitting end of an earthly calling. Theophane had written his bishop: "My heart is like a calm lake." And so he sang the Magnificat as the half-drunk executioner swung his heavy sword.

John Kline (1797–1864)

When the American Civil War began to divide families and make soldiers out of farmers, Brother Kline saw his role as a reconciler and healer, as a peacemaker and pastor. He offered medical help and pastoral counsel to men of both armies, North and South, traveling freely through contested areas and past each sentry line. A pacifist who preached against violence, his mission was to spread the word of the Prince of Peace and to administer balm from pain and loss. After twenty-nine years of itinerant ministry on horseback and four years of work during America's most vicious conflict, bullets finally took his life.

John Kline was born in Dauphin County, Pennsylvania, in 1797. He grew in the faith taught by the German Baptist Brethren, a "plain people" much like the Amish and Mennonite with whom the Brethren shared a common heritage in the Reformation.

Kline's family moved to Virginia in 1811 when he was fourteen years old, setting the stage for the difficult decisions he would have to make as an adult: between the union or slavery; discerning the proper power of government as an instrument of God's power; and the most important question: what does faith require in time of war?

Selected by the Linville Creek congregation for diaconal work in 1827, Kline was appointed to a preaching ministry in 1830. The Brethren did not normally build churches; instead, they met in homes spread throughout their farmlands. Kline's horse thus became his daily companion. He rode, it is estimated, more than 100,000 miles preaching, teaching, and offering elemental medical skills to Brethren congregations throughout the region. Each day Kline would record in a small journal his travels and reports— the basis for an unusual historical record published years after his death.

Kline rose in Brethren leadership. He was moderator of the Annual Meeting during each of the Civil War years. His gentle strength no doubt kept the Brethren united, as other Christian communities divided between North and South. Kline also led the Brethren in reaffirming their central doctrine of Christian pacifism. In 1864 the Annual Meeting report included this statement, "We exhort the brethren to steadfastness in the faith, and believe that the times ... strongly demand of us strict adherence to all our principles, and especially to our non-resistant principle, a principle dear to every subject of the Prince of Peace ... and not to encourage in any way the practice of war."

Kline was not indifferent to the nation's struggle. He opposed slavery and taught obedience to the law "which does not conflict with the Gospel of Christ." During Grant's Wilderness Campaign, close to Kline's home, he secured permission from commanders on both sides to offer medical relief and spiritual aid. Riding home one night from his pastoral duties, he was ambushed near his house. His bullet-ridden body was discovered the next day. Most accounts accuse Southern sympathizers who were most offended by Kline's views against slavery. Only a few months later, Kline's Brethren neighbors would lose their farms and homes during Sheridan's torch-and-burn campaign through the Shenandoah Valley.

For John Kline, trust and obedience to God's call meant enduring the trials that tested faith. In a sermon from Psalm 45, Kline said, "Although iniquity bears rule in the present, God still hates wickedness. God does not acquiesce in the injustice and wrong that is being perpetrated in the world. From this we are being saved."

Robert Thomas (1839-1865)

An isolated Asian government, an aggressive American skipper, and a Welsh missionary armed with Bibles all came together at one spot in September 1865. The foreigners had come too far, their supplies were too thin, and they were overwhelmed. They all perished, including the missionary-interpreter Robert Thomas, the first Protestant to minister in Korea, and the first Protestant to die there.

Robert Thomas was born in Wales in 1839, the son of an independent church minister. He studied at London University; and with his wife Caroline, he was commissioned by the London Missionary Society for work in Asia. A five-month-long voyage put the young missionaries in Shanghai, where Robert quickly learned Mandarin. He was assigned as a schoolteacher in Beijing. But the Hermit Kingdom, as Korea was then called, was on his heart.

Robert found a way. In 1864 or early 1865, he slipped into Korea loaded with Chinese language Bibles provided by Scotland's National Bible Society, and as many Korean language as he could obtain from contacts in China. For four months he traveled and preached, though heavily disguised. Only a year earlier, the Korean king had turned against Christians, killing about 8,000 Roman Catholics in a purge of "foreign religions." Robert's successes brought joy, but his heart sank when Caroline suddenly became ill and died.

In the summer of 1865, an American entrepreneur, W. B. Preston, with the help of a British business firm, launched an expedition designed to open trade with Pyongyang. They supplied a former U. S. navy ship, renamed the *General Sherman*. Thomas offered his services as translator and packed cases of Bibles for his second expedition to this tightly controlled kingdom.

The journey was a missionary's nightmare. The ship captain, under pressure from Preston, ignored Korean orders to turn back. Instead, at high tide, the *General Sherman* steamed upriver. It appeared to be a direct threat to the already testy Dae Won Kun, who apparently believed the ship was an effort by Catholics to reestablish their mission. He ordered his army to kill the ship's crew.

Now stuck on a sandbar, the crew of the *General Sherman* had cannon and rifle in their favor, but time favored the Koreans massed on the banks of the river. Captain Page even took one of the Korean negotiators as hostage, but to no avail. After two weeks of gunfire, Korean troops sent burning barges against the American ship. Its crew fought the blaze, but unable to contain it, they jumped overboard into the waters and the waiting swords of the Koreans. Some reports claim that Thomas made it to shore with Bibles, which he offered to the soldier who killed him.

The *General Sherman* sank into the river, its iron ribbing and anchor all that remained. Thomas's executioner did indeed take that Bible offered to him, and used it to wallpaper his house. Amazingly, guests read the writing of that strange book so casually displayed. The soldier's nephew was converted and became a pastor.

Today forty percent of South Korea is Christian. However, little is known about the church in Pyongyang. North Korea is as isolated and closed to public worship as in the day of Robert Thomas. But that too will change. Then, stories of the martyrs of Pyongyang will be told for the first time, and Thomas's sacrifice—his kneeling on the shore to offer a Bible—will be among the stories of faith gratefully recalled and remembered.

Just de Bretenieres (1838–1866)

Even as a youngster, Just dreamed of faraway places and missionary service. He was born in the Burgundy region of France to devoted Catholic parents. One day at the age of six, Just was playing with his younger brother, digging holes in the ground. Suddenly Just shouted, "Quiet, I hear the Chinese, I see them. They are calling me. I have to go to save them." Just never forgot this incident, and as his devotion to faith grew, so did his sense that his life must be given to carrying God's salvation to foreign soil.

Not yet twenty, Just entered "minor" seminary in Paris, then went on to the Foreign Missions Seminary. Childhood dreams may have taken him there, but those dreams had to grow up, deepen, mature. In 1861 he wrote to his parents: "I sense quite well the road I am taking is rough and difficult. I am not deluding myself about its obstacles and sufferings, nor to the dangers I will meet. I place myself entirely in God's hands."

Graduates of the seminary were never told beforehand where they would be sent. A priest was to simply follow orders, adjusting and accepting his assignment, aware that the ticket to foreign service was often "one-way" and that few places would be welcoming. When Just heard his post would be Korea, his sense of calling and youthful joy of adventure came together. "I believe that our Lord has given me the best portion. Korea, the land of martyrs!" he wrote.

Just de Bretenieres sailed from Marseilles on July 19, 1864. He entered Seoul, the capital city, on May 29, 1865, secretly, taken to shore under cover of night in the same way that a spy might approach an enemy country. The government of Korea had in fact declared war on the church.

Just learned the language and culture, and he began working covertly. Operating mostly at night, he heard confessions, blessed marriages, gave confirmation, and administered last rites. He had baptized about forty adult converts when in February 1866, his location, along with his bishop's, was betrayed by one of the bishop's servants. Just was arrested while celebrating Mass and taken to court tied in red rope, the symbol of a serious crime.

Just de Bretenieres tortured and beheaded in Korea

Just's crime was being a priest and a missionary at a time when the regime had decided that foreign influences must be swept away. When Just responded in his defense—"I came to Korea to save your souls"—he was actually testifying of his guilt and leading the court even more quickly to its preordained conclusion. After two weeks of ceremonial proceedings and daily tortures, Just and his bishop, along with others, were carried away (tied to chairs, for their legs were no longer capable of bearing weight) to the sandy beach that would absorb their blood.

The party of priests testified and preached as the heavily guarded caravan reached its destination. The prisoners were each held up by poles placed under the arms and paraded before the gathered witnesses. Executioners then performed the death dances, swinging swords and inciting the crowd's bloodlust. Each man was stripped of clothing and made to kneel; then quickly the swords fell, and lives spent mostly in study, prayer, and preparation were cut violently short. Just was twenty-eight years old.

Upon hearing the news, his father wept; his mother raised her eyes toward heaven. The boy who had heard a call to missionary service while digging in the ground had finished his mission as a man, a priest, a martyr.

John Coleridge Patteson (1827–1871)

Missionary John Patteson knew every missionary initiative carried risk. He understood nothing could be won for God without a daring faith that trusts God in every circumstance. Patteson was a planner, a trainer, an activist for social justice, a preacher, and an evangelist, courageous to the end in his effort to plant churches and schools in Melanesia. He died at the violent hands of Nukapu islanders, who sought revenge on white men for stealing their people and making them slaves.

Educated at Eton and Balliol College, Oxford, Patteson was ordained in 1853. His tutor at Eton, George Selwyn, became the first bishop of New Zealand and convinced Patteson to pursue a missionary career in the South Seas. From 1855 until the time of his death, Patteson toured the islands of

John Patteson clubbed to death with a hatchet

Melanesia on a ship called the *Southern Cross*, opening schools funded by his private fortune. In 1867 he founded the Melanesian Mission with headquarters on Norfolk Island, where the climate allowed school during winter months and year-round farming. In his travels, he learned twenty-three local languages and prepared the first grammars as connected language families became clearer to him. Patteson became the first bishop of Melanesia in 1861.

Besides the dangers of disease, sea travel, and immense cultural differences, Patteson also had to work in the face of the region's most profitable but illegal business—the slave trade. Some islands, he noted, were becoming depopulated to the point where subsistence was precarious. Many islanders were taking up crude but effective arms for self-protection against the light-skinned people who would steal their wives and sons. While Patteson was widely known, he was quite aware that he shared with the slave traders their most identifiable trait: skin color.

Thus he wrote enroute to Nukapu, only four days before his death:

> "How I pray God that if it be His will, and if it be the appointed time, He may enable me in His own way to begin some little work among these very wild but vigorous islanders. I am fully alive to the probability that some outrage has been committed here ... I am quite aware that we may be exposed to considerable risk on this account ... But I don't think there is much cause for fear."

On September 20 he landed alone on Nukapu, and was clubbed to death. His body delivered back to the ship revealed five hatchet cuts to the chest, one for each islander recently stolen by traders. England was stunned by his death. At last, Parliament passed the Kidnapping Acts of 1872 and 1875, outlawing the slave-trade terror that led to Patteson's martyrdom.

A Melanesian Christian who had been trained by Patteson offered this tribute to the slain bishop: "As he taught, he confirmed his word with his good life among us. His character and conduct were consistent with the law of God. He did nothing carelessly. White or black, he loved them all alike."

James Hannington (1847–1885)

On a hill to the west of Kampala's city center stands the dome of Namirembe Cathedral, with its bronze cross clearly visible to the crowded capital of Uganda. It is one of two cathedrals of the Province of the Church of Uganda (Anglican), one of the strongest Christian movements in East Africa. Beside the church rests a small cemetery, and just inside the gate is a simple stone marking Bishop Hannington's grave. The epitaph contains his last words: "Tell the Kabaka I die for Uganda."

Born in Hurstpierpoint near Sussex, England, Hannington was a precocious, adventurous child. (Once he blew off his thumb with black powder in a childhood prank.) He studied at Oxford, and then went into business and the British Army. Dedicated to Christ, he entered the ministry, and at age thirty-seven he was appointed by the Church Missionary Society to Uganda to lead the first expedition of Protestant missionaries to the East African interior. But he never arrived in Uganda; malaria and dysentery forced his return to London.

In 1884 he tried again, this time as the first bishop of Eastern Equatorial Africa. His goal was the Buganda kingdom, west of the source of the great River Nile, discovered by British explorer John Speke just two years before. This time Hannington might have completed the long journey but for a rumor passed to the Buganda king (Kabaka Mwanga), warning him to beware of white men approaching from the east—they were aggressors intent on a takeover.

Indeed, Hannington's expedition was stopped near Jinja in late July. Bugandan warriors apprehended the bishop, sending word back to Kampala of whites held prisoner. Hannington wrote in his journal on July 22:

> "Starvation, desertion, treachery, and a few other nightmares hover over one's head in ghostly forms ... let me beg every mite of spare prayer. You must uphold my hands, lest they fall. If this is the last chapter of earthly history, then the next will be the first page of the heavenly—no blots or smudges, no incoherence, but sweet converse in the presence of the Lamb."

James Hannington speared to death after months in captivity

Not until late October did the Kabaka's order make its way back: "Kill him." Today, Bugandan leaders will say that in the Luganda language, "release him" and "kill him," sound remarkably similar, but in 1885 warriors holding Hannington could not worry if they had heard the Kabaka correctly. On October 29, Hannington read Psalm 30 and recorded in his journal that it brought him "great power." Later that day he was speared.

Reports of Hannington's death sparked a wave of missionary recruits from England. Within a year the church was growing and Mwanga's own court included several young Christian servants. Even the Kabaka himself, after further bloodshed (see the Namugongo Martyrs), confessed his faith in the same Lord who had called Bishop Hannington to Africa. Today, the Church of Uganda worships in every part of the nation, including the war-torn northern provinces, where the story of martyrdom is still being written.

Joseph Mucosa Balikuddembe (1885)

The arrival of Catholic and Protestant missionaries in modern-day Uganda occurred during the reign of Kabaka Mutesa I (the king of the Buganda kingdom). Mutesa allowed his people free choice among the competing missionary alliances, including Muslims, while he remained neutral and died a traditionalist. He died in 1884, leaving power in the hands of his younger and less adroit son, Mwanga II.

The Christian movement in Uganda required a definitive break from African traditional religion. Converts were taught new behaviors (polygamy, for example, was forbidden) and new loyalties (God first), which upset the traditional religious view of the Kubaka's ultimate sovereignty. Thus Mwanga could afford a certain fascination with the European's faith while he was prince. However, when he succeeded to his father's throne, he came to regard their teaching as subversive.

Certainly the missionaries' teaching was subversive to Mwanga's own personal pleasure, for when he made sexual advances upon his young male servants, they expressly refused in the name of the Christian God who now held their ultimate loyalty. Even though homosexuality was abhorrent among the Buganda people, the refusal of subjects to obey the will of Kabaka had never before happened. Mwanga was caught in a power crisis, without the diplomatic skill or personal maturity to resolve it apart from confrontation and violence.

Only a year after becoming king, Mwanga ordered the execution of his first Bugandan martyrs. Seven years later, Anglican Bishop James Harrington, while approaching the Buganda kingdom through the southern route, was speared on Mwanga's orders.

Joseph Mucosa Balikuddembe, a Catholic convert who was an adviser to Mwanga, criticized the order to kill Harrington. It was customary to give a condemned man opportunity to explain himself, Mucosa asserted. This traveler from Britain—an important man with title and mission—had been executed while still outside the kingdom because of superstitions about the route he traveled. Mucosa's criticism was emblematic of the trouble Mwanga faced, his loss of authority and esteem among his own people, and his failure to live up to images of his father's greatness.

Mucosa, called *Balikuddembe*, meaning "man of peace," knew where his advice would lead. He had directly confronted Kabaka's long-held authority to take life at his pleasure. He had encouraged faith among young converts in Kabaka's court, urging them to observe conscience against enemies, to refrain from wanton killing, and to resist Mwanga's sexual aberrations. Though Mucosa had been a royal page since age fourteen, and a loyal servant since, his faith presented a threat to the new king.

Mucosa had been baptized at age fifteen, one of the first converts of Catholic missionaries. When his mentors retreated to the south side of Lake Victoria, Mucosa became the leader and teacher of the other Catholic pages. At the same time, he was Mutesa's most trusted attendant.

When Mwanga became king, Mucosa was appointed *majordomo* and given permission to reprove the king for inappropriate conduct. He was the king's conscience, as it were, and an adviser and tutor. It was a dangerous position, ripe for intrigue and prevarication. But Mucosa approached his work from his growing faith.

Following Harrington's death and Mucosa's criticism, Mwanga fell ill. Mucosa administered the medicine, probably opium. Mwanga experienced side effects and accused Mucosa of attempting to poison him.

In late October 1885, Mucosa was summoned to account for allegations of subversion and treason. He replied simply, "I am going to die for God." Condemned to burn, Mucosa refused to be bound. "Why bind me? Do you think I shall flee? Flee where, to God?" He was taken to the Nakivubo River near the Nakasero hills on November 15. His executioner so admired him that before the fire was lit, he beheaded Mucosa. Before his death, Mucosa forgave the king and other enemies.

More martyrdom followed, including many of the King's pages (youth attendants). At the Catholic and Protestant sites commemorating these deaths, guides will say that much later in life, Mwanga made his peace with the Church, even adopting the faith of those he killed.

"I have had many storms in this world, but soon my vessel will be on the shore in Heaven ... Jesus, I believe."

— The last words of Thomas Bliney, a law professor at Cambridge University, who was arrested for "heresy" and burned at the stake

Namugongo Martyrs (1886)

The Uganda martyrs were young men who were recruited in the Kabaka's service (the Buganda king), but who had also embraced the Christian faith as presented by the Catholic fathers and the Protestant missionaries who were resident in the King's court.

In 1875 the great adventurer-journalist Henry Morton Stanley wrote in the *London Telegraph*, requesting missionaries to come to Uganda. Kabaka Mutesa I had made this request. When missionaries arrived in Uganda in 1877 and 1879, some of their first converts were these young men in the king's service. When they embraced the Christian faith, they insisted that God was sovereign. This, of course, was treason in the Buganda kingdom where the Kabaka held all power. When the king made homosexual advances on these youth, they refused. Such insubordination was an unprecedented threat to the king.

Both Catholics and Protestants were beaten, rolled tightly in combustible leaves, and then placed in fire. Forty-five men, from age twelve, were burned in a place called Namugongo, near Kampala. Many others were killed in the towns of Busega, Nakivubo, Munyonyo, Lubowa, Mengo, Old Kampala, Mityana, and Ttakajjunga.

Years later the executioner—whose nephew was among those killed—turned to the Christian faith. He tried to explain his actions, pleading that he had only done what the king ordered. A local proverb said that the "queen ant in an anthill feeds on its ants"; thus Kabaka Mwanga executed these martyrs because their allegiance was to God and not to him.

In memory of these young men who gave their lives for God, a shrine was constructed in 1969 at the sight of the execution. Today that structure is a Basilica. Near the Catholic site is a Protestant seminary, which recreates the scene of the blaze and tells the story of young faith that would not quiver at the prospect of death by fire. Thousands gather in Namugongo every June 3, a national holiday in Uganda.

Bernard Mizeki (1896)

In the frontier of Christian missions always stands a spiritual no-man's land—contested territory claimed by pagan faiths and practices where resistance to the Christian invasion is often violent. These territories have casualties of war—saints who sacrifice safety for the sake of establishing a sure testimony to the power of God, defying the pagan spirits, and claiming ground for the gospel by the blood of Christ, made real and visible by their own.

Bernard Mizeki was born Mamiyeri Mitseka Gwambe in Portuguese-controlled Mozambique, sometime around 1861. Before his teenage years, he left home for Capetown, South Africa, to search for work and education. He landed at a school operated by the Society of St. John, an Anglican order. In March 1886, Mizeki was baptized, adopting the name Bernard. For five years he worked as a lay leader doing translations and providing other assistance. Then Bishop Knight-Green asked Bernard to join him in Southern Rhodesia (now Zimbabwe).

During the next few years he helped open schools, begin translations, and conduct worship. Gifted at languages, Bernard learned Shona and several others. In 1891 the bishop placed Mizeki in Nhome, the village of the paramount-chief Mangwenda. The chief gave permission to build a mission complex near a grove of sacred trees. Bernard cut down some of these trees to build, and claiming others for Christ, he notched them each with a cross. Bernard's less-than-reverent treatment of those trees was a serious affront to local witch doctors.

Bernard was fully aware that tampering with the African traditional religion was like waving a red scarf before a raging bull. According to the witch doctors, this act would not only challenge their social status, but also their beliefs, causing the spirits to become restless or angry. Bernard was facing the enemy, engaging in the spiritual battle.

All the while, another battle was simmering, and in 1896 it exploded. A rebellion against colonial masters threatened all who followed their ways. So the Shona-land westerners took refuge back in South Africa. But Bernard stayed, despite threats on his life.

210

Bernard Mizeki speared to death in Rhodesia (Zimbabwe)

On June 18, 1896, loud knocking warned him of enemies at the threshold. Mizeki was taken outside and speared. As he lay gravely injured but alive, Bernard's young wife, pregnant with their first child, ran for help. She then claimed to have seen a bright light over his body. When she returned, the body was gone. Had his killers taken the body into hiding? Had a miracle occurred? In any case, Bernard's body was never discovered, but his witness and the faith he taught lived on among the Shona.

Today Bernard Mizeki College stands near a monument recalling his sacrifice. Churches in Pretoria, Botswana, Capetown, and Swaziland bear his name. Most important, the daughter born after his death was named Masiwa, "fatherless one," and was later baptized *Bernardina*. The church grew as martyrs chose trust and courage over fear and flight.

Therefore, my **beloved** brethren, be **steadfast**, immovable, always **abounding** in the work of the Lord, knowing that your labor is **not in vain** in the Lord.

1 Corinthians 15:58

Boxer Rebellion in China (1900)

European powers were carving China into trading zones, as they had done to sub-Saharan Africa a decade earlier. When the United States acquired the Philippines in 1898, President McKinley and his Secretary of State, John Hay, devised an alternative to the European plan called the "Open Door" policy. This policy would ensure the United States an entry into the vast Chinese market by declaring rather simply that trading zones be abandoned in favor of open competition. The dowager empress, Tsu Hsi, saw the obvious danger to her Ch'ing Dynasty and fostered an informal reaction in an imperial message to all Chinese provinces: "The various Powers cast upon us with tiger-like voracity, hustling each other to be first to seize our innermost territories ... If our millions of people ... would prove their loyalty and love of country, what is there to fear from any invader?"

In drought-stricken Shandong province, a secret society called the Fists of Righteous Harmony recruited thousands of new members. Called by foreigners the "Boxers" because they practiced martial arts, this militant society taught that thousands of "spirit soldiers" would rise from the dead to join their cause.

That cause, promoted by Empress Tsu Hsi as a way to unite her empire, was to rid China of all "foreign devils." Diplomats fled to a compound in Beijing near the Forbidden City. Missionaries in the outer provinces had few choices. Many wives saw their husbands beheaded, and children their mothers. The Boxers took the lives of adults and children alike—Catholics, Orthodox, and Protestant. Diplomats and others who reached the Beijing compound were nearly at the end of their food and bullets when American sailors and Marines fought their way from Shanghai to rescue them.

The empress, who escaped the city disguised as a peasant, returned a year later but never regained the power of the Ch'ing dynasty. John Hay's Open Door policy opened China's market, until the Japanese invaded China in World War II.

Ia Wang

Out of the 1,000 Orthodox believers in Beijing, 300 were killed. On the evening of June 11, 1900, leaflets were posted in the streets calling for the massacre of Christians and anyone who dared to shelter them. That night, gangs of Boxers with torches attacked Christian houses, seizing believers and demanding that they disavow Christ. Those who remained faithful were gutted and then beheaded or burned alive. One Orthodox schoolteacher, Ia Wang, died twice. First, the Boxers slashed her with swords and covered her in a shallow grave. Her groans, however, alerted nearby terrorists. She was exhumed and tortured again. Eyewitnesses reported she died confessing Christ.

Mr. Farthing

An English Baptist missionary named Farthing was the first to be led from his house. His wife clung to him, but he put her aside. Farthing knelt before the soldiers, and his head was severed with one swing of the sword. He was followed by Hoddle, Beynan, Lovitt, and Wilson, each of whom was beheaded. Then Stokes, Simpson, and Whitehouse. When the men were dead, the women were taken. Mrs. Farthing held the hands of her small children, but soldiers separated them, beheaded the mother, then all the children quickly. Mrs. Lovitt was wearing glasses. A soldier took them and then beheaded her as she held the hand of her small son.

After the Protestants were killed, the Roman Catholics were led out. The bishop asked the governor why he was ordering these killings. Without answering, the official drew a sword and split the bishop's face. Priests and nuns followed him in death. The bodies of forty-five victims—all Christians, including Chinese—were left in the street that night so that clothes, rings, and watches could be stripped from the corpses.

John and Sarah Young

John and Sarah Young had been married fifteen months when the evacuation order arrived. They joined others hurrying to escape. On the way, Chinese soldiers met them and offered to protect them if they would agree to stop preaching their foreign religion. The missionaries could not agree because they had been called to share God's good news with everyone, including those speaking to them now. The soldiers killed them immediately.

Carl Lundberg

A small group of Christian and Missionary Alliance missionaries continued their work in remote northwest China. When news arrived that Boxers were coming, they attempted to flee into Mongolia. Bandits intercepted them and stole their clothing and supplies. For two weeks the group survived by eating roots until some Catholic priests came to rescue them. But they were too late. The Boxer army was close behind. Missionary Carl Lundberg wrote:

> "I do not regret coming to China. The Lord has called me, and His grace is sufficient. The way He chooses is best for me. Excuse my writing; my hand is shivering."

The Boxers killed everyone.

Horace Tracy Pitkin (1869–1900)

Horace Pitkin was an American East Coast blueblood. He was a distant relative of Connecticut's colonial-era attorney general and also kin to Elihu Yale, founder of the great Yale University from which Pitkin graduated in 1892, at the height of America's Gilded Age. It was also the era of "muscular Christianity"—a mix of robust physical and spiritual development coupled with nearly unlimited optimism that the new century just ahead would be the Christian century, the fulfillment of the Gospel mandate to all the world.

For Yale men like Pitkin—strong, charismatic, and gifted—the arena where all virtues would meet their test was China. Indeed, Horace organized Yale's first Student Volunteer Band for foreign missions. He then went on to Union Seminary in New York, married Letitia Thomas, and set sail for Hunan Province in central China.

Horace was an organizer, but not blind to the risks. He was, after all, in charge of the station in Hunan for the American Board of Commissioners for Foreign Missions. As news from Beijing arrived and the Boxers began to show restless aggression, Pitkin sent his wife and child back to the United States.

On Saturday, June 30, 1900, the Presbyterian compound on the north side of Paoting was attacked. The missionary surgeon, Dr. G. B. Taylor, went out to plead the missionaries' good will. He was killed immediately, and his severed head was raised for display in a nearby temple. The remaining Presbyterians were burned inside one of the houses.

News traveled quickly to the south side of the city, where Pitkin and two staff women were trapped at the American Board office. By 9:00 a.m., the Boxers arrived. Horace was killed trying to defend the others.

Back at Yale, four friends created a missionary society in 1901 (that still exists today). Their work, honoring Pitkin and others, included a hospital and a school in Hunan Province, which was also the home province of a man who would later undo so much of this work, Chairman Mao.

Lizzie Atwater (1900)

In June 1900, a fierce nationalist reaction in China against Christian missionaries and churches claimed more than 32,000 lives. The worst massacres occurred in the northern province of Shanxi. The pregnant Lizzie Atwater wrote a memorable letter home before she and six others were martyred.

Dear ones, I long for a sight of your dear faces, but I fear we shall not meet on Earth. I am preparing for the end very quietly and calmly. The Lord is wonderfully near, and He will not fail me. I was very restless and excited while there seemed a chance of life, but God has taken away that feeling, and now I just pray for grace to meet the terrible end bravely. The pain will soon be over, and oh the sweetness of the welcome above! My little baby will go with me. I think God will give it to me in heaven and my dear mother will be so glad to see us. I cannot imagine the Savior's welcome. Oh, that will compensate for all these days of suspense. Dear ones, live near to God and cling less closely to Earth. There is no other way by which we can receive that peace from God which passeth understanding. I must keep calm and still these hours. I do not regret coming to China.

On August 15, 1900, soldiers took Lizzie and ten others away from the relative safety of a nearby town and hacked them to death with their swords, tossing the bodies into a pit.

James Chalmers (1841–1901)

He loved the sea, this rebellious Scottish lad. The fishing village of Ardrishaig was his home, and the fishermen his friends. The sea was wild when the wind blew strong, like young Chalmers himself. He breathed the sea air and wondered what lay beyond the rolling waves. Later, when God's call to missionary service touched his heart, he spent many perilous days on the sea, searching out peoples who had never heard God's story.

Chalmers was eighteen when he converted to Christ in an evangelistic meeting led by two preachers from Ireland. Chalmers had come with friends to break up the meeting, to mock the zealots, to make sport of the timid who sought their peace in religion. Perhaps the heavy rain that night dampened the youths' recklessness, but Chalmers listened and believed. The message was from Revelation 22:17: "The Spirit and the bride say,

James Chalmers killed by cannibals in New Guinea

'Come!'" It was an invitation to make his heart's home in God; Chalmers gladly accepted. "I was thirsty, and I came," he said later.

A few years later he received pastoral training and a commission by the London Missionary Society to serve in the Pacific Islands. Chalmers and his wife Jane Hercus were standing at water's edge in New Guinea. Suddenly a mob of painted warriors surrounded them, demanding gifts and weapons.

Chalmers knew the danger, for he had come to a part of the world where killing was honored, where warriors bit off the noses of their victims as a sign of triumph, and where eating human flesh was common. Were those dangers not enough, the waters were infested with snakes and crocodiles, and the entire area filled with malaria and fevers.

"Give us tomahawks, knives, and beads or we kill you, your wife, your teachers and their wives," the leader said, ready to strike with his stone club.

"You may kill us," Chalmers replied, "but we never give presents to persons threatening us. Remember we have only come to do you good."

The mob retreated, threatening to return at dawn's light. Missionaries came to New Guinea with daily prayers for survival and converts. But on this particular evening, waiting for dawn, survival was the small group's chief concern.

Inside their quarters, Chalmers asked the group, "What shall we do? Men stay, women escape? The boat is too small for all of us." Jane replied, "We have come here to preach the gospel. We will stay together." The teachers' wives agreed, "We live together or die together." They prayed, and gradually fell asleep. Chalmers wrote that night in his journal: "The Spirit and the bride say, 'Come!' We came at thy bidding to this land to point these wretched people to the same cleansing, refreshing, healing Fountain. Protect us, that we may fulfill the mission." And God did protect them.

For ten years James and Jane helped build the church on Rarotonga, training pastors and teachers. They constantly reached beyond the established churches and schools to uncover new peoples not yet reached.

In the fall of 1877, they moved to New Guinea, where they found villages filled with disease, sorcery, filth, treachery, and weapons. Slowly, patiently, they told the gospel story and made God's invitation plain. Often they slept as guests in a village's *dubu*—the main lodge and trophy room of human skulls. Most of the people they met had never seen white skin. Chalmers would introduce himself by taking off his black boots, revealing then his white arms and chest to the laughter of some and the shrieks of others. His name there was *Tamate*, the closest sound the natives could make to Chalmers. Wherever Tamate went, the threat of the warrior with the stone club was never far away.

Jane grew sick in 1878 and sought recovery in Australia. Five months later she died. James, who had remained in New Guinea, was devastated. He wrote in the journal: "Oh to dwell at His cross and to abound in blessed sympathy with His great work! I want the heathen for Christ!"

In 1886, Chalmers returned to England to tell his stories of twenty years. There he married Sarah Harrison, who would also die of fever later in the Pacific after remarkable and courageous service. And James turned down a government appointment that would have guaranteed his safety as a missionary-diplomat. His position: "Gospel and commerce, yes. But remember this: it must be the gospel first."

The Chalmers returned to New Guinea in the fall of 1887. James was never content to manage a mission station; he wanted new contacts, far up the unmapped rivers, down the inland trails. On one such journey a year after Sarah's death, warriors armed for piracy and murder surrounded his boat near shore. James decided, as was his custom, to demand a meeting with the local chief as the best way to escape the mob. His young colleague, Oliver Tomkins, insisted on accompanying the sixty-year-old veteran.

Together they approached the village dubu, hoping for a council and anticipating a shared meal. Once inside, however, the stone clubs fell, the strangers' heads were severed and their bodies cooked, mixed with sago, and eaten. The day was April 8, 1901, at the dawn of what was then called the "Christian Century."

Chalmers, two heroic wives, and many co-workers and their families gave their lives to bring the Spirit and bride's invitation to Pacific Island peoples. "Let him that is athirst come," read the words in Chalmers' Bible, "and whosoever will, let him take the water of life freely."

John Kensit (1902)

John Kensit was not someone to go about "business as usual" when truth and reform were at stake.

Kensit was raised by a pious, prayerful mother who focused the young lad's mind on *Pilgrim's Progress*, the *Book of Common Prayer*, and the Bible. Then, as often happens in youth, two odd events created a conflict, which was later resolved by Kensit's lifelong devotion to reform within the Church of England.

The first event was his recruitment to the choir of St. Ethelburgh's, a high church parish where worship was decidedly more Catholic than Protestant. At the same time a nearby evangelical vicar began preaching reformation doctrines. John went to those meetings, and was positively convinced that the Bible alone was God's Word and that Jesus alone was the sufficient sacrifice for sin.

The second event was a visit to London in 1859 by Giuseppe Garibaldi, the Italian nationalist who sought a republic led by citizens rather than a theocracy led by priests. Garibaldi, a man of action, and not one to avoid conflict, made an indelible impression on young John.

Until 1898, Kinset's personal campaign to recover the heart of faith in the Church of England was accomplished by selling books and teaching Sunday school. But in that year, he literally made headlines when he disrupted a Good Friday service at St. Cuthbert's Church. He seized a cross from the people who were kissing it—treating it as an icon—and proclaimed to the crowd, "In the name of God, I denounce this idolatry— God help me." After a sound beating by the crowd, he was arrested. At that moment John Kensit left the life of the quiet soldier and became a public debater—some would say a public nuisance—in the cause of church reform. At every opportunity, he confronted church officials with his probing challenges to return to the faith of Ridley, Latimer, and other English reformers.

Kensit founded the Protestant Truth Society and sent out a corps of lay evangelists he called the Wycliffe Preachers to awaken people to biblical faith. He held public meetings, frequently in parishes dominated by Catholic sentiment. His last meeting was at the Claughton Music Hall in Birkenhead, on September 25, 1902, which was conducted without incident. Later, however, as he was walking to the ferry, a youth hurled a heavy metal file at Kensit and his group. It found its mark on Kensit's brow. He was rushed to an infirmary and seemed to recover, but he contracted pneumonia and died on October 8.

Kensit's crusade for reform, some say, was never realized in the Church of England. He died nonetheless for his reformational faith, one of the last martyrs in England.

"Cheer up, my brothers, and lift up your hearts to God, for after this harsh breakfast we shall have a good dinner in the kingdom of Christ our Lord and Redeemer. ... This is God's armor, and now I am a Christian soldier prepared for battle."

— Anthony Parsons, an English priest, who was burned at the stake

Chet Bitterman's grave in Colombia

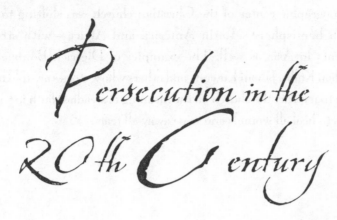

Persecution in the 20th Century

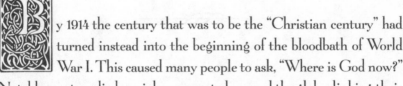

(1914–1999)

By 1914 the century that was to be the "Christian century" had turned instead into the beginning of the bloodbath of World War I. This caused many people to ask, "Where is God now?" Notable martyrs died as violence erupted around the globe, linking their blood with millions of other victims of imperialism, fascism, rebellions, pogroms, and the indiscriminate annihilations of modern warfare.

However, beyond the trenches of World War I and World War II, the Holocaust, the killing fields of Southeast Asia, and China's Cultural Revolution, stand the dominant secular ideologies that have replaced a "Christian climate of opinion" in places where the church was once strong. Pragmatism, existentialism, and the post-modern mood have drawn the once sacred-leaning climate of Europe decidedly away from Christian moorings. Indeed, the constitution of the newly formed European Union makes no reference to deity or to the church at all.

In the United States, commercialism and a widening appetite for toleration had softened Christian convictions to the point where many believers were bewildered as to why anyone would surrender their life for their faith convictions. Martyrdom no doubt still occured. Many Christian Hutus died trying to save Tutsi neighbors in the Rwanda genocide. Bombings of Christian churches in the Middle East took the lives of courageous believers who met for worship at their peril. Christian converts in Afghanistan were put under an automatic sentence of death.

The demographic center of the Christian church was shifting to the southern hemisphere—Latin America and Africa—with strong movements in Asia as well. The examples of Dietrich Bonhoeffer, Maximilian Kolbe, Janani Luwum, and others whose stories are told here, continue to instruct the church on the meaning of steadfast faith in God's promises to heal all wounds and wipe away all tears.

The avalanche of **blessing** and **ministry** began with three words: **"I am willing."**

— Chet Bitterman

Chrysostomos (1922)

Nationalism and ethnic loyalty, normal bonds of a community, also hold potential for evil. This was the case at the turn of the twentieth century in Asia Minor . Bishop Chrysostomos was living in a time of genocide, but refused the safety offered to diplomats and dignitaries.

From 1894 to 1923 in Asia Minor, Turkish nationals purged minorities and Christians in a "pure blood" campaign that rivaled the Nazi's New Order a decade later. In 1922, the pogrom came to Smyrna, the largest city in the Pontus region, a cosmopolitan hub populated by Greeks whose education and energy had created a thriving middle class. Chrysostomos was the Metropolitan (bishop) of Smyrna, serving thousands of Greek Orthodox Christians who lived there. He was urged to leave the city as Turkish forces approached. Instead, he gathered the faithful for worship. He said in his final sermon:

> "God is testing our faith, our courage, and our patience at this time. But God will never abandon Christians. It is during the high seas that the good sailor stands out, and it is during the time of tribulations that the good Christian does the same. Pray and all these will be gone. We shall again see happy days and we will praise the Lord. Have courage as all good Christians should."

At the conclusion of the Mass, a police officer informed Chrysostomos that he had been summoned to the Turkish garrison. That night, death came slowly. The Turks first gouged out his eyes, and then dragged the blind bishop by his beard and hair through a Turkish neighborhood, where he endured the abuse of the crowd and further cruelties of the soldiers. One of those troops confessed a month later:

> "We hit him, swore at him, and cut off pieces of his skin. He neither begged, screamed, nor cursed while he endured all the tortures. His pale face, covered with blood, was constantly looking towards the sky as he mumbled barely audible words, which I could not understand. Every now and then, he would raise his arms and bless the persecutors. One of the troops became so furious that he drew a sword and chopped off the bishop's hand.

Then I felt so sorry for this man that I shot him twice in the head to finish him off. "

To allay his guilt, that Turkish soldier secretly led a Greek university instructor and students to safety, hoping the rescue would purge his conscience. Chrysostomos died by his hand; others would live.

In 1997, on the seventy-fifth anniversary of the burning of Smyrna, a Resolution was passed by the 105th Congress of Greece to commemorate the genocide, citing the martyrdom of Chrysostomos and other persecutions against the church.

It is the privilege of politicians to note the world's disapproval of long-ago crimes. It was Chrysostomos's pleasure to face them with his people. "The duty of the priest is to stay with his congregation," he had said to those who begged him to flee. Those standing near that day saw him wave farewell to the rescue ship, his last hope. As the ship weighed anchor and set to sea, Chrysostomos turned to the duty of preaching the Word and praying for forgiveness for his enemies.

Manche Massemola (1913–1928)

The life and death of this young African girl would be completely forgotten, had not the church of the Province of Southern Africa (Anglican) declared her a martyr soon after her death.

Too young to have attained the honors of university degrees or ordination, Manche endured beatings and ridicule from her own family for simply attending pre-baptism classes with her cousin. Manche represented financial stability because her marriage to a man of means would have brought a considerable dowry. But the girl's pursuit of the Christian life threatened those familial intentions. When the beatings proved ineffectual, or perhaps because they grew in severity and frequency, the young girl's body succumbed. In childhood faithfulness Manche died by the hand of her closest would-be caregiver, her own mother.

Martyrdom is losing one's life because of loyalty to Christ. In most cases, the martyr stands against ruthless power and chooses death over compromise. That was true for Manche as well, though her young world was smaller, and her murderer so close to home.

John and Betty Stam (1934)

Betty held the baby in her arms, singing softly to this infant child, all too aware that this was their last night together. Her husband John, tied to a bedpost, could not sleep either. Only two weeks ago they had arrived at their mission station with three-month-old Helen Priscilla, full of hope, eager for ministry. But on this winter night, their quiet lullabies were parting sorrows, for tomorrow they would die.

Betty Scott, daughter of Presbyterian missionaries to China, graduated from Moody Bible Institute in 1931. She had already accepted the call of God to service with the China Inland Mission. The bond she felt with John, whom she had met at a prayer meeting for China, and their mutual decision to serve Christ in the middle of a dangerous civil war, could not—did not—hold her back. When she was assigned to a mission station in the interior, she left for China. She wrote, "When we consecrate ourselves to God, we think we are making a great sacrifice, and doing lots for Him, when really we are only letting go some little bitsy trinkets we have been grabbing; and when our hands are empty, He fills them with His treasures."

John Stam finished his training at Moody in 1932. He gave the graduating class address that year, urging: "Dare we advance at God's command in face of the impossible?" In the fall he sailed for Shanghai, expecting an assignment too dangerous for a family. He arrived to discover that the Communists were gaining ground, missionaries were on the move, and his beloved Betty, to his great surprise, was in Shanghai, recuperating from illness. They were soon married, and in September 1934 their daughter Helen Priscilla was born. The young family moved to Anhui Province near the town of Ching-te. The local leader assured their safety.

It was a surprise to everyone when the town magistrate appeared at the missionaries' door only three months later to warn them of the approach of Communist troops, but it was too late. Before John, Betty, and baby Helen could get out, the troops got in. John was taken first, bound and pleading for the safety of his wife and child. Soon the troops returned for them. That night in jail, the baby cried. When guards threatened to kill her, an older Chinese man, also a prisoner, intervened. Guards asked if he were so bold as to die for the foreign baby; he assented. The man was hacked to death on the spot.

That night John was ordered to write to mission leaders, demanding a $20,000 US ransom. He concluded the note, fully aware that ransoms were never paid: "The Lord bless and guide you. As for us may God be glorified, whether by life or by death."

The next day soldiers marched the Stams to the nearby town of Miaosheo, where they were placed in the office of the local postmaster, who asked where they were going. By this time John must have known the soldiers' intentions, for he replied: "I don't know where they are going, but we are going to heaven."

The next morning John and Betty were led to their execution. A local Christian doctor approached the soldiers to plead mercy for the missionaries. He was threatened, and John then pleaded for the doctor. The Communist leader had heard enough. He ordered John to kneel, and with the flash of a sword decapitated the young missionary. Betty fell on her husband's body, and the sword fell again.

What then happened to baby Helen? A Chinese evangelist, Dr. Lo, found her wrapped in a sleeping bag, with a change of clothes and money pinned to her diaper. Betty, during her sleepless last night, had done her best to comfort and care for the child she knew she was leaving behind. Lo concealed the child in a rice basket and eventually brought Helen to her grandparents, still serving in China. Helen became a teacher and raised a family in the eastern United States. She chose a private life: no interviews or public statements.

What happened to the church in China? In response to news of the Stams' death, several hundred new missionary recruits volunteered for service. The Chinese church went underground for many years. Today it is emerging, stronger than anyone expected; stronger than Mao's forces, whose day has already passed.

Maximilian Kolbe (1894-1941)

"Ten Polish pigs will die for the one who escaped." A normal day at the Auschwitz extermination camp in 1941, and a normal punishment announced by the SS commandant, "Butcher" Frisch. He then called the ten names of the condemned. All the prisoners were weak and dehydrated, having stood in the sun without food or water all day, waiting for the escapee to be caught. None wanted to die. One of them, Polish sergeant Francis Gajowniczek, cried out for mercy for his young wife and child, and for himself—just the sort of weakness the SS relished. Then in the line of prisoners someone stirred, moved, spoke up. It was forbidden.

"Who are you?" demanded Frisch.

"I am a Catholic priest. I wish to die for that man."

Frisch hesitated. A hero in the camp? No matter. Better to rid the place of such heroes. Better for the hopelessness that breaks the spirit. In any case, none of these prisoners would likely live long anyhow. Frisch accepted the fool's offer. The ten, including Father Maximilian Kolbe, were marched to the camp's starvation cells.

Raymond Kolbe was born to hard-working Polish nationalists near Pabianice on January 8, 1894. His father died later, executed by the Russians for fighting for the independence of a partitioned Poland. His mother, a pious Catholic, saw her prayers for her son answered when Raymond was only twelve. In that year, his "wild youth" gave way to lifelong Christian devotion. In a vision, he had seen two crowns from which to choose. The first was white for purity, the second red for martyrdom. Young Raymond

Maximilian Kolbe died by a lethal injection of carbolic acid on
August 14, 1941.

asked for both. From that day, his life was given to study, missionary work, evangelism, and care for the oppressed. Everything he attempted prospered.

At age thirteen Raymond and his brother Franciszek, illegally crossed the Russian-Austro-Hungary border to join the Franciscans at Lwow. At seventeen he professed first vows, and took his final vows at twenty, when he also took the name *Maximilian Maria*—to denote his veneration of the Virgin. Maximilian aimed high and he received a doctorate of philosophy at the Gregorian University at age twenty-one, and a doctorate of theology at twenty-four. His other accomplishments include missionary service in Japan; the opening of a seminary near Warsaw; a start-up of a radio station, newspapers, and magazines; and the founding of an Order, the Militia of the Immaculata, which grew from 650 friars under Maximilian's leadership, making it the largest Catholic religious house in the world.

Kolbe was a vibrant leader, but to be a Polish leader in 1939 was neither safe nor prudent. He could see the storm gathering. Indeed, Kolbe's media outreach began to assail the dangers of Germany's militarism, and his monastery took in Jewish refugees. Before his arrest by the Gestapo, Kolbe kept nearly 1,500 Jews under cover.

On February 17, 1941, the German war machine caught him. Kolbe knew what he believed. In a well-known statement he said, "No one can change the Truth. What we can do is to seek truth and serve it when we have found it ... There are two irreconcilable enemies in the depth of every soul: good and evil, sin and love. And what use are victories on the battlefield if we are defeated in our innermost personal selves?" When Kolbe was sent to Auschwitz in May, he was prepared for his innermost battle.

During Kolbe's two weeks in the starvation cellblock, a Nazi guard in charge of the prisoner log made note that Kolbe led in prayers and hymns. When he grew too weak to speak, he whispered. Kolbe and three others survived those two weeks, but the Nazis needed their cells for other miscreants. So the end came by a lethal injection of carbolic acid on August 14, 1941. The body of the "escaped prisoner" was later discovered drowned in an Auschwitz latrine. Francis Gajowniczek lived to an old age, dying in Poland in 1997.

Maximilian Kolbe had the kind of devotion to Christ that stands up to evil and takes a condemned man's place. He wrote about his relationship with Christ: "You come to me and unite Yourself intimately to me under the form of nourishment [the Sacrament]. Your Blood now runs in mine; Your Soul, Incarnate God, penetrates mine, giving courage and support. What miracles! Who would have ever imagined such!"

John Willfinger (1942)

In the summer of 1942, the Empire of Japan planned to capture a perimeter of defense and oil reserves that extended from its islands south to Australia. Borneo was to be a land of strategic occupation, and foreigners operating there, especially North Americans, must be captured and controlled.

Missionary John Willfinger and his Bible translator partners, the Lenhams, knew the danger. But their work was critical—producing the Murut New Testament. In July 1942 they learned that Japanese forces had captured missionaries to the south, so instinctively they moved north, to the dense jungle and isolated villages of the Murut. But they underestimated Japanese persistence.

On September 19, a Murut messenger arrived in the village where these three missionaries were waiting out the Japanese occupation. The word he brought was worrisome. All three missionaries were named on the "most wanted" list. Anyone harboring or aiding the three would be severely punished.

Still the Murut people were confident they could successfully hide the missionaries. It would require deception of the kind already used by European Christians and others hiding Jews from the Germans. But this deception the Lenhams and Willfinger were not willing to impose on their Murut friends. Instead, they decided to surrender themselves to the Japanese, trusting God for whatever lay ahead.

The Lenhams went north to the nearest Japanese encampment. They managed to keep copies of Murut Gospels intact throughout the war. Willfinger, who had anticipated a reunion with his fiancée prior to the danger, chose to visit several tribal churches in eastern Borneo before surrendering himself. How far he traveled is not known, but eventually he encountered his captors and was executed three days after Christmas. At the end of the Pacific conflict, Willfinger's body was recovered and his Bible was also found. On the inside cover John had written this poem:

> No mere man is the Christ I know
>
> But greater far than all below.
>
> Day by day his love enfolds me
>
> Day by day his power upholds me.
>
> All that God could ever be
>
> The man of Nazareth is to me.
>
> No mere man can my strength sustain
>
> And drive away all fear and pain.
>
> Holding me close in his embrace
>
> When death and I stand face to face.
>
> Then all that God could ever be
>
> The unseen Christ will be to me.

And underneath the poem his own comment, "Hallelujah, this is real."

Dietrich Bonhoeffer (1906-1945)

He could have escaped the Nazi dragnet, but he chose to return to his troubled country. To stay in New York would be to abandon the mission— a mission he would not survive.

Dietrich Bonhoeffer was born into a prominent Berlin family. His father, Karl, was a renowned psychiatrist and neurologist. Dietrich himself was a gifted child. Skilled at piano, his parents once thought he would become a professional musician. At age fourteen, quite to his scientific family's surprise, Dietrich announced that he would study to become a theologian. By the age of twenty-one, he had earned his doctorate in theology from the University of Berlin.

But Dietrich was as much a pastor as a scholar. In 1932, Bonhoeffer taught catechism to the youth in one of Berlin's poorest neighborhoods. He actually moved there to spend more time with some of the boys. In Spain he pastored a German-speaking church. Later in London, he helped build an international base that would play significantly in his efforts to end World War II.

But in New York City in 1939, he faced his crisis of conscience. It was a lecture tour arranged by American friends who wanted to give Bonhoeffer sanctuary from the Nazis. Only one month into the visit, Dietrich knew he could not fail to struggle with the German church against the National Socialists, who were already showing their hostility toward humanity and especially the Jews. Indeed, Bonhoeffer had already led an "underground" seminary (closed by the Gestapo), and he knew of plans forming in the *Abwehr* (German intelligence) to depose Hitler by whatever means. In effect, the theologian knew too much for his own safety and the well-being of his family and friends. Still, he hastened back to work with the "confessing church" (those who proclaimed that Jesus alone is Lord and that allegiance to Hitler was idolatry).

Back in Germany, Bonhoeffer was forbidden to teach, preach, or to publish without prior approval. He was ordered to report regularly to police officials. But an odd assignment gave him reprieve from Nazi surveillance.

He was recruited to the Abwehr. Pastor Bonhoeffer with his British and American connections was to be a spy for Hitler. At least so his orders read. Actually, the anti-Hitler plotters, led by Admiral Canaris, recruited him. His assignment was to use every means possible to negotiate terms of surrender with the West. Of course, this dangerous double-agentry must also do away with German leadership.

On April 5, 1943, the Gestapo caught up with Canaris and his double agents. Bonhoeffer was sent to Tegel prison in Berlin, where he continued to preach and write among guards and inmates. Two years later, April 9, 1945, after conducting a worship service in prison, with Allied troops approaching, Bonhoeffer was hanged by direct order of the faltering Fuhrer. His last words: "This is the end—for me, the beginning of life."

Bonhoeffer's writings continue to challenge the church today. His notions of "cheap grace" and the "cost of discipleship," life in community, and radical Christian social responsibility are still relevant, vibrant, and widely studied. The personal struggles and faith issues he faced were many: the taking of life (he helped with two failed attempts on Hitler's life), prayer and peace under duress, and love unfilled (he postponed his engagement to Maria van Wedemeyer because his secret negotiations could have been dangerous to her.)

Bonhoeffer died as a traitor to Nazi Germany. The camp doctor who witnessed the execution noted: "I have hardly ever seen a man die so entirely submissive to the will of God." Three weeks later, Hitler committed suicide in his Berlin bunker. In less than a month, the European war was over.

Maurice Tornay (1910-1946)

Maurice was the seventh of eight children born to a Catholic family who lived high in the Swiss mountains near Valais. The family was united in the work required to live and the faith they lived by. Maurice recalled his mother at the fireside telling the story of Saint Agnes, virgin and martyr. "You are virgins," she told her children, "but to be martyrs, that's more difficult. You must love God more than anything else, and be ready to give your life, to shed the last drop of blood for Him." Young Maurice never forgot his mother's lesson.

After secondary school, Maurice joined the Canons Regular of Grand St. Bernard, best known for their rescue work in the Alps and the famous Saint Bernard dogs they breed and train as "assistants." As Maurice progressed, the Canons were asked by the church to send missionaries accustomed to living at higher elevations to begin evangelizing people in the Himalayas, or the Asian Alps as they were called in Europe. Maurice volunteered, but he was kept back until surgery cured an ulcer. In 1936 he arrived in Weixi Province near the Tibetan border, where he finished theological studies, learned Chinese, and was ordained a priest. Maurice wrote: "And now I've almost made a world tour. I've seen and felt that people are unhappy everywhere, and that real happiness comes in serving God. Really, nothing else matters. Nothing, nothing."

Work on the China-Tibet border, difficult on any day, was made more dangerous by the invasion of Japanese forces in 1939. Tornay was in charge of a boy's school, and every life need—food, clothes, heat—was in very short supply. Add to that the antagonism of local Buddhist lamas, especially one Gun-Akhio, who sensed that missionaries would erode his power base. Gun-Akhio was not averse to threats and force against the foreigners.

In 1946 Tornay was made priest of the Yerkalo parish in southeast Tibet. Only days later forty local lamas broke into the priest's residence, looted it, and at rifle-point, forced Torney out of town. He went to Pame in Yunnan Province, China, there to provide whatever help he could for his people—prayer, correspondence, comfort, and care for the sick that made their way to him. By May he was sure that the risk of returning was less than the risk of waiting further. "Leave a parish without a priest ... and the people will be worshipping animals," he said.

At the edge of Yerkalo, Gun-Akhio waited. Again Tornay was kept out of his parish. By now, however, he had a plan: a direct appeal to the Dalai Lama for permission to conduct his mission, for religious tolerance rather than belligerence and intimidation. Tornay began the two-month journey to Lhasa, Tibet's capital.

But Gun-Akhio had his agents, and Tornay could not make a move without his knowledge. The lamas intercepted Tornay's caravan and forced him to retreat. On August 11, at the Choula gorge near the Chinese border, Tornay was ambushed and shot along with his companions. Chinese authorities eventually convicted members of the Karmda lamasery for the killings.

Maurice Tornay had written as a teenager: "Death is the happiest day of our lives. We must rejoice in it more than anything, because it is our arrival in our true homeland." Tornay, the priest who rarely walked on level ground and never served a day in comfort or ease, was finally home.

Therefore whoever **confesses** Me before men, him I will also **confess** before My Father who is in **heaven**.

Matthew 10:32

Jim Elliot, Pete Fleming, Ed McCully, Nate Saint, Roger Youderian (1956)

A news flash alerted the world: "Five Men Missing in Auca Territory." The date was Monday, January 9, 1956. A team of missionary pioneers trying to make peaceful contact with an infamous tribe of Indians in Ecuador had failed to make a scheduled radio call. For almost a full day no word had come from their camp on the Curaray River, which they named "Palm Beach." Then a hovering pilot reported the badly damaged plane at the camp. This was followed by a gruesome confirmation on Wednesday, January 11, when the first body was spotted in the river. Though a search and rescue team was quickly formed, the discovery of more bodies quickly changed the mission from rescue to retrieval and burial.

By Friday of that week the team reached the missionaries' campsite and hurriedly buried four of the bodies. The men had died violently from repeated spear wounds and machete cuts. The fifth body (Ed McCully) was never located after being identified on the beach but then washed away by the river. Five widows and eight orphans mourned the deaths and looked to God for comfort and direction. The world witnessed in stunned amazement.

Shockwaves from the tragedy traveled around the globe. Eventually, thousands of Christians identified the news of the deaths of five young men as the turning point in their lives. In her book, *Through Gates of Splendor*, written a year after the deaths, Jim Elliot's widow Elisabeth described some of the remarkable early results from what seemed like a tragic waste of life. The places of service vacated by those men were filled many times over by young men and women moved and motivated by their selfless sacrifice. Fifty years later, the effects continue to be felt.

Within two years of their deaths, Jim Elliot's widow and Nate Saint's sister made a friendly and lasting contact with the Waodanis. Bible translation into the Waodani language began. One by one, the men who committed the murder became believers in the One who sent the missionaries to reach them. Steve Saint spent much of his childhood among the Waodanis. Despite the fact that they had killed his father, Steve became an adopted son of the tribe and eventually took his own family to live for a time among them. The painful arrival of the gospel among that violent people worked a miracle of transformation.

While martyrdom has always been part of the great battle between good and evil in the spiritual realms, the death of believers has not always resulted directly from those seeking to silence their witness. Violence has often been an expression of fear, suspicion, ignorance or timing rather than a conscious rejection of the message. The five men who died in Ecuador had spent months contacting the Waodanis through over-flights and gifts exchanged via an ingenious bucket drop devised by the team's pilot, Nate Saint. Though the tribe had a history of violent encounters with outsiders, the men had decided they had established some degree of mutual trust that would support a direct contact. At first, their cautious optimism had been rewarded by a visit from three Waodanis. That had occurred without incident. They had expected further contact. Little did the missionaries know that they had stepped into an intra-tribe squabble.

When the attack party killed the five men, their actions weren't personal or even driven by what or who the white men represented. The violence was almost a diversion from internal issues the Waodanis couldn't handle. Two of the three who had visited the camp at Palm Beach reported that the missionaries had mistreated them; the third person argued otherwise. Though others in the group recognized the false accusations, it seemed easier to eliminate the cause (the missionaries) than to address the internal issues. Once the possibility of killing was raised, the general tone in the tribal group shifted to well-established patterns of preparation for battle. They knew the white men had guns; they didn't know they wouldn't use them. Several of the Waodanis reported hearing strange supernatural voices and seeing moving lights in the sky during the attack, as if God sent an angelic choir to celebrate the faithfulness and the homecoming of His loyal servants.

Steeped in generations of horrific hand-to-hand combat, combined with the heightened memory that tends to characterize verbal cultures, the Waodani display an amazing capacity for remembering the details of battles. Lengthy conversations among the Waodani often consist of show-and-tell descriptions of spear and machete scars and gruesome minutiae of the deaths of enemies. But it wasn't until years later, after the death of Rachel Saint, Nate's sister who had come to live among the Waodani and bring God's Word to them, when Steve Saint heard the full story of the raid. Reminiscing by a fire late at night, the aging warriors gave an account of the event, still amazed that the white men had done nothing to defend themselves. Steve learned that Mincaye, who had since become a father to him, had actually been the one who had dealt the deathblow to his father. As soon as he knew, Steve realized it didn't really matter. What mattered was that God had used an amazing mixture of spiritual weapons, including the deaths of five servants, to defeat the power of fear and violence that had kept the Waodani captive as far back as they could remember.

In his book, *The End of the Spear*, Steve reports that he has been frequently asked over the years about the struggle he must have experienced to forgive those who had taken his father from him. He has always responded that it was never a struggle for him. Even to his grieving five-year-old mind, the death of his father and friends had been a part of God's plan. You don't have to forgive someone whom you have never held responsible for an act.

True to the Maker and Mover behind the scenes, the story of the Waodani displays God's ways. Those who were once the impossible-to-reach are now taking their place among those who reach out. Believers among the Waodani have suffered for Christ and at least one has experienced martyrdom. Their long history with violence makes them keen observers of the state of the "modern" world, where the increasing fascination and practice of hatred, violence, and killing appear all too familiar for those recently freed from that life of despair. God's deeper purposes take time to come to light. Occasionally, those who are paying attention get to see those purposes shine and are amazed.

Esther John (1929–1960)

Esther John was born in British-ruled India with the Indian name of Qamar Zia. She was educated in a Christian school where Bible reading and her teachers' vibrant faith led to her conversion as a teenager. When Qamar gave her heart to Jesus Christ, she began a life of service and growth in which each new day was a gift.

When India was partitioned, Qamar moved with her family to Pakistan, where she was pledged to a Muslim husband. Unwilling to accept this family decision, Qamar fled to Karachi. There she found a missionary, Marian Laugesen, who provided a Bible, encouragement, and a job working in an orphanage. At this time Qamar took the name *Esther John*.

Still under family pressure to marry, Esther relocated to Sahiwal, where she lived and worked in a mission hospital under the protection of Pakistan's first Anglican bishop, Chandu Ray. In 1956 Esther enrolled in the United Bible Training Centre. Completing that course of study, and well aware that her faith was not something her family could ever accept, Esther moved to Chichawatni, thirty miles west of Sahiwal. She lived with American Presbyterian missionaries and took up evangelism among rural women, teaching them the Scriptures and working alongside them in the fields. Her life had taken on a second dimension of danger through her evangelism.

On February 2, 1960, Esther was brutally murdered in her bed in Chichawatni. No investigation was conducted; no one was indicted for taking her life. She was buried in a Christian cemetery in Sahiwal. As a tribute to this brave woman, a chapel bearing her name was built on the grounds of the hospital where she had worked. Although her life was suddenly taken away, it still impacts the Christian community where she worked and lived, and she is remembered with devotion today.

Paul Carlson (1928–1964)

When trouble broke out in the Congo, Paul Carlson took his wife Lois and two children across the Ubangi River to the Central African Republic. When he left them there to return to the Congo, the missionary doctor with the Evangelical Covenant Church assured his family that he had several escape routes mapped out. He would leave if the Simba rebels got too close to the hospital at Wasolo, deep in the Congo where this family from California had lived for a year. Soon, on a radio contact, Paul told her, "I must leave this evening." It was not soon enough.

In 1960, Belgium had suddenly granted independence to its diamond-rich colony, the Congo. No government had mastered its terrain and tribal differences, and now, in the early fall of 1964, a rebel movement called the Simbas had captured Stanleyville (Kinshasa) and were moving to consolidate their gains. Carlson feared for the safety of his family and his patients at the eighty-bed hospital in this jungle town "at the edge of the world."

Paul Carlson did not fit the profile of a hero. A quiet man deeply committed to healing, Paul was a graduate of North Park College, Stanford University, and the George Washington University medical school. Then he signed up with the Christian Medical and Dental Society for a six-month term in the Congo. That was 1961. The African service appealed to him, but he had a young family and had planned on a normal medical career; so back they went to Redondo Beach, California, to set up a practice.

Soon, however, he knew where his heart lay. "I can't stand hernias and hemorrhoids any more," he told a friend. Returning to the Congo in 1963, the family was stationed in Wasolo to care for 100,000 regional people and to help build the church.

A year later, on September 9, 1964, Paul was captured by Simba rebels. He was accused of being a spy, and transported 300 miles to Stanleyville as rebels negotiated for his release. Weeks went by while rebels made sport of killing foreigners. Paul was routinely marched to face a firing squad, blindfolded, kicked, pushed, and hit, but never shot. Ransoms remained unpaid. Tension mounted. Finally in mid-November, a joint command of

Paul Carlson gunned down in the Congo

American-supported Belgian paratroopers dropped outside the city in a daring effort to rescue diplomats and hundreds of other trapped expatriates.

That morning, Paul and fellow hostages at the Victoria Hotel were quickly ordered into the streets. Young Simba soldiers, eyes turned upward at the descending rescuers, guns turned level at the massed foreigners, went blank with fear and rage, firing indiscriminately into the hundreds huddled in the street.

Around him, children were falling, women were covering their babies, and men were bleeding and dying. A small group including Carlson at the back of the crowd saw their chance for escape and ran toward a house just past a seven-foot cement wall. Carlson arrived first and helped missionary Charles Davis over the wall. Then Paul grabbed for Charles's hand to pull himself over, but one of the Simba machine gunners fired a volley. Paul slumped to the ground dead.

Minutes later, paratroopers secured the house where the missionaries had taken refuge. Photographers documented Paul Carlson's riddled body lying in the street. *Time* and *Life* magazines featured his story—the self-giving doctor who almost got away. Paul was sure, however, where his true refuge lay. Earlier he had scribbled in his New Testament the date "November 24" and the single word "Peace."

The Paul Carlson Partnership still works to assist the people of Wasolo, and a memorial at North Park University in Chicago remembers the quiet hero who kept his humor and trusted his Lord during a too-short career as "Mongonga Paul," missionary doctor.

Watchman Nee (1903-1972)

Watchman Nee was unique, committed, controversial, and effective. Despite the ongoing controversy concerning his teaching and orthodoxy, the spiritual movement he founded in the 1920s—the Little Flock— certainly helped to stabilize Chinese Christianity during the Mao years and beyond.

Nee was born in 1903 into a family of teachers and evangelists. His mother named him Shi-Tsu, and later changed his name to "bell ringer" or Watchman. This was a sign of the work Nee would do: calling forth a vigorous Christian movement that contained elements of Pentecostalism and the Plymouth Brethren movement and was based on the teachings of English pastor Robert Govett and Theodore Austin of London's Honor Oak Christian Fellowship.

Following Nee's conversion at age seventeen, he taught that churches were properly organized geographically, one to each city. Nearly 700 churches eventually considered Nee their pastor-teacher. He emphasized the inner life: God speaks to each person's intuitive sense. He insisted that the eschaton, specifically the Rapture of the church (emphasized in John Darby's Plymouth Brethren teaching), would involve the pre-tribulation "taking up" of mature believers, while those who still need development must endure the Great Tribulation. These ideas and the call to disciplined faith were promoted in his teachings. A collection of these are found in books that are still known throughout the world: *The Normal Christian Life* and *Sit Walk Stand*.

In 1942, Nee took over management of his brother's chemical factory, hiring Little Flock members and channeling profits to the movement. In 1947, he became active in church planting and training Christian workers. He also became involved in migration evangelism, based on the church in Jerusalem in Acts 8. His work founded hundreds of house-churches throughout China. He sought to make the church in each city and village self-propagating, self-supporting, and self-governing.

Watchman was zealous, idealistic and studious, refusing to become a part of Chinese nationalism. When Chairman Mao came to power in China in 1949, Nee was considered an imperialist and was imprisoned on made-up charges of espionage, licentiousness, and stealing church funds. He was imprisoned up until just before his death when the officials released him so that they wouldn't be held responsible for it.

Commentators examining his writings and those of his followers (especially Witness Lee) are divided on Nee's strategy, biblical interpretation, and the eclectic mosaic of his sources on spiritual development. But no one questions Nee's commitment to Christ and the courage he showed throughout more than twenty years of persecution under Mao. He died a prisoner, yet free in Christ.

God used Watchman Nee's work in China to create a system of underground churches that have survived and grown over the past 35 plus years. Through the ministry of Watchman Nee, more than 150,000 people have come to follow Christ, and the number continues to grow through his ministry, the Little Flock.

"You can **help others** in proportion to what you yourself have suffered. The **greater the price**, the more you can **help others** ... As you go through the **fiery trials**, the testing, the affliction, the persecution, the conflict ... **life will flow** out to others, **even the life of Christ.**"

— Watchman Nee, who was imprisoned in China for his faith.

Wang Zhiming (1907-1973)

Killed by the Communist government, Wang Zhiming holds two distinctions. He is the only Christian executed during the Cultural Revolution to have a memorial built in his honor in China. Second, he is one of ten representative martyrs noted on the Great West Door of Westminster Abbey in London.

Wang was born in Wuding County, in the Yunnan region just a year after the first missionaries arrived there. He became a teacher in the Christian school and the pastor to the 2,800 Christians living through one of China's most difficult decades. The Cultural Revolution intended to remake China into a modern state by casting off all things ancient and traditional. Wang signed on to the Three-Self movement but refused to participate in the public denunciation meetings, claiming the hands that had baptized should not now berate and humiliate those same people.

In May 1969, midway through the Revolution, Wang and members of his family were arrested. Local Red Guards knew he was their critic. Wang's leadership in a "foreign religion" was public and therefore dangerous, they asserted. Wang waited four years in prison before his sentence and the spectacle of his own denunciation on December 29, 1973. He was executed at a mass rally in a stadium before 10,000 spectators. His last reported words were:

> "You should not follow my example." (A statement of humility, meaning that listeners should follow the example of Jesus.)

> "You should follow the words from above and repent." (Encouragement to follow God above all.)

> "In all your work, pay attention to cleanliness." (Be pure and holy.)

Wang's wife was held in prison for three years and two of his sons for nine years. A third son died while in detention. The Chinese government eventually recognized the wrong done to Wang Zhiming and paid a reparation of $250 US to his family—a paltry sum in relation to the value of a man's life. Meanwhile, the church in the Wuding area grew tenfold, as Wang would have wanted.

Minka Hanskamp and Margaret Morgan (1974)

Two nurses, one from Wales and the other from Holland, were conducting a leprosy clinic in Thailand. In 1974 the political situation worsened, and they were kidnapped by guerrillas and held for ransom. Overseas Missionary Fellowship was ordered to pay $500,000 US for their release and to write a letter to the government of Israel supporting Palestinian rights.

Minka Hanskamp was a Dutch citizen who grew up in Indonesia. During World War II she and her family were sent to separate internment camps following the Japanese invasion of Indonesia in 1939. Minka saved many lives as a nurse in the camp and was reunited with her family after being released. She then went to New Zealand, where she attended Bible College. After graduating, she was accepted to serve with OMF in Thailand, where she worked both as a midwife and in a rural leprosy clinic.

When Margaret Morgan felt the call to missions, she was already a nurse. She took further missionary training at the Mount Hermon Missionary College. Then she sailed for Thailand, supported by the Tabernacle Baptist Church in Porth, Wales.

For eleven months Minka Hanskamp and Margaret Morgan were missing, presumed to be held somewhere near Pujud, Thailand. In March 1975, BBC radio reported two bodies had been found in the jungle, with evidence that one was Margaret. She had been shot five months earlier. A Malay informant confessed to killing the two women. The former insurgent reported to officials that when the women were told they were to be killed, they said calmly, "Give us a little time to read and pray."

Janani Luwum (1922–1977)

Janani Luwum was killed by the president of the Republic of Uganda, Idi Amin, on February 16, 1977. That same year the Christian church in Uganda marked 100 years of existence.

Janani Luwum was born in Northern Uganda and began his career as an ordained minister in the Anglican Church in 1956, in the Northern Uganda diocese. Later he trained in theology at St. Augustine College in Canterbury and at the London College of Divinity in the UK. He rose through the ranks from a priest to become archbishop. An active member of the East African Revival Fellowship since 1948, Janani is remembered as one who always told his congregations, "God does not have grandchildren. He only has sons and daughters." He always urged people to have a living personal relationship with God through Jesus and not depend on one's parents' faith. The East African Revival also taught, and Luwum certainly believed, that God is never absent, no matter how difficult life becomes. When Luwum was accused of treason—death sure to follow—he replied to Amin, "We must see the hand of God in this."

Luwum became archbishop of the Anglican Church of Uganda, Rwanda, Burundi, and Boga-Zaire in 1974. Trouble started when he began criticizing the gross human rights abuses perpetrated by the Amin regime, including public executions, disappearances, and expulsions. Property was regularly confiscated without due process. As head of the Church of Uganda, Luwum publicly confronted this lawlessness in the pulpit. Very few critics of Idi Amin who did not flee for their lives survived his eight-year reign of terror.

After Luwum was killed, his family and some of the bishops of the Anglican Church fled the country, but his death certainly strengthened opposition to Amin's brutality. The church continued under intense persecution until two years later in April 1979, when the regime fell to a combined force of Ugandan rebels and the Tanzanian troops.

Life was cheap in Idi Amin's Uganda. People lost their lives for small things such as having a nice car or a beautiful wife. These were the ills

Janani Luwum had the courage to say were against the will of God. Today he is honored as one voice crying in the wilderness when few dared to speak out. His sacrifice is remembered every February 17. The Church of England recognizes him as a martyr of the twentieth century, and a statue in his honor was erected on the front of Westminister Abbey in London. In Kampala a street is named after him.

Chester A. "Chet" Bitterman III (1952–1981)

Chet Bitterman went in with his eyes open. He knew that sharing the gospel could be costly. It could cost everything. But he willingly went to Colombia to bear the Good News. "... I find the recurring thought that perhaps God will call me to be martyred for Him in His service in Colombia. I am willing." Chet penned those words in his diary before he and his wife Brenda arrived in Colombia. Chet's devotion to his Savior was evident: "I am willing."

When the gunmen came into the Wycliffe Bible Translators guest house in Bogotá, Colombia early the morning of January 19, 1981, they were looking for the mission's leader, a more high-profile hostage whose captivity could somehow help their cause. Who they got instead was Chester A. Bitterman III, "Chet" to his friends. The next day President Ronald Reagan took the oath of office, and American hostages left Iran after 444 days in captivity. Their ordeal was over, with Chet and Brenda's just beginning.

Chet and Brenda hadn't been in Colombia long. Their mission career and their translation work lay before them. They had gone to language school and helped in various tasks for Wycliffe, including managing the guest house, serving as buyer for goods needed by mission workers and even as radio operator. Finally, it seemed God was opening the door for them to move into the jungle with the Carijona Indian tribe to begin language study and eventually translation work. In the days before M-19 terrorists kidnapped Chet, he had been scouring hardware and building-supply stores, stockpiling materials for their move to the Carijonas.

The terrorists' demands were twofold. First, they wanted their views printed in several of the world's leading papers. The second demand was that all Wycliffe mission workers be out of Colombia in thirty days, or Chet would die.

Wycliffe's stand was clear: The work God had called them to in Colombia was not complete, and they could not desert the effort. Chet wouldn't want them to leave with so many people still unable to read God's Word in the language of their heart.

Negotiations went on in fits and starts. Brenda and her two young daughters—one barely old enough to walk—waited and prayed and hoped. They prayed Chet would remember the Scriptures that he had faithfully memorized. The guerilas maintained their stance that Wycliffe must leave; Wycliffe agreed to leave when their translation work was done, more than a decade into the future.

His captors released a letter from Chet. His words carried not discouragement and worry, but an exciting sense of mission and possibility:

> "The Lord brought II Corinthians 2:14 to mind: "But thanks be to God, who always leads us in triumph through the Lord Jesus Christ." The word for "triumph" was used for the Roman victory parades, when the soldiers were received back at home by the cheering crowds after a successful battle ... I have had a lot of free time to think about such things as Daniel's three friends ... and Paul and Silas' experience in the jail at Philippi.

> "In the case of Daniel's friends, God did something very unusual through His power for a specific purpose, so that through everything, all concerned would learn (i.e. have their misconceptions corrected) about Him. The result of the experience was that everyone learned who He was. Remember Paul and the Praetorian Guard. Keep this in your thoughts for me. Wouldn't it be neat if something special like this would happen?"

Brenda was thrilled to see that her prayers were being answered. Chet *was* remembering the Scriptures.

Even as he was held hostage, the Lord's work was being accomplished. Colombian media reports about Wycliffe's work included reference to the gospel message and shed a positive light on Christian workers. Bible verses Chet had mentioned in his letter were printed in Colombian newspapers. The Word was going out.

On the morning of March 7, 48 days after Chet's abduction, his life was ended by a bullet to the chest. His body was left on a bus. A sedative in his blood suggests he may have felt no pain.

And still the message went out, even after his death. A radio interview with Chet's parents was broadcast numerous times across the country. "I'm sorry I won't see Chet again in this life," Chet's father said, "but I know I'll see him again in heaven." He went on to say how much Chet loved the Colombian people. Chet's mother said that even though her son had been killed, she still had love for Colombia and its people. "We're hoping the guerrillas come to know God," she said.

Chet was buried at Lomalinda, the Wycliffe base where he'd lived and worked. His burial, in Colombian soil, carried its own message of his love for that land and its people.

At memorial services around the world, men and women stepped forward to answer God's call to full-time service, to take Chet's place on the dangerous front-lines of ministry work. Applications to Wycliffe skyrocketed in the months after Chet's death.

Wouldn't it be neat if something special like that would happen? Chet's words carry the echoes of prophecy. Something special did happen. God's Word went forth; people's hearts were touched and changed. Through one man laying down his life for his Savior, many lives were changed. The avalanche of blessing and ministry began with three words: "I am willing."

Yona Kanamuzeyi (1994)

In the spring of 1994, the rolling hills of Central Africa's tiny Rwanda became a killing zone. Nearly 8,000 people died each day in the 100 days of horror, which was sparked by the death of the country's president in a suspicious plane crash. Stories emerging from that chaos were some of the most brutal ever told. The Western world watched from New York and Brussels and London, debating the meaning of the term "genocide," while Hutu militia, called the Interahamwe, used machetes and clubs to kill their Tutsi neighbors.

The Hutu did not turn to violence against the Tutsi overnight. A history of animosity and jealousy, fueled by tribal privilege bequeathed by German and Belgian colonizers, had simmered for decades, with occasional small bursts that would erupt into full force by 1994. Yona Kanamuzeyi was caught in one of those bursts.

Of his birth and early life we know nothing, not an uncommon circumstance for rural Africans who frequently date their birth around seasons and record their lives in oral history only. Only Yona's death is a matter of historical record, and that might also have been lost but for the mention of his name in the book of modern martyrs in St. Paul's Cathedral in London.

Yona was born to a mixed marriage, Hutu and Tutsi, and raised in the Christian faith. Eventually, he served as pastor (deacon) in the Nyamata district of Rwanda, where he was responsible for twenty-four churches and about 6,000 members.

In January 1994, ethnic violence erupted, following an incursion of Tutsi forces from Rwanda's neighbor, Burundi. Because Yona provided sanctuary and aid to fleeing Hutu, he was identified as a sympathizer and marked for execution.

During the night on January 23, five Rwandan soldiers arrived in an open jeep at Yona's residence, demanding that he come with them for questioning. Two other people were also taken into custody. Aware of the trouble behind the soldiers' benign words, Yona took along his journal in which he scribbled, as the soldiers' intentions became clearer: "We are going to heaven."

Yona asked the other two prisoners about their salvation, then altogether they began to sing, "There is a happy land ... where saints in glory stand."

As the jeep arrived at the military encampment, Yona asked the sergeant to return his diary and money to his wife. The man replied, "You had better pray to your God." Yona did, with these words:

> "Lord God, You know that we have not sinned against the government, and now I pray You, in Your mercy, accept our lives. And we pray You to avenge our innocent blood and help these soldiers who do not know what they are doing."

Yona was tied up and marched to a bridge, where he was shot. His body was dumped into the river. Yona's friend, Andrew Kayumba, also tied and ready to be shot, was instead driven home with a stern warning to never speak about Pastor Yona's execution. Kayumba escaped from Rwanda. He told what he had seen and the prayers and songs that had given Yona comfort as he faced his martyrdom.

"There is a **happy** land ...
where **saints** in **glory** stand."

— Vona Kanamuzei

Abram Yac Deng (1998)

The Bible was small and barely holding together, but it effectively delivered God's Word through the preaching of Abram Yac Deng. With only minimal training, he faithfully shepherded his large congregation near Turalei, Bahr El Ghazal Province in Sudan. He taught the church of 400 Sudanese with the only Bible of the entire congregation. Although many of the people were illiterate, his desire was to provide literary classes for men, women, and children. When a Christian ministry brought in hundreds of Bibles, Abram was thrilled that every member of his congregation would have access to the Scriptures.

Four days after receiving the Bibles, radical Islamic raiders invaded the village. Abram was shot in the head at close range, killing him instantly. The church was torched and many people made it out just in time. Almost one hundred villagers were killed that day and many people were kidnapped and forced into slavery. The newly delivered Bibles that brought them such hope and joy were destroyed in the fire.

One of Abram's favorite verses was Romans 6:23, "For the wages of sin is death, but the gift of God is eternal life in Christ Jesus our Lord." Today, Abram is reaping that free gift in eternity.

By Western standards, the possessions of a Sudanese family would be considered scant and primitive. The grassroofed "tukel" they live in contains almost nothing of value. But it is not for earthly possessions that these brothers and sisters are willing to make such great sacrifices: It is for what they will possess in heaven. They will someday experience the promise of Hebrews 10:34, "For you had compassion on me in my chains, and joyfully accepted the plundering of your goods, knowing that you have a better and an enduring possession for yourselves in heaven." The price that Sudanese Christians pay is very high, but their reward will be great. It is this "better and lasting" possession that gives them courage to withstand such brutal assaults on their faith.

Antonio Revas (1998)

The sound of gunfire echoed down the hall in the early morning hours of January 23, 1998, waking the Revas family. Wearing sombreros, army fatigues and T-shirts, a small squadron of the FARC guerrillas (the Revolutionary Armed Forces of Colombia) armed with revolvers, Uzi machine guns, and AK-47 rifles burst through the door. They demanded to escort Pastor Antonio and his oldest son, twenty-two-year-old Roberto, to a meeting with one of the local FARC commanders. Pastor Revas and Roberto kissed and hugged their families goodbye for the last time.

At the time, Revas's wife, Rosa, wasn't worried or fearful. The men had visited her home before, demanding that her sons join the rebel movement. She began talking with the men and told them she needed to dress Roberto before he left for the meeting. While in an adjacent room, Rosa quietly whispered her suspicions to Roberto. Roberto assured his mother that he would be all right, reminding her of God's continual presence.

Rosa, along with her daughter-in-law and several of her children, waited all night for Antonio and Roberto to return. When morning arrived and the two men were still absent, Rosa's daughter-in-law and two grandchildren headed out to search for them. Not long afterward, they returned shouting, "Mom, we need some sheets! We need some sheets! They've been shot! They've been shot!"

Only one block from their home, Antonio and Roberto had been shot and killed. One bullet had pierced the back of Roberto's head. Pastor Antonio had been shot in the back of his neck and through his forehead.

Why did the FARC guerrillas target Antonio and Roberto Revas? The family had stood up to the guerrillas on many occasions. When the guerrillas would come to the house and demand that their sons join their Marxist movement, Antonio and Rosa would refuse, explaining that they were born-again believers and did not support Marxist ideology.

Pastor Antonio Revas also refused to make the payments required of all the farmers, quoting the book of Malachi 3:8, saying the tithes go to the house of the Lord and not to the rebels.

Even after these deaths, the FARC guerrillas weren't finished with the Revas family. Shortly after the assassination of Pastor Antonio and his son Roberto, the FARC guerrillas occupied the Revas's farm and seized their harvest. The Marxist guerrillas kidnapped Rosa's younger son Juan. Juan failed to return home after several weeks, so Rosa traveled into town to meet with a known leader of FARC.

Snarling in disgust, the man pulled out a revolver, looked Rosa in the eye and said: "You don't need to be asking about your son. You don't need to be telling anybody where he is. And if you tell anybody that he's gone, you're going to suffer the consequences."

Rosa and her family were eventually driven from their land. They are now living in a small house in another village, far from their ancestral home.

The Revas family stood strong in the Lord. Pastor Antonio and Roberto suffered for Christ and gave up their lives for His name's sake. The impact of their lives continues in Colombia and across the world.

For none of us **lives** to himself,

and no one **dies** to himself.

For if we **live**, we **live** to the Lord;

and if we **die**, we **die** to the Lord.

Therefore, whether we **live** or **die**,

we are the Lord's.

Romans 14:7–8

Graham Staines (1941–1999)

Raised in Queensland, Australia, Graham Staines took his medical skills to a leprosy hospital in Orissa State, India. His wife was a nurse and they had a daughter and two sons. Along with his medical work, Graham participated in evangelistic crusades, notably the *JESUS* film campaign in the predominantly Hindu area where they lived.

In January 1999, Staines was conducting a five-day open-air evangelistic "jungle camp" in Orissa. His sons, Timothy (nine) and Philip (seven), were with him. A few days later (January 23), after Graham and the boys had retired for the night in their station wagon, a group of militant Hindus attacked them with clubs and set fire to the vehicle. Trapped inside his car by the mob, the missionary died holding his boys, while rescuers were threatened by the mob to stay away.

Nearly four years later, the leader of the militants, widely known for his radical hatred of Christians, and twelve others, were convicted in an Indian court. In May 2005, the leader's death sentence was changed to a life sentence and the others were acquitted.

Graham Staines had been working for thirty-four years in India. K. R. Narayanan, president of India, denounced the "barbarous killing" of Staines and his sons. Lepers at the hospital operated by Staines's Evangelical Missionary Society buried the three victims two days after the killings. His widow Gladys and daughter Esther, consoled the mourners with their complete trust in God. All together they sang:

> There's not a friend like the lowly Jesus
>
> No not one, no not one.
>
> None else could heal all our souls' diseases,
>
> No not one, no not one.
>
> There is not an hour that He is not near us—
>
> No night so dark, but his love can cheer us.
>
> No not one, no not one.

Graham Staines and his sons Timothy and Philip

Later Gladys told friends and reporters that ten days before the killings she had been urged in prayer to give to Jesus all she had. She meditated and then tearfully prayed, "Lord Jesus, yes, I am willing. Take all that I have. I surrender them all to you."

Gladys remained in India to assist at the lepers' hospital before returning to Australia in 2004 for her daughter Esther's studies. She and Esther speak to each other in Oriya, the local language in Orissa. Most of her friends, she reports, are Hindus. The Evangelical Missionary Society continues to operate the leprosarium established in 1897. She was given a civilian award from the Government of India in 2005, which aroused protests from right-wing organizations in the country.

PART THREE

Modern Martyrs in the Twenty-first Century

Most assuredly, I say to you,

unless a grain of wheat

falls into the ground and **dies**,

it remains **alone**; but if it dies,

it produces **much** grain.

He who **loves** his life will **lose** it,

and he who **hates** his life in this

world will **keep** it for **eternal** life.

John 12:24-25

The Modern Martyrs

Yesu Dasu (September 11, 2000)

They were avoided by people from India's higher castes. These *dalits*, the so-called "untouchables," were the lowest caste in the Hindu culture. To be a *dalit* is to be without hope for a future. Someone cared for them, however, and was willing to risk it all to help them.

Yesu Dasu loved the untouchables, and put that love into action by befriending and helping them. When others ran away, he came closer. He gave them back their dignity. As a mirror of Christ's love, the fifty-two-year-old Christian preacher came to bring healing to their souls.

The roaring of the motorcycle engine outside disrupted their quiet family dinner. As Yesu rose to look out the window, two men began pounding on the door. "Yesu Dasu," they shouted. "Open up! There is someone who wants to speak to you, and you must come with us now."

Yesu slowly opened the door and looked at the men. "Who?" he asked.

"There is no time to talk. You must come with us now," they responded. They grabbed his arm and ushered him to the motorcycle. Yesu's wife and children stared out the window as the motorcycle raced away. After putting the children to bed, Yesu's wife patiently waited for her husband to return. She read her Bible as she waited, and eventually fell asleep.

The morning sun streaming through the window awoke her with a start. She struggled to remember the events of the night before and why she had been sleeping in the chair. Filled with dread, she realized Yesu had never come home. Waking her children, she got them dressed, and together they searched the village for their father.

Yesu's wife heard her name called and looked up to see one of her village neighbors hurrying toward her. He wrapped his arms around her. "I'm so sorry" he said. "They found his body. He's dead."

Near a cattle barn on the outskirts of town, Yesu lay in a pool of blood, his head and other parts severed from his body. Four members of a radical Hindu group had tied his hands and cut him with an axe.

Yesu had been threatened numerous times by members of a radical Hindu group, and he had been warned not to preach in the area. But Yesu had ignored the threats. God had called him to preach, and he would answer that call.

He was a simple and humble man who served society and was respected by the villagers. His ministry to dalits, touching the untouchables, reflected his desire to reach all of God's people. Yesu Dasu not only preached the truth of Christianity, he lived out his faith. Through his life and work, many have come to know the Truth and now spend their lives ministering to others. Yesu demonstrated God's love to the least of those around him without regard for his own well-being. In doing so he earned the highest honor—a martyr's crown.

Liu Haitong (October 16, 2000)

"The government does not wish to create martyrs." The government official in Beijing, China, spoke privately and quietly. "They make religion uncontrollable." Perhaps this officer of a government bent on controlling and abating the growth of the church within its borders knew the effect of suffering and martyrdom upon the Kingdom of God: It expands it.

He might very well have been speaking of nineteen-year-old Liu Haitong.

Liu was a member of an underground Protestant house-church in the city of Jiaozuo in Henan Province. Because of Henan's thriving house-church movement, the province had been at the center of a two-year campaign by the government against unregistered church groups.

Police discovered and raided an underground worship service at a private home on September 4, 2000. Liu was targeted for his simple faith in Christ. He was arrested, taken into custody, and beaten.

"At any one moment," explained one underground house-church leader, "there are probably well over a hundred Christians detained for their faith and receiving severe beatings from sadistic policemen."

Liu was left without adequate food or provisions for hygiene. Within days he began vomiting and developed a high fever, but jail officials refused to provide medical care. On October 16, Liu died of injuries sustained during his beatings and from neglect.

Liu Haitong's death was "a bad mistake," according to government officials who want to suppress Christianity. Because of his faith and the faith of others like him, the Kingdom continues to expand throughout the country like a wildfire, unrestrained and uncontrollable by those who fear it.

Zhong Ju Yu (2001)

The family members of imprisoned Christian Zhong Ju Yu had been invited to a restaurant by the Public Security Bureau (PSB) in the city of Zhong Xiang, China. Zhong's family had waited for months for news of her condition, and had heard nothing. They hoped to learn something— any news of their loved one—from this meeting.

Their feelings were doubtless mixed as each of Zhong's family members entered the restaurant. Would she be released to them? Had she been killed? Would she be sentenced to death, as other members of her church group had been? What news would the PSB officers bring, those who arrested Zhong during a roundup of underground church members in May 2001?

Once inside the restaurant, the family was given an equivalent of $8,000 US by the PSB as they told them in cold finality of Zhong's condition: She was dead. The announcement came with the threat that anyone who shared publicly what had happened to Zhong would be arrested just as she had been.

Zhong had chosen to participate in an underground church because it was where she had found Christ. To fellowship with others of like mind and heart, to "contend earnestly for the faith," (Jude 1:3) became so crucial for her she was willing to risk imprisonment and death. Her fellowship didn't end with her arrest or even with her death. She now joins in fellowship with other saints who surround us as a great cloud of witnesses (Hebrews 12:1), cheering us on as we too run the race of faith.

"Jesus."

— The final word of Roy Pontoh,
a 15-year-old boy attending a Bible camp in Indonesia that was attacked by a Muslim mob. Roy was killed with a sword.

James Abdulkarim Yahaya (August 6, 2001)

James Abdulkarim Yahaya had grown up in a Muslim family in Nigeria, a country where fifty percent of the population follows Islam. He had fully embraced that religion and its Prophet until a few years before his death, when he decided to follow Christ.

Pastor Yahaya may not have read C.S. Lewis, but he fully experienced what Lewis described as being "seized by the power of a great affection." It was an affection he had never known or found in following Muhammad. James was seized by this affection and gave his life over to seeking and serving the Lord. His conversion was neither a subtle nor a quiet one. He became an itinerant preacher who traveled throughout the country preaching the gospel and the "fragrance of His knowledge in every place" (2 Corinthians 2:14). In his vital work he made, at the same time, many friends and many enemies. There were, of course, those for whom James was the aroma of Christ, but there were also those for whom he was the stench of death. In a Muslim-dominated country, abandoning the religion of Muhammad to follow Christ is a dangerous venture. At the least it usually means rejection by family and community. In James's case, it also meant open hostility from fundamentalist members of his former religion, since Sharia Law states that anyone who converts from Islam must be killed.

On August 6, 2001, James had retired for the night to the bedroom in his apartment in Abuja, Nigeria's capital city. It was common for him to leave the apartment door open, as his roommate explained, "because of the unbearable heat and the poor ventilation." Four heavily armed gunmen burst into the apartment and shot the evangelist while he slept.

Christian leaders and friends throughout the country mourned James's death, but they also remembered the power and effect of his life lived fervently for God, and his desire for others to know the same "great affection." The fragrance of the knowledge of God still spills out, as his life and memory stand as a testimony to the love of God and the invitation of the gospel.

Emmanuel Allah Atta (October 28, 2001)

Praises echoed off the walls of St. Dominic's Church just before 9:00 a.m. on October 28, 2001. Catholics shared the church building with the Church of Pakistan, and the Protestant praise and prayer time was running late. Thus, the start of the Catholic service would be delayed.

Pastor Emmanuel Allah Atta had concluded his sermon on the importance of prayer during the turbulent times facing Pakistani Christians, when three terrorists forced their way into the church. They were dressed in black shalwars (a long, loose-fitting shirt common among Pakistani males) and armed with AK-47 automatic weapons.

One of the gunmen marched to the pulpit and ordered Pastor Atta to throw his Bible to the ground. "I will not!" insisted Pastor Emmanuel. He turned away from the terrorist pressing his Bible close to his heart. The gunman shouted, "Allah Ahkbar!" ("Allah is great") and opened fire on Pastor Emmanuel. He shot the pastor in the back, the bullet piercing his heart. As his body dropped to the floor, Pastor Emmanuel captured one last glance at the almond-shaped eyes of his precious four-year-old daughter, Kinza.

The radical Islamic terrorists opened fire on the congregation for six minutes, emptying more than 500 rounds. Fifteen of the seventy-five congregants attending the service perished in the attack, as well as a Muslim security guard standing watch at the church gate. The body of a two-year-old girl was found riddled with forty bullets, and one woman miraculously survived thirteen bullets piercing her arm and abdomen.

Shortly after the assault, Pastor's Emmanuel's wife Sarapheen publicly spoke of forgiveness for the attackers, stating that it was an honor and a privilege that her husband was chosen to be a martyr for Jesus. Little Kinza, who witnessed her father's death, simply said her daddy had gone to heaven.

U Maung Than (March 2002)

"You are of our blood, and unless you return to our traditions, I will take back your blood myself!" shouted the uncle of U Maung Than.

When Brother Than decided to leave his family's traditional religion and become a follower of Christ, he immediately became a marked man by his own family in his homeland of Myanmar. He was soon arrested and imprisoned on trumped-up charges. The military dictatorship used the uncle's hatred of Than's faith to sentence him to death.

In March 2002, Maung Maung and Kam Lian Ceu, two Christian friends of U Maung Than, came to visit and encourage Than, not realizing their friend was in prison. Maung and Kam learned of the seriousness of Brother Than's case, as well as the intense hatred against his faith in Christ. For two days the men diligently sought permission to visit him in prison but were continually rejected. On the third day, military police in that area finally allowed Maung and Kam to see Brother Than, but they were ordered not to speak to him.

After traveling with Than and the police escort to a nearby wooded area, Maung and Kim were surprised to receive permission to talk with Than. Before they could say anything, Than spoke first. He pleaded with them, "I am very glad you are with me. Please go to my area and share the gospel. This is our responsibility: that the gospel covers the entire neighboring area. You must be faithful unto death."

Suddenly one of the police shouted at Than, "You have said too much!" He drew out his pistol and shot Than in the head. The two Christian friends stared in shock and disbelief. The tears began to flow as they stared at the bloodied body of their dear brother in Christ. Than's friends were sternly warned to recant their Christian faith or the same would happen to them.

Brother Than's dying wish was for his friends to be "faithful unto death." With his sacrifice he proved qualified, on behalf of his Savior, to make such a request.

Mohammed Saeed (June 2002)

Mohammed Saeed was twenty-seven when he began searching for something spiritual outside of his family's Islamic faith. In that search, he attended an evangelistic healing festival with a sick friend in the nearby village of Bail Ahata, in his homeland of Pakistan.

Mohammed had never experienced anything like the Christian festival. He was amazed at the joyful spirit and the incredible healings that he saw taking place. The evangelists there prayed for Mohammed's friend. Days later, the friend was pronounced cancer free, and Mohammed was convinced he needed to discover more about this Jesus who had healed his friend. Soon he accepted Christ, was baptized, and started attending church regularly. He had finally found the joy and contentment he had never found in Islam.

Mohammed's faith grew and he became more vocal and aggressive in sharing Christ with others. In his neighborhood, he would knock on doors and pray with those he met. But his bold witness drew hostile reactions from some family, friends, neighbors, and even some church members who feared for his safety. He was now viewed by the Islamic community as an infidel, and co-workers and customers at the restaurant where Mohammed worked refused to eat food he had cooked or even touched. His parents and relatives wouldn't give him food or allow him to touch kitchen utensils. He lost his job, and his wife took their two sons and moved in with her parents.

In June 2002, four years after his conversion, a Muslim relative asked Mohammed to stop by his shop, saying he wanted to learn more about Jesus. Mohammed arrived at the shop carrying his nine-month-old son in his arms. The relative closed the door and urged Mohammed to return to Islam or he would be killed immediately. Mohammed stood firm, insisting he would not renounce Christianity. If necessary, he was prepared to die for Jesus. The relative pulled out a knife, stabbed Mohammed in the stomach, and slit his throat, lips and tongue. Later, Mohammed's infant son was discovered sitting in a pool of blood beside his martyred father's body.

Jesus said, "Do you suppose that I came to give peace on Earth? I tell you, not at all, but rather division. For from now on five in one house will be divided: three against two, and two against three. Father will be divided against son and son against father, mother against daughter and daughter against mother, mother-in-law against her daughter-in-law and daughter-in-law against her mother-in-law" (Luke 12: 51-53). Mohammed Saeed experienced these words in a most horrific manner. But he also experienced another of Jesus' promises: "He who endures to the end will be saved" (Matthew 10:22).

Martin Ray Burnham (June 7, 2002)

"If I have to go, I want to go out strong for the Lord." Those were some of forty-two-year-old Martin Burnham's last words before he was killed.

It was supposed to be a relaxing and romantic time, celebrating their eighteenth wedding anniversary at a beach resort in western Philippines, but it soon turned into a nightmare. Abu Sayyaf, a Muslim extremist group, ransacked the resort and kidnapped the guests, including New Tribes missionaries, Martin and Gracia Burnham. The hostages were threatened and forced to march with their captors through the steaming jungles, trying to avoid the Philippine army that was tracking them. Martin was forced to carry bags of rice through the rain. The months of being in captivity and trudging through the jungles had worn down his boots and he slipped often. Martin never complained. He picked himself up and kept walking, even offering to help others along the way.

Martin and Gracia refused to give in to despair. They spent their time in prayer, thanking the Lord for this opportunity to minister to the other hostages and to suffer for His sake. They led the group in singing inspirational songs, and Martin even tried to share the gospel with the guerrillas. Martin risked his life for Christ and His mission to help others.

After hearing of the capture, the Philippine army increased their search for the guerrillas. As they got closer, Abu Sabaya, the leader of Abu Sayyaf,

Martin Burnham sharing the Gospel with his killers

ordered his subordinates, "If the Philippine soldiers come any closer, I want you to kill the American missionaries." Bullets flew through the air between the guerrillas and the soldiers. When the smoke cleared, Martin Burnham and a Filipino nurse, Ediborah Yap, were dead. Gracia Burnham had a bullet in her thigh.

Martin Burnham wasn't afraid to die. During his time in captivity, he encouraged and strengthened the hostages, praying with and for them. Martin was thankful in all circumstances. While all of the hostages prayed to be released, Martin was also sending up prayers of thanksgiving. Both Martin and Gracia were steadfast in their faith. Despite all of the tremendous difficulties, they kept their faith in Christ.

Just days before his death, Martin felt the need to write a letter to his three children—Jeffrey (fifteen at the time), Melinda (twelve), and Zachary (eleven). He wanted to tell them how much he loved them, how proud he was of them, and how he desired for them to keep their faith no matter what happens. Martin gave the letter to Gracia; it was lost in the firefight, but was eventually recovered by troops who went back to look for it.

Martin Burnham was an example of generosity, love, and faith. He generously lived his life to share the gospel at all costs. As the news of his death and the story of his life were shared around the world, Martin's strong faith inspired Christians everywhere to share the ultimate gift of Christ's salvation. Gracia carried on that ministry, writing books and speaking to thousands. She and her family committed to pray for members of Abu Sayyaf to come to know Christ personally; they saw it as their own little "holy war." She encourages Christians around the world to go to war on their knees for the souls of Muslims, to carry on the work that her husband lived and died for.

Cornelio Tovar (August 17, 2002)

In many rural villages throughout Colombia, Saturday night is known as the "night of the assassins"—the night when those who oppose the Marxist rebel group known as FARC (Armed Revolutionary Forces of Colombia) are targeted for death. But the church members refused to cower in fear at the guerrilla threats, and the Christian and Missionary Alliance Church was packed with 300 worshipers who heard Pastor Tovar talk about staying focused on Jesus. He urged them to resist temptations and distractions and to remain steadfast in Christ. The praise and worship time was electrifying, and the attendees were filled with the Holy Spirit and determination, despite the danger outside. No one was worried—the FARC guerrillas had not made any threats against Pastor Cornelio or any of the leaders of his church.

It was a sweltering night in Algeceris, Colombia, as Pastor Tovar and his wife began the familiar walk home after church. They traveled with five other believers, full of excitement from the night service. They talked excitedly about the attendees at the service who had decided to accept Christ as Lord and Savior. Five blocks from the pastor's home, two men leaped from the shadows, and gunfire rang out in the night.

Panic and confusion reigned as people frantically ran in circles, trying to escape the gunfire that exploded all around them. When the gunfire ceased and everyone began to move around again, Pastor Cornelio Tovar's wife Nelly looked around and found her husband lying on the ground in a pool of blood. She fell down next to her husband's dying form, her anguished screams piercing the night.

As the two masked gunmen fled, Nelly closed her eyes in prayer asking the Lord to bless those who had violently attacked her husband. Later, as doctors tried in vain to somehow revive her husband in the emergency room, Nelly again lifted her eyes toward heaven asking, "Why is this happening to me? Please don't let this happen!" Like Jesus, Nelly prayed and asked God to "let this cup pass ..." (Matthew 26:39). She wrestled with God in that hospital, but peace came as she finally submitted to God, saying "Not my will, but Your will be done."

Nelly surrendered her emotions and her hopes to God's will, and He reminded her that one seed had to fall to the ground in order for the gospel to be spread. She knew her husband was the seed and he had been willing and ready to give his life for the gospel. She determined in her heart not to lose hope, but instead to work toward a bountiful harvest.

Although Nelly was probably not aware of the famous words of the third-century scholar Tertullian, his words continue to ring true: "The blood of the martyrs is the seed of the church."

Bonnie Witherall (November 21, 2002)

Operation Mobilization (OM) missionary Bonnie Witherall was up early on that fateful morning of November 21, 2002. Her husband Gary remained in bed, and she did her best not to disturb his sleep. It was not unusual for Bonnie to get an early start to get the tea and snacks ready at the clinic where she volunteered. But not long after Bonnie left, Gary was awakened by the persistent ring of the phone.

It was difficult for Gary to understand the frantic words he was hearing. But one thing was clear: something terrible had happened, and he had to get to the clinic right away.

When Gary arrived, he rushed up the stairs of the clinic building to the front door. He barged past the soldier by the door but was tackled by two other soldiers and forced into a separate room, away from the body lying on the floor—the body of his beloved wife. Sobs overwhelmed him, and he began to tremble as the realization sunk in—Bonnie was dead.

Bonnie had been met at the clinic by a Muslim extremist with clear intentions. He mercilessly fired three shots into her head at close range. A man full of hate killed a gentle Christian woman who'd come to his country to share about love and forgiveness.

In deep anguish, Gary moved to the wall separating him from his wife of six years. He stretched out on the cold tile floor, pressed himself against the wall, and tried to get as close to her as possible. With tears streaming down his face, he felt as though his heart had been ripped from his chest as he mourned the death of his best friend and life partner.

Images of Bonnie's warm, sunny smile and sparkling eyes, her love and compassion for all people, floated through Gary's mind. He remembered her serving in the clinic, giving pre- and post-natal care to Arabic refugee women. He remembered how diligently Bonnie had worked to learn the Arabic language but still struggled with certain words and expressions and was often lovingly teased by her patients. She had spent many nights in tears for these women whose religion kept them in bondage with very little compassion or hope. Gary and Bonnie had prayed daily for the clinic to meet not only short-term physical needs but also the deeper, spiritual needs of these lost adn suffering women. Bonnie's sole desire was to bring them the message of eternal life, love, and hope.

Only a year-and-a-half earlier, Bonnie and Gary had begun serving the Lord in Sidon, Lebanon. They quickly saw God's plan in action as they worked together to share Christ and to love the Lebanese.

Bonnie and Gary made a great team. She was peaceable, fun-loving, and a perfect counterpart for her unconventional husband. Gary was a seemingly fearless, out-of-the-box evangelist, who would spend his days roaming the streets of the noisy, busy town, building relationships with his predominantly Muslim neighbors and taking every opportunity to tell them of his God—a God who was merciful, loving, and forgiving; a God who could be known.

As the pictures of the past surfaced, Gary found a song running through his mind. He and Bonnie had sung it often.

> I surrender
>
> All to You, all to You.
>
> I surrender
>
> All to You, all to You ...

In that moment, the Lord comforted Gary with these words: "A seed has been planted in your heart today. It is a seed that will turn either from anger to hatred or from forgiveness to love. You need to choose."

Instantly, Gary chose to reject the temptation to hate his enemies and seek revenge on his wife's murderer. Instead, God gave him an unprecedented opportunity to appear live on television across Lebanon and proclaim forgiveness for the assassin from himself and from God.

At Bonnie's funeral, Gary addressed the crowd: "I know we are all very sad, and we all miss Bonnie. But Bonnie is not in a box! She is in the presence of the God she loved and died serving. She isn't sad or afraid or in pain; she is dancing and rejoicing in heaven. We should be celebrating for her!"

Gary opened the huge curtains at the front of the sanctuary. As they were drawn back, the room was flooded with light, and there, framed in the picture window, was a magnificent view of Mount Baker, snow-capped and dazzling in the sunlight. Though mournful at first, the ceremony became a celebration of Bonnie's life, a time of giving glory to her Lord and Savior.

The service formed a picture of Gary's emotional and mental decision. He was choosing to look past the dark, physical curtain and to focus instead on the glorious beauty of the spiritual realm. It hinted at the reality that persecuted Christians seem to understand better than most. Sharing in Christ's sufferings and being found worthy to be beaten, imprisoned, or even killed for His sake is not a tragedy, a punishment, or an accident. Instead, it is the greatest privilege that a Christ-follower has. Neither is such sacrifice wasted in God's eyes, but it is rewarded in eternity with a glorious crown of life!

Bitrus Manjang shot by Muslims

Bitrus Manjang (December 2002)

She could hear the continued gunfire and screams everywhere as she frantically searched for a place to hide, the tears freely flowing down her cheeks. Feeling helpless and afraid, she huddled behind a door, waiting for her turn to die. She covered her ears so she couldn't hear the screams echoing down the street and prayed, "Lord Jesus, help us."

Eventually it was quiet. Garos Manjang slowly crawled out of her hiding spot and made her way to the front door, where she last saw her husband alive. Opening the door she looked out onto the destruction—people walking the streets in shock, bodies either hurt or dead on the ground, and numerous houses destroyed. Looking down the stairs, she saw her husband, sixty-nine-year-old Bitrus Manjang, lying next to his car, keys beside his still body. Garos became dizzy and quickly sat down.

Bitrus Manjang was a well-known Nigerian church leader who retired five years earlier as senior pastor of the three-million-member Church of Christ. He was a gifted evangelist and had helped translate the Bible into several Nigerian tribal languages. Although retired, he was still actively involved in the church and continued to attend numerous church meetings.

The day of the attack, Pastor Manjang had graced several church meetings about thirty miles away. He returned home and hurriedly made his way up the front porch steps toward his beloved wife. He had a wide smile on his face as he wrapped his arms around her and kissed her. Realizing he had left some materials in the car, he took the keys out of his pocket and made his way back to the car.

Garos watched in horror as a mob of Fulani Muslims approached and opened fire on her husband. She saw his blood splatter onto the car and watched the keys slip out of his hands as he fell to the ground. In fear for her own life, she turned and ran.

By the time the Islamic extremists finished raiding the village, nineteen people were dead, and eighteen injured. One hundred twenty-six homes were destroyed; but not the faith of the people. Despite the loss, the church grew stronger.

Garos and the other Christians could have been angry and bitter at the militants and even with God. But just as Jesus had forgiven her, Garos chose to forgive her husband's murderers. She knew that the Islamic extremists believed they were doing their God Allah a service, but they did not know the Father or His Son Jesus. She prayed that they would come to know Jesus and become His followers.

On the day he was killed, family and friends were preparing a party to mark the fifth anniversary of Pastor Manjang's retirement. They didn't plan a time of mourning, but a time to celebrate his ministry and life, a life finished on Earth but now continuing on in heaven with Jesus. They mourned their loss, but they celebrated the pastor's eternal victory.

For I **determined** not to know anything among you except **Jesus Christ** and Him crucified.

1 Corinthians 2:2

Rev. Jose Juan Lozada Corteza (January 27, 2003)

In 2001, the Revolutionary Armed Forces of Colombia (FARC) guerrilla commander Mono Jojoy announced that all evangelical ministers in the country would become targets due to their resistance to the group's movement and ideology. Within five years of Jojoy's announcement, more than 100 pastors had been killed. Largely as a result of its activities and those of the smaller ELN (National Liberation Army) and the paramilitary group known as AUC (United Self-Defense of Colombia), pastors who continue to bring the gospel to Colombia live under constant threat.

Well aware of the danger of his ministry, Rev. Jose Juan Lozada Corteza continued to follow Christ in the calling he had been given—to shepherd the Lord's people in a war-torn nation of unrest, uncertainty, and suspicion. He served as the pastor of the Evangelical Christian Church in the small town of San Antonio in the central Colombian state of Tolima.

On January 27, 2003, Rev. Lozada was traveling on a public bus between his home in San Antonio and Chaparral, a city farther south. Uniformed men suspected to be a part of FARC stopped and boarded the bus. Scanning the faces of the passengers, they landed on the clergyman and a member of his church traveling with him, singled them out, and forced them off the bus.

From inside, the passengers watched in horror as the assailants dragged the men to the side of the bus and shot them both in the head.

As a pastor, Rev. Lozada was targeted by the guerrillas for both his resistance to their ideology of corruption and extortion, and his insistence that the Lord God is the source of life and power. The FARC learned quickly that young people reached with the gospel message of love and peace could not be recruited into their violent cause, and they acted violently to shut up—permanently—any witnesses for Christ. Lozada's death backfired for his killers, for as a martyr Lozada's life and death stand as an unshakeable testimony to the truth of the gospel and of the life found in a relationship with Jesus Christ.

Sunday Madumere (April 22, 2003)

"We are not surprised at all about this incident," said Bishop Nyam of the Church of Nigeria. "We saw it coming."

It was a peaceful April night when Pastor Sunday Madumere and his family were suddenly awakened by the strong smell of smoke. Pastor Sunday looked around the room but could hardly see anything. His eyes filled with tears from the smoke as he crouched to the ground and crawled toward his wife. His breathing became heavier, his vision blurred; finally he collapsed to the floor.

Pastor Sunday was a zealous preacher in Nigeria whose effective ministry often angered Muslim militants. His powerful preaching led many Muslims to convert to the Christian faith. The militants found a way they could retaliate.

Madumere and most of his family died in the house fire. His son, Daniel, was the only one who managed to escape the flames. He survived, but he sustained serious injuries. It took over two hours for the Nigerian Fire Service to get the fire under control.

Similar incidents have happened in the northern part of Nigeria, where Muslim fanatics have killed numerous Christians and church leaders. Years before, a Christian man, Gideon Akaluka, was killed and extremists carried his severed head through the streets. The government appeared unable or unwilling to make a difference.

Christians in Nigeria are aware of the dangers they face daily. Though the number of those killed increases, so does the faith of surviving believers. The testimonies of those who have sacrificed their lives for their King gives His still-living followers courage to face the future, whatever it may hold.

Redoy Roy (April 23, 2003)

His purpose was to bring as many people to Christ as he could—to point them to the Savior. It didn't matter the danger. God had called him to this work, and he would follow to the end. So he packed up his belongings and began working in an outreach ministry with Campus Crusade for Christ in his native Bangladesh.

Redoy Roy walked quickly up the stairs to his home in the late evening of April 23, 2003, after being dropped off by the rickshaw. It had been a wonderful evening as he showed the *JESUS* film to almost 200 villagers. He loved to watch the audience and the beautiful expressions of fascination and hope that showed on their faces. And he loved even more when the film finished and some in the audience chose to follow this Jesus—their newfound Friend and Savior.

Redoy turned the handle, pushed the door open to his rented home, and made his way through the dark house. Before he could reach the light switch, he was hit in the face, being knocked to the ground. Angry radical Muslims grabbed him and dragged him over to his bed. A couple more held him down as they tied his hands and feet to the bedposts. Redoy screamed in pain as the men hit him repeatedly. The knives followed. Redoy uttered a final prayer and departed this Earth to spend eternity with his Savior.

Neighbors who heard the screams called the police, who quickly made their way to the scene. The police were eager to make an arrest, so they arrested the two Christians from the home where the film had been shown that night, as well as the rickshaw driver who had taken Redoy home from the screening. None of them had anything to do with the murder. But in the eyes of the police it showed "progress" in the investigation.

The murder came as no surprise to other Christians in the area. Several times Redoy had been threatened and told to stop showing the *JESUS* film. He refused to stop. He was willing to pay the price for using this tool to reach people with the gospel message.

The Christians could have gotten angry with the police and the murderers, but God has used the persecution to strengthen their faith. Just like Redoy Roy, they decided to be faithful to Christ's call, no matter what the cost. The ministry grew immensely. Many Muslims heard about the case and were curious to see the film that this murder victim had given his life to show. They wanted to know more about Jesus and how to follow Him. God used the attack to spread His word.

Redoy and his co-workers did not pray that the persecution would go away. They prayed that God would find them faithful. Redoy passed the ultimate test. And through his example, others committed to do the same.

Jamil Ahmed al-Rifai (May 6, 2003)

A smile spread across Jamil's face as he watched yet another person walk away with a New Testament in his hand and the Word of God on his mind. He tried to pray for each one—by name if he could—as they walked away.

The past ten days had passed in a blur. There were so many people in Lebanon who needed to hear about Christ, and Jamil was thrilled about the number of people he spoke with. He gave out almost 3,000 New Testaments! "After all that God has done for me, it's the least that I can do," he said. The highlight of his day was telling others about Christ. He was active in Campus Crusade for Christ, multiple Bible Studies, and evangelism. *God has really blessed me and provided for me the past few years*, he thought.

Jamil Ahmed al-Rifai grew up in a high-class Jordanian Muslim family. Just a few years earlier, he became a Christian through the ministry of *Trans World Radio*. When Jamil's family heard he was a Christian, they angrily told him that he was no longer allowed to live with them. Jamil packed up his belongings and left his family in exchange to follow Christ. He moved around several times, finally ending up with a couple, Anna and Frank Marsden, and their three children.

Living with the Marsden family was an incredible encouragement to Jamil. Frank was a powerfully anointed evangelist who spent his days sharing the gospel with neighbors or whomever the Lord brought to him while in town. Anna was a prayer warrior. She tended to the home and children and constantly took opportunity to pray for the place and people she loved. It was no surprise that they took in the twenty-nine-year-old Jamil when he approached them about living arrangements. He became a part of the family.

Two nights after Jamil finished handing out New Testaments at the Exhibition, Frank and Anna were reading in the living room. Anna looked up from her book and noticed that it was 11:30 p.m. She pulled herself out of the chair and got ready to go to bed. As usual, she looked in on the children on her way. The two younger ones slept in their parents' bedroom, and she paused to snuggle the blanket around one of them. As she turned away, a movement outside the window caught her eye. Looking out, she saw a man walking past the house, inside their garden. He turned the corner, and through the other window Anna saw him pass along the back of the house.

Rushing back to the living room, Anna alerted her husband, who hurried into the kitchen to investigate. Lifting the curtain, Frank too saw the man, who was now crouched down with his back to the door. The man tried to force open the door, but Frank quickly closed it. Then he and Anna summoned Jamil.

The two men returned to the kitchen and opened the door. On the patio, just a couple of feet from the door, was a bomb. With his bare hands, Frank attempted to extinguish the fuse; then he and Jamil tried to push the device away from the house. They were able to shift it to the opposite end of the patio, about six feet from its original position.

Thinking the immediate danger had been averted, Frank and Jamil quickly searched the property for the intruder. There was no sign of him, so Frank re-entered the house. "We need to call the police," he told Anna, leading the way into the hall. Almost before he had finished the sentence, a huge explosion rocked the house. If they'd been in the kitchen instead of the hallway, Frank and Anna likely would not have survived the blast.

Running to the children's rooms, they were amazed and relieved to see that all three of them were safe. Gathering them up, they hurried outside the house, where a crowd of onlookers was rapidly assembling. The police arrived and began to take control of the situation. But where was Jamil?

The rest of the night was spent at the police station, going over and over the events of the day, trying to make some sense of what had happened. They heard that a body was found in the garden, but it was some time before the awful realization dawned that it must be Jamil.

No one knows exactly what happened. Perhaps Jamil had simply been too late following Frank back into the house. Maybe he realized they had not been successful in extinguishing the fuse and was trying again when the bomb exploded. There was little doubt about what the motive was; a Dutch missionary said it was "almost 100 percent certain" that the attack was religiously motivated—an angry Muslim striking back at effective witnesses for Christ. Even in their grief, the couple realized that this was no surprise to God. Several people reported that they'd had prophetic dreams and visions in the weeks prior to the incident.

Perhaps the most significant was by a friend who saw a vision of Jamil in eternity. It was so powerful that he told Jamil about it, just a few weeks before the explosion, saying, "Jamil, I saw you in the presence of the Lord. I saw you in eternity! If this is going to be, that you will be with the Lord, what is your advice for us—what are the words that you are going to leave with us?"

With a rare opportunity to choose his epitaph, Jamil Ahmed al-Rifai answered with simple clarity, "Run the race; finish the race that I have started."

Reverend Wau (June 9, 2003)

Local Indonesian Muslims told him to stop holding church services. They warned of the danger if he continued his Christian activities. But Reverend Wau chose to ignore the warnings. He wasn't ashamed of his faith in Christ.

The day their threats were carried out started like any other Lord's Day. Reverend Wau led Sunday services in the morning, challenging and encouraging his fellow believers in their Christian walk. Afterward, he and his family spent a relaxing afternoon at home.

Around 5:00 p.m., a man knocked on the door. He didn't say much, only that he needed the pastor to go with him for a short while. Without saying much more, Pastor Wau picked up his Bible and followed the man out the door. When Reverend Wau didn't return home after a couple of hours, his wife began to worry. It wasn't supposed to take long. Also, aware of the many threats to her husband's life, she knew that being absent for that amount of time with someone they didn't know couldn't be good.

She asked her neighbor for help, and together they began searching for her husband in the surrounding neighborhood. After searching for several hours and finding nothing, they made their way home. As they neared the house, Mrs. Wau noticed something lying in the front yard. Running toward her house, Mrs. Wau began screaming as she realized that it was her husband's body. He was covered with bruises, and the deep wounds around his neck indicated that he had been strangled.

Reverend Wau knew the consequences of his very public faith and witness, but he had courageously chosen to speak about it to the people of Sumatra. He knew that every day he walked fearlessly with Christ was a day more people would come to know Christ and grow in their faith; he also knew that it was a day closer to the escalating danger. His last Lord's Day was truly the best one for him, as it was the day that he entered for eternity into the Lord's presence and heard the great welcome, "Well done, good and faithful servant."

Pastor Mariano Díaz Méndez and
Pastor Jairo Solís López (October 2003)

Mariano Díaz Méndez was a minister of the indigenous Tzotzil Evangelical Church in San Juan Chamula, a small town in the central highlands of Chiapas, Mexico. He was traveling near the village of Botatulan early on the afternoon of October 24, 2003, when a group of heavily armed men stopped his car. As a pastor in a tumultuous area, Méndez was well aware of the threat against his life and intimately familiar with the increasing attacks aimed against evangelical Christians from the *caciques*, or community chieftains, in the area.

Since Christianity's advent in the Chiapas Highlands in the 1960s, the caciques have used violent tactics to discourage its spread. Scores of evangelicals have died and hundreds more have suffered injury by groups who practice "traditionalist" religion, a semi-pagan mix of Mayan religion and Roman Catholic beliefs.

Pastor Méndez bolted from his car in an attempt to evade his attackers, but they overpowered him with their weapons, their bullets piercing his body and bringing the pastor to the ground. The assailants shot him to death.

The deadly assault against Pastor Méndez had occurred exactly one week after a pastor in the city of Mapastepec, namely Jairo Solís López, had also been killed by the caciques.

Both Pastor Méndez and Pastor López had given their hearts to serve Christ in the face of formidable challenges in Chiapas. Together, they embody what God promises in Revelation, that "they did not love their lives so much as to shrink from death"; rather, they overcame "by the blood of the Lamb and by the word of their testimony" (12:11).

Zhang Hongmei (October 30, 2003)

Mrs. Zhang Hongmei was thirty-three years old when she was arrested by local Chinese police in the village of Dong Maio Dong, China, for her Christian witness and for participating in so-called "illegal religious activities."

The afternoon of her arrest, October 29, police approached her family and demanded a bribe of 3,000 RMB (about $400 US) in order to release Zhang. The family was unable to raise the money, so later that day her brother and her husband, Xu Feng-hai, went to the police station to request her release. What they found there shocked them.

Zhang was bound to a bench with heavy chains. She was badly wounded and unable to speak. In spite of her deteriorating condition, police refused to let her go. Her husband and brother were forced to leave without her.

The following day, her family returned to the station where they were notified that she had died at noon that day. The autopsy report showed that she had died from internal injuries sustained from vicious beatings.

Affected by Zhang's life and outraged by her death, more than 1,000 people joined in a protest the next day in front of the city offices.

Zhang Hongmei was ready to die rather than deny Christ. In her life she touched many in her community. In her death she offered a challenge and example to believers around the world.

Mukhtar Masih (January 5, 2004)

Tears streamed down the aging cheeks of Parveen Mukhtar as she detailed the final days of her husband's life. She clutched her husband's Bible tightly in her hands as she told how her husband, Pastor Mukhtar Masih, had loved the Lord and wanted to share the gospel with all who would listen.

Pastor Masih had led more than 200 people to Christ during seventeen years of ministry in his homeland of Pakistan. He started a church in the year 2000. Though his church was small, Pastor Mukhtar was convinced that the fifty-member congregation would grow as a result of their morning prayer services each day. The services were broadcast throughout his predominantly Christian neighborhood via several loudspeakers atop the church steeple. Muslims blasted their calls to prayer into the streets of Khanewal five times daily; Mukhtar thought Christians should do the same.

The fifty-year-old pastor had studied the Koran and was prepared to discuss matters of faith and religious doctrine with Muslim scholars. He was a convincing debater and an effective speaker, and Muslim leaders grew disgruntled at his growing popularity among Christians and non-Christians alike.

One day, a Muslim mulvi (mosque leader) came to the church during the children's Sunday school. He demanded that they halt the Sunday school and immediately discontinue the loudspeaker broadcasts, saying the noise was interfering with the Muslim prayers. Church members tried to calm him, but he wouldn't listen and kept shouting angrily.

Pastor Mukhtar was then summoned to the police station after Muslims lodged a formal complaint against the church. He was told the loudspeaker boadcasts were too loud. Pastor Mukhtar apologized and willingly lowered the volume of the loudspeakers. Days later, some elderly Muslims came to the church and warned Mukhtar that he would be killed if he continued his loudspeaker evangelism. Mukhtar didn't fear death and continued the broadcasts.

The morning of January 5, 2004, Pastor Mukhtar Masih rose to catch a 4:00 a.m. train to Lahore. His eldest daughter, Esther, had been unable to visit for Christmas, and Mukhtar had made arrangements to go and visit her and his grandchildren. The morning air was cold and damp. A thick fog had settled in, making it very difficult to see. In spite of the conditions, Mukhtar slowly made his way down the winding roads leading to the train station.

The pastor was only a few blocks from the train station when his assailants appeared. Due to the fog, Mukhtar may never have seen them or even heard the first shot come ripping through the fog. Later that morning as the fog lifted, Pastor Mukhtar's body was discovered in a pool of blood. Beside him was his travel bag with clothing, a few of his possessions, and his Bible.

On Sunday, January 4, 2004, the day before his murder, Mukhtar preached his last sermon to his Church of God congregation. He urged his church family to love one another, pray regularly, and remain united. "I may not be among you for a long period; therefore, be united and be a congregation of faithful believers," said Pastor Mukhtar. He encouraged them to spread the good news of Christ just as the early church did after the resurrection of Jesus. The early disciples were told,

> "Remember the word that I said to you, 'A servant is not greater than his master.' If they persecuted Me, they will also persecute you. If they kept My word, they will keep yours also." (John 15:20)

Timeless words for those who follow Christ.

Sergei Bessarab (January 12, 2004)

The shots rang through the air and shattered the glass window of Pastor Sergei Bessarab's front room the evening of January 12, 2004. The first bullet hit Sergei's hand that was gently strumming his guitar while singing songs of praise to God. The second shot got him in the leg and the third in his chest, ending his life on Earth.

Pastor Bessarab's wife, Tamara, heard the shots and frantically ran into the room. She stared in disbelief at the scene before her—the shattered glass and blood spattered on the chair, carpet, and on her husband's guitar. She dropped to the floor to avoid additional bullets and began to sob as she lay next to her husband's body.

Tamara could smell the acrid scent of gunpowder as the gunman continued his rampage and fired into the house and at Sergei's car. Finishing his task, the gunman turned and fled down the narrow, dusty alley behind the house, disappearing into the darkness.

Suffering wasn't new for Sergei Bessarab, and he was prepared to die for Christ. Just five years ago, however, the idea would have been inconceivable. Bessarab had gone to prison five different times as a leader in Tajikistan's organized crime underworld. A fellow prisoner who had come to know Christ through a prison ministry began to minister to Bessarab as he served one of his sentences. This prisoner continually prayed that Jesus would become real to Sergei.

"Pray for someone else," Sergei would growl. "Don't waste time praying for me." But the man persisted and prayed every day that he would come to accept Christ as Savior and Lord. Finally, three years later, in August 2000, his prayers were answered. Sergei Bessarab began walking with the Lord and eventually began a Bible study in the prison. After his release in November 2001, he returned often to bring Christ's message to his former prison mates.

Sergei traveled all over the country. He was a passionate preacher with a great love for people. He planted a church in Isfara, a city in Tajikistan with no Christian presence but a strong, radical Muslim one. Accompanied by his wife Tamara, Sergei traveled to Isfara on Sundays to hold services; in early 2003 they moved to the city. The church began to grow, and new people were accepting Christ, but their ministry was not unnoticed by enemies of the gospel. A week prior to Sergei's death, the local paper carried the headline: "What's going to be done about Sergei Bessarab?"

Sergei's life for Christ was like an exploding star, burning hot and fast and spreading much light. Even after Bessarab's death, Tamara received numerous letters from prisoners all over Tajikistan. They had either heard Sergei speak or heard about the remarkable way Christ had changed his life. They were challenged to know God more, and to rely on Him.

Pastor Sergei Bessarab was a man of prayer. For two hours every morning and two hours every evening, he spent time with the Lord. He read his Bible, prayed, and sang praise songs while strumming his guitar. His favorite passage was John 12:24: "Most assuredly, I say to you, unless a grain of wheat falls into the ground and dies, it remains alone; but if it dies, it produces much grain."

Those four hours of prayer were the source of Sergei's continual spiritual fervor. In fact, in the weeks before his death, he had been asking the Lord to open up two more hours—in the middle of the day—for him to commune with God. God answered his prayer in a way no one expected—not just two more hours, but an eternity with Christ.

Before Sergei's death, he and Tamara prayed alone for Isfara, and then with a small group of believers in Tajikistan. One of their requests was that God would raise up an army on their knees for the city He had called them to. God answered Sergei and Tamara's prayer, using the death of one prayer warrior as a seed to raise up a bountiful harvest of prayers for Isfara from around the world.

Ahmad El-Achwal (January 21, 2004)

"When a person's faith is true, and they realize that their suffering doesn't go unnoticed by God, they see that they're doing something for the cause of Christ and furthering his kingdom...then they grow with more courage...and still the work goes on." These words, spoken by a West Bank evangelist, reflect the life of Ahmad El-Achwal of Palestine.

A cook at a Jerusalem fast-food stand and father of eight, Ahmad El-Achwal was born a Muslim. And in Palestine, if one is born a Muslim, he is expected to stay a Muslim or face the consequences.

While serving time in prison after the Palestinian Authority accused him of dealing in stolen gold, Ahmad met Christ. He was later acquitted of all charges, and word quickly spread of his newfound faith in Christ. But his decision to turn his back on Islam and embrace the One born in neighboring Bethlehem came with a generous dose of consequences, including one that would cost him his life.

Ahmad was repeatedly harassed and abused. Palestinian Authority security forces would search his home, confiscate his Bibles and Christian books, interrogate him for days and arrest and hold him for long periods of time. However, members of the Palestinian Authority promised him an end to his suffering. Their offer? Return to Islam. They would even give him a job—financial security for his wife and eight children. Ahmad rejected the offer, so the suffering continued.

The assaults intensified. Repeatedly, Ahmad was beaten. He and his family received threats to their lives. Men affiliated with the Palestinian Authority security forces fire-bombed his home. Then Ahmad's livelihood was threatened when the landlord of the fast-food shop he rented refused to renew his rental agreement. This forced Ahmad to work in distant Jerusalem.

In the face of the beatings, losses, arrests and threats, Ahmad kept professing his faith in Christ. His home was converted into an informal Christian center where he held Bible studies, handed out Christian literature and shared the gospel with others.

His body began to bear the scars of Christ (Galatians 6:17). Burns covered his body where hot pieces of sheet metal were pulled from a fire and held to his skin. But the Muslims' hatred of his faith in Christ and persistent witnessing soon went beyond torture to murder.

On January 21, 2004, Ahmad heard a knock on his door. Ready to greet his guest, he turned the knob and pulled the door open only to be met by a flood of bullets.

The persecution of Palestinian Christians has increased. Christians have fled the West Bank and Middle East due to political insecurity, economic adversity and human rights violations. In 1914, the Christian population in Israel, Syria, Lebanon, Jordan and the Palestinian Authority was 26.4 percent; and in 2006, it is less than 10 percent. Because Islamists dominate the Palestinian Authority, Christians are treated as second-class citizens in the Holy Land. Christians are forced, along with everyone else, to abide by Islamic laws and teaching.

However, many Christians have chosen to stay in the Holy Land during this era of turbulence and uncertainty. And for this they have, like Ahmad El-Achwal, paid dearly—even with their lives. But like the West Bank evangelist said, these brave believers know God has taken note of their suffering; He is the God who sees (Genesis 16:13). They consider it a joy, an honor, to bear His scars.

"... and most of the **brethren** in the Lord, having become confident by my chains, are much more **bold** to **speak** the word without fear."

Philippians 1:14

Pastor George Masih (April 2, 2004)

George Masih had been an elder in a Church of Pakistan congregation in Lahore. When he and his wife Aniata had felt called to relocate their family to the small, predominantly Muslim village of Manawala to plant a church, he willingly went.

For two years, Masih pastored the church based in his home. Filled with the love of Christ, he ministered house-to-house, reaching out to his neighbors and praying for the sick—even if they were Muslims. He and his wife became well-known in the village for the worship songs that could be heard pouring from their house. Their desire was to know God and to make Him known to those in their community.

Their work drew the anger of a Muslim neighbor named Shokat Ali. Ali was irritated by the Christian meetings in the Masih home, and urged the landlord to kick the family out. On more than one occasion Ali threatened to kill Masih if he continued preaching.

But Masih remained steadfast. Around noon on Friday, April 2, 2004, Masih, his wife and four children were watching the *JESUS* film in their home. When the movie finished, Aniata got up to go out of the house. When she opened the door, two masked attackers burst in. One grabbed Aniata and covered her mouth, threatening her with death if she tried to cry out for help. The other attacker fired a shotgun point blank at George Masih's face. As the Christian man lay dying, the assailant hit him in the head with the butt of the gun. Then both men fled, dropping the stunned Aniata to the ground. Neighbors ran toward the home when they heard Aniata cry. Shokat Ali was one of the few neighbors that did not show up to offer aid.

George Masih had an unbounded passion for the Lord God and a deep compassion for people. His mark upon the community was immense, as evidenced by those gathered for his funeral. Around 300 people crowded into his brother's home to remember Masih and express gratitude for his life, including many Muslims who had been blessed by his ministry. "He was a true and passionate believer," said Pastor Mukhtar, the man who led George to Christ, "and he always tried to win the souls with his preaching."

Pastor George Masih shot by Muslims

Samuel Masih (May 28, 2004)

"The blasphemy law in its present form has become more of an instrument of persecution and vendetta than of justice," a Pakistani newspaper editorial stated. Blasphemy means showing extreme irreverence toward something sacred, and for centuries Christians have been accused of blaspheming Islam. Often in Pakistan, contrived witnesses with false accusations have spoken out against believers, sending them to jail and even to death. Such was the case with Samuel Masih, whose body was found bloodied and battered, his skull smashed.

Samuel Masih spent his days as a whitewasher and painter. He had just finished one job and stopped at the local mosque in order to use the restroom. As he returned outside, bystanders grabbed him and shouted accusations. Samuel Masih's accusers, knowing he was a Christian, claimed that he had spit on the walls of a mosque; two false witnesses confirmed this story. Samuel was immediately arrested and put on trial.

Under the maximum penalty for violating Section 295 of the Pakistan penal code, Masih could have been jailed for two years and fined, if convicted of "defiling a place of worship with the intent of insulting the religion (Islam)."

The pungent odor of urine and sweat filled the dirty prison. The sounds of coughing and scuffling feet echoed along the walls. Just down the hall lay Samuel Masih, struggling to breathe and continuously coughing up blood. Although the head of the prison deeply resented his Christian prisoner, he sent Samuel to the hospital to treat his advanced tuberculosis.

During his stay in the hospital, there was a policeman posted near his bed. When Samuel should have been safely recovering, the horrible crime occurred.

Early one morning, the police constable entered Masih's room and swung the hammer down on Samuel's head. Bleeding profusely from the hammer wounds, Masih fell into a coma and was rushed to the emergency neurosurgery ward, where he died a few days later. The Pakistani police constable who took Samuel Masih's life claimed, "I wanted to earn a place in paradise by killing him."

"This is a case that brings out, like nothing else, the myriad contradictions that these [blasphemy] laws have infused in this state and society," a *Daily Times* newspaper editorial commented the day after Masih's death. "The fact is that it is a bad law both in its conception and its implementation, and the legislation has created a psyche that encourages vigilante behavior."

Samuel Masih was arrested for a crime he never committed. His only crime was following the call of the one true Savior, Jesus Christ. Masih's murderer thought killing him would earn a place in paradise. Samuel Masih, however, knew the one true way to get to heaven, through Jesus Christ, and he is with his Savior.

Jiang Zongxiu (June 18, 2004)

She was arrested for handing out Christian materials in a village marketplace. She was not a threat to anyone, certainly not a threat to the great nation of China. Yet thirty-four-year-old Sister Jiang Zongxiu would never taste freedom again. Instead, she was beaten until she died. It happened at the Public Security Bureau (PSB) office of Tongzi County, Guizhou Province—a neighboring province of her hometown.

The previous day, Sister Jiang and her mother-in-law, Mrs. Tan Dewei, went to the marketplace of Pusdu Town, Tongzi County. The women had been active in their local house-church for ten years and were distributing Bibles and other gospel tracts in the street. They were arrested by the local PSB, who bound their hands with one set of handcuffs on the way to the county detention center. Mrs. Dewei was kicked repeatedly during her interrogation. She noticed that Jiang's treatment was even worse. They took off Jiang's shoes and beat her. They told her mother-in-law they would beat her too if she didn't obey.

Both Jiang and Mrs. Dewei were accused of spreading rumors and "disturbing the social order" by the PSB. They were sentenced to fifteen days of "administrative detention." In the police report, they were described as having "seriously disturbed the social order by distributing Christian literature to the masses in the market."

In the early morning of June 18, they were taken to the Tongzi detention center. The police took their fingerprints and brought them to separate cells. Mrs. Dewei protested that they had not broken any laws and were being held illegally, but it didn't matter. Mrs. Dewei also remembered seeing a person's feet lying on a bed across from her cell, and officers later came in to take pictures. She asked an officer what had happened, but he told her it was not her concern.

Mrs. Dewei asked to see her daughter-in-law, but they told her that she was resting. When she inquired again, she was told Jiang was very sick and in serious condition. Mrs. Dewei kept asking to see her, but the officers refused and cursed her. Then without notice or explanation they released her. She again inquired about her daughter-in-law but Mrs Dewei was forced on the train back to her village. She learned of Jiang's death after she arrived home, and only then realized why they were taking pictures at the detention center and why they wanted her to leave so quickly.

The family received the autopsy report later that month. It stated that Jiang died of natural causes, of heart failure. There was no mention of her wounds from the beatings, no mention of the brutal treatment at the hands of a government that claimed to have freedom of religion. The family asked for a second autopsy. They were refused. They went to their local court to plead their case of how Jiang was beaten to death and were again refused. PSB officials then pressured the family to cremate Jiang's body, desiring to destroy any evidence of her murder.

The surviving members of Jiang's family naturally sought justice. They were not afraid of a government that persecuted its citizens for preaching the Gospel of Jesus Christ. They were shocked at the assault and murder of sister Jiang, a loving wife and mother.

The PSB killed Jiang because she was caught sharing her faith. How could a young peasant woman threaten the "social order" of China? A simple act of handing out Christian literature resulted in a brutal death.

Jiang's sister-in-law asked permission to take pictures of Jiang's body; permission was refused. So she rented a camera and sneaked in. From the pictures she took it was easy to see the wounds on Jiang's body, the scars on her neck from the beatings. It was clear that she was beaten to death. One PSB officer even told the family secretly that they didn't need another autopsy; that it was "easy to see that she was beaten to death."

Jiang's family sought justice, a justice that was not to be granted in this life. Jiang now joins the martyrs written about in the Book of Revelations. Her family joins in asking, "How long?"

> "When He opened the fifth seal, I saw under the altar the souls of those who had been slain for the word of God and for the testimony which they held. And they cried with a loud voice, saying, 'How long, O Lord, holy and true, until You judge and avenge our blood on those who dwell on the Earth?' Then a white robe was given to each of them; and it was said to them that they should rest a little while longer, until both the number of their fellow servants and their brethren, who would be killed as they were, was completed" (Revelation 6:9-11).

Mullah Assad Ullah (July 1, 2004)

The sun reflected off ripe fruit laid out in the market stalls in Ghazni Province, Afghanistan. Mullah Assad Ullah breathed in the clean air, thankful to God for the beautiful day. He made his way through the market, picking out ripe fruit and crisp vegetables. He loved the market, with the rush of people and the easy conversation. Some of those conversations had led to discussions of faith, discussions where Assad could quietly share that he was no longer a follower of Muhammad but of Jesus Christ.

As Assad stopped at the next booth and reached forward for some fruit, there was rushed movement behind him. Assad looked up and briefly saw the faces of his attackers before the knife swung across and slit his throat.

People in the market began to scream as the Taliban fighters dragged the now-lifeless body of Mullah Assad Ullah down the streets of the market. "This is what happens to Christians who seduce people, and to the people who listen to their teachings," the men shouted as a warning. "This is what happens to people who convert Muslims to Christianity." The Taliban even called the media to brag about murdering Assad.

Mullah Assad Ullah's passion was to tell people about the gospel of Christ. He spent his time getting to know people and living a life that reflected God's love. Of course, his family was a priority. Ullah made sure that his wife and four daughters, ages seven to fourteen at the time, were growing in their faith as well.

As a former mullah, Assad knew the Muslim law. He could speak knowledgeably about the Koran and Muhammad's teachings, which made his witness for Christ even more effective. He came to know Jesus Christ as Lord and Savior after receiving a New Testament five years before his murder. He was baptized secretly two-and-a-half years later under the brutal rule of the Taliban regime.

There were others killed not long after Assad Ullah. Each left behind a wife and children. They did not live in fear, nor did they die in vain. Their deaths have shown the power of Jesus and the strength of faith in Him, even in a land where so few choose Christ.

The men were accused of studying the Bible, praying in the name of Jesus, and converting people to Christianity. No better epitaph could be written for a follower of Christ than that he or she was "guilty" of those charges.

Susianty Tinulele (July 18, 2004)

At only twenty-six years old, Reverend Suianty Tinulele was one of the younger leaders within the Presbyterian Christian Church of Central Sulawesi, Indonesia (GKST). She had been ordained only two weeks and hadn't yet been assigned a permanent pastorate, yet she had already earned a reputation as an outstanding Bible preacher, a leader who would speak the truth in love, even if that truth was unpopular.

"Susi," as she was called by friends, was invited to speak at a nearby church, Efatah, that Sunday night in July. Nobody expected that it would be her last sermon. She was just finishing her sermon when the gunmen arrived— radical Muslims, their faces wrapped in black jihad masks, and automatic weapons in their hands. One of them stood in the entryway to the church and fired, blowing out the back of Pastor Susianty's head as she stood at the pulpit. Four other worshippers were also wounded in the attack; the gunmen fled on motorbikes and in a car.

Just two days earlier, Pastor Susianty had delivered food to an imprisoned pastor and encouraged him to remain strong in his faith. She was a vocal supporter of justice in the region, calling for Christians to receive fair treatment and equal protection from local authorities.

Her ministry and her life had just seemed to be starting; now both were over. She had been scheduled to be married only weeks later; now she would never be a bride.

Yet Susi's final sacrifice was not made blindly. Pastor Susianty knew that to stand up for Christ and for justice in Muslim-dominated Indonesia made her a target. Only the night before, a Christian woman living nearby had been stabbed to death in her front yard. Witness reports from that crime were very similar to the reports of the jihad bandits that invaded the church and left Pastor Susianty dead.

Pastor Susi's ministry seemed shortened to human eyes, but in God's eyes it lasted exactly the right amount of time. Her days had been numbered before the world was created; however, it is not the number that matters but how we use those days. Pastor Susi used her short time on Earth to build something for eternity.

Joseph Mondol (September 18, 2004)

It had been a long day at the pharmacy and the walk home for Dr. Joseph Mondol was a lengthy one. The night air was crisp and cool, and Dr. Mondol faithfully used this time in prayer. He would have been deep in thought when the men approached.

Dr. Joseph Mondol, a Bangladeshi pharmacist, had made the decision two decades earlier to leave Islam and follow Christ. He found joy in following Christ and wanted to bring glory to Him. He was known as a faithful follower of Christ in his village and often provided medicines to poor families without charge. He was a living example of God's love.

Mondol, who was still known by his former Muslim name of "Dr. Goni," was employed by the government health department and also had a small pharmacy of his own. He rose to leadership in the Bangladesh Baptist Fellowship (BBF), becoming secretary of one of the BBF districts. His area of responsibility included sixteen churches, made up almost entirely of former Muslims who had chosen to follow Christ.

At 9:30 p.m., on September 18, 2004, while walking home from his pharmacy, Dr. Mondol was passing under a Banyan tree when he was attacked by four radical Muslims. As instructed in the Koran on how to deal with Muslims who leave the faith, they slit his throat from one side to the other, almost decapitating him. His dead body was left lying on the road. The radicals thought they had silenced his witness for Christ.

The next day Dr. Mondol's wife Teresa buried her husband's body in the village over the objection of Muslim leaders who didn't want a memorial to the Christian martyr so close to their soil. Teresa stood firm, wanting her husband's grave to be a reminder and testament to Christians in the village that they need not fear being a witness for Christ. She hoped the grave would remind Christians in the village of the words of Christ, "Do not fear those who kill the body but cannot kill the soul. But rather fear Him who is able to destroy both soul and body in hell" (Matthew 10:28).

Francisco Montoya (December 8, 2004)

Squeals of delight from the children could be heard from down the street. Father Francisco Montoya was laughing with them, grinning from ear to ear. The local priest was performing illusions for the kids, reveling in the smiles that radiated from their faces. This was Montoya's favorite time of day.

Montoya called the kids closer and had them sit down as he pulled out his clarinet. The children sat mesmerized as the beautiful music pierced the air and touched their souls. The adults also gathered around and allowed the sounds to wash over them.

Putting down the clarinet, Father Montoya began telling the story of Jesus Christ. The people of Quibdó, Colombia, needed to hear the gospel message more than the music. God used the music to draw people closer and to open their hearts, and Montoya was now prepared to share the good news with them.

The next day, Francisco Montoya rose early to attend services and began his trek from Quibdó (the capital city of Chocó Department) to the village of Nóvita. He traveled on foot all around the region, carrying necessary belongings in a typical indigenous basket. The time passed quickly as Montoya walked steadily down the road.

Suddenly, a man raced toward him and grabbed his right arm. Montoya pulled away but soon another man arrived, grabbing his other arm. Others appeared and there was no hope of Father Montoya to escape.

The area he was visiting was under the control of the FARC guerrillas, and he had entered the area with their authorization. The guerrillas knew he was a religious worker, but they also suspected him of being an army informant. Through the diverse terrain they force-marched Montoya from town to town and eventually to a mountain base in another region of the country. Forcing him to his knees, the men stared at him and pointed the gun, shouting false accusations and insults at him. Without any proof or even investigation of his alleged spying, Montoya was killed with a single bullet to the head.

His congregation became worried days later when they had not yet heard anything from him. A group from the church was sent to look for him and encountered the FARC guerrillas, who blatantly confessed to shooting him. The guerrillas had buried his body in the mountains. No one would be permitted to see his grave.

Under the control of the FARC guerrillas, organized church services were not permitted. Many church leaders had tried to negotiate with the guerrillas, telling them they had no intention of stirring up problems. They simply wanted to minister to the people. Their pleas feel on deaf ears.

Knowing the possible fate that awaited him, Montoya still had asked the church to send him to minister in this dangerous region. The risk was great, but the need for people to hear the gospel was greater. Armed only with God's love and a conviction to serve, he left the safety of the city to minister in rural, guerrilla-controlled communities. Faith had overcome fear as Francisco Montoya demonstrated the greatest love of all.

Sunday Nache Achi (December 9, 2004)

Passionate, sincere, faithful, and loving—some of the words used to describe Nigerian Christian Sunday Nache Achi. Despite the opposition to Christian evangelism on the campus of Abubakar Tafawa Balewa University, Sunday passionately shared his faith openly with other students. While studying architecture at the University, Sunday served as president of the campus ministry of the Evangelical Church of West Africa (ECWA). Despite the tension between Muslim and Christian students on the university grounds, Sunday continued his ministry and Bible studies—people needed to hear the good news of Jesus Christ. Sunday was at one of these meetings when the men showed up at his room looking for him.

Sunday closed his Bible and looked around at the people gathered in the small room. It had been a good turnout, with some new students, and everyone was eager to hear the gospel. Even though three of their members had recently been expelled from the school for distributing leaflets comparing Jesus' teachings with Islamic beliefs, they continued to meet. Sunday bowed his head and led the group in prayer, unaware of the turmoil back at his room in the student hostel.

Idakwo Ako Paul, Sunday's roommate, stared at the papers in front of him, wishing he were praying with the others instead of studying for his exam the next day. The stillness was broken as the door burst open and Paul jumped out of his chair. Three Muslim students dressed in Islamic jihad clothing rushed into the room and demanded: "Where is the Christian leader? Where is Sunday?" "I don't know where he is," said Paul. The men angrily stormed out of the room and continued their search for Sunday.

A few hours later, Sunday returned to the room and Paul shared what had happened. Though his life was in danger, Sunday simply smiled, thanked Paul for telling him, and took a seat at his drawing board to work on some drawings for his architectural class the next morning. Paul lay down on his bed and went to sleep.

Sunday Nache Achi strangled by Muslims

"Wake up, Paul! Wake up!" screamed Sunday. Paul jumped out of bed and saw masked Muslim men dragging Sunday out of the room. Paul ran toward the door where Sunday was being accosted, but one of the kidnappers pointed a pistol at him, forcing him back into the room and locking him inside. Paul pounded on the door and screamed. The Muslims living in the hostel stayed in their rooms. Paul slumped to the floor, exhausted. No one came to help.

Paul was awoken the next morning by one of the Christian students as he unlocked the door. Paul told him about Sunday and made a plan to tell the other Christians of the danger they faced. They ran out the door, down the stairs, and right into another Christian brother who knew what had happened to Sunday.

"He's dead," he said, tears streaming down his face. He collapsed into the men's arms as he began to tell them about the discovery of Sunday's body, which was found next to a mosque, near the home of the university's vice chancellor. His neck was broken from being strangled, and bruises covered his body. The men wept as they shared in the grief of a strong, brave, and faithful friend who was now gone.

The persecution didn't end with the death of Sunday Nache Achi. It grew stronger. The offices of the Nigeria Fellowship of Evangelical Students (NIFES) were burned down, and authorities closed Abubakar Tafawa Balewa University.

One of the Christian students from the university said it best:

> "Evangelism is something we must be prepared to die for. I see in
> the Bible examples of many who had to lay down their lives for
> the sake of the gospel. Why not me?"

Dulal Sarkar (March 8, 2005)

Dulal Sarkar was a thirty-five-year-old lay pastor and evangelist with a local branch of the Bangladesh Free Baptist Church in Jalalpur village, in the southwest division of Khulna. As a lay worker, his desire was not only to care for his church but also to plant churches in other areas. His goal was to minister to all the people of Bangladesh.

On March 8, 2005, Sarkar was slowly walking toward his home. God had given him a strong love for the people and he spent most of his spare time in prayer for them. He looked forward to his time at home with his wife Aruna and their five children. "Thank you for my family, Lord God. I am so blessed," prayed Sarkar daily.

That day Sarkar spent hours talking about his faith with many of the villagers. The week before, he had shared his faith with several Muslim villagers and they had accepted Christ as their Savior. He made sure that they came to church so they could continue to be discipled and grow in their faith.

Suddenly, ten Muslim extremists, armed with knives, surrounded and threatened the native evangelist. "We know that you have led many people to believe in this Christ of yours. Stop preaching or we will kill you right now," said the men. But Sarkar stood firm and replied, "I will not stop the ministry God has called me to perform." With that answer, the men attacked. Sarkar's throat was cut so deeply that his head was separated from his body.

Sarkar's wife Aruna immediately filed a police report and officers arrested three of the ten attackers. However, local Christians reported that the remaining seven, who have connections with the Jamaat-e-Islami political party, had tried to bribe the police to get their friends out of jail. After filing the police report, Aruna was also threatened by Islamic extremists and forced to move numerous times to protect herself and her children.

Dulal Sarkar left a legacy for his family and church members. While only obtaining the authority of a lay pastor, he fulfilled the highest mandate in demonstrating faithfulness as a good shepherd who laid down his life for the sheep.

Tapon Roy and Liplal Marandi (July 28, 2005)

The screams echoed down the hallway and woke neighbors from their sleep. The closest neighbors tried to rush out of their homes to see what was happening, but their front doors were chained closed and they were unable to get out. Neighbors farther away got out of their houses and ran toward the screams, but they were too late to prevent the carnage.

It was July 28, 2005, and Tapon Kumar Roy and Liplal Marandi were sound asleep in the calmness of the night. A loud noise woke the two men as their door came crashing in and eight Muslim men rushed into the room. They held Tapon and Liplal down while they tied and bound their hands with strips of the sheets they ripped apart. Then they began to viciously stab them.

Soon the neighbors' footsteps and voices could be heard outside. The assailants quickly fled the scene after stabbing Liplal fourteen times and Tapon twelve. The two severely wounded men were rushed to the nearby Boalmari Health complex in a van. Tapon died in transit, and Liplal died immediately after reaching the hospital.

Tapon and Liplal began their ministry in Dhopapara in April 2005. They rented a small room to share and began showing the *JESUS* film. They were warned by local Muslims more than once to stop showing the film. Tapon and Liplal knew that their God was greater than any threats, so they continued in the ministry He had called them to, showing the film.

Only a few days before their murder, a mob of people rushed to their house around noon and demanded that they leave Dhopapara village immediately. "If you fail to obey, then we will make sure that you will be gone forever while your *JESUS* film will be left behind." Once again, the men followed God's call and remained in the village. They knew the danger they faced and were prepared to die if it was God's will. Tapon and Liplal left behind more than a film. They left behind a witness of a Savior who chose to face the cross that all might be saved.

Ezzat Habib (October 24, 2005)

The taxi's tires screeched as it careened into the street and hit Pastor Ezzat Habib, his son Ibram Habib, and a friend as they were crossing the street in Cairo. The men were thrown across the street as the taxi raced away.

People hurried to the scene and Ezzat was rushed to the hospital, suffering from internal bleeding and a broken skull. He underwent surgery, but it didn't help; he died the next day. The friend suffered a broken leg, and Ibram had severe bruising in his legs and persistent lower back pain.

While he was still stunned and in shock, the hospital had Ibram sign an incident report after his father was delivered to the hospital. He signed the report even though he was unable to read it clearly at the time. Later he saw the report was completely different than what had actually happened. The taxi driver went unpunished.

This was no accident. The Habib family was frequently threatened, and faced physical abuse from neighbors and from Egypt's national security police. In June 2003, Pastor Ezzat was arrested for supposedly "disturbing the neighborhood." He was put in an underground cell that was so narrow he couldn't sit down. He was physically and sexually abused by the police officers; yet he never rejected his Lord Jesus Christ.

After being in prison for five days, an officer bandaged his eyes, chained his hands, and interrogated him. There was a police officer on each side that hit him, kicked him, and insulted his wife. He was warned to stop his Christian meetings and to forbid non-Christians from attending. The source of the abuse was clear: Police knew that Pastor Habib had been sharing the gospel with Muslims; he'd been encouraging them to leave Islam and follow Jesus Christ. This could not be tolerated.

In spite of repeated threats, Habib's congregation continued meeting. Later, two trees smashed through the windows of the Habib's apartment building. There was a man in the front yard chopping the trees with an axe. The phone line was cut, and the front door was blocked from the outside. The man claimed a police officer told him to cut down the trees.

"Didn't I tell you to stop doing your meetings?" the officer told Habib. "Look what is happening to you."

In spite of harassment and continued threats from police and neighbors, Ibram and the family resolved to continue the house fellowship. They had seen Pastor Habib stand firm in his faith, even unto death; they were determined to do the same.

Theresia, Alfita, and Yarni (October 29, 2005)

The four high school girls walked down the path leading to Poso Christian High School. The sun was shining in a cloudless sky and the girls looked forward to another day of school. It was a holiday for the Islamic schools in the area, celebrating the holy month of Ramadan. But Christian schools like the one the four girls went to were still in session. Their friendship and fellowship brought smiles across their young faces as they enjoyed the peacefulness of the early Saturday morning.

The stillness of the air was broken as six men dressed in black and with veils covering their faces jumped out of the bushes and ran toward them. Before the girls could move, the men surrounded their young victims and viciously began swinging machetes. Screaming for help, the girls fought for their lives. Only Noviana Malewa was able to escape. Covered in blood from cuts mostly on her face, she ran to find help. The bodies of Theresia Morangkir (fifteen years old), Alfita Poliwo (seventeen), and Yarni Sambue (fifteen) were left on the ground, their heads severed from their bodies and missing.

A couple of women walking to the nearby market had heard the girls screaming for help. Filled with fear, the women ran toward the military post, reporting what they heard. The Indonesian soldiers began looking for the source of the screams but instead discovered the three decapitated teenagers.

The attackers had put the girls' heads in a sack and dumped them in different areas around the county. Two of the heads were found near a police post, while the third was discovered outside a local church.

It wasn't enough for the radicals to attack churches or Christian leaders. They purposely targeted young Christian girls—girls who refused to recognize the Islamic holiday of Ramadan. Girls who would never be able to be forced into marriage with a Muslim man. They also made a deliberate statement by taking their heads and leaving them by a police station and a church. The message was clear: Neither the church nor the government could stop their cowardly attacks on young girls in the area.

These teenagers knew of the dangers to Christians in the area, but with confidence and joy they made their daily trek to the Christian school. They chose to rise above fear and trepidation. Though their lives were mercilessly taken that Saturday morning, their faith lives on. Word of their testimony traveled worldwide, giving encouragement and hope to others to possess lives full of youthful joy in Christ, and a sober reminder that we are all just visitors in this corrupt world.

Yea, though I walk through the **valley** of the **shadow** of death, I will fear no evil; for **You** are with me; Your **rod** and Your **staff**, they **comfort** me.

Psalm 23:4

Collin Lee (November 5, 2005)

The smoke billowed as flames engulfed the jeep. Hedwig Unrau Lee's face was flushed not only from the heat of the flames, but also from dragging her wounded husband, Collin Lee, away from the disaster. What had started as a typical day for the couple working for International Aid Services (IAS) quickly turned to fear and turmoil.

Collin Lee, his wife Hedwig, and their driver, Karaba Juma, were driving along the Ugandan border in Sudan, toward the town of Yei, when they suddenly came upon a roadblock. Juma spotted twenty militants— members of the brutal Lord's Resistance Army (LRA)—and tried to reverse the jeep and avoid the block, but it was too late. Bullets flew through the air toward the jeep, and hit the chest and neck of Collin Lee who was sitting in the passenger seat.

Despite her own injuries, Hedwig refused to leave her bleeding husband. She begged the gunmen to let her remove him from the vehicle before they set it ablaze. Struggling with his seatbelt as tears streamed down her face, she eventually pulled Collin from the car. The pregnant thirty-five-year-old woman draped her husband's arm around her and made the hour-long trek to the closest village.

Hedwig's minor wounds were taken care of and Collin was immediately taken to Yei hospital, where doctors unsuccessfully tried to keep him alive. Six hours after the shooting, Collin was pronounced dead.

It was only a couple of years earlier that Collin had felt a call from God to begin working for IAS doing trauma counseling for war victims in Somalia, Sudan, Ethiopia, and Uganda. He joined his wife, who had worked for IAS before. Together, with urgency, they worked diligently to counsel the victims and share the gospel of Jesus Christ.

Over a million lives in Uganda and surrounding nations have been affected by attacks of the Lord's Resistance Army (LRA). Children have been kidnapped by the LRA and used as soldiers, porters, and sex slaves. Many walk up to ten miles every day to find a place to sleep securely. A large part of the Ugandan rural population has left home and taken refuge in large cities.

These were the conditions where Collin and Hedwig worked—where they felt called to minister. Collin worked strategically to help these victims, putting his concerns and safety behind him. Hedwig stood with her husband in this service. Hundreds have come to know Jesus through his work and only God knows how many more have been reached because Collin followed God's call and glorified Him.

Ghorban Dordi Tourani (November 22, 2005)

It was a late November afternoon when the phone rang. "Ghorban," the caller began, "I heard you speak at the meeting last week and was moved by the testimony of your Christian faith. I want to hear more about your beliefs. I prefer to meet somewhere other than your house, so that others don't see me. Can you meet me at a park in the city so we can talk more about Christianity?"

Pastor Ghorban Dordi Tourani eagerly agreed to meet with the caller and made his way quickly out of the house and to the park. Someone wanted to know about Jesus!

One week earlier, Ghorban had been contacted by the head of religious leaders in his area of northern Iran. He was invited to a meeting held by the ethnic Turkmen Islamic leaders in the area so he could answer their questions about his faith. Ghorban believed it to be an opportunity to share the gospel of Jesus Christ with these Islamic leaders.

But when he arrived at the meeting, he was disappointed to find that it wasn't a time for questions and open discussion. The Islamic leaders' goal was far more direct. They wanted Ghorban to return to Islam and strongly advised him to give serious consideration to what they were saying.

"We are well aware that your ancestors and your parents have been dedicated followers of Islam," they told him. "And you are supposed to be a committed Muslim too. Why have you turned to Christianity? We are giving you one more chance to deny your Christian faith and return to Islam."

Ghorban Dordi Tourani knifed by Muslims in Iran

"I am not going to deny Jesus."

Now a week later, Ghorban thought about that meeting as he hurried to the park, excited that his words seemed to have touched the heart of at least one of his listeners. He knew it could be a trap, but then again the caller could be sincere and Ghorban would not want to miss the opportunity to speak about Christ. He waited for some time, but no one showed up. Deciding that the man must have gotten scared, he began making his way home. At the end of the alley down which Ghorban's house sat was a car with three people inside.

One of the three got out of the car and called Ghorban. Hesitantly, Ghorban approached the man who quickly pulled out a knife and thrust it into Ghorban's stomach. The second person out of the car attacked him with a knife to his back. The third slit the pastor's throat.

Standing over the body of the slain pastor, the men shouted a warning to all who could hear. "This is the punishment of those who become infidels and reject Islam."

Ghorban's path to the true God began when he and his family moved from Iran to Turkmenistan in 1983 to find a better job. Things didn't turn out as they planned. Ghorban got into a heated argument and killed someone with a knife. As a result of his crime, he was arrested and sentenced to fifteen years imprisonment. His time in prison was difficult and he soon earned a reputation as the most evil prisoner.

A Russian Christian in prison for his faith was eventually transferred to Ghorban's cell. He befriended this "most evil" prisoner and shared the message of the gospel. For a long time Ghorban opposed his cellmate's message. But the more he got to know him, the more he was impressed by the Christian's love and peace, in spite of the prison conditions.

Ghorban, unable to deny the truth being revealed, gave his life to Christ. Shortly after his conversion, he boldly asked the head of the prison if he could hold evangelistic meetings. The prison warden, amazed at the changes in Ghorban's life, miraculously agreed. "Because the God you worship has changed your life in such a dramatic way, I will give you permission to have meetings in the prison."

Ghorban was finally released from prison and went back to Iran and to his city, Gonbad-e-Kavous. Ghorban shared with his family and friends and relatives the faith that had transformed his own life. He also shared with them the Christian teachings he had learned and all that the Holy Spirit had revealed to him as a result of his study of the Word of God in prison. Twelve ethnic Turkmen gave their lives to Jesus within the first couple of years of Ghorban's ministry. He then moved to another large city in Iran, as he needed further training to better disciple and teach these new converts. He eventually met a key leader in one of the churches in that city who was willing to help Ghorban in his ministry among the Turkmen.

Ghorban attended a Bible training program to become more equipped for pastoral and teaching ministry. Over the next seven years, God's work among the Turkmen people grew, and at least thirty-five Turkmen became Christians as a result of Pastor Ghorban's ministry.

Ghorban was a fearless Christian leader and would boldly share about Jesus on the streets and in shops and bazaars. He was convinced that true faith in Christ was not to be kept silent and he shared it with others everywhere he went.

Several times Ghorban was threatened by the Islamic religious leaders in his community. His own brother slashed Ghorban's face with a knife for his Christian witness. In spite of these oppositions, he continued to share about Jesus, no matter what it would cost him.

Ghorban's wife Afoul Achikeh had learned from her husband's boldness. After finding him dead on the street, she shouted to those crowded around her husband's body, "O people, remember that Ghorban is a Christian martyr who laid down his life for the sake of Christ!" She repeated the words in a loud voice several times, not wanting death to end her husband's powerful witness.

After the murder, the secret police took all Ghorban's family members and the other believers for interrogation. They asked a lot of questions and told them they were trying to identify the three murderers of Ghorban. They also took all the Christian materials (books, videos, Bibles, etc.) from their homes.

Afoul and her children also came under extreme pressure from Ghorban's brothers, urging them to turn back to Islam. But she and the children have stood firm in their Christian faith and have told those who would ask that they will follow Jesus, no matter the cost.

Before meeting Christ, Ghorbandordi Tourani was an angry, violent man, a murderer and a prisoner. But anger and violence did not die with him; Pastor Ghorban had become a man of inner and outer peace. No three attackers—nor three hundred—could take that from him, no matter what their weapons or resolution to kill. God had turned a murderer into a martyr.

Aroun Voraphorn (December 2005)

Metta Voraphorn answered the door with dread in her heart, already sure of what the men were going to say. Grief and pity filled their eyes as they looked at her and said the two words she feared most, "He's dead."

Her husband, Aroun Voraphorn, had been missing for two days when these same friends first came to visit. They were supposed to join Aroun for a Christmas service in another part of Borikhamxai Province in Laos. Metta told them she assumed her husband had been called on short notice to preach at another church, but it had been awhile since she'd talked with him. She shared her newfound concerns about his whereabouts due to some recent unusual events.

Three unidentified men came to their house the day before Voraphorn's disappearance. Metta didn't know the men or why they were there, but assumed they wanted to know about the church or Jesus. Voraphorn left home the next day to preach a Christmas service about ninety kilometers south. The three men arrived at the end of the service and entered the church. Voraphorn introduced the men to the pastor of the church and told him that two of them were his relatives. They all ate together, and then Voraphorn and the men thanked the pastor and left. Metta had talked with Voraphorn later that afternoon. He told her he would be late for his youngest daughter's birthday party because he was going to buy a birthday cake on the way home. That was the last time she talked to him. Aroun never returned.

After hearing Metta's story, Voraphorn's friends left the house and started toward their preaching engagement. On the way, they stopped by the church where Voraphorn had preached a few days before and asked the pastor if he had heard or seen Aroun. The pastor hadn't. The men thanked him and made their way down the jungle road. Up a little ways and about twenty meters into the jungle, the friends saw some policemen in a huddle. As they moved closer, the men covered their mouths and clutched their stomachs as they saw the body. It was Aroun Voraphorn.

The men turned away so they could compose themselves, then they approached the body. The body was bloody and mutilated, but the friends would recognize that peaceful face anywhere. Voraphorn's hands were tied tightly behind him and he had been stabbed numerous times. The rock lying next to his body had been used to smash his head, and his throat had been cut.

The two friends asked permission to take Vorphorn's body. The officers said yes, and they took the body back to their church in Vientiane.

Aroun Voraphorn preached the gospel fearlessly, always aware of the danger surrounding him. At his funeral service the day after the body was discovered, Metta encouraged the Christians in Laos to do the same—to preach the good news without fear.

When Laos became a Communist republic in 1975, the government severely restricted Christian activity. Pastors, evangelists, and anyone associated with the Christian church were often harassed and beaten by police and local officials. Christians have been tortured and imprisoned for refusing to sign documents renouncing their faith. Ten years before his death, Voraphorn himself was imprisoned for his faith.

Aroun Voraphorn knew there would be consequences for his faith on both sides of eternity. Yet he chose to follow Christ no matter what the consequences would be here on Earth. And at his funeral, held on Christmas Eve, Voraphorn's wife Metta pleaded with Christians in Laos to continue preaching the gospel fearlessly, just as her husband had done.

"We don't pray to be **better** Christians, but that we may be the **only kind** of Christians God means us to be; **Christ-like** Christians; that is, Christians who will bear **willingly** the **cross** for God's **glory**."

— A note smuggled from the underground church in Communist Romania

Pastor Jimendra Nayak (Mantu) (January 1, 2006)

Thirty-five-year-old Pastor Jimendra Nayak (Mantu) was accustomed to the threats against him for witnessing to his Hindu neighbors. As a pastor for two years in the Indian Church Assembly in the northern Indian village of Baliguda, Kandhamal district, he preached God's Word to those in his community. His proclamation of the Truth angered radical Hindus. They wanted him silenced. But it was Nayak's love for Christ that compelled him to continue reaching out to them.

It was that devotion that led Pastor Nayak to the nearby Beradakia church on the first day of January for a New Year's Day service. Here he was to preach the Word in his desire to lead the hearers deeper in their relationship with God, in hopes that they would believe and call upon the Lord as Paul expressed to the church in Rome (Romans 10:13-14). He didn't know it as he prepared, but this would be his last sermon.

The afternoon had gone down to evening when Nayak left the church building to head home for the night. As was customary, he hired an auto rickshaw taxi to navigate through the streets of the village and drive him to his house. The pastor never left the vehicle alive. His body was later recovered from the cabin of the rickshaw. Death had apparently come to the pastor by a severe blow to the head.

The police insisted that the pastor had died in a strange automobile accident, but investigation into his mysterious death reveals several major discrepancies that allude to a more sinister story—one of premeditation and murder at the hands of those opposed to his message and witness.

Pastor Nayak was among the impassioned who sought out God's Kingdom with intense desire, and sought to share its light with others as well. Through him, the kingdom advanced forcefully. His work has been completed, his race run. Now others take the torch and carry the light of the gospel of Christ as a beacon for the lost and dying in Nayak's community.

Andrea Santoro shot during morning prayer

Andrea Santoro (February 5, 2006)

Sun shone through the stained glass windows onto the pews. Only the soft murmurs of prayers disturbed the peaceful silence. The activity of morning Mass at Santa Maria Church in Turkey had subsided. Father Andrea Santoro could take his time in fellowship and conversation with God.

Suddenly the back doors of the church flew open and before Father Santoro could even turn around, two bullets had pierced his body, hitting his heart and liver. In an instant, he went from simple conversation with God on Earth into eternal fellowship.

"Allahu Akbar!" (Allah is great!) cried the Muslim assailant as he fled the church and escaped down the road. This phrase is an Arabic exhortation used as a rallying cry by Islamic militants. Police launched a major manhunt and found him hiding in a relative's home near the city center. He was only sixteen years old, already filled with enough hate and deception that he could kill an innocent priest in cold blood, believing he was doing Allah a favor.

Prior to his murder, Father Santoro was threatened numerous times by Muslim militants about his ministry of converting Muslims to Christianity. The priest never requested police protection. He did not want it to hinder his ministry.

There are numerous theories as to why Father Santoro was killed, but the constant theme running through them all is that he was a Christian— one who dared to share his faith with Muslims. Had he confined his ministry to his church, he may have avoided the assault.

The Santa Maria Church was built in the second half of the nineteenth century to serve foreign Christians visiting the city. Santoro was a member of the Sons of Divine Providence, a Catholic religious order in Italy. He came to Turkey in 2000 to live and work, and eventually to die for his commitment to bring "church" outside the safety of its four walls.

Eusebio Ferrao (March 18, 2006)

Broken and splintered, the wooden cross lay upon the grass outside the church. Clearly written on one of the wooden pieces were the words "Shri Pardesi" ("Mr. Foreigner"). Christians were seen as unwanted foreigners by radical Hindus in India. A priest's robe was found covered with a mosquito net, hanging on a tree branch in a park near a church where another cross had been destroyed.

A couple of weeks later, threats became reality. In Macazana, parishioners of St. Francis Xavier Church arrived around 6:30 a.m. for morning service. The church seemed unusually quiet and their priest, Father Eusebio Ferrao, wasn't there. He was always at the door welcoming his parishioners. The early arrivers crept quietly toward the front of the sanctuary. As they reached the front, the silence was broken as their screams filled the air. Lying on the floor in a pool of blood was the body of their beloved priest. Some of them fell to the floor and began weeping as they looked at the body of Father Ferrao that had been beaten, stabbed, strangled, and smothered.

Police soon arrived at the scene and ushered the parishioners out of the church. They began searching for clues as to why Ferrao was killed. Nothing was taken from the church, so theft wasn't the motive. It was clear that someone with a great deal of anger against the church had committed the crime. The night before his murder, Father Ferrao had dinner with two young men. It was suspected they might have been the killers.

Hindu extremists have created tension between Hindus, Muslims and Christians. The extremist group Rashtriya Swayamsevak Sangh (RSS) was accused of crusading for an all-Hindu state. Areas with a high percentage of Christians became targets by the extremists. Riots had broken out between Hindus and Muslims, leaving two policemen and two civilians severely injured. The rioters also looted eighteen shops and a gas station, and damaged twenty-four vehicles owned by Muslims. About a month before his death, Father Ferrao had written an article for two local newspapers about the recent rioting. As an outspoken Christian unafraid to address the needs of a nation, Father Ferrao became a target of extremist hatred. He was aware of the danger of his words, but knew the truth must be spoken. Without fear for his life, he defended not only his faith but also human rights for all his countrymen.

Father Eusebio Ferrao could have chosen a path of safety and silence. But he chose to speak out, and in doing so he brought an end to his ministry on this Earth. His testimony rings loud of boldness and courage.

Prem Kumar (June 8, 2006)

When God imparted the Ten Commandments to Moses, He told him, "For I will cast out the nations before you and enlarge your borders..." (Exodus 34:24a). Such was the ministry of sixty-seven-year-old Pastor Prem Kumar, whose effective outreach extended beyond the boundaries of his church in Nizamabad, India. He taught at prayer gatherings, corner meetings and conventions. However, his fruitful work of expanding God's kingdom did not go unnoticed.

On Thursday, June 8, 2006, Pastor Prem Kumar left for his regular prayer service at the local church in Kotagiri. After he left, an unidentified, well-dressed man arrived at Prem's house and asked his wife if this was indeed his home. He told her he had come from Nizamabad to take Prem to lead a service. Since he had already left, the man wrote down Prem Kumar's cell phone number and went away.

At about three o'clock in the afternoon, Pastor Prem Kumar called his son Sunil saying he was going along with the man on his scooter to lead a prayer service in Rampur Thanda, in Kotagiri Mandal.

Around nine o'clock that night, Prem again called his son, this time saying he was at the Bodhan bus stop and was accompanying four unidentified people to another prayer service. He mentioned he was scared to go with them and asked Sunil to call him every half hour. He was scheduled to arrive in Kotagiri in thirty minutes.

A little later when Sunil tried calling his father, he could not reach him, as his cell phone was in an area without service. He called again and again, still with no answer. After learning that his father's cell phone was turned off, family members began to panic.

Pastor Prem's sons, Sunil and Sudhir, called their friends in Kotagiri to find out if they had seen their father. They had not, so the sons immediately left for Kotagiri.

After searching and searching that night, they gave up and started again early the next morning, asking many if anyone had seen their father. One person said they had seen a dead body and a scooter in an open space nearby. They rushed to the spot and found a pair of glasses...then slippers...and then a scooter and a Bible. To their utter shock, they found their father dead in a pool of blood in the hills near Rampart in Kotagiri Mandal, of the Nizamudeen district. Prem's body was mutilated beyond recognition, forcing the Kotagiri sub-inspector to identify the remains from a description of Prem's clothes.

The family took his body home. At ten o'clock that night, the family said good-bye to Prem in a funeral.

It is suspected two landlords, who are the owners of about 100 acres, are behind this ruthless murder. A landlord and villagers were very annoyed because one of Prem's family members had been sharing her Christian faith with her family and drawing not only them, but also others, to belief in Christ. A police official stated that personal rivalry was more than likely the motive for the murder of Kumar. "There is definitely no religious angle," he insisted and said that Prem was one of the accused in a murder case and that relatives of the victim could be behind the killing. He also claimed that Kumar's son was involved in a kidnapping some time ago, and after the kidnapped woman was released, she had threatened him.

However, one of Kumar's sons said his father had no enemies, and he strongly suspected the hand of Hindu extremists. He also said he could identify the person who invited his father to hold the prayer meeting in Rampur Thanda.

In the face of persecution and threats at the hands of Hindu radicals, believers in Jesus are standing strong and continuing to witness the love of Christ. Like Prem Kumar, God is enlarging the borders of their outreach, gathering more into His kingdom daily.

A Nigerian Woman (June 28, 2006)

"Release her to us!"

"Release her or we will burn down the building!"

"She deserves death!"

By now the mob had fully surrounded the police station, and their demands for the officers to hand over the woman to them had grown to a deafening level. Several held rocks of various sizes in their hands, ready to release them at the first sight of the woman—the infidel—while others held clubs and sticks.

The police had only moments ago found the bruised and bloodied woman and brought her into the station to protect her from Muslim extremists who were beating her with clubs and fists.

Earlier that day, this unidentified woman had been evangelizing in the streets of Izom, Nigeria. She had entered into a conversation with some Muslim youths, sharing the gospel and handing them some Christian literature to read. Her encounter had not gone unnoticed.

Muslim elders standing nearby had seen the exchange and approached the youths to find out what she had told them. They were infuriated to learn that she had shared the gospel with them. They claimed she had insulted the prophet of Islam, Muhammad, and insisted that the woman be killed. Their rage and allegations incited hundreds of other Muslims to pour through the streets to track down the woman. They finally caught up with her near the River Gurara and began beating her.

That's when the police intervened and brought her into protective custody at the Izom police station.

The mob stormed the premises, demanding she be released to be stoned to death in accordance with Shariah, Islamic law. The Islamic legal system was implemented in several states of Nigeria in 2000, making it illegal to speak out against Allah or the prophet Muhammad.

The police had persistently refused to hand her over and were now faced with the real threat that the mob would burn down the police station. In an effort to protect the woman and get her to safety, the police tried to smuggle her out through a back door, but the angry Muslims had blocked all escape routes. Fleeing for their lives, the police abandoned the woman at the door, and members of the mob clubbed her to death.

In the panic, the police did not have time to identify the woman before she was killed. All that is known of this courageous young woman is her actions of love in reaching others for Christ and bringing them the Good News. Although nameless in death, she unashamedly pointed others toward the true Name above all names, Jesus Christ, and it is certain that He was ready to welcome her by name into eternity.

For I **determined** not to know anything among you except **Jesus Christ** and Him crucified.

1 Corinthians 2:2

Y Ngo Adrong (July 13, 2006)

A Montagnard Degar Christian named Y Ngo Adrong, age forty-nine, from Dak Lak Province was tortured to death in the police interrogation room at Ea H'Leo District, Dak Lak Province. ("Montagnard" is French for "mountain dweller" or "mountain people," and "Degar" is how Montagnards in Vietnam refer to themselves.)

On July 13, 2006, Y Ngo Adrong was summoned to the police station at Ea Hleo district, where police officers interrogated him about his Christian house-church activities.

At about eleven o'clock in the morning, the police from Ea Hleo district went to Y Ngo Adrong's village of Buon Le. They told his family that he had hanged himself at the police station. On July 14, 2006, his body was transferred to the morgue; then one of his relatives brought his body to the village of Buon Blec, the village of his birth.

But Y Ngo Adrong's family's grief did not end with the news of his mysterious death. Dozens of police surrounded the village, preventing residents of nearby villages from attending the funeral. The police also refused to allow his family to inspect the body or to remove his clothing. Even though family members wanted to see his wounds to try to understand the cause of his death, police refused to permit relatives to get near the body.

Added to the restrictions on inspecting Y Ngo Adrong's body and attending the funeral, the police gave his family fifteen million Vietnamese dong in compensation, and admitted they were wrong in causing his death. However, the police refused to provide details of what happened in the interrogation room.

Like Y Ngo Adrong, Montagnard Degar Christians are carrying on in their ministry, sharing the Good News of Christ throughout Vietnam. They know well the risks they face—risks of imprisonment and even death—yet the message they carry is so valuable, so important, that they willingly take any risk to share it.

Pastor Irianto Kongkoli (October 16, 2006)

"It is God's will." Rita Arianti Kopa exhaled. "He gives life."

Rita's memory flashed back to the last moments of her husband's life. The two of them and their five-year-old daughter had gone to the hardware store in Central Sulawesi, Indonesia, to buy ceramic tiles, a trip that was not uncommon for them. There was nothing extraordinary about this Monday morning, except that the two of them had come to understand the dangers involved in living out a risky faith in such a violent place.

Irianto and Rita had just finished bargaining for some tiles and were heading back to their van when Irianto noticed some interesting tiles on display in the yard outside the store. He started walking toward them. It was then that two masked men approached Irianto and shot him in the back of the head at near point-blank range, then fled on a motorcycle.

Rita ran to her fallen husband, adrenaline and shock taking over her body in waves. As a member of the East Palu police force, Rita had been trained to respond in such an incident, but for her this incident became a crisis and soon a tragedy. Irianto was rushed to a nearby hospital where doctors battled to save his life, but the wounds were too severe, the blow too violent. Irianto was gone.

It had only been a short time that Pastor Irianto had taken over as acting head of the Protestant Church in Central Sulawesi, following in the steps of Rinaldy Damanik. It was a hazardous undertaking. Pastor Damanik himself had only been released two years earlier after being imprisoned for twenty-three months on trumped-up charges.

In the late 1990s, fighting erupted in Indonesia through what Pastor Damanik has called "corruption and favoritism." Commenting on this violence, he said that "this is not a religious conflict. The real causes are the injustices we live with."

It is for justice and an end to the corruption that Pastor Irianto fought. He offered life in the form of justice and freedom for the oppressed and victimized. He often spoke out against governing authorities who failed to properly investigate incidents of violence in the region.

He and Pastor Damanik had a passion to give protection to the victims of the violence, beyond the bounds of ethnicity or religion. Amazed by their love, a Muslim refugee wrote a letter stating that he had been a victim of the violence and had received aid by evacuating to one of the Crisis Centers. "Even though we differ in religion," he stated, "their hearts ... were extraordinary."

Pastor Irianto Kongkoli bore many titles and lived out many roles: father, husband, pastor, beloved friend, defender of the oppressed, and a voice of justice for the wronged. But perhaps he will be most remembered as one who bore the scars and the wounds that come through suffering, the marks of love.

"A shadow of a dog can't bite you, and a shadow of death can't kill you. You can kill us or put us in prison, but nothing bad can happen to us."
— A pastor who was faced with the threat of arrest and torture by police who burst into his home as he, his wife, and his six small children had just finished reading Psalm 23

Immanuel Andegeresgh and
Kibrom Firemichel (October 17, 2006)

Night had fallen as the men left their houses, silently closing the doors behind them. They each stood still a few frozen, breathless seconds and looked cautiously both ways down the street before they dared move. Confident of their concealment, they quietly and carefully set off in the direction of the meeting place, following the contours of shadows and dark lanes to veil their journey.

When they arrived, they were greeted by the warm and familiar faces of their brothers and sisters who had also gathered here to fellowship together. For all of them, including two men, Immanuel Andergeresgh and Kibrom Firemichel, this was the only opportunity to worship their Savior together in a community, their only hope for true fellowship, and they were entrusting their lives to all of those present. They had become all too accustomed to the laws forbidding open worship in Eritrea. The fear and hesitation melted away as they began to worship and share together.

It came as both an intrusion and a distress when a loud hammering at the door broke their praise. The singing stopped. The gathered believers exchanged wide-eyed and knowing glances. They knew immediately what it meant: Their meeting had been discovered, and they would be arrested, detained, and possibly tortured for breaking the law.

Since 2002, only the Orthodox, Roman Catholic, and Lutheran churches have been recognized in Eritrea, along with Islam. Numerous evangelical Christians have been arrested for practicing what officials call a "new religion." Since that time, thousands of Christians have been placed in prisons where they face deplorable conditions, some held in metal shipping containers in temperatures that can soar above 100 degrees Fahrenheit or drop below freezing.

Within moments the door was forced open to reveal several uniformed security police, members of a task force specifically established to eradicate all "menfesawyan," or "spirituals," a term often used to describe Christians not belonging to one of the recognized churches.

Immanuel, twenty-three years old, Kibrom, thirty, and eight others were arrested and taken to a military confinement camp. There they were subjected to torture and "furious mistreatment," according to one of the other believers. At the end of two days, Immanuel and Kibrom both died of severe dehydration and injuries sustained in the torture.

In the end, the two men dared to gather with other believers because they understood the life-giving effects of sharing in the bonds of brotherhood. They understood the risks, but could not deny that to be united with Christ meant to be bound to one another in love and encouragement, gifts that far outweighed the risks.

"The blood of the martyrs is the seed of the church."

—Third-century scholar Tertullian; his words continue to ring true.

PART FOUR

Persecution Survey

2000-2006

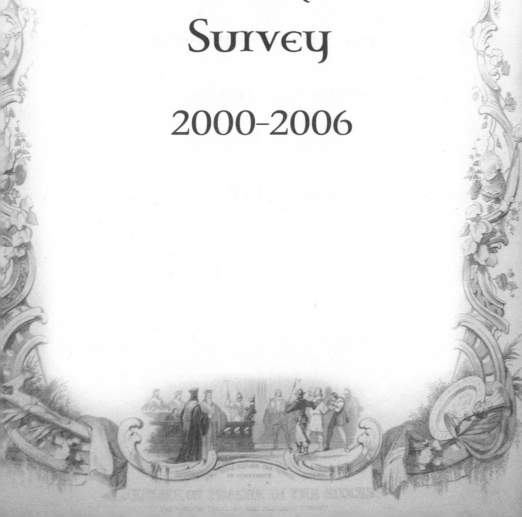

"The church has been and always will be persecuted. Everyone watches us. If we die in faith, hope, and love, it can change the history of nations."

— A missionary who works in China and North Korea

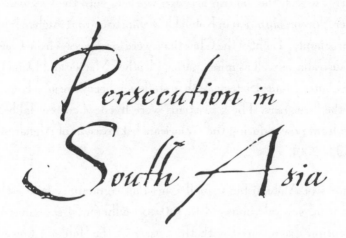

Afghanistan

By 2000, the ultraconservative Islamist group the Taliban had solidified control of about ninety percent of Afghanistan. The Taliban imposed its interpretation of Shariah law on the populace and established a religious police to enforce it under the direction of the Ministry for the Promotion of Virtue and the Prevention of Vice.

The Taliban forbade non-Muslims from building places of worship, but worship at existing holy sites was allowed. Non-Muslims were prohibited from criticizing Muslims and they were required to identify themselves by placing a yellow cloth on the rooftop of their homes. Non-Muslim women were also required to wear yellow dresses, and Hindus reportedly were required to wear a yellow cloth attached to their clothing to identify them as non-Muslims.

In January 2001, Taliban Supreme leader Mullah Muhammad Omar announced that any Afghan discovered professing the Christian or Jewish faith would be executed.

Six months later, in June, the Taliban passed a decree prohibiting proselytism by non-Muslims. Those found guilty of violating the decree faced possible death. Foreigners faced deportation.

In early August, the Taliban arrested workers with the German-based Shelter Now organization in Kabul for "trying to convert Afghan Muslims to Christianity." Eight of the Christians were foreigners—from Germany and Australia, as well as missionaries Heather Mercer and Dana Curry of the United States. Sixteen Afghan staff members were jailed separately from the foreigners. The Christians were freed when the Taliban was forced from power during the American-led invasion of Afghanistan in the fall of 2001.

Members of Afghanistan's small Christian community (size estimates range from several thousand to 100,000 adherents) say government persecution disappeared with the ouster of the Taliban; however, if Christians practice their faith openly, they face persecution from non-Muslim family members, neighbors and radical Islamists.

In July 2004, Reuters reported Taliban fighters said they had slit the throat of a former Muslim cleric caught propagating Christianity. A Taliban spokesman told the news agency that Maulawi Assadullah was killed in Awdand, a remote district of Ghazni Province.

Three more Afghan Christians were reportedly stabbed or beaten to death in late July and in August. The body of Christian convert Naveed ul-Rehman was found near his abandoned car in Awdand. Ul-Rehman apparently had gone to visit Assadullah's family.

Forty-one-year-old Abdul Rahman was arrested in February 2006 for converting from Islam to Christianity—a crime punishable by death. An international outcry led to his release and claims from government officials that he was mentally unfit to stand trial. He was granted asylum in Italy.

A re-emerging Taliban and a record opium poppy harvest in late 2006 threatened the stability of the young democracy.

Bangladesh

Muslim extremists often denied Christians access to public water wells, as well as forcing them from their homes and beating them during the 2000-2006 period. These extremists also destroyed rickshaws owned by Christians, thereby taking their only source of income. As a result, Muslim converts to Christianity were often subjected to ostracism, expulsion from their communities, and violence from family members and neighbors.

During the past forty years, churches have been growing at twice the population rate. Persecution against Bangladeshi believers intensified as a result of their higher visibility and increased efforts to win Bangladeshis to Christ.

The kidnapping of a Bangladeshi evangelist known as "Moses" confirmed a worrying trend of violence against Christians. An evangelist with Gospel for Asia (GFA), Moses was taken hostage by a Muslim terrorist group which then demanded a large ransom. GFA reported on June 10, 2003, that Moses escaped the previous night after his guards fell asleep. With his hands tied behind his back, he ran for hours until he reached a town the next afternoon, suffering from exposure and lack of food. His brother had tried to negotiate with the terrorist group, but GFA said, "The terrorists found and severely beat the brother and others with him. They threatened to kill Moses if the money was not brought soon."

Dr. Abdul Ghani, a respected Christian leader, was decapitated by a gang of assailants in September 2004. He was killed on the street as he returned home from the market. Four militant young men fled away on their motorcycles. Local villagers said the four assailants belonged to an Islamic extremist group. Ghani was the coordinator of Bangladesh Baptist Mission in Jamalpur district, and his wife used to work in the same mission in Dhaka. In addition to his pharmaceutical business, Ghani used to preach Christ and was involved in humanitarian work.

Most of the documented reports of persecution occurred in the final year of the survey period, but Bangladeshi Christians say many of the cases were similar to those they have experienced in recent years. The only difference was that they occurred with greater frequency in 2005 because a greater number of Islamic extremist groups were present in Bangladesh, and they were targeting Christians for attack.

In January 2005, a Bangladeshi human rights group announced a dangerous trend was emerging in the country: Thirty-one Islamic militant groups were now operating in Bangladesh. The goal of the militants was to establish an Islamic nation with adjoining Indian states, and they were mainly targeting non-Muslim groups for attack.

Sources confirmed the murder of Dulal Sarkar, a lay pastor and evangelist in Bangladesh. Sarkar worked with the Bangladesh Free Baptist Church in Jamalpur village as an evangelist and church planter. On the night of March 8, 2005, as he returned home, he was attacked and beheaded by Muslim extremists. His wife Aruna immediately filed a case against the killers, and three suspects were arrested. However, militants are now threatening Aruna and her children. The beheading was the second in the space of one year.

Two Christian health workers in Bangladesh were hacked to death on July 29, 2005. Police and local officials believed Islamic extremists were likely responsible for the murders. The incident took place about 150 kilometers from the capital, Dhaka. Tapan Kumar Roy, twenty-seven, and Liplal Mardi, twenty-one, worked for Christian Life Bangladesh (CLB). They often showed the *JESUS* film at the invitation of local villagers. A well-known Christian leader familiar with the two evangelists said an official at a local *madrassa* (Islamic school) had threatened the men verbally prior to the murders. Some villagers had also threatened to kill Roy and Mardi if they continued to show the *JESUS* film.

Also in July, Islamic extremists forced the Grace Presbyterian Bible College in Khulna to shut down. They beat the students with the intent to kill the men and kidnap the women. The school moved to a new location fifteen miles north of the capital city of Dhaka only to receive more threats from extremists in October 2005. This time the Islamic militants threatened to amputate the hands of Bible school attendees if they sang or prayed too loudly.

As the Christmas season approached, security around the nearly 100 churches in Bangladesh tightened. Two live bombs were recovered from a school compound in Pagla, near the capital of Dhaka. Police also detained ten suspected Islamic militants on December 25. Police believe the ten were involved in a late 2005 spate of suicide bombings by the Jamaat-ul-Mujahideen, a group demanding Shariah law in Bangladesh.

While Bangladeshi Christians most often face persecution from the Muslim majority, Buddhist hostilities against Buddhist converts to Christianity intensified in 2006. In March, a Buddhist mob set fire to a church in Pancchari sub-district. The converts were threatened with additional acts of violence if they did not return to Buddhism

Bhutan

Some Bhutanese refugees living in Nepal were expelled from their country when the Bhutanese government discovered they were Christians. Buddhism is the official religion of Bhutan and to be Bhutanese is to be a Buddhist. Those discovered to be Christian risk losing their jobs, their children face possible expulsion from public school, and their families face possible expulsion from Bhutan.

The importation of printed religious materials other than Buddhist is not allowed. Bhutanese law prohibits conversion from Buddhism to other religions, and permission must be obtained from the government to build new places of worship.

Only one church building exists in Bhutan and it is located in the south where the greatest number of Christians is concentrated. Though their numbers are small, most Bhutanese Christians worship in small house-churches.

While Christian non-government organizations are actively involved in education and humanitarian relief in Bhutan, the government prohibits them from proselytizing. The teaching of religions other than traditional

Drukpa Kagyupa Buddhism in schools is not allowed. The passports of non-Buddhists cite the holder's religion, and often when non-Buddhists apply for government services they are asked their religion before services are rendered.

Among the most noted incidents during the 2000-2006 period occurred at Easter time 2004. Police raided three Protestant house-churches in Sarpang district in southern Bhutan. No arrests were made following the Easter Sunday service on April 11, but attendees were warned to stop meeting together. Police reportedly told the Christians that the government viewed their meetings as "terrorist activities." Four church leaders were ordered to report to the police station daily.

Catholic churches also reportedly faced increased restrictions against them during the survey period. Bishop Stephen Lepcha said the Bhutanese government outlawed "public non-Buddhist religious services, and imprisoned those who violate(d) the law."

Two Christian evangelists were arrested in January 2006 after showing the *JESUS* film to a woman and her neighbors in the city of Paro. They were imprisoned for six months without trial and finally received sentences of at least three years because of their evangelistic activities.

India

Violence against Christians in the world's largest democracy was sporadic, but consistent during the period 2000-2006. Attacks against Christians residing in the states of Orissa and Gujarat were more numerous during this time.

Chandrakant Shourie, the nephew of a prominent Indian journalist and Member of Parliament, began the year 2000 recovering from wounds he received in an attack against his family New Year's Eve night. Six Hindu militants from the Vishwa Hindu Parishad (VHP) group armed with clubs beat Shourie, his wife, son, friends and neighbors. They shouted, "Kill this Christian," and pledged to turn Madhya Pradesh state into another Orissa, a reference to the Indian state where Australian missionary Graham Staines and his two young sons were martyred in January 1999. Shourie, had converted from Hinduism to Christianity. His uncle, Arun Shourie had been a leader of a campaign against Christians. Police looked on and did nothing to halt the attack against Chandrakant Shourie and his family.

In May 2000, militant Hindus stepped up attacks against Christians in Uttar Pradesh and Gujarat. In December, less than two weeks before Christmas, a mob of 200 militants from the VHP and Rashtriya Swayamsevak Sang (RSS) groups, armed with swords and knives, stormed the Evangelical Church of India in Chindia, Gujarat. The Hindus destroyed crosses and desecrated the church building. The building was seized, and Hindu idols were placed in the sanctuary.

Fifty-two-year-old Pastor Yesua Dasu was beheaded September 11, 2000, in the state of Andra Pradesh. Police refused to consider evidence in the pastor's death supplied by the All Christians Welfare Center (ACWC), maintaining that radical Hindus had threatened to kill the pastor if he continued to preach in local villages.

During the 2000-2006 period, radical Hindus increasingly resorted to violence to prevent Christians from evangelizing Hindu villagers. Two evangelists were hospitalized in serious condition after they were beaten in January 2001 for showing the *JESUS* film in the village of Jehra, near the Gujarat-Rajasthan border.

Less than two months later, militants stormed into Krishnanagar Baptist Church in Tripura state and ordered the pastor to halt the church service.

Nineteen Christians were forced to re-convert to Hindusim during a ceremony in Kendrapada, Orissa, in July 2001. They were socially ostracized by villagers and forced to pay obeisance to the village deity. The ritual cleansing ceremony of re-conversion is known as shuddhikaran. The Christians also faced possible prosecution for violating provisions of the Orissa Freedom of Religion Act—an anti-conversion law. Another similar incident was reported in Orissa state in February 2004 as eight females—two of them only fifteen years old—were dragged from their homes as their husbands were away at work. When the women refused to re-convert to Hinduism, they were beaten, stripped naked and forced to parade through the village. In a further act of humiliation known as tonsuring, the women's heads were shaved bald.

In August 2001, a Catholic nun was shot by militant Hindus in Madhya Pradesh. During the same month, two Bible school students were assaulted for distributing gospel tracts. They were forced to sign statements saying they were forcibly converting Hindus to Christianity, and on August 6, Father Oscar Mendonca, a Catholic priest, was beaten by a Hindu mob near Bombay.

Raids against churches—especially those actively engaged in evangelizing Hindus—continued and intensified in the period 2000-2005. Among the churches attacked was the charismatic New Life Fellowship Church in Moodabidari, Karnataka state. Radicals describing themselves as "custodians of the Hindu Faith" accused worshippers of converting young educated Hindus through a campus outreach ministry.

In March 2003, the Pata Fellowship Church in the village of Patapaypangara, Maharashtra state, was attacked by radical Hindus. A cross on an exterior wall of the church was destroyed and a Hindu idol was put in its place. Death threats were made against church members as Hindu radicals continued to demand that Christian converts return to Hinduism.

In May 2003, Muslim militants threw a grenade into the front entrance of the Saint Lukas Convent School near Srinigar, killing Sister Kamlish, a missionary nun from West Bengal. The Muslims had made death threats against Christians at the school after hearing local media reports claiming that 20,000 Kashmiris had converted from Islam to Christianity.

Hindu radicals often lodged false accusations against Christian leaders to defame them and Christianity. Five Naga missionaries were arrested in July 2003 in Arunachal Pradesh and charged with participating in insurgent movements.

In August, officials at a Catholic primary school in Bangalore were accused of attempting to convert a twelve-year-old Hindu girl to Christianity by promising to help her become a doctor. They denied the allegations, but Hindu radicals demanded the school's operating license be revoked. Also in August, Christian evangelist Yusi Hey Yobin was arrested in Shillong, Meghalaya, and charged with drug possession. Yobin was a research scholar at North Eastern Hill University. Church officials claimed his arrest was part of an ongoing campaign to blacken the reputation of pastors and evangelists. Yobin was terminated from his university fellowship.

Police, local government officials and politicians often encourage and support radical Hindus as they plan and implement violent attacks against Christians. One such incident occurred July 31, 2003, in Sirs district, Mariana. A former member of the legislative assembly and Barratry Janet Party (BJP) politician led a mob of 250 militant Hindus in an attack against a church and Bible school. Five females were among the students injured in the assault. The assailants shouted anti-Christian slogans and voiced objections to the showing of the *JESUS* film as they attacked church members and the students. Another incident involving police occurred in Sultanpur district, Uttar Pradesh state, in February 2004. Pastor Ram Prakash was accused of converting local Dalits to Christianity. A mob of 200 militant Hindus beat Prakash and his wife at the house of a relative. When police arrived, they arrested Prakash and beat him severely at the police station.

Rumors that Christians were paying Hindus to leave their faith incited many attacks against believers during the 2000-2006 period. One such attack occurred in Mumbai in September 2003. Vishwa Hindu Parishad (VHP) radicals stormed into the Faith Fire Fellowship prayer meeting, forced the Christians out and locked the doors to the worship hall. The VHP assailants claimed Christians were offering $100 US to each Hindu that was willing to convert.

Also in September 2003, Dara Sing and twelve other Hindu militants were convicted of killing Australian missionary Graham Staines, his eleven-year-old son Phillip and seven-year-old son Timothy. In addition to the three murders, the defendants were found guilty of committing conspiracy, unlawful assembly and burning a vehicle and house.

In late October, radical Hindus attacked eighty Christians attending a prayer gathering in Uttaranchal. Some women and children attendees were injured; Bibles, posters, banners and tracts were burned; and equipment was damaged at the guest house where the event was held. False rumors that the Christians had converted Hindus incited the attack.

Christians had high hopes and great expectations when the Congress Party returned to power in May 2004. It was thought the Congress Party would better protect the rights of minorities. But that hasn't been the case. Attacks against Christians have escalated. Several Indian Christian missionary organizations now report thirty to forty acts of violence are occurring each month.

Shortly after the Congress Party victory, the right wing Hindu supremacist group the Rashtriya Swayamsevak Sang (RSS) announced plans to step up training of armed militants. Dilip Singh Judeo, former Minister of Forestry and Agriculture, encouraged recruits to "move into the interior parts of the country to check religious conversion." The RSS oversees a network of at least seventy Hindu groups known as the Sang Parivar. Parivar believes "true" Indians are those that accept and respect the truth of Hinduism. They want to transform India from a secular society to a Hindu one.

In May 2004, Pastor Subas Samal and an assistant were arrested in Orissa state and charged with violating the Orissa Freedom of Religion Act. Villagers claimed the two men used financial enticement to convert twenty-five Dalits over a period of ten years.

Those coming to Christ in the greatest numbers are the Dalits—commonly referred to as "the untouchables." Many are poor, uneducated and jobless. Sixty percent of the Indian Christian community are Dalits. Dalit voters gave overwhelming support to the Congress Party and were instrumental in the party's national electoral victory.

Christianity gives the Dalits hope—a way out of their low caste status in Indian society. Because they want to weaken Dalit support for the Congress Party, and because Hindu nationalists see Dalit conversion as a threat to their culture and the traditional caste system, they've forced and enticed many Dalit Christians to attend re-conversion ceremonies. Some converts have been lured back to Hinduism with promises of housing, material goods and money. Others have been threatened with physical violence and death.

A seventy-one-year-old Syrian Catholic priest was murdered in August 2004 in Kerala state. Father Job Chatillapilly was killed on the day of an annual harvest festival. A Hindu priest told adherents attending a ritual at a Hindu temple that the death of a Christian priest was required to appease the soul of a Hindu priest murdered at the temple twenty years earlier.

And **do not fear** those who kill the body but **cannot** kill the **soul**.

Matthew 10:28

The year 2005 was a brutal one for Indian Christians with more than two hundred acts of violence committed against them in the first ten weeks of the year.

A newly opened Catholic school in Assam was set ablaze by radical Hindus in January 2005. They accused officials at the school of converting Hindus. Two hundred eighty Christian students attending a seminary graduation ceremony were robbed and beaten by members of the radical RSS group in Kota in February 2005. Many of the students were attacked as they disembarked from trains carrying them to the Emmanuel Mission graduation. Police arrested many of the Christian students instead of their Hindu attackers who claimed the school had lured them to Kota with promises of a bicycle and about $6 US each.

Also in February, the body of martyred twenty-five-year-old Christian evangelist Narayan Siddiaha was discovered in the village of Channapatana, Karnataka state. Doctors performing an autopsy on the body say Narayan had been brutally murdered and suffered from broken ribs, teeth, and injuries to his abdomen. The official medical report suggested the young pastor had committed suicide.

On February 27, evangelist Kiran Kumar was brutally attacked while traveling to the home of a Hindu man who had requested he come for prayer. Hindu extremists tied him up and threatened to throw him into a nearby lake. Police arrived on the scene and arrested Kumar. Once at the station, police beat him mercilessly with a bamboo stick, asking, "Why don't you call to Jesus to save you?"

Radical Hindus with the Bajrang Dal group assaulted eight members of the Friends Missionary Prayer Band in March, falsely accusing Christian orphanage director Pastor Arthur Joel of child abuse. The radical Hindus demanded the closure of Christian institutions around the state and the implementation of an anti-conversion law. An anti-conversion law was repealed in Tamil Nadu state shortly after the Congress Party's national election victory in May 2004, but anti-conversion laws remain in place in five Indian states: Madhya Pradesh, Arunachai Pradesh, Chattisgarh, Gujarat and Orissa.

Radical Hindus in states without anti-conversion laws often use another law to curtail evangelistic activities of Christians. Section 153A of the Penal Code addresses accusations of fraudulent conversions. In April, 153A was used against Christian businessman Vidya Sagaran of Kerala state who was accused of attempting to forcibly convert his neighbor. Sagaran's attorney said the charges were actually the result of a personal dispute between the two men.

During the same month, militant Hindus set fire to the Believers' Church of Manipur. Church members were told to abandon the church site or "face the consequences."

On May 1, 500 Hindu villagers —members of the militant Bajrang Dal group—attacked a house-church in the Mangalwarapete village, Karnataka state. They burned Bibles and other Christian literature at the King Jesus Church and then proceeded to molest some of the female church members and beat Pastor Paulraj Raju. Bleeding profusely, Raju was hospitalized as a result. Raju had been beaten and arrested in January for converting Hindus.

Two of the most brutal murders occurred in early June 2005. Radical Hindus abducted and murdered Pastor K. Daniel and Pastor Isaac Raju because of their outreach to Hindus. Both had baptized Hindu converts to Christianity. Raju was maimed and murdered so brutally (his body parts were found in a burlap bag) that his wife Satya Veni could identify his body only because she recognized his undergarments and scars on his legs.

In late summer 2005, Christians in Chattisgarh organized a five-day rally to protest increased attacks against churches in the state. One of the attacks occurred September 11 when Hindu extremists tore the cross off an exterior wall of the Teacher Disciple Vineyard Church building and threw it into a septic tank; on the same day, militants punched and harassed members of the Christian Evangelist Assembly Full Gospel Church.

In Punjab state in late September, police took four Christians into custody to protect them from angry members of the Bajrang Dal group. Once in custody, the men were beaten by police.

Arrests of believers accused of forcibly converting Hindus, and attacks against Christians and churches by militant Hindu groups continued through the end of the year.

The year 2005 ended as perhaps one of the most violent against Christians in recent memory, and the violence continued in 2006. Several pastors and evangelists were martyred, and attacks by radical Hindus against churches, schools, orphanages and a hospital owned and operated by Emmanuel/Hopegivers International in Rajathstan state forced the cancellation of seminary graduation ceremonies in Kota. False charges against Hopegivers missionaries led to the arrest and jailing of several of the ministry's leaders.

Greater **love** has no one that this, than to **lay down** one's life for his **friends**.

John 15:13

Maldives

Islam is the national religion and nearly all citizens are believed to be Muslim.

Shariah law is practiced and no other religions are permitted. There are no church buildings in Maldives—none are allowed. Resident foreigners are allowed to practice Christianity privately, and the importation of Christian literature and Bibles is permitted for their use.

Proselytism is forbidden, and Muslims discovered to have converted to Christianity forfeit their citizenship and are deported.

The Maldives Constitution requires that the president be a Sunni Muslim, and in 2000, he stated that no other religions will be allowed in Maldives.

Nepal

Nepal was the world's only declared Hindu kingdom until the parliament in May 2006 stripped King Gyanendra of most of his powers and declared Nepal a secular state. In the early 1990s, Nepal changed from being a Hindu monarchical state to a democratic state, and a new constitution in 1990 supposedly guaranteed each person the freedom to profess and practice his own religion.

Proselytizing is banned and carries a three-year jail penalty, but no one was prosecuted during the survey period. Also during the 2000-2006 period, extremist Hindu organizations from India set up offices in Katmandu, and aggression against Christians increased. Militant Hinduists in Nepal aimed to drive all Christians from the country. Christians residing in the countryside also faced persecution from Maoist extremists bent on imposing communist atheism on the people of Nepal.

In February 2000, the Hindu Volunteers Organization accused Christians of stepping up efforts to convert Hindus. The HVO coordinator pledged the group was launching a campaign to stop the conversions.

In May 2000, the government of Nepal refused to register the Bible Society in the country because its board members were Christian converts from Hinduism. The Supreme Court issued a directive to register the Nepal Bible Society, but the chief district officer ignored the court order.

Also in May, villagers in Gorkha beat Christians, destroyed six Christian homes and a church. The Christians were attacked and chased from the village because Hindus were angry that the Christian converts would no longer participate in traditional practices.

In September 2000, Maoist rebels angered over a religious school's refusal to appoint Maoists to the school board, incited villagers to stone the school. Saint Joseph's Catholic School in Gorkha (central Nepal) was expected to be closed for the remainder of the school year as a result.

In November 2000, Christians Trond Berg, thirty-six, a Norwegian, and Timothy Rai, forty, a Nepali pastor, were sentenced to six weeks imprisonment for their Christian activities in Rajbi Raj. Nepali pastors Perm Bahdur Rai, fifty-two, and Devi Prasda Batrai, thirty-eight, who had also been arrested, were released on bail.

The four men were conducting a meeting in a rented hall on October 29 at the request of local Christians in Rajbi Raj. Without warning, Hindu radicals disrupted the meeting and demanded that they be given $2,000 US. When the Christians refused to pay, the mob began to beat them. When police reached the place, they took the four Christian leaders into custody, and detained them in the Rajbi Raj jail. Rajbi Raj is a four-hour drive from Kathmandu, the capital city. Charges were dismissed in February 2001, and the four men were released after prosecution witnesses failed to appear in court.

On the day of the trial, a huge crowd of Hindus and their priests gathered in front of the court buildings shouting slogans and threatening to burn down the buildings if Berg was released. Another trial was scheduled for six weeks later. Berg's wife and children returned to Oslo on advice from the Norwegian embassy because of fears for their safety.

In mid June 2003, a Nepali evangelist witnessed an attack on a newly built church in Jhapa district, Beldangi. He said 1,000 people came to destroy a newly constructed church as 100 worshippers attended services inside. The police came, confiscated Christian materials, and arrested the three church leaders.

One month later on July 26, Christians belonging to a small but rapidly growing house-church in northern Nepal were attacked by Buddhist and Hindu villagers, resulting in hospitalization for at least one member. Authorities in the village had repeatedly asked the Christians to give up their faith. When they refused, Buddhist and Hindu villagers retaliated, destroying houses and cornfields belonging to Christians.

In April 2004, authorities in Kathmandu held two Christian leaders for questioning about their efforts to organize an Easter celebration event for 16,000 Christians from about 200 churches. The government originally approved the event, then canceled it because of a ban on opposition rallies— a ban which was not supposed to be enacted against religious events.

Missionaries traveling through areas controlled by Maoist revolutionaries risked abduction and death at the hands of the rebels. In August 2004, a Gospel for Asia missionary called Besh was kidnapped by the Maoists. The Maoists would often kidnap evangelists and pastors in an attempt to convince them to join the Maoist insurgency movement. They also faced extortion and false allegations from radical Hindus as they attempted to profit monetarily and prevent Christianity from spreading.

In May 2005, police arrested Babu Varghese and his wife Sabitri and charged them with forcibly converting minors. The couple managed an orphanage in Nepal. They said a former disgruntled employee sent a photo of them baptizing an adult to the local newspaper. He said they were baptizing children. The newspaper printed the photo, and editors demanded the Vargheses pay them $2,500 US. When they refused, the editors printed articles demanding the Vargheses be jailed for six years. Orphanage staff members cared for the couple's two young boys during their parent's incarceration.

As 2006 came to a close, Christians were hopeful that the newly declared secular state would eventually lead to greater religious freedom in Nepal.

Pakistan

Christians in Pakistan were targeted for attack by militant Muslims and terrorist groups immediately following the U.S. bombing and liberation of Afghanistan in autumn 2001. The bloodiest attack against Christians since the 1947 independence of Pakistan occurred in the city of Bahawalpur on October 28, 2001, at the conclusion of a Protestant Sunday service. Masked Islamic terrorists armed with AK-47 automatic weapons stormed Saint Dominic's Church, killing pastor Emmanuel Ditta, fourteen worshippers and a security guard.

The Bahawalpur incident was followed by another church attack, this one at the International Church in Islamabad. Five people were killed in the March 2002 attack, including the wife and daughter of an American diplomat.

In August 2002, five people were killed in an attack at the Muree Christian School. Security guards stationed at the school entrance prevented gunmen from advancing their assault into school classrooms.

Several days later, three nurses were killed when terrorists threw several hand grenades at them as they departed morning prayers at the chapel of the Texsila Mission Hospital near Islamabad. It was the fourth such attack against Pakistani Christians within ten months.

Also in August 2002, the Pakistan Supreme Court overturned the blasphemy conviction of Ayub Masih. Masih was imprisoned in October 1996, falsely accused of blasphemy against the Islamic prophet Muhammad. Masih would have been executed if his conviction had not been overturned by the high court.

Ayub Masih was among at least nine Christians imprisoned under Pakistan's 295 Blasphemy Law. Sub-section A of the law prohibits blasphemy against Islam; sub-section B, the Koran; and sub-section C, the prophet Muhammad. The maximum penalty against those convicted of violating sub-section B is life in prison while sub-section C violators face possible death by execution.

In March 2001, Jhang Amjad and Asif Masih were sentenced to life in prison for allegedly violating 295B. The two Christian street sweepers had been arrested two years earlier and charged with vagrancy. The men say police attempted to extort money from them by falsely accusing them of burning a copy of the Koran.

In August 2001, bail was denied for another Christian accused of blasphemy. School teacher Parvez Masih was arrested and accused of violating law 295C, blasphemy against the prophet Muhammad, a crime punishable by death. Family members say jealous Muslims had leveled the false accusations against Parvez because a growing number of Muslim students were enrolling in his successful Christian school. They accused Masih of committing blasphemy when he responded to questions from several of his Muslim students when they asked him about Muhammad's nine-year old wife, Aesha.

Several Pakistani pastors active in evangelizing and ministering to Muslims were martyred during the 2000-2006 period. Forty-two-year-old Pastor George Masih was among those murdered. Two assassins stormed into Masih's home in Manwala in April 2004. Pastor George and his wife were known in the village of Manwala (near Lahore) for the worship songs that could be heard coming from their house. They would often visit the homes of Muslims and pray for the sick. On the day of his murder, Pastor George, his wife and four children had just finished watching a video of the *JESUS* film when two masked gunmen stormed into their home. One of the assailants pointed a shotgun at Pastor George's face and opened fire. Though only one other Christian family lived in the village, more than 300 people—many of them Muslims—gathered for Pastor George's funeral. Some described him as a caring man, a "true and passionate believer."

Often militant Pakistani Muslims seek vengeance against Christians accused of committing blasphemy. In May 2004, a policeman assigned to guard accused blasphemer Samuel Masih murdered him in his hospital room. Masih was falsely accused of defacing the side of a mosque. He suffered from tuberculosis and had been hospitalized. The policeman told investigators he killed Masih because it was his religious duty as a Muslim to kill a Christian man who had committed blasphemy against Islam.

Muslim fanatics often target Pakistani Christians for attack during Christian or Muslim holidays. One such attack occurred Christmas evening 2002 and another on Easter Day 2005. On Christmas night 2002, two young male assailants interrupted a children's pageant lobbing several hand grenades into a small Presbyterian Church in the village of Chianwali near Lahore. Three girls were killed and thirteen children and their parents were injured. Many of the wounded suffered from severe eye injures.

In March 2005, the Easter morning service (March 28) at Victory Church International in the village of Khambay near Lahore was disrupted when four armed assailants opened fire on church property outside the church building. Church members who left the service to investigate were shot. One worshipper was killed and six others were injured.

In late 2005, angry Muslims launched an attack somewhat reminiscent of the 1997 violence that occurred against Christians in the village of Shanti Nagar. This time Christian homes and churches were destroyed in the village of Sangla Hill. The incident was on a much smaller scale than Shanti Nagar, but it demonstrates how some Islamic leaders often exploit false accusations and rumors to incite Muslims to wage jihad against Christian neighbors and their places of worship. A false accusation of Koran burning was made against a Christian that was owed money by a Muslim. A mob of 2,000 angry Muslims burned and vandalized three churches, a pastor's home, a youth hostel, a convent, two schools and many Christian homes. Four hundred fifty Christian families were forced to flee for their lives. Investigators admitted local police were involved in the attack.

In February 2006, false rumors of Koran desecration caused Muslim mobs to attack and burn two churches and a Christian school in Sukkur. The same month, a mob of several thousand Muslims attacked a United Presbyterian girls school in Kasur because they were upset about the publication of cartoons depicting Muhammad.

In June 2006, accused blasphemer Christian Abdul Sataar was stabbed to death by Muslim militants in front of the Multan district court building.

Sri Lanka

Although freedom for other religions is assured, there has been a steady erosion of that freedom with discrimination against minority religions through taxation, employment and education. Many Sri Lankans perceive Christianity as a foreign religion and a colonial imposition. From 2003 to 2005, 170 acts of violence against Christians or their organizations were recorded.

During this survey period, militant Buddhists frequently bombed and burned churches in remote cities and villages of Sri Lanka. They often interrupted church services demanding they be discontinued—all in an attempt to halt the explosive growth of Christianity on the island nation.

On January 22, 2001, in the southern city of Hulandawa, militants attempted to destroy a newly built Roman Catholic church by detonating explosives positioned at the four corners of the church building. No one was injured, but it was the third attempt by militants to remove the Catholic congregation from the community. The structure of the church building survived the attack, but previous similar attacks destroyed two church buildings in the town.

On March 15, 2001, the New Life Christian Church in Hingurakgoda was destroyed in an arson fire. The church had been vandalized by a machete-wielding mob one month earlier, and three Christians walking to church in the town were attacked and beaten by a Hindu mob on March 4.

As Christianity spread during 2000–2006, Christians moved their worship services from small house-churches into larger church buildings. As their religious practices became more public, attacks against them increased.

On May 25, 2001, assailants broke into the Heavenly Harvest Church in Kaluvenkerni, beat the pastor mercilessly and ransacked the building. Police were unable to control the frenzied mob of about 500 Hindus armed with sticks, clubs and homemade weapons. Attackers pelted the church with stones, then ran inside and began breaking windows and furniture and beating worshippers, including some children. One week later, a mob of approximately 100 destroyed the partially constructed St. Stephen's Lutheran Church in Orutota, Gampaha, at midnight. Villagers threatened a Christian family living next door with death if they reported the incident and then threatened to bomb the church if the Christians attempted to rebuild it. On June 13, assailants broke into the home of Pastor Rozairo in Neluwa, assaulted the minister and a male guest, and then burned the house to the ground. They threatened to kill the Christians who met in Rozairo's home if they did not leave the village immediately.

In August 2003, organized attacks against five churches caused the Evangelical Alliance of Sri Lanka (EASL) to suggest the attacks were part of a government plan to introduce anti-conversion legislation.

Police thwarted an attempted attack on the Methodist church in Rathgama launched by a crowd of Buddhist monks and youth on July 27. The monks returned the following Saturday and stoned the building, destroyed pews and benches, and beat two church workers so badly that they required hospital treatment. Other churches in the area were attacked on August 2, including the Assemblies of God in Thanamalwila and Lumugamvehera, and the Calvary church in Hikkaduwa. An EASL representative said the attackers were attempting to create an environment of religious disharmony which would allow the government to argue convincingly for the introduction of anti-conversion laws.

"More **persecution** ... more **growing**!"

— Pastor Samuel Lamb,
a Chinese house-church pastor
who spent 20 years in prison for his faith

The following month, a new government ministry compiled a list of officially recognized churches. However, only the Roman Catholic Church and mainline Protestant denominations were included on the list, while independent and evangelical churches were excluded. Evangelical Christians comprise less than one percent of the population in Sri Lanka, numbering about 120,000, according to the Evangelical Alliance of Sri Lanka (EASL). "If a church is not included in this list, it will become a 'rebel' organization as far as the government is concerned," said a member of the EASL. "This will result in that church becoming an underground church, which will have no civic rights." The announcement by the ministry followed a series of violent attacks against churches. One took place on August 14 in the town of Kesbewa. In that incident, a young man belonging to the Assembly of God church sustained seven shrapnel wounds from a homemade bomb.

Four female Christian workers were assaulted on September 17, 2003. A week later, unidentified motorcyclists set fire to the Assembly of God church in Kotadeniyawa, completely gutting the structure. The four Christian women were erecting a fence around the church property when a Buddhist monk from the nearby Erabadda Temple demanded with foul language that they stop work immediately or face death.

Around 10:00 P.M. that night, a group of some thirty men dragged the women from their lodging next door to the church, beat them, and smashed the concrete fence posts they had erected. Police took the women into custody but required them to appear in court the next morning and publicly charged them with prostitution. The judge ordered three of the women to undergo a medical examination to disprove the accusation.

On October 19, members of the New Covenant Life Center of Athurugiriya were meeting in a reception hall when a Buddhist monk accompanied by about fifty young men arrived and demanded that the believers vacate the building within ten minutes. According to the Evangelical Alliance of Sri Lanka (EASL), a leading Buddhist monk in the area had warned the Christians that they would no longer be permitted to meet in the village. One week earlier, Sunday worship at an Assemblies of God church in Embilipitiya was interrupted by seven Buddhist monks and a small crowd of local villagers. They forced the Christians to stop the service and said they should leave the area and practice their faith elsewhere.

Buddhist monks in Sri Lanka carried out further attacks against Christians in November, acting with impunity as the government failed to prosecute several cases of arson and physical assault that occurred the previous month. The Assembly of God church in Mathugama, the Emmanuel Church in Nawala, Colombo, and an independent church in northern Anuradhapura endured attacks, as did the offices of World Vision in Colombo.

Christians suffered further violence in the Buddhist-majority country of Sri Lanka on January 20, 2004, when a Catholic church was attacked near the capital, Colombo. Attackers set fire to the door of St. Anthony's church and vandalized a cross outside the building. A week earlier, Buddhist protestors set fire to another Catholic church on the outskirts of Colombo.

A Christian Fellowship Church (CFC) in the Kalutara district of Sri Lanka was attacked on April 11, Easter Sunday. About ten people, including women and children, were injured in the attack. The church had been closed for three months following an initial attack in late December 2003, when a mob of about 300 Buddhist villagers rushed into the church. A near-riot ensued, with police finally convincing the mob to disperse. When church members gathered on the following Sunday, they were attacked again by a much larger crowd. Representatives from the Buddhist temple and CFC church were then asked to sign an agreement for the "temporary" suspension of church services; however, no date was given when services could be resumed. "How long can we go on like this, keeping the church closed?" said Pastor Sunil, who resumed services on Good Friday despite the risk of a further attack.

Unknown assailants set fire to St. Michael's Catholic Church in Katuwana, Homogama, Sri Lanka, in the early hours of December 19, 2004. The fire was ignited by gas cylinders and rubber tires. The blaze damaged pews, an organ, the altar, and church statues.

In 2004 and 2005, Buddhist clerics and lawyers aggressively pursued attempts to pass an anti-conversion law through the Supreme Court. Two anti-conversion bills—one proposed by the Buddhist Jathika Hela Urumaya (JHU or National Heritage Party)—were presented to parliament in 2005, but were put on hold. The JHU bill called for prison sentences of up to five years and/or a stiff fine for anyone found guilty of converting others "by force or by allurement or by any fraudulent means." The *Island* newspaper quoted the country's highest-ranking Buddhist cleric as saying that anti-conversion legislation is an "urgent requirement, since Buddhists are being converted to other religions at an unprecedented rate."

As the survey period came to a close, Sri Lanka Christians expressed concern about pressure on the newly elected president, Mahinda Rajapakse, from radical Buddhists bent on enacting a national anti-conversion law.

"With him, my **beloved** Master, it is **good** everywhere. With him I have **light** in the dark dungeon. I had asked him to be where I am **needed**, not where it is better for the **outward** man, but where I can bear **fruit**."

— From a letter written by Russian pastor
P. Rumatchik after he was imprisoned
for the fifth time

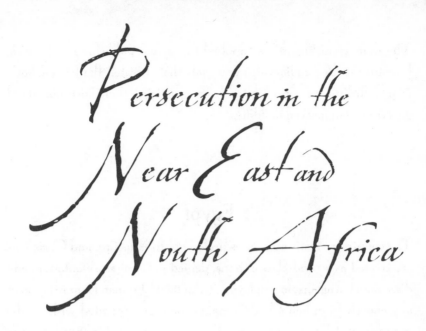

Persecution in the Near East and North Africa

Algeria

Islam is the state religion in Algeria, but the constitution prohibits discrimination because of religious belief. Proselytism by non-Muslims is prohibited and the importation of non-Islamic literature for mass distribution is not allowed. Personal copies of the Bible are allowed and some Christian literature has been sold in bookstores. Non-Islamic audio and videotapes can be found for sale in Algiers.

In recent years Christians have suffered violence from the Islamic Salvation Front, whose members have been known to march through towns and slit the throats of those who have not lived up to their call to Islamic fundamentalism. Proselytism is not allowed.

Algeria has very few Christians. Believers in the cities are few in number and keep a low profile. However, in many Kabyle villages, people are aware of Christian meetings that are also held openly. The Catholic and Protestant churches are the only Christian bodies officially recognized.

A new anti-conversion law restricting Christian evangelism was implemented in March 2006. Those found guilty of "shaking the faith" of a Muslim faced punishment of two to five years in prison and a maximum fine of about $12,000 US.

The same punishment was applied to anyone publishing or keeping literature and/or audio-video materials that threaten the Islamic faith. Non-Muslims were prohibited from practicing their faith outside of government-approved buildings.

Egypt

The country's constitution gives preference to Muslims, and Christians are treated as second-class citizens, denied political representation, and discriminated against in employment. An 1856 Ottoman Empire law kept any church from being built, repaired or even repainted without the permission of Egypt's president. The law was revised in 2003, and the decision-making was left up to local governments.

In January 2003, President Mubarak declared Christmas (January 7 on the Eastern Church calendar) a public holiday. That was a first for Egypt, but Christians were still susceptible to attacks by Muslim extremists who often went unpunished. Some Christian girls were raped and then forced to marry Muslim men. Others were abducted and forced to convert to Islam. Financial incentives were offered to convince some Christian girls to convert to Islam.

Conversion from Islam to Christianity is not illegal, but some were imprisoned for "despising Islam" or "inciting intercommunal strife."

Amicable relations existed between most Muslims and Christians, but Islamic militants often attacked Christians during the Islamic holy month of Ramadan and during Christian holiday celebrations.

One of the worst attacks during the survey period occurred New Year's weekend in January 2000. Twenty-one Christians were killed in riots in the southern Egyptian town of El Kosheh. Radical Muslims went on a rampage causing dozens of serious injuries, destroying 104 Coptic homes and businesses following a heated dispute between a Christian merchant and his Muslim customer.

On January 6, Abu al-Fadl al-Qassem Ibrahim, forty-five, was caught in the hills and charged with killing eight of the Christians and injuring another.

On February 7, 2000, Father Gabriel Abdul Masih, thirty-five, was booked in a Cairo court on charges of attempted murder, conspiracy to commit murder, leading a mob attack, looting and damaging property, and possession of unlicensed weapons and ammunition. After ten hours of interrogations, the priest was released on bail and allowed to return to his parish at the Angel Michael Church in El-Kosheh. The priest denied the allegations and noted that he was not even in El-Kosheh that Sunday morning, when witnesses accused him of leading rioters.

By March 13, twenty-four of the El-Kosheh suspects had been released for "lack of evidence." All twenty-four were Muslims.

In a long-deferred judgment handed down June 5, the Sohag Criminal Court ruled Coptic Christian villager Shaiboub Arsal guilty of the 1998 double murder of his cousin and another young Copt in southern Egypt's El-Kosheh village. Arsal, thirty-eight, was sentenced to fifteen years at hard labor, the maximum sentence under Egyptian law for unpremeditated murder. Coptic activist and lawyer Mamduh Nakhla termed the judgment "extremely puzzling and highly political." Nakhla said that the defense had provided the court with "twenty pieces of evidence that (Arsal) was innocent."

Officials from Egypt's powerful State Security Intelligence (SSI) agency detained a Coptic Orthodox Christian for the fourth time in early June, interrogating him under torture on accusations of preaching Christianity to Muslims. Aziz Tawfik Rezkalah, fifty-six, was arrested by SSI officials on the night of June 7 at his home in El Mahalla el-Kubra, sixty miles north of Cairo. Police officers stripped Rezkalah of all his clothing, blindfolded him and then insulted and beat him, demanding that he confess to the accusation.

On July 16, 2000, an Egyptian court in the Sohag governate handed down an unusually harsh sentence of three years in prison at hard labor to Coptic

Christian Sourial Gayed Isshak. He had been convicted on charges of insulting the Muslim religion. Several Muslim witnesses testified that they had heard the Coptic shopkeeper curse Islam in the streets of El-Kosheh village December 30, 1999, the day before violence broke out in the village over New Year's weekend. Isshak, thirty-seven and married, was imprisoned March 9 over the slander allegations, which he categorically denied in court. Isshak was the first person sentenced in relation to the New Year's weekend violence, which targeted El-Kosheh's Coptic Christian population.

By contrast, several weeks earlier an Egyptian Muslim author accused of blaspheming against Islam and the Koran was given only a six-month suspended sentence.

Instead of convicting the Muslim murder suspects accused of killing 21 Christians in the El-Kosheh massacre, a judge in southern Egypt accused the local Coptic clergy of responsibility for the three-day rampage. In his opening statement on February 5, 2001, presiding Judge Muhammad Affify accused three priests in the predominantly Christian village of failing to put a stop to the rioting. The Sohag court acquitted all but four of the 96 suspects in the El-Kosheh trial, including seven defendants who had eluded arrest. A total of 57 Muslims were being tried, 38 of them for murder. The most serious charges against the 32 Christian defendants were looting, arson and attempted murder. Coptic Bishop Wissa of nearby Baliana village denounced the blanket acquittal of all the murder suspects as an open incitement to more killings and injustice.

The Egyptian military launched a series of attacks against a Christian farm in the Suez desert just east of Cairo, injuring several staff members and inflicting considerable property damage on the Coptic-owned Patmos Center for handicapped children. On February 19, 2001, army officers and soldiers bulldozed a 25-meter section of the compound wall and began uprooting trees along the property boundaries. The assault was only halted when civil police and state security officers summoned from Heliopolis arrived at the scene. A case involving The Patmos Center was stalled in the Egyptian courts for at least five years to recover extensive damages inflicted in similar army attacks in 1996 and 1997.

An Egyptian court issued a long-awaited retrial verdict on February 27 which virtually acquitted the accused murderers of twenty-one Coptic Christians massacred in the southern Egyptian town of El Kosheh in January 2000. A year after the carnage, the Sohag Criminal Court found four of the 96 suspects guilty—not of murder, but of vandalism and illegal possession of weapons. The Coptic *Al-Keraza* magazine called the February 27 verdict "a source of disappointment to all Copts." In its March 7, 2001 issue, *Al-Keraza* declared that the court decision "left a deep wound in their souls and a scar in their memory that time will not erase.

One Christian was killed and two others seriously injured on January 5, 2004, when another confrontation erupted between a military contingent of about 300 soldiers and the staff of the Patmos Center. The military used construction equipment to knock down several meters of wall on either side of the center's main gate. Thirteen staff workers surrounding Bishop Botros, the Coptic Orthodox cleric directing the center, were struck down. Military officials contend that the driver simply lost control of the vehicle, but church sources accused army officers of ordering the driver to run over the bishop and his staff.

An unprecedented verdict occurred on April 13, 2004, when an Egyptian court ordered the Interior Ministry to return formal Christian identity status to a Coptic Christian who had converted to Islam eleven years earlier and then returned to her Christian faith. The decision resolved a six-month stand-off with state security officials and required them to return the Christian I.D. card of Mira Makram Gobran Hanna to her possession. Hanna had signed papers in March 1993 to convert to Islam but obtained the approval of the ecclesiastical council to return to the Coptic Orthodox Church thirteen months later.

Government officials often made false accusations against Coptics and Muslim converts to Christianity to justify arrests, imprisonments and confinements to mental institutions.

In May 2005, Egyptian convert to Christianity, Gaser Muhammad Mahmoud, was held in a Cairo mental hospital, where supervising doctors told him he would stay until he recanted his faith and returned to Islam.

Mahmoud, thirty, was committed to the El-Khanka Hospital in early January by his adoptive parents after they learned he had become a Christian two years earlier.

Egyptian Christian females—teens and young adults—were kidnapped by Muslim men, raped and forced into marriage and conversion to Islam during the survey period. Police often refused to investigate missing person and suspected abduction reports from Christians because they were either sympathetic to the Muslim kidnappers or collected bribes from them.

One such case occurred in September 2005 with the disappearance of twenty-year-old Marianna Rezk Shafik Attallah. Marianna's father, Rezk Shafik Attallah, was convinced she had been kidnapped by a former police constable. Marianna had not been seen since she left work May 30 in El-Fayoum, sixty miles south of Cairo. Police obstructed efforts by her fiancé and father to find her. An Egyptian security official reported that former policeman Ali Mahmoud Abdel Rasoul had taken the young woman and moved 250 miles south to Sohag. But the official warned her fiancé, Bishoy Hosni, and father to stop looking for her, saying she had left of her own free will.

The survey period neared an end in late October 2005, with the hit and run murder of Protestant pastor Ezzat Habib. Pastor Habib was under continuous threat from Egypt's security police for holding services at his house-church. Habib and his son Ibram and a friend were crossing the street in Cairo's Matereya district on the evening of October 23 when a parked taxi pulled into the street and hit them from behind. The pastor died the next day from internal bleeding and a crushed skull. The incident culminated two years of harassment in which Pastor Habib was jailed and tortured.

The year 2005 came to an end with some good news for Egyptian Christians when President Hosni Mubarak eased long-controversial restrictions on church repair. His December 2005 decree allowed churches to implement basic repairs without waiting for government approval. For major church renovations, governors were now required to process requests within thirty days and could only reject an application by producing detailed reasons for the decision.

One Christian was killed and at least twelve others injured when three churches were attacked April 14 in Alexandria. Witnesses at one church said a crazed Muslim shouted "god is great" and "death to infidels" and assaulted Christians with two long knives as they left the church service. Seventy-eight-year-old Noshi Girgis was the lone fatality.

Gaza and the West Bank

Persecution against Palestinian Christians residing in the West Bank and Gaza Strip intensified during the 2000-2006 survey period.

International Human Rights Attorney Justus Weiner researched the plight of Palestinian Christians for more than eight years. His findings were published in late 2005 by the Jerusalem Center for Public Affairs.

Weiner said Palestinian Christians lived in fear during the period because persecution against them actually increased.

He said specifically, "I think the situation has been on a steep downhill, for at least twelve years, since Israel withdrew from the Palestinian populated areas of the Judea-Samaria/West Bank and Gaza. The Christians fear for their own lives, they fear for their own family, they fear for the future of their community."

Muslim converts to Christianity experienced the worst persecution during the survey period. They suffered harassment, physical violence, torture and even death at the hands of radical Muslims and members of the Palestinian Authority.

"Their life becomes a living hell," Weiner said. "They have no place to go, their family lives in jeopardy, they're fired from their job, and they're accused of false charges. When they're thrown in jail, they're not even fed adequately, unless their family brings food and, in effect, bribes the prison guards."

Some were accused of collaborating with Israel, working for the Mossad intelligence service or the CIA.

Abed (not his real name) converted from Islam to Christianity in 1995. He began to love everyone, and he shared his new faith with family and friends. But shortly after his conversion, Palestinian security officials began to question him. He was arrested nearly a dozen times and was eventually jailed, beaten and tortured. They hung him up in the air, and forced him to go without sleep for days.

"They tried to sit me down on the leg of a chair. They tried to let me, to sit me down on a bottle. It was hard ... I cannot describe it. And it makes me like, cry, when I remember that situation. But I feel, I feel that this suffering is a privilege from the Lord, because I suffered for Him," Abed said.

In 2000, Abed and a fellow believer, Khalid, were told that local Muslim clerics had issued a "fatwa" or judgment against them.

Also in 2000, another believer, "Ali" (not his real name) began hiding from radical Muslims by sleeping in the open or in a bomb shelter. He was still hiding out there in early 2002. Because he refused to return to Islam by a specific date, a contract was put on his life for fifty thousand shekels ($11,000 US).

Palestinians approved a draft constitution in 2005. While Western leaders praised the PA for embracing democracy, the draft constitution actually demonstrated a government consigned to institutionalizing Islam over any other religion, even over secularism.

The draft constitution pledged to guarantee freedom of worship. But in fact, Islam was stated as "the official religion of Palestine," so Shariah law was considered to be the primary source of legislation.

Under Shariah law, any Muslim who leaves Islam and chooses to convert to another faith must be killed. So it was for Ahmad El-Achwal who owned a falafel stand. The father of eight children chose to convert to Christianity and even held regular Bible studies in his home. He suffered repeated arrests and torture at the hands of Palestinian authority police.

Justice Weiner met and interviewed Achwal prior to his death in January 2004. Weiner said, "He showed me, at the time, the results of his—what were then recent—arrests. The arrest results included burns all over his body where hot pieces of sheet metal were taken from a fire and touched to his skin. And on January 21, 2004, someone knocked on the door. He opened the door and was met with a hail of bullets. Thus, he was shot dead in the entrance to his apartment."

There were several reported attacks on West Bank Christian villages late in the survey period. One of the worst occurred in September 2005 in the West Bank village of Taybeh. All that remained of fourteen homes set ablaze in the West Bank Village of Taybeh, in the Judea-Samaria/West Bank area, was charred ruin.

An angry Muslim mob from a neighboring village attacked the Christian town, saying they were "avenging the dishonor of a Muslim woman" allegedly impregnated by her Christian employer from Taybeh.

"I was standing on the hands of God's angels. They could not see angels, but I felt that they were there to help me stand."

— Pastor Wally, a missionary to Saudi Arabia, who was severely tortured for his faith in Christ

Taybeh is the only village completely inhabited by Christians—about 2,000 of them—in Judea-Samaria/West Bank. The village was originally called Ephraim and is mentioned in the Old Testament. It is also spoken of in the New Testament, in the Gospel of John, as a village where Jesus stayed. The Mayor of Taybeh—David Khoury—said the attack would not have occurred if Taybeh were a Muslim village instead of a Christian one.

The Islamic terrorist group Hamas won democratic elections in Gaza and the West Bank in late January 2006. Repeated efforts to form a unity government with the more moderate Fatah organization led by Palestinian President Mahmoud Abbas failed. Less than two percent of Palestinians are Christian, many of whom can trace their roots back to pre-Islamic times. There are about 2,000 Arab evangelicals in thirty churches, twenty of which are in the West Bank. "They feel rejected by Jews, Arabs, traditional Christians and even Western evangelicals, and thus isolated. Those from a Muslim background have been specifically targeted by Islamists" (*Operation World*). The Palestinian Bible Society bookstore in Gaza was forced to close after two small pipe bombs were exploded outside its entrance in February 2006, and several West Bank churches were fire-bombed following the controversial comments of Pope Benedict in September 2006.

Increased persecution and the Islamization of the West Bank and Gaza Strip have caused a mass exodus of Christians from the Palestinian areas. The city of Bethlehem—the birthplace of Jesus—used to be a Christian city. Several decades ago, it was perhaps more than eighty percent Christian. Today, the Christian population has declined to less than fifteen percent.

Iran

While churches are allowed in Iran, pastors and priests may only conduct services and give sermons in the Armenian language, not the national language of Farsi. Church activities are closely monitored by the Iranian religious police. The evangelization of Muslims and public demonstrations of Christian faith are prohibited. Evangelical church services are only allowed on Sundays, and Iranian law requires the government be notified when a new member joins a church.

Some Protestant associations have not been allowed to register with the government since the Iranian revolution in 1979. Churches closed by the government during the 1980s have not been allowed to reopen. Since 1990, at least eight evangelical Christians reportedly have been killed at the hands of government agents and as many as another twenty-three are reported missing. In 2001, the UN Special Rapporteur on Iran reported that the government had convicted some of the missing evangelicals on charges of apostasy.

During the 2000-2006 period, Iranian Christians continued to face discrimination in just about every aspect of life. Because university applicants are required to pass a test on Islamic theology prior to admission, most Christian students were denied access to higher education. Christians are not allowed to run for president, serve in the judiciary, security services or military. Private Christian education is allowed for Christians, but the schools are administered by the Islamic government and Christian school directors must be Muslim.

Most Iranians have tired of the undelivered promises of the Iranian revolution. They had great hopes that much-desired reforms would be implemented during the reign of President Muhammad Khatami, but their hopes were eventually dashed when dozens of reformists were sentenced to lengthy prison sentences by the Revolutionary Court.

An Assemblies of God pastor and dozens of his church members were arrested in the northern city of Chalous in May 2004. All except Pastor Khosroo Yusefi and three key church leaders were later released. Most of those arrested were former Muslims who met in house-churches. Yusefi was freed six weeks later.

The crackdown against the Assemblies of God Church in Iran continued in September 2004 as church leaders gathered for their annual general conference west of Tehran. The eighty attendees were arrested and interrogated. All but Pastor Hamid Pourmand were later released. Pourmand was moved to a military prison, put on trial and sentenced to three years in prison. A military colonel, he was found guilty of not disclosing his conversion from Islam to Christianity. It is illegal in Iran for a non-Muslim to serve as a military officer. Following international outrage and protest, an Islamic court acquitted Pourmand of charges of apostasy and proselytizing in May 2005.

Elections were held for Iran's 290-seat Parliament in February 2004, but one third of those seeking candidacy were disallowed by the Guardian Council. As a result, most reformers boycotted the election, and hardliners gained an even larger majority in the Parliament.

The extremist mayor of Tehran, Mahmud Ahmadinejad was elected President in June 2005, and the plight of Christians worsened as a result. In September, ninety church leaders were reportedly arrested and beaten. By late 2005, Ahmadinejad publicly proclaimed that the holocaust never occurred, that Israel should be wiped from the face of the Middle East map, and that Christianity should be eliminated in Iran.

In late November 2005, a house-church leader in northern Iran, Turkmen Ghorban Dordi Tourani, was found beaten and stabbed to death. His body was found in front of his home. Tourani was a Muslim convert to Christianity who had reportedly led at least twelve Muslim Turkmen to Christ over a two-year period. His family says radical Muslims in the area had made many threats against him. After his death, religious police searched Tourani's home and confiscated his Christian materials. They told family members he had been killed by local Muslims who were angry about his conversion and Christian activities.

In May 2006, long-term convert to Christ Ali Kaboli was arrested in the northern province of Golestan. Police had threatened to arrest him in the past for holding illegal religious meetings in his home. He could have been sentenced to death for comitting apostasy, but was released without charge six weeks later. Another Christian convert was arrested in August after witnesses said the eight-year-old daughter of Motamedia Mojdehi had tried to lead Muslims to Christ. Mojdehi was released one month later.

Former military officer Hamid Pourmand was released from prison in July after serving more than half of a three-year sentence for concealing his conversion from Islam to Christianity from the Army. He was warned that his release orders would be revoked if he attended church services.

The twenty-eight-year-old daughter of Christian martyr Rev. Mehdi Dibaj was arrested along with her husband in late September. Plainclothes police entered the apartment of Reza Montazami, and his wife Fereshteh Dibaj, arrested them and forced them to leave their six-year-old daughter behind. The couple ran an independent house-church in the city of Mashad. They were released on bail one week later.

Iraq

Saddam Hussein spread his brand of secular dictatorial rule throughout Iraq leading up to the U.S. liberation of the country in early 2003. While Saddam slaughtered and persecuted Iraqi Shiites and Kurds, Christians for the most part escaped persecution if they remained in government-approved churches. Evangelicals established a network of underground churches during Saddam's reign. Some were discovered by Iraqi secret police, were shut down and their leaders imprisoned. Most were sent to a detention facility in Baghdad known as the "White Ship" because the main building resembled a large ocean liner. Christians experienced harsh conditions in the facility. Some were subjected to physical and psychological torture.

Just before the U.S. liberation of Iraq, Kurdish Christian taxi driver Ziwar Muhammad Ismael was found shot dead in the northern city of Zakhoin. Family members said he was murdered because he had converted to Christianity from Islam and often shared his new faith with Muslims.

Militants also attacked American Christian missionaries and humanitarian workers during this time. In March 2003, four Baptist missionaries were gunned down and killed as they provided material relief in the city of Mosul.

A new dynamic occurred with the liberation of Iraq. When Saddam was forced from power, underground churches moved aboveground. They registered with the interim government and some built new or expanded church facilities. New churches were also started. Membership roles grew, but as Iraqi evangelicals became more overt in their faith, persecution against them increased. Those who worked for or supported the Americans were targeted for attack.

The plight of Christians worsened in 2004 as the Iraqi insurgency gained a foothold throughout the country, especially in the Sunni Triangle region in and around Baghdad.

In April 2004, seven South Korean missionaries were kidnapped but later released. Members of an Islamic rebel group calling itself Brigades and Mujahideen threatened to kill Christians, assassinate and kidnap priests, and destroy churches if the United States did not end its siege of the city of Fallujah.

In June 2004, radical Muslims killed four Assyrian Christians as they departed their neighborhood for work. Later in the day, three Assyrian Christian women returning home from work with the Coalition Provisional Authority were gunned down in a drive-by shooting. Also in June, two sisters employed by the American firm Bechtel were victims of a drive-by shooting in Basra. Assailants gunned down thirty-eight-year old Janet Audishow and twenty-five-year old Shatha Audishow as they arrived home from work. And a South Korean Christian translator was beheaded by Islamic militants calling themselves the Jamat al-Tawhid.

Fear permeated the Chaldean and Assyrian churches when many of their church buildings were bombed and shot up by Islamic radicals. Twelve Christians were killed and many women and children injured when a series of explosions occurred near four churches in Baghdad and one in Mosul August 1, 2004.

Five more Baghdad churches were bombed at the start of the Muslim holy month of Ramadan in October 2004. At least three Christians were killed when car bombs exploded outside two churches in southern Baghdad in November 2004. Two churches in Mosul were bombed in early December 2004.

Christian shopkeepers have been shot and killed, their shops destroyed, and other Christians have been targeted for assassination. In October 2004, seven Christian workers with the Baghdad Hunting Club were gunned down in a Christian suburb of Baghdad.

Radicals killed a Christian woman in October 2004 because her head was uncovered. Other bareheaded Christian women were reportedly squirted with nitric acid. Many Christian female students stopped attending Mosul University after displeased Muslim extremists made threats against them because of the clothing they were wearing.

Insurgents seeking to extort money or gain media attention often targeted Christians for abduction. In autumn 2005, an Anglican priest was kidnapped and presumed dead, and the son of an evangelical pastor was also kidnapped. Christians said abductions against them were occurring because they were leading many Iraqi Muslims to faith in Jesus Christ.

In late September 2005, the entire lay leadership of Iraq's main Anglican Church was massacred in an ambush as they returned home from a church conference in Jordan. Among those killed were lay pastor Maher Dakel, his wife Mona, their son Yeheya, and Firas Raad, the church music director.

Although the Iraqi parliament met in May 2006 for its first full legislative session since it was elected in December, competing Muslim factions caused the nation to drift further apart. American and Iraqi troops also seemed unable to halt an Islamic terrorist-led insurgency.

As 2006 came to a close, kidnappings, shootings, car bombings and attacks with improvised explosive devices continued daily. Christians and Assyrian and Chaldean church buildings often came under attack.

Thousands of Iraqi Christians have fled their country and are now living in Syria, Jordan, Canada, Europe, and the United States.

Kuwait

Islam is the state religion and Shariah law is the source of legislation. Christians are free to worship without government interference within their communities.

The population of the Christian community is estimated at between 250,000 and 500,000. The majority are Roman Catholic and Maronite Christians. Other denominations present in Kuwait are the Anglicans, Greek Orthodox, National Evangelical Church, Armenian Orthodox and Coptic Orthodox. Tens of thousands of Christians are members of other unrecognized denominations.

Government procedures for registration and licensing of churches and religious groups in Kuwait are ambiguous. The government has not responded to several requests to build churches. With only two church buildings and more than 100,000 attendees, the Roman Catholic Church faces severe overcrowding, yet the construction of new facilities has yet to be approved.

Only Muslims may become citizens. Evangelism to Kuwaitis is forbidden. The government discourages Christianity by providing financial incentives for Muslims and has even purchased large quantities of Bibles to burn them.

Relations between Muslims and Christians are amicable in Kuwait, and there were no major incidents of persecution of Christians reported during the survey period.

In June 2006, women were allowed to stand for election and vote for the first time in Kuwait; and while there's been a loosening of strict religious rules, full freedom to worship is still not a reality.

Lebanon

Though Lebanon's sixteen-year civil war between Christians and Muslims had ended one decade earlier, tensions between the groups continued during the 2000-2006 period. Christians and predominantly Christian villages were often targeted for attack by Islamic guerrilla groups. Unfortunately, it was not always easy to tell if the problems were political or religious. They appeared to be a mixture of both.

Freedom of religion is enshrined in the Lebanese constitution, and for the most part it is respected; however, Article 473 of the Penal Code stipulates that one who "blasphemes God publicly" will face imprisonment for up to one year. The major danger faced by Christians in Lebanon was from anti-Christian militants within the populace.

On November 21, 2002, an unknown assassin gunned down American missionary Bonnie Penner Witherall, thirty-one, with three pistol shots to her head. She had just begun her morning shift at the Unity Center, a prenatal clinic that provides care to women in Sidon and the Ein al-Helweh Palestinian refugee camp. Weatherall and other workers at the clinic had previously received threats and complaints about their efforts to convert Muslims.

On February 14, 2005, former Prime Minister Rafiq Hariri was assassinated in a bombing, which also killed Mr. Basel Flaihan, a Christian Evangelical Church member in the Lebanese Parliament.

In the wake of the Hariri assassination, five bombings targeted Christian districts and locations.

Two people were killed and five wounded March 23, 2005, when a bomb ripped through a shopping center in the anti-Syrian Christian heartland north of the Lebanese capital of Beirut. The explosion was the second in a commercial Christian area in five days.

Another shopping center was bombed in the Christian resort village of Broummana east of Beirut April 1, 2005, wounding twelve people and causing extensive damage.

On May 6, 2003, a Jordanian convert from Islam was killed while attempting to defuse a bomb planted at the home of a missionary couple in a suburb of Tripoli. Authorities believed the bombing was related to their missionary activities in the country.

Two people were killed and twenty-seven injured during the May 6, 2005 attack of *The Voice of Charity* radio station run by the Congregation of Maronite Lebanese Missionaries.

In the mostly Christian neighborhood of Zalka, on August 22, 2005, a bomb placed between a shopping center and a hotel damaged shops and windows, wounding eight people. It consisted of twenty to thirty kilograms of TNT set on a timer.

A car bomb explosion rocked the largely Christian area of Ashrafieh on September 16, 2005. One person was killed and twenty-three injured. Two cars were blown up and buildings near the blast were severely damaged.

Christian journalist and critic of Syria, May Chidiac was seriously injured when a bomb exploded as she got into her car in Jounieh on September 25, 2005. She lost her left leg and arm. Chidiac was a television news anchor with the Lebanese Broadcasting Corporation.

In July 2006, Israel launched a massive military operation against Hizballah terrorists in Lebanon. Israel's goal was to eliminate Hizballah and gain the release of two kidnapped Israeli soldiers. South Lebanon Christians were caught in the crossfire as Hizballah launched katusha rocket attacks against Israel from Christian villages. Israel responded by bombing the Hizballah positions. Christians were killed, injured, and their homes and businesses were destroyed as a result.

As the 2000-2006 period came to an end, Christians struggled to rebuild their neighborhoods, and they feared that the ongoing political strife in the country meant they would continue to be targeted for attack by Muslim militants and those who opposed them in their midst.

Libya

The Libyan government restricts freedom of religion, but Christians for the most part are free to practice their faith openly without hindrance from the government, unless their practices appear to be politically motivated. Sunni Islam is the preferred faith and rarely are Christians harassed by Muslims.

The Vatican established diplomatic relations with Muhammar Qadhafi in 1997, saying his government had taken steps to protect the religious rights of Libyan Christians. An estimated 50,000 Christians reside in Libya. Most of them are foreigners, and about 40,000 of them are Roman Catholic. The Anglican Church in Tripoli is comprised mostly of African migrant workers. The Christian community also includes Egyptian Coptics and members of the Greek Orthodox Church.

The government restricts the number of churches allowed to one building for each denomination per city. Libyans are off limits for evangelism. A number of expatriates are seeking to reach Libyans, but they are hindered by the country's elaborate secret police network. Christian literature may enter only through secretive means.

There were no major cases of persecution against Christians reported during the survey period.

Morocco

Islam is the official state religion and the constitution guarantees religious freedom for Moroccan citizens. The estimated number of Christians in Morocco is as high as 25,000.

There are about 5,000 practicing Christians in the foreign community. Christians are allowed to openly practice their faith, but proselytizing is prohibited and restrictions are placed on Christian materials. Bibles are allowed in languages other than Arabic.

Voluntary conversion from Islam to Christianity is allowed under the Moroccan Criminal and Civilian codes; however, converts have faced questioning by authorities and in some cases they've been jailed. Inducing a Muslim to leave his faith is illegal, and attempting to prevent him from attending religious services or exercising his religious beliefs is punishable by as much as six months in prison and a possible fine of 575 dirhams ($50 US).

Foreign missionaries are allowed to conduct humanitarian activities. Some foreign Christians have opened orphanages, hospitals and schools in addition to churches. They've done so without government restrictions; the government did not require licensing and registration.

In 2000, some members of the foreign Christian community were summoned by the Gendarmerie Royale for questioning about the practicing of their faith. None were deported as a result.

Moderate Muslims and secularists fear a rising tide of Islamic extremism in Morocco. A January 2006 opinion survey indicated forty-four percent of Moroccans aged sixteen to twenty-nine believe al Qaeda is not a terrorist organization. Thirty-eight percent said they did not know. In early October 2006, the government announced it was removing Koranic and Hadith verses from school textbooks on Islamic education. Photos of girls wearing the hijab were also removed. The government said it was taking the action in an attempt to prevent the rise of radical Islam among the youth.

Oman

Islam is the state religion of Oman and Christians are free to practice their faith as long as they do not breach the "public order." Proselytizing Muslims is prohibited. Shariah law is the basis of legislation and the government restricts the activities of non-Muslims. Christian organizations are required to register their activities with the government. Land has been given to Christians by the Sultan for worship center construction.

Discussion of religious beliefs is allowed; however, Christians are prohibited from publishing religious literature in Oman. The importation of religious literature is not allowed, and leaving the Islamic faith is prohibited.

Qatar

During the 2000-2006 period, the Qatar government continued its prohibition against public worship for faiths other than Islam. Jews and Christians were quietly allowed to worship privately as long as they gave prior notice of intent to the government. The importation of non-Muslim religious publications and materials was prohibited except for personal use.

For the most part, the Christian community in Qatar is comprised primarily of foreign workers—Filipinos, Indians, Europeans, Arabs and Americans, representing Catholics, Anglicans, Orthodox and Protestants.

The state religion is Wahhabi Islam. Conversion from Islam to Christianity is considered apostasy. It is officially a capital offense, but the last known execution for apostasy in Qatar occurred in 1971.

In early January 2000, word spread that the government was liberalizing the country's religion policy and would allow a plot of land to be shared by various Christian denominations. The proposed compound would house several church buildings. The Catholic church of Doha would be the first allowed to construct a church facility.

The *Gulf Times* newspaper said the government decision indicated an opening of "new vistas of freedom and religious tolerance" in Qatar.

Few incidents of persecution against Christians were made public during the survey period, but among those reported was the deportation of India national Stanislas Chellappa, a Christian medical technician. Chellappa had lived and worked in Qatar for twenty-two years; and in January 2003, the Interior Ministry ordered him to leave the country along with his wife and son. Chellappa had led a small Tamil-speaking church in the capital city of Doha. He believed he was deported because he was a Christian, but government officials maintained that his deportation was linked to a corruption crackdown against employees at the hospital where he worked. Chellappa said there was no mention of corruption each time officials questioned him prior to his deportation. "Police asked me several times if I was a Christian," he said. "but they said nothing about corruption."

Saudi Arabia

Religious freedom is non-existent in Saudi Arabia. Missionary activity and Christian evangelism are prohibited and public religious expressions other than the government's interpretation of Sunni Islam are banned. The Saudi Monarchy uses religious police (mutawa) to enforce the government's religious restrictions throughout the kingdom. Christian activities are monitored regularly and the mutawa often raid worship services in Christian homes. Christians have been arrested, beaten, tortured and imprisoned for practicing their faith in Saudi Arabia. Many Christian expatriates have been deported.

Forty-year-old Filipino engineer Edmar Romero was arrested December 1, 1999, and was still imprisoned in late January 2000, even though authorities promised he would be released at the conclusion of the Muslim holidays in mid-January. Romero's Bible and other Christian literature found in his home and office by religious police were confiscated at the time of his arrest. Romero was forced to submit to Islamic dictates during his imprisonment which included fasting during the Muslim holidays.

The mutawa continued its ongoing investigation of a secret Christian worship network in the kingdom by attempting to extricate information from four Filipino Christians arrested during a raid on a house-church meeting January 7. Fifteen of the one hundred Christians who had gathered at the home of Art and Sabalista Abreu were arrested. Most were released within two weeks, but Vic Mira Velez, Rupino Sulit, Art Abreu and Eminesio Rabea were still jailed a month after arrest. Their arrest and imprisonment occurred despite claims from Saudi authorities that Christians are allowed to worship privately in their homes without government interference.

In summer 2001, religious police launched a major effort to track down Saudi nationals believed to have had contact with expatriate Christians. At least thirteen Indian, Ethiopian, Nigerian, Filipino and Eritrea Christians from house-church groups in Jeddah were arrested, jailed and interrogated. A June gathering of more than 400 Christians at a rented hall in Jeddah may have prompted the religious police investigation. Saudi law forbids Christians from gathering together in public places. The thirteen Christians remained jailed at Christmas time.

In November 2001, seven Ethiopians—several of them women—were taken into police custody as they left a house-church meeting.

At the end of March 2002, the last of the expatriate Christians rounded up in religious police raids the previous summer were released from prison and deported.

After his return to Manila, freed Filipino Dennis Moreno said government authorities jailed the expatriate Christians because they were afraid many Saudis were changing their faith.

An Eritrean and an Ethiopian were arrested in spring 2003 for their involvement in "Christian activities." Their arrest and deportation came after religious police subjected members of an Ethiopian-Eritrean Christian congregation in Jeddah to extensive questioning about the church's religious activities.

In October 2003, two Egyptian Christians were arrested for "illegal" religious activities and were released three weeks later. In December 2003, a foreign worker reportedly was arrested and charged with apostasy—a crime punishable by death in Saudi Arabia. Three months later charges against him were reduced to blasphemy. He received 600 lashes and two years in prison.

The persecution of Christians intensified in the Saudi Kingdom in 2004. In February, a Christian was deported for giving an Arabic Bible to a Saudi citizen. An Indian foreign worker reportedly was arrested and tortured for preaching Christianity in March and deported in November 2004.

Forty Pakistani workers held a Christian service at a private home in Riyadh in April 2005. The mutawa detained them and some were held for two days before they were released. Also, one week later in Riyadh, the mutawa burst into an East African house-church meeting attended by sixty Ethiopians and Eritreans. Five church leaders were arrested and Bibles in the Amharic and Tigrinya languages were confiscated. They were jailed, blindfolded and interrogated for seven days and released one month later.

In June 2006, a private worship meeting attended by 100 Eritreans, Ethiopians and Filipinos was raided by police in Jeddah. Two Ethiopian and two Eritrean house-church leaders were arrested and jailed for "preaching to Muslims, planting churches and gathering ladies and gentlemen together for prayer." The four were held for more than a month, were reportedly tortured and then deported back to their home countries.

Syria

Religious freedom is guaranteed in the Syrian Constitution, and Christians experience less persecution in Syria than in other Muslim nations. There is no state religion, but Syria's president must be a Muslim. Christians are free to worship as they choose and evangelism is allowed, but discouraged. All religious groups are required to register with the government and permits must be obtained for religious gatherings other than regularly scheduled church services. Government agents regularly monitor sermons and church services.

There were no major incidents of persecution against Christians reported during the survey period; however, Muslim converts to Christianity suffered ostracism, banishment, harassment, and physical and emotional abuse from their families and communities because of their decision to embrace Christianity.

Tunisia

While Islam is the state religion in Tunisia, the government does allow Christians and other religious groups to worship freely as long as they do not disturb the public order. Proselytism is prohibited.

The Christian community in Tunisia numbers about 20,000. Most are temporary and permanent foreign workers; some are native-born citizens of Arab or European origin.

Practicing Christians are only believed to number about 2,000. At least 200 Christians are converts from Islam. The Catholic Church is believed to have the most practicing members—about 1,400 people. The Catholic Church has five church buildings, fourteen private schools, seven cultural centers throughout the country, and one hospital in Tunis, the Tunisian capital. The Russian Orthodox, French Reform, Anglican, and Greek Orthodox churches have a total of slightly more than 300 practicing members. All have congregations in Tunis. The Catholic Church and

Russian and Greek Orthodox churches have congregations in other Tunisian cities in addition to Tunis.

Most Tunisians are nominal Muslims, and amicable relations exist between religious communities. The government prohibits Christians from building new churches, and foreign missionaries are not allowed to operate in the country. If foreign Christians are found proselytizing, they are deported. Christian literature is not openly distributed.

While no major incidents of persecution against Christians were reported during the survey period, there were reports that several Muslim converts to Christianity were denied passports, voting rights, and military service because of their conversion.

Also during the survey period, Tunisian government officials reportedly confiscated Christian materials distributed to secondary school students in the city of Sfax.

United Arab Emirates

Islam is the state religion in the UAE, and freedom of religion is limited to the Christian expatriate community. Christians are free to worship and witness within the expatriate community, but not outside of it with Muslims. Also, Christians can be tried in Islamic (Shariah) courts.

Foreign missionaries are allowed in the UAE, but their activities are limited to humanitarian work. They are not allowed to proselytize. The government limits the ability of Christian groups to worship or assemble without a designated building.

Local rulers determine whether to grant a group access to land and permission to construct a church building within their emirate. Twenty-four church buildings have been constructed in the UAE on land donated by ruling families.

In May 2003, a Shariah court found Filipino Pastor Fernando Alconga guilty of "abusing Islam" and conducting missionary activity. He was arrested five months earlier for giving a Bible and Christian literature to an Arab Muslim at a shopping center. Pastor Alconga spent five weeks in jail and was charged with violating the UAE Federal Criminal Code for "preaching other than the Islamic religion," a felony. The court suspended Alconga's punishment because it did not believe he would repeat his offense. He was deported in July—more than nine months after his arrest. In March 2006, the government banned a social studies textbook on world cultures for "insulting the country's religions and culture." In May 2006, an expatriate school principal was banned from teaching or working in education in the UAE because she prohibited Koranic recitals during school activities.

Yemen

The Yemeni Constitution guarantees religious freedom, yet the official state religion is Islam, and the Constitution declares that Shariah law is the source of all legislation. Christians are allowed to practice their faith privately in homes or other facilities without government interference, but proselytism by non-Muslims is prohibited as is conversion from the Islamic faith. Muslims who leave the faith are apostates and face execution for deserting Islam.

In July 2000, an Islamic court in the capital city of Aden ordered Somali Christian convert Muhammad Omer Haji to return to Islam within one week or face execution for committing apostasy. Following an international outcry, Haji, his wife, and small child were deported and were granted emergency religious asylum in New Zealand.

Christians must obtain government approval before constructing a new church building. In 1998, the government agreed to a Vatican request to construct a Christian center in Sana'a.

The historic Christ Church was among buildings attacked in a series of five New Years Day bombings in Aden in January 2001. No one was injured when a bomb exploded around 5:30 A.M. at the Anglican church, knocking out a dozen walls and destroying two rooms of the pastor's residence. The church pastor and his wife were abroad on holidays at the time of the blast.

One of the most notorious persecution incidents occurred December 30, 2002, at the Baptist Hospital in Jibla. Hospital administrator William Koehn, Dr. Martha Myers and purchasing agent Kathleen Gariety were martyred by Islamic militant Abed Abdul Razak Kamel. The thirty-year-old Kamel had entered the hospital with a semi-automatic gun hidden under his clothing. He opened fire on the three American missionaries as they attended a staff meeting. Kamel, a suspected al-Qaida militant said he murdered the three Christians because "they had converted dozens of Muslims to Christianity." The missionaries were well loved by the Yemenis. The day after the killings, hundreds of Muslims came to pay their respects and lined up along the road for more than a half mile leading up to the hospital entrance. Forgiveness was the central theme of funeral "thanksgiving" services in Yemen and the United States. Kamal was found guilty and sentenced to death in May 2003.

In late February 2006, a second gunman with alleged ties to the al-Qaida terrorist network was executed for killing the three Baptist missionaries.

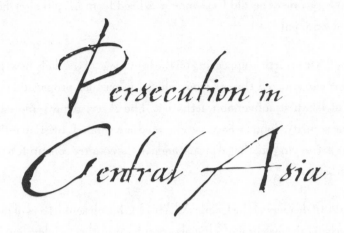

Persecution in
Central Asia

Azerbaijan

After enduring seventy years of atheism under Soviet communism, the Azeri church grew in the 2000-2006 period, and now numbers at least 2,000 believers. The New Testament and a children's Bible are now available in the Azeri language, but persecution against Azeri Christians intensified during this time as the government attempted to control the growth of the Christian church and temper the spread of more radical forms of Islam. During the survey period, Christians experienced persecution from government officials—many of them Muslims or former communists.

In January 2000, Baptists operating a street library in the western city of Gyanja were threatened by police who warned them to "stop preaching the gospel among Muslims." After an unidentified man assaulted one of the Christian workers, two of the Baptist men were held by authorities and later released.

In April 2001, two evangelical Christians were arrested and jailed for seven days in the city of Ismailly, 120 miles west of Baku. The two men— Asif Mardanov and Azer Gasymov—were arrested by police at their homes and charged with conducting mass evangelism while picnicking with other Christians on April 7. The arrests occurred, though no one was known to have complained to police about the Christian's activities.

The twenty-one-year-old Gasymov was fired from his job after he was released from jail.

In May 2001, an article appearing on the front page of the daily newspaper, the *Zerkalo*, equated threats from "illegal Christian propaganda" with those of Islamist subversion activities. The Azeri deputy minister of national security, Tofiq Babayev, was quoted as saying, "Christian religious structures carrying out illegal propaganda in the country constitute a threat to Azerbaijan."

In July 2001, leaders of the Ganja Adventist Church sent letters of protest to Azerbaijani government officials complaining that a television news program deliberately propagated intolerance and created a disrespectful attitude toward the church.

Adventist pastor Khalid Babaev was forced from the city of Nakhichevan after he had received numerous death threats. In May 2004, he was fined for leading an unregistered congregation in the city if Sumgait near the capital city of Baku. Also in May, two Adventist pastors in the city of Gyanja were fined for not registering their places of residence.

In September 2004, a Baptist congregation in northwest Azerbaijan was raided by police for not registering its religious activities. While most Protestant congregations were functioning quietly with little government interference, it was unclear why the Baptists were singled out. The only church allowed to register during the 2000-2006 period was the Armenian Apostolic Church.

Many local government officials during the survey period reportedly refused to issue birth certificates to children given Christian names. One Christian parent was asked why he was choosing the name Luke for his newborn son. The government official suggested the parents name the child after a famous Azeri poet or writer instead. The child's father responded by saying that Luke was one of the writers of the Gospels and will be famous long after the poets or writers are forgotten. Birth certificates are required in Azerbaijan in order for a child to attend school, gain hospital treatment, or travel abroad.

In December 2004, a notary in Zapata in northwestern Azerbaijan said, "We don't need any Baptists here." For more than a year, Najiba Mamedova refused to notarize signatures on a registration application for the local Baptist church in Aliabd. The church had applied for registration since 1994. One official said there was no need for the church in the community because they already had a mosque. Also in December, Adventists in the city of Nakhichevan reported their church had been crushed, and authorities in the enclave near the Turkey, Armenia and Iran border region banned the church from meeting.

In February 2005, the head of the State Committee for Work with Religious Organizations, Rafik Aliev accused the Adventist and Greater Grace Protestant churches of conducting "illegal religious propaganda," and of "disturbing citizens residing near places where prayers are held." Aliev reportedly used a similar approach in 2002 to close down an Azeri-language Baptist church in the capital city of Baku.

In April 2005, a commanding officer of the unrecognized army of the Nagorno-Karabakh republic, Gagik Mirzoyan, was beaten and held for ten days for evangelizing. Christian calendars were discovered in his possession and authorities threatened him with a two-year prison sentence.

In July 2005, The Azerbaijan Center for Religion and Democracy was the latest religious non-government organization denied registration by the Justice Ministry.

Also in July, the Swedish pastor of the charismatic Cathedral of Praise church in Baku was deported after having lived in Azerbaijan for more than ten years. His visa renewal was denied in June, and he was given two weeks to leave the country. Azeri Christians maintained that they had the right to invite foreigners to lead their service and church communities if they so desired.

Raids on open-air preaching and summer camps intensified in the summer of 2005. One of the most serious attacks occurred in the northwestern town of Gakh near the Georgia border. The Love Baptist Church summer camp attended by thirty-five children was raided by more than thirty police officers and KGB agents on July 21. Witnesses said police were heard shouting and swearing even at the women. One man said his tooth was knocked out in front of the children. Twelve workers were handcuffed, arrested and taken in for questioning. The Christians were accused of "selling out to the Armenians." They were released the next day, but ten of the camp leaders were fined a combined total of about $152 US. The average monthly salary of an Azeri is $32 US.

Another Christian camp was raided in August in the southern port town of Neftechala. One neighbor complained that the Baptist day camp was noisy and said the workers "shouldn't be telling Azerbaijani children about Christ." Neighbors hit two of the children attending the camp and dragged them away.

Christians expressed concern when the ruling party won parliamentary elections in November 2005. They predicted the government's policy of using registration to discriminate against and control religious communities would continue.

Chechnya

Chechnya declared its independence from Russia in 1994. Its citizens live under Islamic law. Protestant Christians there have suffered persecution and death threats. Almost all of the 950,000 Chechens are Muslim and have been radicalized by Sufism and international Islamists. Chechnya's Christian presence is practically nonexistent, and Christian aid organizations have withdrawn in order to work with refugees in North Ossetiya.

Sixty-five-year-old Aleksandr Kulakov, leader of the Grozny Baptist Church, was reportedly beheaded in 1999, and his severed head displayed at a local market.

Also, when the Grozny Baptist Church was captured by militant Muslims October 2, 1999, a thirteen-year-old church member, a Christian girl named Anya Hrykin, was kidnapped and held for three months until she was found by Russian soldiers in late December and taken to a safe house in early January 2000. She had been raped repeatedly by her Muslim captors, physically abused, and nearly starved to death.

Tajikistan

The government fears the spread of Islamic fundamentalism and national disharmony in Tajikistan. It has attempted to control religion by embracing a policy of active secularism; as a result, government officials have often expressed anti-religious attitudes.

Nine Christians were killed and another seventy injured October 1, 2000, when two bombs ripped through the Sunday morning worship service at Grace Sonmin Church in the Tajik capital of Dushanbe. Police originally held and interrogated more than a dozen members of the church, but three weeks later they arrested three Muslim students from the local institute of Islamic studies. One local newspaper reported the attack was "God's punishment on traitors" of the Islamic faith. Some members of the predominantly Korean church were Muslim converts to Christianity.

At the end of July 2003, a Baptist evangelist was fined five times the minimum wage (about $8 US) for talking to passers-by about God. The fine was imposed against the man, even though the country's 1994 law on Religion and Religious Organizations does not prohibit evangelization.

On January 12, 2004, Baptist Pastor Sergei Besarab was gunned down as he prayed in the northern city of Isfara. Isfara is a district known for Islamic fundamentalism. Besarab's missionary activities had come under fire from the local newspaper. A previously unknown Islamist group called Bayat—with ties to the Afghan Taliban—was believed to be responsible for the murder.

The Grace Sonmin Church in the northern city of Khujand was ordered closed for violating the law. Some Muslims said they were annoyed by the church and wanted it shut down. Officials wouldn't explain what law had been violated even though the church had operated in the city for eleven years without incident.

In 2006, government officials announced the postponement of a proposed draft Religion Law that would have been the most restrictive in Central Asia.

Turkmenistan

Repression of religious activity in Turkmenistan has increased in recent years. A new religion law was imposed on the Turkmen people in 1996. It required all religious communities to register with the government, and each church needed to have 500 members before they could register. Churches refusing to register their activities faced fines of five to ten times the average member's monthly wage. The government has refused to accept the registration applications of many churches. The Armenian Apostolic Church is one of the largest church communities in Turkmenistan denied registration.

The 2000-2006 period saw an intensification of government efforts to enforce the law and to expand the influence and acceptance of President Niyazov's own brand of religion. Church buildings were closed and confiscated and some were demolished. Christian activists were imprisoned, and foreigners suspected of religious activity either saw their property confiscated or were expelled.

Ukrainian Pastor Vladimir Chernov and his wife Olga were deported two days before Christmas 1999. The Baptist couple was put on a plane and sent to Kiev with only the clothes on their back. Another Baptist couple was deported to Russia at the same time. The expulsions were part of a coordinated government effort in late 1999 and early 2000 to remove prominent Christian leaders from Turkmenistan.

In addition to expulsions, National Security Committee secret police (former KGB) often raided church services as five of them did against the Baptist church of Balkanabad in July 2001. They took down the names of all members attending the service and threatened to confiscate the church building if the Christians gathered again. The church leadership was warned against taking legal action.

A major crackdown on Christians and people of other faiths occurred in the spring of 2003. Unregistered approved places of worship were confiscated and destroyed, and restrictions against government-approved churches were tightened. Many Christians were denied a place to worship. The sharing of religious beliefs in public and in the media is not allowed, and formal religious education is prohibited in Turkmenistan.

In April, NSC police reportedly removed Christian children from their classrooms in the same western city. The students were interrogated about their church activities and "Christian education" at home. The children were prohibited from attending church, and the older children were reportedly threatened with imprisonment.

In late May 2003, a non-denominational church was raided in the city of Abadan. Guzelya Syraeva was among the church members fined for attending an "illegal" church meeting. In June, Syraeva was pressured to quit her job as a kindergarten school teacher. She said she never preached to her students, and she insisted that government officials were trying to "sack" her because of her religious beliefs.

In late 2003, President Niyazov signed a revised religion law. All unregistered church communities were officially banned, and members of minority faiths faced possible criminal charges. The population of Turkmenistan is estimated at five million people. Less than three percent are Christian, and most Christians are Orthodox. The registration requirement was almost impossible for most Protestant groups to meet— most of their churches had fewer than 100 attendees.

President Niyazov's brand of religion was a strange cult of personality, where statues and portraits of him appear throughout the country. A two-volume ideological book published in his name called the *Ruhnama* (Book of the Soul), which officials have likened to the Koran or the Bible, is compulsory reading for schoolchildren and the public. At the end of 2000, Orthodox priests reportedly received orders to quote from the *Ruhnama* in sermons and to preach about the virtues of living in Turkmenistan and of the policies of Turkmenbashi.

Religious leaders are required to display the *Ruhnama* prominently in their places of worship. One Ashgabad mosque has a dedicated *Ruhnama* room. Nyazov has ordered that Russian Orthodox churches must have a minimum of two copies of it in parish libraries. No new Christian publications appear in those libraries because the printing of Christian literature is no longer allowed in Turkmenistan.

Government raids on religious meetings continued in a new wave of persecution in summer 2005, as Nyazov moved to further impose his religious ideology on the citizenry. Protestant Christians were among devotees harassed. Churches were confiscated or demolished, and believers were beaten, fined, detained, deported and removed from their jobs in punishment for unapproved religious activity. Among them was Asiya Zasedatelevaya, who regularly held Bible study in her apartment. It was raided by police in July 2005. Christian literature and other materials were confiscated; she was hit on the head with a Bible and punched in the face. One of the men interrogating her threatened to hang her because of her "illegal" activities.

A registered Baptist church was raided by anti-terrorism police in the northeastern town of Dashoguz in August 2005. Police told church attendees that even though their church was registered in the nation's capital of Ashgabad, the registration was not valid in Dashoguz. Police warned that church members could not meet together again. They said, "Individuals can only believe alone on their own at their home."

The government used its church registration requirement in 2006 to deny several churches official recognition. Among them was the Armenian Apostolic Church in Ashgabad. Evangelical Christians have suffered the most persecution under the government's religious legislation, which is considered to be one of the harshest systems of state control over religious life. Participation in unregistered Baptist house-churches has resulted in fines, the seizure of family possessions, and deductions from their salary. Russian Baptist Aleksandr Frolov was expelled from Turmenistan in June

2006 because of his religious activity. Pastor Frolov led church meetings in his home. His expulsion separated him from his Turkmen wife and two young children.

Uzbekistan

Christians in this former Soviet Republic have been affected by government attempts to control the advancement of radical Islam and potential political opposition. House-churches are illegal, and Christians convicted of evangelization or unregistered missionary activity can end up spending three years in prison. All churches must register with the government, and police reportedly have raided church services demanding to see registration papers. Those unable to produce the documentation have been closed.

Christians and other religious minorities report that they are often followed and their activities monitored by national security police. Pastors and other church workers—especially Baptists and Pentecostals—have been singled out. Some have been arrested, beaten and harassed. Bibles and Christian publications have been confiscated by police and destroyed.

Police in Nukus arrested Christian camp leader Nikolai Rudinsky in July 2000 on false charges of illegal drug possession. Rudinsky was jailed and severely beaten after police closed down a youth church camp sponsored by a legally registered church. Police said Rudinsky's church—the Mir Presbyterian Church—had no right to operate a religious camp, and they threatened him with life imprisonment if he did not cooperate with their investigation by naming other camp organizers. Mir Presbyterian was the last legally registered Christian church. It was forcibly closed by government officials July 24. Rudinsky was released two months later.

Two Pentecostals meeting in the western autonomous region of Karakalpakstan were arrested, beaten and jailed for five days in December 2002. Pentecostal church leader Salavat Serikbayev remarked that Protestants in the city of Muinak were prohibited from meeting together and lived "like the first catacomb Christians under the Roman Empire."

On February 28, 2003, ten Baptist women—Kazakh and Karakalpak ethnics—had gathered in an apartment in the town of Khojali for a Christian meeting. National Security Service police raided the apartment and took the women to the police station for interrogation. The women say they were subjected to verbal slurs against their Christian faith and were questioned and detained for twenty-seven hours. They were held in a cell overnight with male prisoners—some of them homeless vagrants.

In October 2004, in the Uzbek capital of Tashkent, 120 members of Bethany Baptist Church were midway through Sunday service when they were abruptly interrupted by eight police officers. They ordered the worship to stop, saying that the Christians were participating in an "illegal religious meeting."

It was not the first raid on the church. The pastor was arrested and fines were imposed in May 2000 and June 2001. Bethany church has existed since 1996—two years before strict registration laws were imposed. Its leaders say they have filed all required paperwork and have paid a hefty registration fee, yet the government has refused to grant the congregation registration. At least three other Tashkent churches have experienced similar persecution.

"Today, my love, I will see you in Heaven."

— These were the words of a mother to her young daughter who was hanged for her faith by communist guards. The mother was executed shortly thereafter.

Uzbek Christians have also experienced persecution from Muslims. In October 2005, in the village of Janbashkala, near the southwestern city of Turtkul, Muslim converts to Christianity were denied access to drinking water, adults and children reportedly suffered severe beatings, and workers lost their jobs and businesses. Christian homes were attacked and confiscated, and hefty fines were imposed against those attending "illegal" church meetings. Kaldibek Primbetov, the first person to convert to Christianity in the village five years ago, said the most influential Muslim in town told him, "There is no place here for Christians." The wealthy man said Muslim converts needed to live in Kazakhstan or Russia if they wanted to be Christian. Half the Christian families of Janbashkala fled the village because of the persecution against them.

In summer 2005, a twenty-two-minute documentary depicting members of the Full Gospel Church (FGC) of Urgench as an extremist religious group was broadcast on regional television. People throughout Uzbekistan began saying the FGC was worse than Wahhabi Muslims. The documentary showed scenes of a police raid against the church, and depicted Pastor Ruzmet Voisov and his congregation as Christian extremists bent on destroying national stability.

In late 2005, the Uzbek government launched a major crackdown against Christian charitable organizations and groups suspected of receiving financial aid from abroad. No fewer than 1,000 organizations were closed. Government officials said the organizations were shut down because they violated federal law by conducting illegal missionary activities. On Christmas Day 2005, Pastor Bakhtier Tuichev was brutally beaten by assailants who said he had betrayed the faith of his ancestors. Tuichev fell unconscious and was hospitalized for more than a week. Pastor Tuichev believes his assault was ordered by government authorities because he was interrogated for nine hours by police a month earlier and told "a lot of trouble" was in store if he did not abandon his unregistered church activities. Authorities had questioned Tuichev about his possible links to Western human rights organizations and potential foreign financial support. He was forced to sign a statement pledging that his church would not meet.

Also in late 2005, fines for unregistered illegal religious activity were reportedly increased extensively from five to ten times the minimum wage to from fifty to one hundred times the minimum wage.

The Uzbek Supreme Court upheld the government-ordered closures of the Emmanuel Full Gospel Church in Nukus and the Forest Full Gospel Congregation in Tashkent. All Protestant church activity in northwest Uzbekistan is now prohibited. One Protestant church member said, "Unfortunately in Uzbekistan today there is no Protestant church that doesn't face persecution, whether registered or not."

Police continued to make unannounced visits to churches in 2006, demanding to see their registration papers. Churches that cannot immediately produce their registration are closed and their doors sealed by the police. Pastors have been arrested and detained and members threatened. In April 2006, police raided a house-church meeting near the Turkemistan border city of Urgench. A computer and Christian literature were confiscated, and Pastor Lunkin Sergey and church member Chursin Vasily were charged with "breaking the laws on teaching religion." House-church meetings in Uzbekistan are illegal. In one raid, police reportedly said there was no need for Christians or faiths other than Islam in Uzbekistan. The government closed at least a dozen foreign charities in 2006. Most of them were religiously affiliated, and alleged missionary activity of staffers was cited as the reason for the closures.

Persecution in Europe

Belarus

Belarus became an independent state in 1991, after the dissolution of the Soviet Union. Many state officials are still influenced and committed to militant atheism.

In November 2002, a repressive new religion law came into effect. According to the new law, all unregistered religious activity, communities with fewer than twenty members, and any religious activity in private homes (apart from occasional, small-scale meetings) were considered illegal. Religious communities without a registered umbrella body were not allowed to invite foreign citizens for religious work, and all religious literature was subjected to censorship. In addition, all religious organizations were required to re-register within two years.

All unregistered churches were banned and liable to prosecution, but despite the new law and requirements, the number of unregistered churches in Belarus during the 2000-2006 survey period continued to expand. Much of the persecution against Christians occurred late in the survey period—after Parliamentary elections in the fall of 2004.

In January 2004, Baptist Union church member Yuri Denishchick was fined for holding a religious meeting in a private home. Christians said the fine was an exception—there had been little government harassment of unregistered church activities in advance of October's Parliamentary elections. During Easter 2004, two Christians had personal property confiscated, including a car, and another believer's pay was docked after the three visited a hospital, sang hymns, and handed out tracts to patients. A local religious affairs official said the action was taken against the three Baptists because they had not received permission to "hold a mass event with music and give out literature."

Following Parliamentary elections in October, Christians feared a major crackdown against unregistered churches and their activities. Reports surfaced in the town of Lepel that a Baptist street evangelist was beaten by police. Police denied the allegation, but admitted that they had repeatedly detained Baptists running a street library in the town.

Though the Full Gospel Association of Minsk was officially registered with the government, government authorities continued to obstruct worship services of the charismatic congregation. Full Gospel Pastor Andre Sido was fined one month's salary for holding a religious service in his home. Authorities said that while his church was registered, fire safety and sanitation workers had not cleared his home for religious activities. The deadline for compulsory church re-registration was November 17, 2004.

November 17, 2004. It became clear that only those churches that authorities felt they could influence or control—those not viewed as a threat to the ruling government—would be allowed. Most non-Moscow Patriarchate Orthodox churches were barred from registration. Government officials boasted that 96.2 percent of churches successfully re-registered and those that failed to register would be liquidated.

In December 2004, the 600-member charismatic New Life Church in Minsk was denied registration and barred from meeting for worship. Church members wanted to convert a cow shed into a worship hall, but government authorities refused to grant them permission or allow them to rent a facility elsewhere. On December 28, church pastor Vasily Yurevich was fined 150 times the minimum monthly wage for organizing an "illegal" church service. Another pastor at the church possibly faced similar punishment. The government had denied the church registration in violation of international law.

"The opportunity to be a
servant of the **Lord** exists at
all times and in **all** places.
Opposition should make
no difference.
Spiritually, we have only
one Leader.
He **orders** our steps."

— Tom White, who suffered in a Cuban
communist prison for dropping gospel tracts
from a small airplane over the island nation

Government action against New Life continued in March 2005, when electricity was cut off to the church building. Pastor Vyacheslav Goncharenko was fined the equivalent of thirty times the minimum monthly wage for organizing religious services without permission.

On August 17, 2005, the Belarus government announced it would confiscate the plot of land beneath the cow shed used by New Life Church. The church argued that it owned the land and had even paid $13,000 US in taxes on it.

Minsk Moscow city district court fined New Life Church Pastor Vasily Yurevich $1895 US—160 times the country's average minimum wage— for "violating established procedures for holding religious events." In October, he was fined for a third time. This time he was ordered to pay a fine of $1,727 US. The average monthly salary in Belarus is $100-$150 US.

On September 20, 2005, the Minsk City Court liquidated the legal status of the Belarusian Evangelical Church. The church had attempted repeatedly to register with the government, but registration was denied.

The Belarusian Reformed Evangelical Church (Calvinists) refused to register and continued to meet underground. It faced hefty fines for "illegal" unregistered church activity in the wake of its liquidation the previous month.

A village parish in the southwestern region of Brest was denied registration in November 2005. It was originally part of the Moscow Patriarchate diocese, but several months earlier the 120-member parish of SS Sophia and her Three Daughters, Faith, Hope and Charity, had left to join the U.S.-based Russian Orthodox Church.

The year 2005 ended with the expulsion of Polish priest Father Robert Krzywicki. Krzywicki had worked in Belarus for ten years and had worked closely with Catholic and Protestant youth in the town of Borisov. Another Polish priest was also expelled.

Turkish Republic of Northern Cyprus (TRNC)

A British-controlled state until 1960, the country was split into Greek
(South) and Turkish (North) communities after the Turkish invasion of
1974. In the Turkish North, where almost everyone is Muslim, there is
freedom of religion, but evangelization by minority groups is watched.
Less than one percent of TRNC is Christian. According to *Operation
World*, the Muslim population is very secularized, with about ten percent
regularly attending the mosque.

Turkey

Two Christian evangelists were arrested near Izmir on March 1, 2000.

Ercan Sengul and Necati Aydin were charged with forcing people to accept
Bibles and with insulting Islam. Members of the Izmir Fellowship of Jesus
Christ, the two had changed their religious affiliation on their permanent
identity cards from Muslim to Christian. Their arrest came just one day
after a national television investigative report depicted Turkish evangelical
Christians as part of "missionary sects." A judge ordered the two men
released after they spent one month in jail. Judge Levent Akcali declared
there had been no evidence that they had committed a crime. Witnesses
admitted that local officials had pressured them into signing false
statements against the accused Christians. The men were employees of
the Kaya Publishing Company, and the judge said the Ministry of Culture
had granted them permission to sell and distribute Christian materials.

On May 24, 2000, police raided a Bible study meeting in a registered
place of worship in Istanbul. Six Turks, an Australian (Ian McLure), and
an American (Garth Conkright) were arrested and held overnight. The
eight were accused of violating the penal code on public meetings and
demonstrations. After questioning, they were forced to sleep on the floor
of a bare jail cell. The State Prosecutor quickly threw out the charges and
ordered the men released. McLure said he had been struck in the face and
abdomen by the police chief who cursed and shouted at him during
interrogation. In September, the eight were charged with opening a

Christian training institute without government permission. They faced a possible eighteen months in prison. Turkish law requires Christians to inform local authorities of premises designated for religious worship, listing the days and times of regular meetings.

Among the bright spots for Christians during the 2000-2006 period was the Supreme Court ruling June 9, 2000, allowing the establishment of the first Christian foundation for a Protestant church in Turkey's history. The decision allowed a forty-member evangelical church in Istanbul to establish an official legal religious identity.

Syrian Orthodox priest Father Yusuf Akbulut stood trial December 21, 2000, on charges that he had "provoked religious hatred and enmity," when he told journalists in an off-the-record interview that his Christian minority community had been among victims of the Armenian genocide carried out by Turks in 1915. Akbulut faced three years in prison if convicted of violating Turkish penal code Article 312. He was acquitted of the charges in April 2001, when the state prosecutor revealed that a video recording of the priest's comments indicated his private views did not constitute a public attempt to incite hatred.

A Muslim convert to Christianity went on trial January 30, 2001, for allegedly insulting the prophet Muhammad and Islam. Kemal Timur was alleged to have made the insulting statements as he distributed New Testaments in front of a high school in Diyarbakir, the regional capital of southeastern Turkey. Timur denied making insulting statements. He faced a maximum one-year prison sentenced if convicted. A criminal court acquitted Timur of the charges in June 2002.

In March 2001, security police ordered the Fellowship of Jesus Christ Protestant church in Gaziantep to stop gathering for worship. The police said the church was violating city zoning and public meeting laws. The police action came sixteen months after the church leaders had notified local officials that they were forming an independent Protestant church in Gaziantep.

In December, a state prosecutor dropped criminal charges filed against the Ephesus Protestant Church in Selcuk. The pastor had been accused of holding church meetings and religious education without permission. The prosecutor said the charges against the church were baseless under Turkish law.

A crackdown against Protestant churches ordered by the Turkish Interior Ministry began in November 2001, and continued into spring 2002. Judicial proceedings were held in nine provinces, questioning the legality of designated Christian places of worship. Government prosecutors argued that Christians meeting in "undesignated" places of worship were in violation of municipal zoning laws. In contrast, the government admitted that 81 percent of mosques under construction in Turkey had obtained no license. Fifty-five percent had no architectural plan.

In mid-June 2002, security police ordered the New Testament Church of Iskenderun closed. The church had gathered for worship in the same location for more than seven years without complaint from neighbors or government officials. The police said that the church had "no legal basis," and that its activities were harmful to society. The church had met in the southeastern port city for forty years.

In late July, Diyarbakir city officials granted permission for the construction of a worship and ministry center for a small Protestant congregation, the Diyabakir Evangelical Church, but opposition to the church continued, and the church and its pastor had many obstacles to overcome before being granted official recognition by the local government. City officials had ordered construction of the building halted nine months earlier because they wanted to limit its use to residential purposes. Pastor Ahmet Guvener was later charged with opening an illegal church; but in May 2004, the charges were dropped before trial. The state prosecutor announced that reforms implemented by the Turkish Parliament and international agreements granted citizens the right to conduct worship and to teach and propagate their faith. Zoning of the new church building was formally approved in November 2004 by a committee under the Turkish Ministry of Culture.

The Diyarbakir Evangelical Church became the first Protestant church to be built in the southeastern Turkish city.

Two months after Turgay Papakci was married in November 2003 at the Istanbul Presbyterian Church, her application to change her religious affiliation was refused. Officials at the local population bureau said she could not change her religious affiliation from Muslim to Christian because the church she attended was not an officially recognized church.

Turkish convert to Christianity Yakup Cindilli was attacked and brutally beaten while distributing New Testaments in his hometown of Orhangazi in late October 2003. He was admitted to the hospital in critical condition and later slipped into a coma. Also assaulted was Christian colleague Tufan Orhan. Three suspects were arrested, and one of them—Metin Yildiran —was identified as president of the local chapter of a far-right Muslim nationalist group.

In April 2004, the producer and host of a television news program was sentenced to two years in jail for broadcasting false provocations against Turkish Protestants. In his program, Kerim Akbas reported that Protestant Christians were linked to foreign intelligence services and were paying young Muslims to convert to Christianity.

Ten days after the broadcast, a church was attacked and another received bomb threats. The court ruled that Akbas had incited violent attacks against Turkish Christians.

From the end of 2004 through May 2005, Protestant churches and their church workers were threatened and attacked by Islamic vigilante groups. The attacks occurred in at least five Turkish cities, but the incidents received little media attention because Christians did not want to draw attention to the attacks for fear that the publicity would incite reprisals against them. The wave of attacks were believed fueled by comments from government ministers suggesting that foreign missionaries operating in Turkey had political motives to "damage the social peace and unity" of the country.

Members of the European Union insisted they could not consider Turkey for EU membership until it improved efforts to protect and guarantee the religious rights of its citizens. Despite that requirement and the government's desire to please the EU, Turkey's efforts to protect religious liberties on the local level seemed to fall short. As the year 2005 came to close, Christians experienced fresh harassment from security police and the judiciary. In the city of Selcuk, members of the Ephesus Protestant Church were summoned by the prosecutor to answer bizarre accusations made against them. In Samsun, security police sitting in a minivan filmed members of the Agape House Church as they entered and exited worship services. Vandals tried to set fire to the St. Paul Cultural Center in the city of Antalya.

A Christian church leader was beaten unconscious following a church service in the city of Adana in January 2006, and a sixteen-year-old boy shot and killed a Catholic priest in the city of Trabzon as a reaction to cartoons of the prophet Muhammad published by a Danish newspaper.

"I hate the communist **system**,
but I **love** the men. I hate the sin,
but I **love** the **sinner**.
I **love** the communists
with **all** my heart.
Communists can **kill** Christians,
but they cannot **kill** their
love toward even those
who **kill** them."

— A Christian who was imprisoned for
14 years in a communist prison

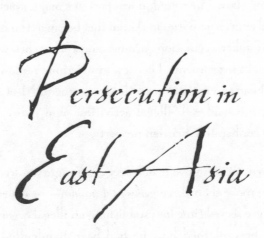

Persecution in East Asia

China

As the year 2000 began, the national Religious Affairs Bureau intensified efforts to curtail the rapid growth of religions throughout China. At a Beijing conference January 10, the Chinese Communist Party Central Committee adopted a new religious policy that tightened government control of religion—particularly the government-controlled Patriotic Catholic and Three-Self Protestant churches. The new policy also called for heightened awareness of foreign religious influences.

In February 2000, five house-church leaders with the "Born Again" movement arrested in December were sentenced to two years hard labor. The fifty-nine-year-old leader of the movement—Pastor Xu Yongze— had been incarcerated three years earlier.

While the government launched a major crackdown against the Falun Gong movement in July 1999, authorities were targeting leaders of well-organized unregistered churches extending over several provinces six months later.

Twenty-two Christians were arrested by authorities in Anhui Province on February 26 and another thirty evangelists were arrested less than one week later. Thirty more were arrested April 26 as they gathered for a Bible training class. The roundup was part of a major crackdown against unregistered church activities in Anhui that began at the start of the year when new tougher regulations against house-churches were passed by the provincial government. The new restrictions outlawed all house-churches refusing to register with the government. Meetings and Bible training were considered "illegal activities," and police were granted authority to confiscate Christian property.

In May, "Born Again" movement leader Xu Yongze was freed from prison after serving more than three years of *Laojiao*—"re-education through Labor." Yongze served time for establishing an illegal organization. After his release, he explained how he had been handcuffed to a gate by interrogators. They opened it so he was stretched off the ground in a crucifix position.

Also in May 2000, Guangzhou pastor Li-Dixian was arrested for the fourteenth time in six months for "illegal preaching." Li had been arrested a month earlier and held for fifteen days. At that time, authorities placed his hands and ankles in shackles. Prior to Li's arrest in May, Public Security Bureau (PSB) police blasted the worship services with loud music and placed banners up around the church perimeter, stating that the service was an illegal meeting. Regardless, 500 church attendees showed up for the meeting, prayed, sang songs and completed their service.

Three Americans were among more than 100 house-church attendees arrested August 23 in Zhou Kou Dan City, Henan Province. The Americans were immediately deported from the country for involvement in "activities incompatible" with their tourist status. Of the 100 Chinese arrested, at least 70 were believed transferred to prison on charges of belonging to a "cult."

Twenty-one-year-old Liu Haitong was among Protestant believers arrested for attending an unregistered church service in Jiaozuo, Henan Province, September 4. He was beaten by police following his arrest, and soon developed a high fever and began vomiting. Liu died in the county jail on October 16, after police refused to provide him with medical attention.

In October 2000, authorities issued new rules against foreigners. All foreigners were now prohibited from "expounding the Scriptures" at unofficial house-churches. House-church leaders said the new rules were nothing new; they just codified government requirements that all religious activity of foreigners be pre-approved and only take place in government-approved places of worship.

In early November, government authorities launched a major campaign to close or destroy unregistered churches in southern Zhejiang Province. At least 450 churches, temples, and shrines were affected in the port city of Wenzhou and seven surrounding counties where people were experiencing religious revival.

Government raids and arrests against Christians and their unregistered churches were not limited to large cities in south and east China. In May 2001, thirty-five house-church members were arrested in Inner Mongolia. Fifteen of the Mongolian believers were sent to labor camps after PSB officials stormed into their worship meeting in Dongsheng.

Also in May 2001, government Public Security Bureau (PSB) police launched a major crackdown against the unregistered South China Church. SCC leader Pastor Gong Shengliang was sentenced to death in December 2001, after a court in Hubei Province declared him guilty of using an "evil cult" to "undermine the enforcement of the law" and of "complicity of rape." Fifteen other members of the South China Church, including publisher Li Ying, received prison sentences ranging from two years to life. Bowing to international pressure, the defendants were given a re-trial and their sentences were reduced in the fall of 2002. Pastor Gong's sentence was reduced to life in prison; Li Ying's was reduced to fifteen years.

Word about the martyrdom of Sister Zhong Ju Yu was made public in the West in January 2002. Six months earlier, the family of the South China Church member was notified that she had been beaten to death while imprisoned in Hubei Province.

Chinese Christians also reported that another imprisoned South China Church member—Xuequei Gu—was believed to have been martyred in the fall of 2001. Gu was arrested in September and was last seen being taken away in a prison van October 10.

South China Church leaders said they received information that Gu died from injuries sustained during severe beatings and torture while incarcerated.

A Hong Kong businessman Li Guangqiang was sentenced to two years in prison January 28 for smuggling more than 33,000 Bibles into southern China. The court had accused Li of "distributing cultic material." Li was trying to supply copies of *The Recovery Version of the Bible*—published with notes from evangelist Witness Lee—to church members in Fujian. Li was freed less than two weeks after his sentence was handed down, prior to the February visit to China by U.S. President George W. Bush. Li's sentence was reduced to "illegal sales of overseas publications."

The New York-based Committee for Investigation on Persecution in China revealed that 182 house-church Christians from 24 cities and 16 counties were arrested between June and August 2002. Many were reportedly tortured by police.

"Before prison we heard about God. But in prison we experienced God."

— Pastor Sze, a Chinese house-church leader who was imprisoned for his faith

In December 2002, Phillip Xu was sentenced to eighteen years of re-education through labor for leading an unregistered house-church service near Shanghai the previous month.

Xu had previously spent six years in *Laojiao* (re-education through labor) and had been released from prison only two years earlier. This was his fourth imprisonment. His sentence was served and he was released in June 2004.

New regulations regarding the levying of fines were implemented in 2002. For years when Christians were arrested in rural areas for involvement in unregistered church activities, they would often be taken into police custody, questioned and released after they paid fines of about $100 US. The new regulations allowed more massive fines of $500 US, and church leaders caught operating Bible training camps could be fined from $600 to $4,000 US. Christians complained that the new law encourages police corruption and the excessive fines are far beyond what most Chinese could afford to pay.

Human rights advocates hoped the ascension of Hu Jintao to the position of Communist Party Secretary General in late 2002 would eventually lead to a liberalization of China's policy on religion, but most Christian leaders had no such expectations. They knew Hu was a hard-line communist who had led the crackdown against Tibet in 1987. The Christians were right. As he solidified control over the party and government, Hu continued—and some say even expanded—the government's policy of confrontation with unregistered churches and their leaders.

Communist Party plans to crack down against unregistered house-church activity in Hebei Province were exposed with the release of a confidential document in January 2003. The document entitled, "Work Plan of the Baoding Municipal Public Security Bureau to Prohibit Christian Illegal Activities," detailed specific steps to be taken in the months leading up to the Communist Party Congress in November 2002. The document stated that the aim was to "protect legal" church activities and "to prohibit illegal ones...and to ruthlessly strike down all cult activities masquerading under the banner of Christianity." Christian rights advocates said the document provided proof that continuing, coordinated action was being taken against unregistered house-churches by the government and Communist Party.

One of the "most wanted" house-church leaders in China, elder Chen, was arrested along with his seventeen-year-old son in Anhui Province in early April 2003. Their arrest followed a National People's Congress in March where government officials pledged to continue the "Strike Hard" campaign against unregistered religious groups.

Raids and mass arrests continued against unregistered house-church Christians from May through September 2003. In May, forty believers were tied up during a raid on a house-church in Anshan City. In June, a total of 53 Christians were arrested in Funing County and Lisoning. Three house-church leaders with the "Little Flock" church network—including 80-year-old Shen Shaocheng—were taken to an unknown location by PSB officers following a raid on their house-church meeting in Xiaoshan City in July, and 170 church attendees were arrested at a rural house-church meeting in Nanyang, Henan Province, September 2.

Word came in November that thirty-three-year-old Christian Zhang Hong-mei died while jailed in Ping Du City, Shandong Province. On the day of her arrest (October 29), her family members were told they needed to pay a bribe of about $400 US to gain her release. They saw Zhang bound with heavy chains and visibly wounded, but they were unable to pay the excessive amount to secure her release. The following day, they were called to the PSB station to pick up her body. An autopsy showed wounds to her face, hands, legs and serious internal bleeding—possibly from kicks and blows to her body.

In September 2003, church historian Zhang Yinan and 100 other Christians were arrested in Henan Province. They were sent to labor camps for a minimum of two years.

In late April, 2004, twenty-eight-year-old Gu Xianggao was beaten to death while in PSB custody in Heilongjiang Province. He was a teacher in a house-church group known as "Three Grades Servants" and was arrested one day earlier during a major raid against the church in Harbin

City. Gu's family was shown his body minutes before it was cremated. His parents were paid the equivalent of $28,000 US—a small fortune for the average Chinese famil—and ordered not to tell what had happened.

The government carried out large-scale raids against unregistered house-churches throughout 2004. In June, more than 100 house-church leaders with the China Gospel Fellowship (CGF) were arrested throughout China. Also, among church leaders held and interrogated by police was well-known house-church pastor Samuel Lamb of Guangzhou. It was the first time in more than fourteen years that repressive action was taken against Pastor Lamb.

Also in June 2004, thirty-four-year-old Jiang Zongziu was arrested for "disturbing the social order" when she distributed children's gospel literature in the marketplace. She was beaten to death by police while incarcerated in Tongzi County.

On August 6, three famous Chinese house-church Christians were sentenced one to three years imprisonment respectively by the Intermediate People's Court of Hangzhou City, Zhejiang Province. All of them were charged with "illegally soliciting, providing national intelligence to overseas organizations." The sentences against Liu Fenggang, Xu Yonghai and Zhang Shengqi were three, two and one year(s) respectively.

Also in August, the government issued a series of internal directives calling for tighter control of religion in China. The goal was to suppress the conversion of Communist Party members, the growth and spread of religion and religious activities across the country and on college and university campuses.

As the year 2004 came to a close, prominent house-church pastor Zhang Rongliang was arrested in a rented apartment at Xuzhai village, Zhengzhou City, Henan Province. PSB officers searched Zhang's home and confiscated Christian DVDs, literature and photos revealing his relationship with foreigners and foreign agencies. Zhang was the leader of the Fangcheng Mother Church, one of the largest house-church networks in China, estimated to number more than ten million members.

New regulations on Religious Affairs were adopted by the government March 1.

Government officials boasted the new regulations were a step forward in allowing greater religious freedom in China, but older generation house-church leaders—many who had experienced and survived the Cultural Revolution—were suspicious of government motives. Their suspicions were warranted because government officials used the new regulations to launch a massive wave of arrests against unregistered churches in spring and summer 2005. In May, 600 house-church members, students, and professors were held and questioned in Jilin Province. During the same month, 100 pastors were arrested for attending a leadership training seminar in Henan Province. In July and early August, a total of more than 210 house-church pastors were arrested in Hebei and Henan Provinces.

Two American theology students from Westminster Theological Seminary of Texas and California were among the Christians arrested.

On July 1, seventy house-church believers were arrested during a baptism of sixty new believers at a home in Sui County, Henan Province; and on July 22, approximately 100 Christian high-school-aged students were arrested in Wanzhuang Town, Lanfang City, Hebei Province, as they attended a Vocational Bible School (VBS).

Chinese Christians received good news in late September when church historian Zhang Yi-nan was released from prison after completing his two-year sentence of *laojiao*—"re-education through labor"—at Bailou Labor Camp in Henan Province.

In early November, Pastor Cai Zhuohua, the leader of six Beijing house-churches, and three family members were found guilty of conducting "illegal business practices" for printing more than 200,000 pieces of Christian literature. Cai was sentenced to three years imprisonment.

A major crackdown against unregistered church groups continued in early 2006. On January 8 and 15, Beijing Public Security agents raided the well-known unregistered Beijing Ark House-church during Sunday services. One PSB officer declared the church was disturbing the neighbors, while another quoted new State Council Regulations on Religious Affairs saying the congregation was meeting in an "illegal religious gathering place" because it was not registered. A house-church member was beaten after a PSB officer noticed that the raid was being videotaped. Thirty-six students of a house-church Bible school in Huaibei City, Anhui Province, were arrested March 1, 2006, when PSB officers in anti-riot uniforms and vehicles stormed the school. Christian materials were confiscated.

In May, for the first time, a sitting U.S. President met a group of Chinese house-church intellectuals at his private residence in the White House. The one-hour meeting ended with President George W. Bush leading prayer for his Chinese guests and the Chinese people.

"More love, O Christ, to Thee. More love to Thee."

— Sung by North Korean Christians
as their children were being hanged
by the communists because the parents
refused to deny Christ

Prominent Chinese house-church leader, Pastor Zhang Rongliang, was sentenced to seven-and-a-half years in prison on July 4, 2006. Zhang was charged with "attaining a passport through cheating" and with "illegal border crossing" because he had traveled to the U.S., Australia, Egypt and Singapore for world mission conferences. He is the leader of the China for Christ Church, which is one of the largest house-church networks estimated to have more than ten million members.

One of the worst incidents of the year occurred July 29 in Che Lu Wan village, Dangshan town, Xiaoshan district, Hangzhou City, Zhejiang Province, as several thousand anti-riot police in 300 military vehicles converged on a newly constructed church building. Several hundred Christians were beaten and many arrested as they attempted to prevent the destruction of the building.

The 2000-2006 period ended much like it had started: with reports of frequent arrests of house-church leaders and attendees, Bibles and other Christian literature confiscated, and churches closed or demolished by Chinese authorities. There were also numerous reports of torture and beatings of Christians while held in police custody for interrogation.

North Korea

Religious freedom is non-existent in North Korea. Unauthorized practice of religious faith can result in arrest, imprisonment, torture or death. More religious prisoners are jailed in North Korea than any other country in the world.

Kim Il Sung came to power in 1945 with the help of the Soviet Union and introduced the "worship of Stalin." By 1949, relationships with the Soviet Union were crumbling and he introduced his own cultic dictatorship under a philosophy of *Jucheism* ("self-reliance"), further splitting relations with the rest of the communist world. In 1970, *Juche* was formally adopted by the 5th Party Congress as the sole guiding principle for all actions. Everyone from the age of two is taught to "think, speak and act as Kim Il Sung and

Kim Jong Il," and it encompasses one-third of all educational curriculums. By the time Kim Il Sung turned eighty, the country was littered with 70 bronze statues, 40,000 half-length plaster figures, 250 monuments, 350 memorial halls, 3,500 "towers of eternal life," and a 70-foot high statue covered in gold leaf costing nearly a billion dollars.

After the end of the Korean War in 1953, Kim Il Sung moved aggressively to destroy all churches (estimated at 2,000), and he proceeded to kill or imprison the remaining 109,000 known North Korean believers. In a 1962 speech, Kim claimed to have executed all Protestant and Catholic priests, and all other religious figures were sent to the camps.

There are four churches in North Korea's capital, Pyongyang, but they are mostly for show. The nation's first Russian Orthodox Church held its inaugural mass in Pyongyang in August 2006. The government manages and operates the church. A true, accurate number of secret house-churches is impossible to state. Estimates put it as low as 5,000 and as high as 20,000, with a potential 250,000 to one million believers. An estimated 100,000 Christians (and/or family members of Christians) are believed to be locked away in prison camps.

The regime of the current leader, Kim Jong Il (the son of Kim Il Sung) has created the Korean Christian Federation to monitor and regulate North Korean Christian activities. However, three showcase churches in Pyongyang are controlled and operated directly by North Korea's National Security Agency. The carrying of Bibles, passing out of Christian literature, and other public expressions of Christian faith are prohibited and punishable by imprisonment. At least 6,000 Christians are reportedly held in prison #16 in the northern region of the country. Imprisoned Christians who refuse to renounce their faith are beaten, and some have been tortured to death.

Famine and harsh conditions during the past eight years caused as many as 300,000 North Koreans to flee their country and enter China as refugees. Most were forcibly repatriated and subjected to extensive questioning by authorities upon re-entry into North Korea. They were subjected to arrest, imprisonment and torture. Each reportedly was asked if they had made any contact with Christians in China or South Korea. Those who answered affirmatively were imprisoned and forced to perform hard labor.

Because of the secretive nature of North Korean society, and because the government controls and restricts the free flow of information, fresh, up-to-date reports of persecution are difficult to obtain. Bits and pieces of information trickle out from time to time Pieced together, these reports have revealed an ongoing, brutal campaign of persecution against Christians.

Among the credible reports surfacing in the 2000-2006 period:

In 2003, a North Korean army general who became a Christian was shot dead by a senior army officer after he began to evangelize soldiers under his command.

At least twenty Christians were believed shot or beaten to death while jailed in North Korea in 2004.

Several Christian leaders were reportedly tortured and executed in early 2005.

In April 2005, a South Korean court convicted a Korean ethnic from China of kidnapping a South Korean pastor and taking him to North Korea. The man was sentenced to ten years in prison for his involvement in an abduction plot involving North Korean agents. Thirty-five-year-old Ryu Youn-hwa helped the North Koreans kidnap Christian missionary Kim Dong Shik who was working with North Korean defectors in northern China.

In August, North Korean defector and gulag survivor Kang Cheol Hwan revealed fresh information detailing the kidnapping of a North Korean man who was abducted after he was caught with film he had taken of the Yodok political labor camp. Kang said the man had wanted to expose to the world atrocities occurring there. Kang, who experienced many brutalities during his ten years at Yodok, told of torture, forced labor, near starvation conditions, and public executions.

As the end of 2005 approached, word came in mid-November that sixty-four-year-old underground church leader Moon Seong Jeun, some of his siblings, and dozens of his church members were scheduled for possible execution on charges of attempting to overthrow the communist government. Religious rights advocates feared many of the eighty church members questioned by State Security Agency officials had been arrested.

Many North Koreans have fled to China—some of them Christians—and have been known to return to North Korea to share the gospel. Any North Korean sent back by the Chinese government faces almost certain death. One such case caught the attention of the international community in 2006. Son Jong Nam defected to China in 1997, but was repatriated to North Korea and imprisoned in 2001. He was released in 2004, but arrested again in January 2006, tortured and sentenced to be executed for criticizing the quality of life in North Korea.

Tibet (China)

Christians are trapped between the oppression of Buddhism and the oppression of communism. Buddhists who convert to Christianity are forced to overcome many obstacles to grow in Christ. They often face ostracism in their communities, and some are forced to leave home. Some also suffer physical and emotional abuse from family members.

There may be about 1,000 evangelical and 2,000 Catholic Christians among the five million Tibetans in the world. There are at least two secret groups of Tibetan believers in Tibet.

"Before being shot by you, we wish to thank you heartily for what you have meant to us. You baptized us; you taught us the way of eternal life, you gave us Holy Communion with the same hand in which you now have a gun ... God bless you, and remember that our last thought of you was not one of indignation against your failure. Everyone passes through hours of darkness. We die with gratitude."

— Two Christian girls, Chiu-Chin-Hsiu and
Ho-Hsiu-Tzu, who were killed by their pastor,
who had been promised to be released by the guards
if he shot the girls

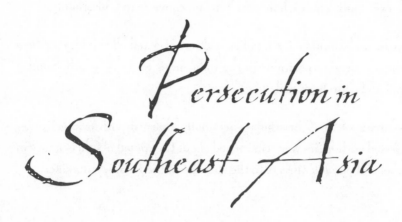

Persecution in Southeast Asia

Brunei

Islam is the state religion in Brunei, and non-Muslims are free to practice their faith without interference from the government as long as they do not proselytize Muslims. Those caught proselytizing face fines and imprisonment.

There are only two church buildings in the Brunei-Muara, which includes the capital city of Bandar Seri Begawan. Muslims and Christians coexist peacefully, but there is little interaction between the faiths.

Few incidents of persecution were reported in Brunei during the 2000-2006 survey period, but it appears the worst time of reported persecution occurred during late 2000 and into the first half of 2001.

Seven Christians were arrested in mid-December 2000 and late January 2001 for alleged "cult" activities. They were detained, and four of them were released by mid-February 2001. Upon their release, they were reportedly told they were not to leave the country or talk about their arrest. Muhammad Fredie Chong Abdullah, Malai Taufick Haji Malai Hashor, and Yunus Marang remained in jail until July 2001.

The Christians were reportedly arrested because of their involvement in a well-organized prayer program. Marang was reportedly charged with

431

smuggling Indonesian Bibles into Brunei. He was given a two-year prison sentence. Taufick and Chong are Muslim converts to Christianity.

Also, by mid-summer 2001, police had interrogated all church members holding leadership positions in the indigenous church—youth, Sunday school and church council.

The arrest of the Christians—originally charged with evangelism— suggested authorities were concerned about the spread of Christianity in Brunei and possible threats to the stability of the Islamic sultanate.

Burma (Myanmar)

The persecution of Christians and other religious minority groups has intensified in Burma—also known as Myanmar—during the past five years. The State Peace and Development Council (SPDC) has stepped up efforts to monitor and control the activities of Christians.

Nearly all foreign missionaries were expelled from Burma in the mid-1960s, and the government nationalized many hospitals and schools owned and operated by Christian groups.

The SPDC government has closed churches, and since 1996, it has prohibited the construction of new ones in Chin state. Government army troops have destroyed churches in rural areas and reportedly attempted to forcibly convert Naga and Chin Christians to Buddhism. Karen and Karenni Christian villages have been destroyed, their women and young girls have been raped, and boys and young men have been abducted and forced to serve as porters or army conscripts.

While Christians among the ethnic groups along Burma's borders face severe persecution, Christians in the cities have more freedom. According to one Burmese church leader in Rangoon, "we cannot say we are persecuted for our faith, but there are a lot of restrictions." Government restrictions are placed on those who may be invited to attend church services, what they may say, and where they can meet; but they do not face the same harassment as churches in the Chin, Karen and Karenni areas. While the printing and importation of Burmese-language Bibles and Christian literature is allowed, their numbers are closely regulated by the government. The printing and importation of Christian literature and Bibles in ethnic languages is prohibited.

According to the U.S. State Department, Burmese government and military authorities have been actively involved in the forced conversion of ethnic Chin and Naga Christians to Buddhism. Children have been separated from their parents under the guise of free education. The children are then instructed to convert without the consent of their parents. Buddhist soldiers have been offered financial and career incentives to marry Chin Christian women.

In 2000, the military government closed a Bible School that had operated in Tamu township, Sagaing division, for more than two decades.

In February 2001, government soldiers entered the Rinpi Baptist Church in the western city of Haka, where they arrested Chin ethnic, female Baptist pastor Gracie and accused her of harboring Chin separatists. About 800,000 of Burma's one million ethnic Chin are Christian.

In April 2002, the government prohibited the Kachin Baptist Convention from holding its 125th anniversary gathering; however, in May 2002, it did permit a Baptist Youth Assembly rally, but only 300 of 3,000 members were allowed to attend.

The government confiscated twenty-two orphanages for military use in early-to-mid- 2003. Two pastors, Run Hesh Ling and Sa Tin Khup, were among five Christians arrested for attempting to prevent the property seizures. They were falsely accused of selling children and faced sentences of life in prison or possible execution. A Burmese court ordered their release several weeks later.

Fearing that Buddhists were being evangelized and Western ideas spreading, the SPDC launched a major crackdown against unofficial evangelical churches near Mandalay in the summer of 2005. Twenty-eight houses of worship were raided and closed after Buddhists in the area had reportedly converted to Christianity in large numbers.

Government officials forced pastors to sign statements pledging they would discontinue worship services. Seventeen churches—most of them Pentecostal—and a Bible school were closed in the capital of Yangon. The Full Gospel Assembly Church—one of the fastest growing churches in Kyauktada Township, Yangon—was among the churches closed. Government officials ordered Pastor Mung Tawng to cease all church activities. An intelligence officer was quoted as warning that worship in Burma could only take place inside church buildings and services in private homes and unregistered church activities are illegal. Working with foreigners or inviting foreigners to preach is prohibited.

A report released in 2006 by the Women's League of Chinland revealed the widespread use of rape as a weapon of war against the Chin by members the Burmese Army. Ninety percent of the Chin is Christian. The report also stated that Burmese Army soldiers are paid $15,000 US to marry a Chin woman—part of the government strategy of Burmanisation. In September 2006, a CSW report detailed extensive violations of human rights against the Kachin Christian ethnic group. Highlighted were government restrictions on the construction, extension and renovation of churches. The government Commander of the North was quoted as saying that he did not want to see crosses or Christian symbols on roadsides in the Kachin state. Also in September, the United Nations agreed for the first time to formally debate human rights violations in Burma.

Indonesia

Violence against Christians in Indonesia's Maluku Islands and Central Sulawesi intensified into jihad waged by several militant Islamist groups in 2000. Churches were burned and hundreds of Christian homes and businesses destroyed. At least 8,000 people were killed in three years of violence. Thousands of women and girls were raped, while some believers were sliced to shreds and beheaded by crazed Muslim mobs. Captured and kidnapped Christians were forcibly converted to Islam and many were forcibly circumcised—men, women and children.

A large group of school children on the island of Haruku were orphaned because of the jihad against Christians—some lost one or both parents. Tragedy struck fourteen-year-old Maria Nenkeulah and her siblings when their parents left home for a night out in January 2000.

"I waited for them until ten o'clock and wondered why they hadn't come back," Maria said. Maria's parents didn't return because they had been hacked to death by militant Muslims. Their bodies were found buried beneath some banana leaves at the bottom of the village water well.

In January, 2001, Stefanus Wenno and his wife Mila, a forty-three-year-old nurse, were attacked by a Muslim mob as they journeyed to church. One irate Muslim brandishing a machete tore into the flesh of Mila's right arm. Her bone was broken and the blow nearly sliced her arm in two. Only six centimeters of dangling skin kept Mila's arm attached slightly above her elbow. She no longer has any feeling in her hand and forearm because one of her nerves was severed.

"I felt terrible and sad when this incident happened to me, but I know that God will bless me and my family the same as He has blessed Job and his family," said Mila. "I feel happy. I do not feel sad about this incident which happened to me, and I also forgive all the people who have done this to me."

Mila, Stefanus, and other Christian families were left homeless that fateful winter day after radical Muslims burned their village on the north end of Seram Island. Nearly 4,000 villagers were forced to live as refugees in the jungle.

One of the worst incidents occurred on the small island of Kasiui at the start of Ramadan 2000, when armed Jihad warriors forced as many as 600 Christians to undergo an Islamic conversion ceremony. One fourteen-year-old girl says she cried when the Muslims poured water over her head to cleanse her before she entered the mosque. She says she wept because it symbolized the giving up of her Christian faith.

Several days after the forced conversions, Muslims went from house to house and forcibly circumcised as many as ten people at a time—all with the same razor blade. Victims were told they had to undergo circumcision if they were to be considered "real" Muslims. Thomas Rusin, thirty, says he was told that he must "follow the Muslim way or be killed." He says he did not fight his armed attackers. "I felt scared because I hadn't faced this problem before," he said. Rusin says none of the victims were given antiseptic, painkillers or bandages—only a small piece of cotton was placed on their wounds. He says he was sore, sick and bedridden after his forced circumcision.

"I could not get up from the bed or walk for two days," he said.

More women than men were circumcised, and even small children were cut. A six-year-old girl named Emiliana was restrained while her genitals were forcibly butchered. She was too young and embarrassed to fully understand or talk about her experience.

Violence against Christians subsided after the signing of the Malino Peace Accords in December 2001 and February 2002. One of the main militant groups waging jihad against Christians, Laskar Jihad, was disbanded following the October 2001 Bali bombing. However, some Laskar Jihad members joined other Islamic groups and are now believed to be involved in jihad training camps in Sulawesi.

"We have learned that **suffering** is not the **worst** thing in the world ... **disobedience** is."

— A Vietnamese pastor who was imprisoned for his faith

After his arrest and trial, the head of Laskar Jihad, Jaffar Thalib, was acquitted of charges of illegal weapons possession and instigating violence. Meanwhile, Christian pastor Rinaldy Damanik faced similar charges and was sentenced to three years in prison. He served two years and gained an early release in November 2004.

In July 2004, several months prior to Damanik's release, twenty-six-year-old Reverend Susianty Tinulele of the GKST (Presbyterian Christian Church of Central Sulawesi) in Palu was preaching from the pulpit during the evening service when militant Muslims stormed into the church and sprayed her and the worship team with gunfire. Reverend Susianty died instantly after she was shot through the head. Four other worshippers were seriously wounded and were hospitalized with gunshot wounds.

In October, gunmen shot at random into Christian homes in Poso, Central Sulawesi, killing three people. No one was killed but at least three Christians were injured when simultaneous attacks were launched against two churches in the Central Sulawesi capital of Palu. Terrorists detonated a bomb at Emanuel Church and opened fire on the congregation of Anugerah Church just ten days before Christmas.

In 2005, violence against Christians intensified again in Central Sulawesi. In late May, at least 23 people were killed when two bombs exploded at the marketplace in the Christian city of Tentena.

Christians around the world were shocked and saddened to learn of the brutal beheadings of three Christian school girls October 29, 2005, near Poso, Sulawesi.

The previous month, three Christian women in Bandung, West Java, were sentenced to three years in prison for the "Christianization" of Muslim children attending their Sunday school class.

During late summer and early fall 2005, radical Muslims forced the closure of more than sixty churches, most of them in West Java.

For the first time in fifty years, Aceh Province was opened to Christian missionaries in early 2005, as many conducted tsunami relief efforts.

The year ended with a New Year's Eve bombing at a Christian marketplace in Palu, the capital of Central Sulawesi. At least eight Christians were killed in the attack believed to have been committed by Jemaah Islamiya, a militant Muslim group with ties to the Al-Qaida terror organization.

A backlash against Christians surfaced in September 2006, when a mob of irate Muslims set fire to the Evangelical Mission Church building in Aceh Singkil. Pastor Luther Saragih and his pregnant wife were forced to flee the area. At least sixty churches have been forced to close in West Java since late 2003. Radical Muslims forced the closure of eight house-churches in the city of Bandung in January 2006. The government requires churches to receive approval from neighbors before permits are granted, but Christians say this requirement is nearly impossible to achieve in Muslim communities.

In May 2006, seven Islamic militants confessed to the beheading of three Christian schoolgirls in Central Sulawesi seven months earlier.

Despite outrage voiced by Pope Benedict and the international community in September 2006, three Christian men were executed for allegedly leading attacks against Muslim villages during a religious conflict that ended in 2003 in Poso, Central Sulawesi.

Laos

The three or four Christian churches in the capital city of Vientiane are considered potentially subversive and are closely monitored by the government. House-church meetings are raided, and Lao Christians are arrested, while foreign Christians are expelled. Communist leaders in some districts have implemented a program called "New Mechanism," in which anyone who does not convert to Buddhism or animism is forcibly removed from their district. Christian villagers also have been forced to sign a document renouncing their faith. If they refuse, they are forced to leave their homes, and their property is either seized or destroyed.

One such incident occurred in the Laotian province of Luang Prabang in the spring of 2000, when a committee of officials detained twelve Christians from March 11 to April 10, and forced them to sign an affidavit recanting their faith. Officials told the believers that being a Christian is illegal because Christianity is a lying religion, it violates Lao custom, and the Bible teaches deception.

By early summer 2000, twenty-seven Christians were believed imprisoned by the government for their faith. But their numbers increased by late summer when the government arrested more Christians and continued to close down churches. The crackdown appeared to be getting closer to the capital Vientiane. The Lao government had previously avoided taking action in Vientiane for fear of international condemnation. The authorities in Luang Prabang and Savannakhet Provinces continued to force hundreds of Christians to renounce their faith in front of other believers, sign affidavits; in some cases, Christians were forced to return to animistic practices by taking part in blood sacrifices. Some civil servants were also threatened with loss of their positions if they did not sign the affidavits.

By spring 2001, Lao government officials continued to pressure Christians into signing affidavits renouncing their faith in Christ. The churches and homes of those refusing to sign were destroyed. Authorities reportedly closed two churches—one of them founded in 1902—in the southern part of the country. The number of families affected by the closure earlier in the year was between 50 and 100. A total of twenty churches were open in Savannakhet in 1998. Only five remained three years later. Fifty-eight churches were closed by Lao authorities throughout the country from late 1999 to spring 2001. Believers have been told that being a Christian is illegal because "it violates Lao custom and the Bible teaches deception."

In May, a round-up of eleven Christians brought the total number of Christians in jail in Laos to thirty-three. Protestants barely number 70,000, but that total had reportedly doubled since 1997.

On March 30, 2003, officials raided a church meeting in Nong Ing, in southern Savannakhet Province. Church leaders persuaded authorities to let the meeting continue; however, police returned four days later to arrest two ministers of the church. On April 5, local officials tore down the building used for church meetings.

Twelve Lao Christians arrested in May 2003 were still being held in prison in September. The twelve were among twenty-one Christians from the Bru minority tribe arrested by local authorities who were alarmed at the growth of the church in their district. Officials had forcibly relocated a Christian family to Muang Nong district in southern Laos to isolate them from other Christians. However, the attempt backfired when the Christians converted sixty other families in the surrounding area.

On February 19, 2004, government officials told Christians attending a local meeting in Attapeu Province that they would face death if they did not abandon Christianity or leave the village.

Pastor Boutao of southern Laos was taken into police custody October 19, 2004, for conducting worship services in his house attended by 300 believers in Phin district. Boutao had been holding services at his home for two years. His arrest was ordered by the chief of the Phin District police headquarters.

Twenty-four Bru Christians were arrested in the last week of March 2005. The believers were beaten, tied to a post under the hot sun, tortured with red ants, and asked to sign documents renouncing their faith. Eventually twenty-two of the believers, under great duress, signed the documents and were released. The other two remained in prison. Meanwhile, Christians living in Muangphin district were threatened with serious harm if they continued to meet together for prayer or worship.

Eight evangelists were arrested in late March 2005 on false charges of illegal weapons possession. The arrests occurred in Hueyhoy village in Savannakhet Province. Two of the men—fifty-nine-year-old Kamchan and thirty-one-year-old Vangthong—were later sentenced to three years in prison (July 2005). Laotian Christian leaders say false charges of illegal weapons possession are often an excuse used by authorities to arrest Christians who are successful in leading villagers to Christ.

The Laotian church experienced tremendous growth during the 2000-2006 period, despite persecution and restrictions. There were numerous reports of entire villages turning to Christ. Those coming to Christ in the most significant numbers, and those suffering the worst persecution, were the tribal Hmong and Khmu people.

Malaysia

Religious freedom is guaranteed in the Malaysian constitution; however, the government often acts to restrict and limit the spread of Christianity. Fundamentalist Muslims also act to inhibit the ability of Christians to evangelize ethnic Malays.

Christian literature is limited only to non-Malays. Ethnic Malays are not allowed to have a Christian place of worship. Governmental efforts to prevent the unauthorized use of religious terms have led to the banning of the Indonesian Bible and several other Christian books containing certain phrases common to Islam. Permission to build new churches is rarely granted, and house-churches are strongly discouraged.

Police say members of a militant Muslim group known as the Kumpulan Militan Malaysia, or KMM, set the Marthoma Christian Community Center ablaze in the city of Sungei Patani July 21, 2001. The building was unoccupied at the time of the attack. Church members were forced to meet in homes for worship services in the city located about 190 miles northwest of the capital of Kuala Lumpur.

A series of attacks against five churches coincided with the American bombing of Afghanistan during the last two weeks of October 2001. Police said the attacks were the work of arsonists and vandals, but Malaysian Christians questioned the true motives behind the destruction. The attacks occurred within a short period of time; and after the Malaysian prime minister declared that Malaysia is an Islamic state. Among the churches damaged was the Christ Community Center in Subang Jaya near Kuala Lumpur, which was looted and set ablaze.

In November 2002, 1,500 CDs and cassette tapes belonging to a church in Sabah were confiscated by the Home Ministry of Malaysia. Two of the eleven songs recorded by Christian singers from the Kadazan Dusun tribe contained the word "Allah," and were not marked "For Christians Only," as required by Malaysian law. Members of the National Evangelical Christian Fellowship (NECF) explained that the word "Allah" had been used during pre-Islamic times and for years in Christian publications.

In April 2003, the Malaysian Home Ministry included the Iban-language Bible, "Bup Kudus," on a list of 35 books banned for being detrimental to the public peace. Twelve of the 35 banned books were Christian publications. "Bup Kudus" was first published in 1998 and is the only complete Bible in the Iban language.

The acting prime minister lifted the ban less than two weeks after Christians in Sarawak filed a complaint against the ban. They had explained that the Iban-language Bible did not disseminate extremist religious views and had been used in Sarawak for fifteen years.

One thousand Indonesian-language Bibles were impounded by Malaysian customs officials during the final week of April 2003. Authorities said the Bibles were seized because they contained the word "Allah." The Bible Society of Malaysia (BSM) threatened to take legal action if the Bibles were not released.

Lina Joy's eight-and-a-half-year battle to legally renounce Islam and change the religious designation on her identity card was rejected by judges in Malaysia's Court of Appeals in September 2005. The court said Ms. Joy needed to apply to a Shariah court for permission to legally renounce Islam. The court reportedly said she had the right to practice the religion of her choice.

Joy had first approached the National Registry Department in 1997 for permission to change her name from Azlina Jailani to Lina Joy, and to change her religious status to Christian on her national identity card. The name change was allowed, but the NRD did not permit a change of religious status on her identity card. The Muslim designation on her card prevents her from marrying a Christian and places other restrictions on her life. In a previous decision in April 2001, High Court Judge Datuk Faiza Tamby Chik ruled that Ms. Joy could not change her religious identity, because ethnic Malays are defined as Muslims under the Constitution. "As a Malay, the plaintiff exists under the tenets of Islam until her death," the judge told the *Berita Harian* newspaper. Sending the case back to the Shariah court did not bode well for Joy. Malaysian lawyers said the Shariah court has never granted permission for a Malaysian Muslim to convert out of Islam, according to a *Straits Times* article on September 20.

Joy's lengthy legal battle and challenge to the Malaysian Constitution intensified in 2006. Furor over the watershed religious freedom case erupted and caused Prime Minister Badawi to prohibit further debate on the issue and incited radical Muslims to threaten Joy's life. She went into hiding as a result. Article 11 of the Malaysian Constitution gives every person the right to change his or her religion; but Article 3 declares Islam to be the official religion of the state. The dual court system in Malaysia complicates religious freedom matters.

"A **church** that does not remember its **persecuted brethren** is no church at all."
— Pastor Richard Wurmbrand, author of *Tortured for Christ*

Mindanao (Philippines)

The Muslim minority in Mindanao, Philippines, has been trying to establish an independent Islamic state in the south. Several Muslim terrorist organizations exist in the Philippines, such as the Abu Sayyaf and the Moro Islamic Liberation Front, which have been linked to Al-Qaida. According to police sources, the groups are attracting new converts to Islam in greater numbers than Muslims born into the faith. "Converts are ideal terrorists because they are eager to prove themselves worthy of their new faith," Chief Superintendent of Police Rodolfo Mendoza told a journalist. There are over 200 missionaries working in this area and are doing so at great risk. Filipino Christians and missionaries working in the southern area are often targeted for attack by the Muslim militants.

On May 27, 2001, Abu Sayyaf Guerrillas (ASG) abducted New Tribes Missionaries Martin and Gracia Burnham while the couple celebrated their wedding anniversary at the Dos Palmas Beach Resort on the southern Philippine island of Palawan. Pilot Martin Burnham was killed a year later during a Philippine military rescue attempt and shootout with the ASG on June 7, 2002.

Gracia Burnham survived the rescue effort and later created the Martin and Gracia Burnham Foundation to support missionary aviation, tribal outreach, Muslim missions and persecuted Christians.

In February 2003, fifty Islamic militants entered the Christian village of Kalawit on the Zamboanga peninsula. They threw grenades into houses before rounding up the villagers and opening fire on them. Fourteen people, including three children, were killed. Another three children were reported missing after the attack.

On November 17, 2004, a twenty-four-year-old Christian was shot by an assailant as he returned home from work in the city of Zamboanga. The evangelist had often debated Christianity and Islam publicly with local Islamic leaders. He had been warned to stop proselytizing Muslims. He was left for dead, but survived the attack. Though he was paralyzed from the waist down, he insisted that he would continue sharing the gospel with Muslims and others who would listen.

In June 2006, three gunmen shot and killed Pastor Mocsin Hasim and his twenty-two-year-old daughter Mercilyn as they returned from a wedding in Zamboanga, Mindanao. The forty-seven-year-old Christian and Missionary Alliance pastor often ministered to Muslims in the region.

Several Muslim terrorist organizations exist in the Philippines, such as the Abu Sayyaf and the Moro Islamic Liberation Front, which have been linked to Al-Qaida. Islamic terrorists belonging to the Al-Qaida-linked Southeast Asian terror network Jemaah Islamiyah were believed responsible for several bombings in Christian markets and other areas in Mindanao in 2006.

Six people were killed and twenty-nine wounded in one attack during an annual festival in the remote southern town of Makilala. According to police sources, the groups are attracting new converts to Islam in greater numbers than Muslims born into the faith.

Vietnam

The Vietnamese government continued a policy of repression against Christians during the five-year period. Church members suffered beatings, arbitrary arrests and imprisonment as the communists attempted to limit the growth of Christianity throughout the country—especially among ethnic minorities. The government tightened control of Catholic seminaries by placing limits on the training and ordination of priests and nuns. Some Christians belonging to the Assembly of God church, and members of other unregistered Protestant denominations, were subjected to property seizures and loss of employment; also, their children were prohibited from attending school.

By mid-2000, at least 3,500 house-churches existed in Vietnam—all considered illegal by the communist government. At least forty Christian leaders were believed to be imprisoned for church-related activities. Government officials demolished a small crude church building July 1 just hours after a group of Christians erected it in Ho Chi Minh City. A militia videotaped church members as they gathered for services among the ruins the following day.

When U.S. President Bill Clinton met with Catholic Archbishop Pham Minh Man during a visit to the city in November, police launched a raid against Grace Church. Police confiscated Bibles and threatened members of the house-church as they attended Sunday worship at the home of Reverend Nguyen Ngoc Hien. Pastor Hien's identity card was confiscated and he was ordered to report to the police station for questioning.

Christian Sung a Chua of Ha Giang Province was arrested in August 2000 for involvement in "illegal" church activities. He was forced to make bricks at a labor camp 80 kilometers from Hanoi in Vinh Phu Province. Chua, like Hmong Christian Da who was released after serving two years at the labor camp, was forced to carry 2,000 bricks to a kiln each day. Both men were brutally beaten when they didn't meet their daily quota.

In October 2001, Father Nguyen Van Ly was sentenced to fifteen years in prison for contacting the U.S. government about religious rights abuses. He was released in February 2005.

Two Christian leaders were reportedly beaten to death in 2002 and 2003, but the Vietnamese government denied responsibility. Repression of ethnic

"Just like shaving a tiger's hair doesn't do away with its stripes, so I am still a Christian."

— Mrs. Vo Thi Manh, a Vietnamese grandmother who was imprisoned for her faith

Hmong and Montegnard Christians has continued; in some cases it has intensified during the past five years. More than 200 Montegnard Christians were reportedly detained for unregistered church activities and participation in protests during the 2001-2006 period.

In mid-2003, nine Montegnard leaders were sentenced to between 18 and 30 months in prison for spreading "Dega Protestantism" in the Central Highlands. Mennonites have also been targeted.

A new religion law implemented in November 2004 was hailed by the government as a step forward, one that allowed greater religious freedom in Vietnam, but Christians say it has actually codified many restrictions against them. They've seen no lessening of government repression, and in some instances it appears that persecution against them has gotten worse. In May 2003, a major crackdown occurred against Hmong Christians in northwestern Vietnam.

Former Vietnamese Army officer Than Van Truong converted to Christianity and joined the Vietnamese Baptist General Conference house-church organization. As his ministry grew, he started to send Bibles to high-ranking government authorities in Vietnam, leaving encouraging messages for them to refer to God's Word for truth and wisdom. He was arrested in May 2003 and spent 239 days in prison, even though official charges were never brought against him. Once Rev. Truong was released, Vietnamese officials made sure he was under close surveillance. He was arrested a second time on June 3, 2004. Even though prosecutors could not bring him up on criminal charges again, he was incarcerated in Dong Wai police cells until September 29. Later, Truong was told that he was being detained for illegally proclaiming the gospel.

On September 30, 2004, Truong was transferred to Bien Hoa Mental Hospital in Dong Wai Province, where hospital officials entrenched in a Marxist worldview diagnosed him as insane for believing in God. He was locked in a solitary room and injected with strong tranquilizers. The undisclosed drugs made him sluggish and very ill, but his health returned when the staff began giving him oral medication instead, which he refrained from swallowing.

After a few weeks, he was moved to different rooms. Seeing his chance to continue evangelizing, Reverend Truong baptized a number of his fellow patients, many of whom were mentally sound, but pleaded insanity in order to avoid the harsh conditions of prison. An international letter-writing campaign ensued. Publicity and international public pressure were enough to convince the Vietnamese government to release Truong in September 2005.

In 2004, several church workers and Pastor Nguyen Hong Quang were arrested, beaten and received prison sentences of between nine months and three years. In July 2005, seventy government workers with sledge hammers and electric saws tore down much of the Vietnam Mennonite Church in Ho Chi Mihn City, including a meeting hall and an apartment that housed the imprisoned Pastor Quang's family.

Local authorities continue to destroy the homes of Christians who refuse to renounce their faith. One recent incident occurred in Quang Ngai Province in August 2005 when police incited a mob to burn down the home of evangelist Dinh Van Hoang.

In late May 2006, police armed with nightsticks, numchucks and cattle prods raided Pastor Nguyen Hong Quang's Mennonite house-church at C5H1 Tran Nao Street in Vietnam's Ho Chi Minh City. Many of the church members were beaten, while Pastor Quang and ten others were arrested. Repairs that were being made to the church were torn down. Degar Christians and believers from several other ethnic groups in Vietnam's Central Highlands experienced increased harassment, arrests and persecution in 2006. Two Degar Christians were killed in prison in July 2006; and in late August 2006, a Montegnard Christian died following alleged torture in prison.

Persecution in Africa

Comoro Islands

Less than one percent of Comorians are Christian, while more than 98 percent are Muslim.

A new constitution approved by 85 percent of voters in October 1997 greatly increased the influence of Islam in Comoros. Christians are prohibited from meeting openly, and public witness is prohibited. While there are nearly 800 mosques in Comoros, there are no official churches. Christians are denied many social and civil privileges, and some have suffered persecution.

The only reported act of persecution in recent years occurred when two young men were arrested and imprisoned for "anti-Islamic activity "and "disturbing the peace." Neither man knew the other, but both appeared for a joint trial in October 1999. Twenty-two-year-old Taki Islam served three-and-a-half months of a ten-month sentence for possessing several copies of the *JESUS* film in the Shimaore language. He was granted provisional release from prison on January 17, 2000. Twenty-four-year-old Ali Toibibou left the Comoros Islands with his pregnant wife in November 1999, after serving one month of his sentence.

An Iranian-trained Sunni Muslim cleric, Ahmed Abdallah Mohamed Sambi, was elected President in May 2006.

Eritrea

Persecution against evangelical Christians has intensified in Eritrea during the past several years. Public expressions of faith by religious groups other than the four recognized by the government are prohibited. Those officially recognized by the government are the Orthodox Church of Eritrea, the Roman Catholic Church, Lutheran-affiliated Evangelical Church of Eritrea, and Sunni Islam. The government appears to be aligned with the Orthodox Church, but even officials within the Orthodox Church—especially those who have broken with orthodox tradition—have experienced persecution at the hands of Eritrean government officials.

In 2002, a new law was imposed requiring religious groups to register their churches with the government. Registration required churches other than the four officially recognized ones to provide the government with financial and membership details. Because of the registration requirement, all churches and worship services other than those of the four recognized groups were shut down pending government approval. So far, none have been approved for operation in Eritrea. As a result, Christian denominations other than Orthodox, Roman Catholic and Lutheran have been forced underground.

During the period 2002-2006, Evangelical and Pentecostal Christians experienced the worst persecution.

Seventy-four Eritrean soldiers were among Christians imprisoned in 2002. They were given hard labor at a military prison in the port city of Assab for refusing to return to the Orthodox Church. The military refused to grant them contact with their families.

Eritrean security forces launched a major crackdown against unregistered churches in February and March 2003. One hundred seventy Protestants were arrested, jailed, beaten and threatened with death for their illegal activities. Security police had stormed into worship services—including one wedding—in four cities to make their arrests. Women and children were among those arrested.

On Easter eve 2003, two young believers with the government-recognized Lutheran Church were detained for publicly singing hymns about the resurrection of Christ. They were later released and given a warning to not repeat their Easter tradition again.

Military police launched another crackdown against unregistered Protestant churches in late April 2003. Fifty-six Pentecostals were arrested in their homes and workplaces in the northern province of Sahel.

Fifteen Protestants were hospitalized after suffering severe beatings by police in September and October of 2003 in the capital of Asmara. Police sealed off the Full Gospel Church building and ordered church workers to leave. As many as 4,000 worshippers could be accommodated in the building, which had served as the church meeting place for eleven years.

The arbitrary arrest of evangelical Christians and their pastors continued throughout 2004 and 2005. Police would often interrupt Bible study and prayer meetings in Christian homes. Some of those not imprisoned were reportedly ordered to pay fines of more than one month's salary.

The government crackdown against Christians was extended to Eritrean Roman Catholics in January 2005. Twenty-five Catholics attending a wedding rehearsal in Asmara were arrested, even though the Roman Catholic Church was an officially recognized church. Those arrested were part of the Tebadasso renewal movement within the church.

A private printing press was shut down and confiscated by Asmara police in March 2005 for printing Christian literature.

Two hundred fifty Christian wedding guests were arrested in May 2005, and one hundred twenty-nine of them remained in jail under severe conditions three months later. The Bibles of some of the prisoners were confiscated and burned in front of them. The police station commander reportedly told the jailed Christians they had been arrested because they were working with the United States to "disrupt the peace and unity of the Eritrean people," and would eventually attempt to overthrow the government.

In October 2005, the government ordered the only Anglican priest in Eritrea, Rev. Nelson Fernandez, to leave the country. An Indian citizen, he had served the church in Asmara for five years.

By the end of 2005, Eritrean evangelical church leaders confirmed that a total of 1,778 Christians were still imprisoned for their faith. That was nearly double the number of Christians jailed six months earlier.

Persecution against Christians intensified in 2006, with at least 163 new arrests reported from January through September. It's believed that 1,918 Eritreans are still imprisoned, tortured and subjected to forced labor because of their faith in Christ. Thirty-five pastors, priests and church elders were reportedly jailed in the Asmara Wongel Mermera investigation center in 2006, and some of them were held in storage containers.

Ethiopia

Muslims started massive campaigns to Islamize Ethiopia by penetrating Christian areas with bribes and mosque-building programs during the 2000-2006 period. In the town of Alaba (K'olito), evangelical Christians were victims of severe physical abuse, confiscation and destruction of property, extortion, kidnapping, forcible marriages and unlawful imprisonment. Alaba's regional office was the first to have requested the government for permission to implement Shariah law.

Persecution against Ethiopian Protestants—especially evangelicals— intensified in 2000-2001. One report quoted an Ethiopian Protestant Church leader, saying, "We may have freedom on paper, but I can say that persecution has doubled and it is coming from the Orthodox Church and the Muslims."

Since 1998, reports have surfaced of churches being ordered to stop singing or praying together. Mission work in some areas provoked violent reactions, and some church leaders were whipped and beaten.

In late 2001, The Full Gospel Church in Axum asked police for protection against stone throwing by members of the Orthodox Church. Though evangelical and Pentecostal churches constituted more than seventeen percent of the population at the turn of the new century, the government seemed reluctant to recognize the rapid growth of the churches. Some believed it was to avoid angering the traditional Orthodox Church, which was quickly losing members to the more charismatic churches.

In early March 2002, a Muslim mob attacked the indigenous Protestant Mekane Yesus church in the eastern Ethiopian town of Asaita. Police prevented the radicals from setting the church ablaze, but property inside the building—church robes, hymnals and Bibles—was destroyed. The Muslims attacked two evangelists, Molla Tesfay and Guerta Ahmad. Police said Ahmad was jailed for his protection; Tesfay was hospitalized because of injuries he sustained in the attack. The Muslim radicals accused the two men of proselytizing.

A mob led by priests of the Orthodox Church attacked and killed an evangelical Christian pastor in his home in Merawi, in northwestern Ethiopia. Brother Dantew, a teacher by profession and the leading elder in the Full Gospel Church, was martyred on the evening of July 17, 2002, several hours after he had asked for police protection. The homes of eight other evangelical families also came under attack that night, leaving their furniture and belongings destroyed. A formal investigation into the attack resulted in the arrest of some forty Orthodox Church members, including six priests.

On March 12, the homes of eleven evangelical Christians were burned to the ground by a hostile mob in the town of Deneba, 150 kilometers northeast of Addis Ababa. About 26 believers including children were displaced as a result.

On April 23, 2003, two evangelical church leaders were arrested in Maychew after violent riots broke out against their churches. Kiros Meles, forty-six, and Abebayeh Desalegn, thirty-five, were both jailed after an Orthodox Church member was shot to death April 23 as local police tried to bring the two-day, anti-evangelical rampage under control. An off-duty policeman, believed to have shot the fatal bullet into the air using a pistol belonging to the local chief of police, is also in custody. The two Christian leaders were still being held without charge five months later. They were released in March 2003 when a magistrate said she found no evidence against Pentecostal pastors Kiros Meles and Abebayeh Desalegn.

Hajji Husman Mohamed, a former Muslim Imam, has suffered since his conversion to Christ. In December 2004, all of his property was taken from him. On February 1, 2005, he and his family, including his pregnant wife, were severely beaten. Since the Ethiopian Constitution allows flexibility in administering justice in local areas, any investigation of these events is unlikely.

In early January 2005, thirty-two believers were chased out of the village of Besheno, located approximately 30 km northeast of Alaba. The Muslims who organized the attack checked every vehicle entering the community to ensure that no Christians return.

In the Alaba area, an eight-year-old girl named Denkenesh was stabbed to death on June 5, 2005, by a witch doctor who had repeatedly told her Christian family that their prayers hindered his contact with the spirits. As a result, the witch doctor lured the girl into his home and killed her. When blood-soaked cloths were found in his home, he admitted to the attack and was arrested.

Also in the Alaba region, in the village of Colicha, a government official led a mob in raiding a church service on June 12. Those present were forced from the home where they were meeting. The governor had written a letter to the owner of the house, forbidding further church services.

On June 19, eleven Muslim converts were late arriving for church. They and others had been accosted on their way to the service and beaten. These managed to escape and proceed to the service while the others were driven away.

Muslim mobs attacked Christians and their churches in several towns and villages throughout 2006. Among the churches destroyed was the

Emmanuel Christian Church in Jiiga. Five Christians were injured when the church was attacked with a fire bomb April 15, 2006. Nesero Abraraw, a guard at the Lutheran church in Arisi Negellie, 225 km south of Addis, died after he was shot three times by an unidentified assailant.

Some of the worst violence against Christians occurred in September 2006, when Ethiopian Muslims rioted in the town of Denbee in an attempt to stop Orthodox Christians from celebrating the festival of Meskel. The festival occurred during the Islamic holy month of Ramadan. As many as nine people were killed in the violence. The violence started when an Orthodox woman and her son were killed for refusing to recant their faith. More than fifteen hundred members from the evangelical Kalehiwot ("Word of Life") denomination were displaced from their homes. Five churches in the area were burned: three Kalehiwot, one Lutheran and one Catholic. Five Kalehiwot churches were confiscated and turned into mosques. More than 750 believers were kidnapped and forcibly converted to Islam after being starved for four days.

Nigeria

Civilian rule was restored to Nigeria with the election of former Army General Olusegan Obasanjo as president in 1999. He was re-elected in 2003. Nigerian Christians had great hopes that their Christian president would be able to curtail attacks against Christians by Muslims—particularly in many of Nigeria's Northern states where Muslims are the majority. He has implemented reforms against government corruption, but has found efforts to halt the advance of radical Islam and Shariah law (Islamic law) more difficult.

Nigeria is becoming a bloody battleground in Africa as radicals advance plans to Islamize the country. Islamists have been emboldened since the implementation of Shariah law in twelve Nigerian states. Muslim militants from neighboring countries—primarily Chad, Niger and Cameroon—have come to join the jihad against Christians.

The period 2000-2006 was a horrific one for Nigerian Christians. Muslims—particularly in Nigeria's Northern and Central States—made frequent raids and attacks on Christian villages. Many of the attacks during this period occurred in Nigeria's Plateau State.

Plateau state is predominantly Christian. It's surrounded by Muslim states, and the governor of Plateau State, Joshua Daryle, said that the goal of militant Muslims is to wage jihad against the Christians of Plateau State to make them Muslim by force.

The Plateau State capital of Jos was the scene of mass bloodshed in September 2001, when Muslims clashed with Christians. More than 5,000 people were killed, most of them Christian.

Forty Christians died in Fajul, Plateau State, in October 2002, when a force of about 2,000 militant Muslims invaded the village. Homes were burned, women were raped, and seventeen policemen who came to aid villagers were murdered. Seventeen Christians were killed in a similar attack in the nearby village of Kassa. Armed mercenaries from the neighboring countries of Chad and Niger joined the jihad against the two villages.

"I will not run away.
I am ready to take a stand."

— Saratu Turundu was a 35-year-old
unmarried woman who loved the
children she taught in Sunday school.
She was killed for her faith in Christ by a
fanatical Muslim mob in Nigeria

In December 2002, the vice-president of the Church of Christ Nigeria, Pastor Bitrus Manjang, was killed in front of his home by a rioting Muslim mob. He died just three days before a planned retirement party. Manjang was a prominent church leader who had translated the Bible into several Nigerian tribal languages.

Also in 2002, state officials reportedly ordered the demolition of churches in Maiduguri, in the Northern State of Borno. In Gusau, Zamfara State, Muslim officials seized a convent owned by the Nigerian Catholic Church. One of the nuns said conditions for Christians residing in Zamfara started to worsen when state officials implemented Shariah (Islamic) law in 2000. Zamfara was the first of twelve Nigerian states to impose Shariah law on its citizenry.

One of the worst attacks of 2003 occurred in the Western Nigeria state of Adamawa in February. At least 110 people were killed, 500 injured, 130 houses and some churches were destroyed, and 21,000 people were left homeless when a well-armed mob of Muslim militants attacked Christians in Dumne village. The Muslims said they were retaliating for an attack Christians launched against them three months earlier when sixteen Muslims were killed.

Muslim militants were believed responsible for setting the fatal fire that claimed the life of Pastor Sunday Madumere, his wife and three of his children, in the Northern Nigerian city of Kano in May 2003. Madumere had led many Muslims to Christ.

One week before Christmas 2003, a combined force of police and members of the Nigerian military raided the headquarters of Muslim militants in the city of Jos, Plateau State. One humdred seventy-five radicals were arrested. The roundup preempted attacks planned against Christians on Christmas Day. Muslim radicals from Niger and Cameroon were among those arrested.

In February 2004, Nigerian Church of Christ pastor Samson Bukar and 48 members of his church were killed when Muslim militants attacked their church in the Telwa, Plateau State. More than 150 others were killed during a raid on the town. Two other churches in the area were burned down by Muslim radicals just one day after the slain pastor's funeral.

The violence against Christians in Plateau state continued throughout late winter and spring of 2004. Fifteen hundred Christians—including eight pastors—were killed, 173 churches destroyed, and more than 25,000 people were displaced from their homes.

The Nigerian government imposed a six-month state of emergency on Plateau State between May and November 2004. On December 29, 2004, Christian community leader Davou Bulle was shot in the chest by Muslim militants in the village of Gana-Ropp, Plateau State. Attacks against Christians, church leaders, and church buildings continued throughout 2005 in the Nigerian States of Adamawa, Benue, Kaduna, Kano, Plateau and Niger.

A fatwa was issued against Christian lecturer Andrew Akume. A militant Muslim group at Ahmadu Bello University passed the death sentence against Akume, claiming he committed blasphemy against the prophet Muhammad when he asked one of his female Muslim students not to wear her hijab (head-to-toe covering) because it hid her identity.

In May 2005, the governor of Kano State ordered that all Christians in the state must dress according to Islamic tenets, including head coverings and long-flowing robes for women.

In Lagos State in July, a fifty-seven-year-old Christian man was attacked when Muslim radicals came to the man's home searching for his sixteen-year-old daughter. The militants had pronounced a death sentence against the family because the daughter allegedly sold pork in violation of Shariah law. Shariah law is not in effect in Lagos State.

Attempts to impose Shariah law on Nigerian Christians led to more violence and difficulties in Niger State in September 2005. Muslim militants stormed into a classroom at the Federal University of Technology in Minna and attacked Christian students. The violence erupted after a Christian girl was stabbed in a lecture hall by a Muslim fanatic distraught because she was not wearing a veil.

Also at the FUT, a request by Christian students to construct a chapel on campus was denied while Muslim students were allowed to build a mosque.

In 2006, violence against Christians continued. Believers were killed; churches, Christian schools, homes and businesses were burned and destroyed. Some of the worst attacks against Christians occurred in February when Muslims responded violently to the publication of cartoons of the prophet Muhammad. At least 75 Christians were killed.

In Niger State, Muslims stoned and clubbed a Christian woman to death in late June because she handed out tracts and preached to young Muslims in the village of Izom.

In September, 70 homes, businesses, and churches were destroyed, and 2,000 Christians were left homeless in the city of Dutse. Police said Muslims rioted after a Christian businesswoman insulted the prophet Muhammad.

Also in June 2006, Muslim students in the northern state of Nasarawa rioted, looted the home of their teacher, burned it, threatened to behead him, and attacked Christians because the teacher had disciplined a Muslim student. High school teacher, Muslim convert to Christianity Joshua Kai faced trial for committing blasphemy against Muhammad. Lai caned one of his students—a customary punishment—when the student said he was late for class because he had been saying morning prayers at the mosque. Lai didn't believe him because the boy arrived in class long after morning prayers had ended. Lai lost his job and all his possessions as a result.

Sudan

The U.S. Commission on International Religious Freedom called the Government of Sudan (GOS) the "world's most violent abuser of the right to freedom of religion and belief." During the past five years, acts of violence and persecution continued against Sudanese Christians. In an attempt to eliminate a viable Christian presence in Sudan, GOS planes frequently bombed Sunday school services, church buildings, hospitals, schools, and Christian villages in the South. Christians captured by radical Muslims faced beatings, torture and death for refusing to convert to Islam.

Aerial bombings of civilian areas intensified as profits from Southern Sudanese oil fields began flowing to the GOS in late summer 1999. More than 150 bombing incidents were reported in 2000. Among the facilities destroyed were buildings belonging to various churches and humanitarian relief organizations.

In February 2000, a Sudanese government plane, an Antonov, was sent to drop bombs on Holy Cross School in the Nuba Mountains near Kauda, Sudan. Four were dropped, three exploded, and 23 people were killed as a result. Most of the victims were young children between the ages of eight and fifteen.

"If I die, I will be very happy because I will leave an example for other Christians to follow in my wake."

— Kuwa Bashir, a Sudanese youth pastor who stood before his Muslim guards as they poured acid on his hands

In March 2000, a Christian worker was killed when a hospital sponsored by VOM in Nimule, Sudan, was bombed; and during the same month, a hospital sponsored by Samaritan's Purse in Lui was bombed twice.

Thirty-two people—including women and children—were killed in June 2000, when a Roman Catholic mission was attacked in the town of Gumriak. At least three people were killed when bombs were dropped on the central market in the city of Yei in November. The following month—not far from Yei—the city of Lui was attacked once again; two people were killed when a church was bombed during Christmas week.

The U.S. State Department reported that by the end of 2000, as many as 15,000 people—mostly Christian Dinka women and children—were still being held captive after having been abducted by government-backed militias and sold into slavery. Most were forced to convert to Islam. Once enslaved, many young girls and even young boys were reportedly brutally raped by their Arab masters. In July 2002, Sudan fact-finders interviewed numerous newly freed slaves. One of them, a boy named Deng Ayuel, testified: "I watched the Arabs rape my two sisters, and I watched many slave boys being raped as well. They would often take a girl or boy and do whatever they wanted with them sexually. I too was raped many times by my master and his Arab friends." Another redeemed slave named Deng Deng reported: "Many times during rape boys would cry so loudly that the Arabs would stuff rags in their mouths so they could not be heard. I witnessed this often. If you refuse [sex], sometimes they would shoot you."

By early September 2002, Sudan President, Gen. Omer Hassan al-Bashir pulled out of peace negotiations with the SPLA in Machakos, Kenya. At that time, he declared at a mass mobilization rally that his government would press ahead with "jihad" until peace (i.e., Islam) was achieved. He made good on his promise less than two weeks later. The Samaritan's Purse hospital in Lui was bombed again. No deaths were reported, but the following day GOS aerial bombing of the Southern Blue Nile city of Yabus claimed the lives of two young school boys and injured eight others. One week later, the aerial bombardment of Twic County caused the death of two children (aged three and thirteen) and three women. Ten others were injured. Twic County is adjacent to the western Upper Nile oil fields where the armed forces of the Sudanese government displaced, killed and enslaved over 100,000 civilians during a series of military offensives in July and August. Many of the survivors sought refuge in Twic County.

Despite signing several memorandums of understanding and cease-fire agreements with the Sudan Peoples Liberation Army (SPLA), the GOS continued major military operations against the people of the South— particularly in and around the southern oil region. In May 2003, fifty-nine people were killed and fifteen were injured when GOS troops attacked ten villages in eastern Upper Nile. Many victims were burned alive in their homes. Among them was Presbyterian pastor Jacob Gadet Manyiel, the region's only Christian pastor. He was burned to death along with his wife and four children as government troops surrounded their home, threatening to shoot any family member attempting to escape the flames.

Persecution hasn't been limited to south Sudan. Christians in the capital city of Khartoum have faced persecution for violating Shariah law, and for refusing to surrender their church buildings to government authorities.

In April 2004, twenty-seven-year-old Cecilia Holland was arrested by public-order police because she was not wearing a headscarf. She told them she was a Christian from the South, but they insisted that Shariah law applied to Muslims and Christians alike. An Islamic court fined Ms. Holland the equivalent of $40 US, and she was forced to submit to forty lashes on her back.

An Episcopal priest was jailed in May 2003 for refusing a government order to demolish a church building he had constructed in 1992. One year later, Khartoum police forcibly evicted church workers from the Episcopal Church in Sudan provincial headquarters. An Islamic court ordered the eviction, saying the church property had been sold to a new owner.

As the 2000-2006 period came to an end, there were glimmers of hope and a promise of peace in much of Sudan. A peace agreement signed by the government and the Sudan Peoples Liberation Army (SPLA) in January 2005 had ended more than twenty years of armed hostilities between them.

The government's war of jihad and genocide has now shifted to Sudan's Darfur region. As they did throughout South Sudan, government troops and surrogate militias now regularly pillage and burn villages, rape and abduct women and young girls, kill men and conscript and enslave boys in Darfur. Two million people have been displaced as a result. In late 2005, fighting spilled over into neighboring Chad, and human rights organizations were calling for an expanded international force for Darfur and more UN peace-keepers throughout South Sudan.

Mauritania

Mauritania is an Islamic republic, and Islam is the national religion. Christians are free to practice their faith openly and freely without hindrance from the government. However, Christians are prohibited from evangelizing and distributing Bibles and Christian literature outside their own small Christian community.

Christian non-government organizations are allowed to operate in the country, but their activities must be limited to humanitarian work. They must register with the government, but they are not taxed.

There were no major incidents of persecution against Christians reported during the survey period.

Somalia

During the 2000-2006 survey period, there was no constitutional guarantee of religious freedom in Somalia because no constitution existed in the country. No strong central government was in place, but Islam was the official religion in the regions of Somaliland and Puntland. Three Shariah courts were in place in the capital of Mogadishu, but they were not considered independent because they were aligned with and influenced by various clans. Shariah law was often enforced, and punishment for violators rendered by various militias.

In both regions, religious schools and churches were required to obtain permission from the government to operate. Christian groups were required to get Ministry of Religion approval before obtaining entry visas.

Proselytizing is prohibited for all faiths except Islam. Christian organizations were allowed to operate as long as they did not evangelize Muslims.

On February 3, 2000, Somaliland authorities briefly held nine Ethiopian Christians for evangelizing. All were deported after they were released.

In 2006, Islamists led by Sheikh Hassan Dahir Aweys, on the U.S. list of those allegedly linked to terrorism, gained control of most of the southern half of the country. Fighting between moderate Muslims and Islamists caused many Somalis—some of them Christians—to seek refuge in neighboring Kenya. Christians fear that the rise of the Islamists will lead to Shariah law and greater persecution against them.

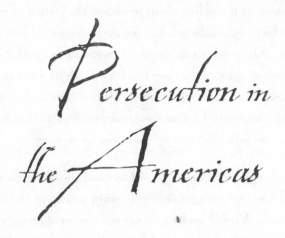

Persecution in the Americas

Chiapas, Mexico

Religious intolerance in the southern Mexican state of Chiapas decreased in the late 1990s and early 2000, but violence against evangelical Christians in small communities intensified, starting in 2002. Church building construction was disallowed for some evangelicals, and others had their property damaged or seized. Some were victims of violence, and others faced expulsion from their communities.

In November 2001, a new legal team obtained the release of six Christian prisoners jailed as suspects in the Acteal killings of December 1997. Originally, 90 people were arrested as participants of the tragedy, 35 of them being evangelical Christians. Eighty-five suspects were jailed unjustly for refusing to join an ongoing political struggle between the Zapatista insurgency movement and followers of the dominant political party (PRI). The six Christians were released because of insufficient evidence and a lack of due process.

Despite the release of the six Christians, 78 men—including 34 evangelical believers from the Chenalho community—remained in prison for the Acteal killings. Some, like Javier Luna Perez, continued to serve a 36-year sentence for a crime they say they did not commit.

Perez, a lay preacher in his evangelical church, was working in his cornfield in Acteal Alto on December 22, 1997, when his wife Loida and other women

465

of the village came to tell him about trouble at the Catholic hermitage. He returned to his home and heard shooting in the distance. Three days later—on Christmas Day—he was on his way to a community meeting in Chenalho when authorities stopped the open truck in which he was a passenger and took him into custody, charging him with homicide and illegal weapons possession. Javier, thirty-four, was sentenced to 36 years in prison. His wife raises their two sons. His two uncles are also imprisoned.

On September 29, 2002, Pastor Jesus Hernandez and ten other Christians were jailed for conducting a public worship service in the town of San Juan Chamula. A tribal leader intervened to prevent an angry mob from beating the evangelicals. Though Hernandez was a native of the town, he was told to "leave and not come back," because his religion was not wanted in the town.

The two pastors' murders were the most recent in a 30-year saga of severe persecution of evangelical Christians by local *caciques*, or powerful community chieftains. Caciques practice "traditionalist" religion, a semi-pagan mix of Roman Catholic beliefs and ancient Mayan religion.

Since the advent of evangelical Christianity in the Chiapas Highlands in the 1960s, caciques have used violent tactics to discourage its spread in indigenous regions. Scores of evangelicals have died and hundreds more have suffered injury. About 35,000 evangelical Christians live in ghettos surrounding the district capital of San Cristóbal de las Casas, having been driven from their ancestral homes by caciques and their henchmen.

Caciques have enjoyed near impunity while carrying out the anti-Christian campaign. In three decades, only six caciques and their accomplices have been punished for these crimes.

In July 2005, three evangelicals in the town of San Antonio Las Rosas were arrested and jailed for 24 hours, as town officials attempted to force them to leave the area. The men were required to pay a fine of about $93 US each to be freed. Town leaders later decreed that only Catholics were allowed to live in San Antonio Las Rosas.

Two months later, on September 25, local authorities cut electricity to evangelical families in another attempt to force them to leave the community. The evangelicals protested to the state, and an interfaith council was created in an attempt to resolve the dispute between the Catholics and evangelicals.

Colombia

Marxist guerrilla groups like FARC (Armed Revolutionary Forces of Colombia) demanded "war tax" money from churches, continued to kidnap people, threaten missionaries, and force Christian schools and churches to close. Guerrillas persecuted both Catholics and Protestants. Their violent acts were funded by the transporting of illegal drugs. Former president Andres Pastrana effectively ceded to FARC control of a 16,000-square-mile area of south central Colombia. Missionaries expressed concern for the safety of pastors and believers in this zone. In October 1999, guerrillas issued a cease-and-desist order for all evangelical pastors and churches, which meant possible death if they continued to meet. Some churches were closed in the zone, with a curfew imposed on services for churches allowed to meet. Public religious activity was also banned.

Despite the fear and intimidation of Marxist guerrilla groups, the church continued to grow in the 2000-2006 period. In 1993, there were only 15,000 evangelicals; but in 2000, there were almost two million. Aggressive evangelistic outreaches resulted in an increase in churches. However, such success made pastors the target of violence, seeing the church as a threat to guerrilla groups controlling the area. The guerrillas were motivated by a desire to stop the spread of Christianity. They felt if pastors and other evangelicals continued to win young Colombians to Christ, there would be fewer recruits for their Marxist-led revolution.

Jorge Aldana, twenty-eight, was shot to death in the early morning hours of the day after Easter 2000, presumably at the hands of left-wing terrorists. Aldana left behind his wife, Orpha, a nine-year-old daughter, and a seven-year-old son. The Aldanas had pastored in Nueva Antioquía since 1996.

Aldana's death brought the toll to forty evangelical ministers murdered in Colombia since mid-1998.

In October 2000, New Tribes Missions (NTM) reported tribal Christians in Colombia were being displaced and had their homes and Bibles burned by members of Colombia's largest rebel organization, FARC. NTM reported that on September 12, 2000, FARC soldiers began looting the homes of believers of the Kogui tribe, piling their New Testaments, hymnals, and readers in the middle of the village and setting them on fire. Then the rebels ordered the man responsible for translating the Scriptures and all of the other Christians to leave. According to NTM, thirty-three have left the village. FARC is the same group believed to be responsible for the kidnapping of three NTM missionaries in 1993.

In mid-November 2000, Colombian television broadcast footage of Revolutionary Armed Forces of Colombia's (FARC) military commander Mono Jojoy ordering his troops to kill pastors as enemies of the revolution.

Colombian rebel groups frequently harass Christians in an attempt to coerce them into supporting the rebels in their long war against the Colombian government. In addition, young people who become Christians prove to be more resistant to recruitment into the guerrilla organizations.

In some rural villages in Colombia, Saturday night is known as "night of the assassins"—the night of the week when Armed Revolutionary Forces of Colombia rebels target for death those opposed to their Marxist ideology. Christian leaders are at constant risk. Many pastors were martyred during the 2000-2006 period as the FARC terrorists continued their assaults against the church. More than thirty pastors were killed in one year alone. But in spite of the risks, Colombian pastors continued to be a bold witness for Christ. One said, "Every time we leave church, we never know ... if we will continue with life. We live under the shadow of death continually."

Cornellio Tovar was among pastors assassinated in 2002. He and his wife would often travel into rural areas to share the gospel with poor Colombian farmers. One Saturday evening as Pastor Tovar and his wife Nelly were returning home from church services, they noticed someone lurking in the shadows. Two gunmen emerged from an alleyway and opened fire on

Pastor Tovar. Tovar died in an ambulance on the way to the hospital. Nelly said her husband was prepared to give his life for the gospel. While saddened and burdened by the loss of Cornellio, she expressed the martyr's spirit, saying, "I knew one seed had to fall to the ground in order for the gospel to be spread."

Also in 2002, Hector Peña, pastor of the United Pentecostal Church of San Vicente de Caguán, died at the hands of unknown assailants as he was returning to his home February 7. It was not certain which of the armed groups assassinated Peña or why he was killed. Three weeks later, on February 28, FARC rebels shot dead Bernardo Urrego Osorio, a member of the San Vicente Christian and Missionary Alliance Church, as he was driving livestock along a trail near his home. Guerrillas reportedly killed Urrego in retaliation for his refusal to aid the FARC cause.

On Saturday, March 16, professional gunmen—allegedly working for Cali drug traffickers—assassinated Roman Catholic Archbishop Isaías Duarte. The archbishop was at the door of a church, greeting the last of the guests of a communal wedding involving some 100 couples. Two men approached and fired five shots at Duarte at close range. Two days after Duarte's death, the National Prosecutor General voiced his suspicion that local guerrilla cells may have allied themselves with drug traffickers to murder the archbishop.

Three weeks after the assassination of Archbishop Duarte, unidentified gunmen murdered another priest, Juan Ramón Núñez, as he celebrated Mass in his church in La Argentina.

A gunman shot Father José Hilario Arango to death at close range in front of the Santa Teresa church in Cali on June 27, 2002, just after the priest had celebrated evening Mass. Arango became the third Roman Catholic priest to die at the hands of assassins in Colombia in less than four months.

Two evangelicals were assassinated less than two months later on August 3. Unidentified assassins from the Revolutionary Armed Forces of Colombia (FARC) ambushed and killed Rev. Adelmo Cabrera Polanco and his adult son, Luis Carlos as the two were returning to their home.

"In spite of the painful reflections and memories, I have no time for bitterness. My life is filled with too much happiness, too many loving, caring people to allow myself to be devoured by the cancer of hate. I rejoice. I sing. I laugh. I celebrate, because I know that my God reigns supreme over all the forces of evil and destruction Satan has ever devised. And best of all—my God reigns supreme in me!"

— Pastor Nobel Alexander,
who was imprisoned in Cuba for 22 years

Pastor of the Christian and Missionary Alliance Church in the town of Puerto Rico for eighteen years, Cabrera left a widow and five children.

Two more Roman Catholic priests were murdered in fall 2002. Hooded gunmen assassinated forty-nine-year-old Jose Luis Arroyave on September 20 while he was passing out flyers for a church parish. A week later, another priest died in a hail of machine-gun fire while traveling in southern Colombia. Jorge Sánchez, sixty-three and parish priest of Restrepo, along with three companions were attacked and killed while driving on a highway in southern Colombia.

On January 27, 2003, unidentified gunmen assassinated Rev. Jose Juan Lozada Corteza, pastor of the Evangelical Christian Church of San Antonio. According to the Evangelical Council of Colombia (CEDECOL), uniformed men stopped the public bus in which Lozada was traveling and singled out the clergyman from the rest of the passengers. Forcing him off the vehicle, assailants shot Lozada in the head in full view of bystanders.

A military report released in April 2003 said the Revolutionary Armed Forces of Colombia (FARC) posed the most serious threat to Christians in Colombia. Despite the findings, Roman Catholic and Protestant evangelical church leaders said that stationing troops or police officers at churches would likely place them in even greater danger.

The following month, twenty-five armed men entered a rural church in northern Colombia Tuesday night, May 6, and murdered its eighty-year-old evangelical pastor and three other believers. Among the dead was Miguel Mariano Posada, pastor of Sardis, a church in the Association of Caribbean Evangelical Churches denomination. The murders took place in his church, located in the town of Tierralta in Cordoba department, near Panama. The other victims were teacher and church treasurer Ana Berenice Girardo Velásquez; eighty-year-old Natividad Blandón, the wife of another pastor; and seventeen-year-old Julio Torres, who was visiting the church.

Two more Roman Catholic priests were slain in apparently unrelated incidents on November 4 in Colombia. Rev. Saulo Carreño, parish priest of Christ the King Church in the town of Saravena, in eastern Colombia's violent Arauca department (state), was shot after leaving a hospital where he had been ministering to sick parishioners. The same day, Rev. Henry Humberto López was found stabbed to death in his home in the city of Villavicencio, sixty miles southeast of Bogotá.

The year 2003 neared an end with the murder of another Roman Catholic priest in November. The bullet-riddled body of the second priest murdered in less than three weeks in Colombia's volatile Arauca department (state) was found November 21 on a street near the community where he ministered. Jose Rubin Rodriguez, fifty-one, was kidnapped at a roadblock November 14, news sources report. Arauca Bishop Carlos German Mesa says that military intelligence and local citizens believe the 10th Front of the Revolutionary Armed Forces of Colombia killed him.

Three gunmen wearing black hoods burst into an evening worship service at the Christian and Missionary Alliance Church in Puerto Asis, Colombia, on Saturday September 4, and opened fire with automatic weapons, killing three worshippers and injuring thirteen more. One of the murder victims was a woman; two children were also among the wounded. The pastor of the congregation, Francisco Sevillano, was unhurt in the attack. The assault did not appear to be aimed at the church body, but rather at an individual who was present at the worship service.

In 2005, a demobilization program led many para-militaries to turn in their weapons in exchange for Bibles. Government officials said the demobilization process would not have moved forward without the help of local church leaders.

One more evangelical pastor was martyred before the 2000-2006 persecution survey period came to a close. In September 2005, Pastor Benestey Paderna Escobar was threatened by Marxist guerrilas. They stormed into Sunday services and dropped the body of a murder victim into the center of the church, telling the thirty-five-year-old pastor he would end up like the slain man if he did not leave the community. Pastor Escobar did not leave. Two weeks later, the guerrilas returned and shot Escobar in the leg. They told him he had two more weeks to leave. Again Pastor Escobar refused, saying he would obey God and continue his ministry to the people. The Marxists returned two weeks later, again stormed into the church, shot the pastor and dragged his body into the street, shooting him six times in the chest in front of his wife and seven children. The guerrillas demanded that his wife Rubiela take the children and leave immediately. In shock over the murder of her husband, she requested more time to gather clothing for the children and other personal items. The guerrillas refused, saying she could get them later. She left, but returned the next day only to find all the family's possessions missing; even the toilet bowls and lights had been removed from her home.

Cuba

In the 1960s, Cuban dictator Fidel Castro labeled Catholics and Protestants "social scum" and forced lay people and clergy into labor camps under inhumane conditions. Cuba's constitution was amended in 1992 to guarantee freedom of religion. Yet today, Christians are still imprisoned and churches destroyed. The year 1999 saw many changes in Cuba. Open evangelical crusades were held for the first time since Castro came to power, and were carried on Cuban TV. However, applications for registering or repairing churches are still routinely ignored.

Conditions improved and persecution against Christians decreased early in the survey period, but a resurgence of persecution by the Cuban government occurred near the end of the survey period starting in 2005.

In early 2000, the Castro government loosened religious restrictions against registered Christian churches as three new Baptist church buildings neared completion. In an unprecedented move for his government, Castro had given the Baptists permission to construct a total of seven new church buildings.

In another unprecedented move, on January 24, 2004, Archbishop Athenagoras of the Central American Greek Orthodox Church laid the cornerstone for a new, registered Greek Orthodox Church building in Havana.

While Castro allowed greater freedom for registered denominations during the period, efforts to harass and restrict the growth of unregistered house-churches continued.

During Easter of 2000, authorities closed a Baptist church in the suburbs of Havana. Church members faced hefty fines and possible imprisonment if they failed to comply with government orders to close the church.

In October 2000, Pastor Jorge Ferrer and his wife Ailin Leon returned home from an out-of-town trip, only to find that government security agents had seized their house and had evicted the couple's children and their ailing grandfather. The family's furniture and possessions had been tossed into the street, and a guard was stationed outside the home to deny the family access to it. The couple had purchased the home from the government three weeks earlier. Authorities said the home should not have been sold to them.

A human rights group revealed in July 2004 that prominent, jailed Christian dissident Dr. Oscar Elias Biscet had been denied food for nearly three weeks. In ill health, he was transferred to a prison hospital in December 2004. He had been sentenced to 25 years in prison in April 2003 for criticizing the Castro regime.

In February 2005, the members of Light of God Pentecostal Church in Managua, Cuba—not far from Havana—vowed to "let the church roof fall on them" if government officials followed through with threats to demolish the building. Government authorities said the church had been built without permission. A 600-peso fine was imposed on Pastor Ernesto Oliva, the owner of the property.

In September 2005, the Cuban government implemented new restrictions banning religious meetings in homes. The restrictions were part of a new government directive announced the previous April. The directive did not specifically mention Protestant house-churches, but church leaders called the restrictions repressive and complicated, and they feared that the growing house-church movement would bear the brunt of the impact of Fidel's more antagonistic and repressive attitude toward unregistered Christians.

In October 2005, police closed a Christian printing press and held a pastor for distributing "subversive" materials. The materials were printed Gospels of John seized at a house in the city of Colon.

On December 19, 2005, an Assembly of God pastor survived an assassination attempt as he left his house in Havana. Assailant Eduardo Valdes Oliva beat Words of Life Church Pastor Octavio Rios Verdecia with a police stick. Oliva also attempted to stab Pastor Verdecia and had attacked a Baptist church several years earlier. Oliva was arrested but released 72 hours later. He immediately continued his assault against Christians and their places of worship by attacking another church with stones.

Arrested in February 2006, Pastor Carlos Lamelas, former national president of the Church of God in Cuba, was unexpectedly freed from jail four months later without being formally charged.

As the survey period ended, Cuban Christians feared the government was returning to the repressive policies of the past. Persecution against Christians was on the rise.

For the first time since he seized power in 1959, Cuban dictator Fidel Castro relinquished government control to his brother Raul. The ailing seventy-nine-year-old Fidel underwent successful surgery for abdominal bleeding. Christians worried that Raul would impose greater restrictions on the church.

Then a white robe was given to each of them,

and it was said to them that they should rest a little longer,

until both the number of their fellow Servants

and their Brethren, who would be killed

as they were, was completed.

Revelation 6:11